Spheres of Justice

Spheres of Justice

A Defence of Pluralism and Equality

MICHAEL WALZER

Basil Blackwell · Oxford

© Michael Walzer, 1983

First published in the United Kingdom in 1983 by
Martin Robertson & Company Ltd.

Reprinted in 1985 by Basil Blackwell Ltd.,
108 Cowley Road, Oxford OX4 1JF.

British Library Cataloguing in Publication Data

Walter, Michael
Spheres of justice.
1. Pluralism (Social sciences)
I. Title
305   HM276

ISBN 0 631 14063 8

Printed and bound in Great Britain by
The Pitman Press, Bath

JOSEPH P. WALZER

1906–1981

"The memory of the righteous

is a blessing."

CONTENTS

Contents

Contents

PREFACE

Equality literally understood is an ideal ripe for betrayal. Committed men and women betray it, or seem to do so, as soon as they organize a movement for equality and distribute power, positions, and influence among themselves. Here is an executive secretary who remembers the first names of all the members; here is a press attaché who handles reporters with remarkable skill; here is a popular and inexhaustible speaker who tours the local branches and "builds the base." Such people are both necessary and unavoidable, and certainly they are something more than the equals of their comrades. Are they traitors? Maybe—but maybe not.

The appeal of equality is not explained by its literal meaning. Living in an autocratic or oligarchic state, we may dream of a society where power is shared, and everyone has exactly the same share. But we know that equality of that sort won't survive the first meeting of the new members. Someone will be elected chairman; someone will make a strong speech and persuade us all to follow his lead. By the end of the day we will have begun to sort one another out—that's what meetings are for. Living in a capitalist state, we may dream of a society where everyone has the same amount of money. But we know that money equally distributed at twelve noon of a Sunday will have been unequally redistributed before the week is out. Some people will save it, and others will invest it, and still others will spend it (and they will do so in different ways). Money exists to make these various activities possible; and if it didn't exist, the barter of material goods would lead, only a little more slowly, to the same results. Living in a feudal state, we may dream of a society where all the members are equally honored and respected. But though we can give everyone the same title, we know that we cannot refuse to recognize—indeed, we want to be able to recognize—the many different sorts and degrees of skill, strength, wisdom, courage, kindness, energy, and grace that distinguish one individual from another.

Nor would many of us who are committed to equality be happy with the regime necessary to sustain its literal meaning: the state as Procrustean bed. "Egalitarianism," Frank Parkin has written, seems to require a political system in which the state is able continually to hold in check those social and occupational groups which, by virtue of their skills or education or personal attributes, might otherwise . . . stake claims to a disproportionate share of society's rewards. The most effective way of holding such groups in check is by denying them the right to organize politically.[1]

This comes from a friend of equality. Opponents are even quicker to describe the repression it would require and the drab and fearful conformity it would produce. A society of equals, they say, would be a world of false appearances where people who were not in fact the same would be forced to look and act as if they were the same. And the falsehoods would have to be enforced by an élite or a vanguard whose members pretended in turn that they were not really there. It is not an inviting prospect.

But that's not what we mean by equality. There are egalitarians who have adopted Parkin's argument and made their peace with political repression, but theirs is a grim creed and, insofar as it is understood, is unlikely to attract many adherents. Even the advocates of what I shall call "simple equality" don't usually have in mind a leveled and conformist society. But what do they have in mind? What can equality mean if it can't be taken literally? It is not my immediate purpose to ask the conventional philosophical questions: In what respects are we one another's equals? And by virtue of what characteristic are we equal in those respects? This entire book is an answer of a complicated sort to the first of these questions; the answer to the second I don't know, though in my last chapter I shall suggest one relevant characteristic. But surely there is more than one: the second question is more plausibly answered with a list than with a single word or phrase. The answer has to do with our recognition of one another as human beings, members of the same species, and what we recognize are bodies and minds and feelings and hopes and maybe even souls. For the purposes of this book, I assume the recognition. We are very different, and we are also manifestly alike. Now, what (complex) social arrangements follow from the difference and the likeness?

The root meaning of equality is negative; egalitarianism in its origins is an abolitionist politics. It aims at eliminating not all differences but a particular set of differences, and a different set in different times and places. Its targets are always specific: aristocratic privilege, capitalist wealth, bureaucratic power, racial or sexual supremacy. In each of these cases, however, the struggle has something like the same form. What is at stake is the ability of a group of people to dominate their fellows.

Preface

It's not the fact that there are rich and poor that generates egalitarian politics but the fact that the rich "grind the faces of the poor," impose their poverty upon them, command their deferential behavior. Similarly, it's not the existence of aristocrats and commoners or of office holders and ordinary citizens (and certainly not the existence of different races or sexes) that produces the popular demand for the abolition of social and political difference; it's what aristocrats do to commoners, what office holders do to ordinary citizens, what people with power do to those without it.

The experience of subordination—of personal subordination, above all—lies behind the vision of equality. Opponents of the vision often claim that the animating passions of egalitarian politics are envy and resentment, and it's true enough that such passions fester in every subordinate group. To some extent they will shape its politics: thus the "crude communism" that Marx described in his early manuscripts, and which is nothing but the enactment of envy.[2] But envy and resentment are uncomfortable passions; no one enjoys them; and I think it is accurate to say that egalitarianism is not so much their acting out as it is a conscious attempt to escape the condition that produces them. Or that makes them deadly—for there is a kind of envy that lies, so to speak, on the surface of social life and has no serious consequences. I may envy my neighbor's green thumb or his rich baritone voice or even his ability to win the respect of our mutual friends, but none of this will lead me to organize a political movement.

The aim of political egalitarianism is a society free from domination. This is the lively hope named by the word *equality:* no more bowing and scraping, fawning and toadying; no more fearful trembling; no more high-and-mightiness; no more masters, no more slaves. It is not a hope for the elimination of differences; we don't all have to be the same or have the same amounts of the same things. Men and women are one another's equals (for all important moral and political purposes) when no one possesses or controls the means of domination. But the means of domination are differently constituted in different societies. Birth and blood, landed wealth, capital, education, divine grace, state power—all these have served at one time or another to enable some people to dominate others. Domination is always mediated by some set of social goods. Though the experience is personal, nothing in the persons themselves determines its character. Hence, again, equality as we have dreamed of it does not require the repression of persons. We have to understand and control social goods; we do not have to stretch or shrink human beings.

My purpose in this book is to describe a society where no social good serves or can serve as a means of domination. I won't try to describe how we might go about creating such a society. The description is hard enough: egalitarianism without the Procrustean bed; a lively and open egalitarianism that matches not the literal meaning of the word but the richer furnishings of the vision; an egalitarianism that is consistent with liberty. At the same time, it's not my purpose to sketch a utopia located nowhere or a philosophical ideal applicable everywhere. A society of equals lies within our own reach. It is a practical possibility here and now, latent already, as I shall try to show, in our shared understandings of social goods. *Our* shared understandings: the vision is relevant to the social world in which it was developed; it is not relevant, or not necessarily, to all social worlds. It fits a certain conception of how human beings relate to one another and how they use the things they make to shape their relations.

My argument is radically particularist. I don't claim to have achieved any great distance from the social world in which I live. One way to begin the philosophical enterprise—perhaps the original way—is to walk out of the cave, leave the city, climb the mountain, fashion for oneself (what can never be fashioned for ordinary men and women) an objective and universal standpoint. Then one describes the terrain of everyday life from far away, so that it loses its particular contours and takes on a general shape. But I mean to stand in the cave, in the city, on the ground. Another way of doing philosophy is to interpret to one's fellow citizens the world of meanings that we share. Justice and equality can conceivably be worked out as philosophical artifacts, but a just or an egalitarian society cannot be. If such a society isn't already here—hidden, as it were, in our concepts and categories—we will never know it concretely or realize it in fact.

In order to suggest the possible reality of (a certain sort of) egalitarianism, I have tried to work my argument through contemporary and historical examples, accounts of distributions in our own society and, by way of contrast, in a range of others. Distributions don't make for dramatic accounts, and I can rarely tell the stories that I would like to tell, with a beginning, a middle, and an end that points a moral. My examples are rough sketches, sometimes focused on the agents of distribution, sometimes on the procedures, sometimes on the criteria, sometimes on the use and the meaning of the things we share, divide, and exchange. These examples aim to suggest the force of the things themselves or, rather, the force of our conceptions of the things. We make the social world as much in our minds as with our hands, and the particular world that we have made lends itself to egalitarian interpretations. Not, again, to a literal egalitarianism—our conceptions are too complex for that; but they do tend steadily to proscribe the use of things for the purposes of domination.

This proscription has its source, I think, less in a universalist conception of persons than in a pluralist conception of goods. Hence in the pages that follow I shall imitate John Stuart Mill and forego (most of) the advantages that might derive to my argument from the idea of personal—that is, human or natural—rights.[3] Some years ago, when I wrote about war, I relied heavily on the idea of rights. For the theory of justice in war can indeed be generated from the two most basic and widely recognized rights of human beings—and in their simplest (negative) form: not to be robbed of life or of liberty.[4] What is perhaps more important, these two rights seem to account for the moral judgments that we most commonly make in time of war. They do real work. But they are only of limited help in thinking about distributive justice. I shall invoke them primarily in the chapters on membership and welfare; even there, they won't take us very far into the substance of the argument. The effort to produce a complete account of justice or a defense of equality by multiplying rights soon makes a farce of what it multiplies. To say of whatever we think people ought to have that they have a right to have it is not to say very much. Men and women do indeed have rights beyond life and liberty, but these do not follow from our common humanity; they follow from shared conceptions of social goods; they are local and particular in character.

Nor, however, can Mill's principle of utility function as the ultimate appeal in arguments about equality. "Utility in the largest sense" can function, I suppose, in any way we please. But classical utilitarianism would seem to require a coordinated program, a central plan of a highly specific sort, for the distribution of social goods. And while the plan might produce something like equality, it would not produce equality as I have described it, free from every sort of domination: for the power of the planners would be dominant. If we are to respect social meanings, distributions cannot be coordinated, either with reference to the general happiness or with reference to anything else. Domination is ruled out only if social goods are distributed for distinct and "internal" reasons. I shall explain what that means in my first chapter, and then I shall argue that distributive justice is not—what utilitarianism certainly is—an integrated science, but an art of differentiation.

And equality is simply the outcome of the art—at least for us, working with the materials here at hand. For the rest of the book, then,

I shall try to describe those materials, the things we make and distribute, one by one. I shall try to get at what security and welfare, money, office, education, free time, political power, and so on, mean to us; how they figure in our lives; and how we might share, divide, and exchange them if we were free from every sort of domination.

Princeton, New Jersey, 1982

ACKNOWLEDGMENTS

Acknowledgments and citations are a matter of distributive justice, the currency in which we pay our intellectual debts. The payment is important; indeed, there is a saying in the Talmud that when a scholar acknowledges *all* his sources, he brings the day of redemption a little closer. But it isn't easy to make that full acknowledgment; we are probably unaware of, or unable to recognize, many of our deepest debts—and so the great day is still far off. Even here, justice is unfinished and imperfect.

In the academic year 1970–71, I taught a course at Harvard University, along with Robert Nozick, on the subject "Capitalism and Socialism." The course had the form of an argument, and half of that argument can be found in Professor Nozick's *Anarchy, State, and Utopia* (New York, 1974); this book is the other half. I have not tried to respond to Nozick's views in any detailed way but have simply developed my own position. I owe more than I can say, however, to our discussions and disagreements.

Several chapters of the book were read and discussed at meetings of the Society for Ethical and Legal Philosophy and at seminars sponsored by the School of Social Science at the Institute for Advanced Study. I am grateful to all the members of the society and to my colleagues at the Institute during the academic years 1980–81 and 1981–82. I want particularly to acknowledge the counsel and criticism of Jonathan Bennett, Marshall Cohen, Jean Elshtain, Charles Fried, Clifford Geertz, Philip Green, Amy Gutmann, Albert Hirschman, Michael McPherson, John Schrecker, Marc Stier, and Charles Taylor. Judith Jarvis Thomson read the whole of the manuscript and pointed out all those places where, though I had every right to say what I said, it would have been better had I made an argument. And I have tried to make the arguments, though not always at the depth that she (and I) would have liked.

Robert Amdur, Don Herzog, Irving Howe, James T. Johnson, Marvin Kohl, Judith Leavitt, Dennis Thompson, and John Womack each read a chapter of the book and offered helpful advice. My wife, Judith Walzer, read much of it, talked with me about all of it, and supported me in my effort to say something, if only sketchily, about kinship and love.

No one writing about justice these days can fail to recognize and admire the achievement of John Rawls. In the text, I have mostly disagreed with *A Theory of Justice* (Cambridge, Mass., 1971). My enterprise is very different from Rawls's, and it draws upon different academic disciplines (history and anthropology rather than economics and psychology). But it would not have taken shape as it did—it might not have taken shape at all—without his work. Two other contemporary philosophers come closer to my own view of justice than Rawls does. In *Justice and the Human Good* (Chicago, 1980), William M. Galston argues, as I do, that social goods "are divided into different categories," and that "each of these categories brings into play a distinctive ensemble of claims." In *Distributive Justice* (Indianapolis, 1966), Nicholas Rescher argues, as I do, for a "pluralistic and heterogeneous" account of justice. But, in my view, the pluralism of these two arguments is vitiated by Galston's Aristotelianism and by Rescher's utilitarianism. My own argument proceeds without these foundational commitments.

The chapter on membership, in an earlier version, first appeared in *Boundaries: National Autonomy and Its Limits,* edited by Peter G. Brown and Henry Shue, published by Rowman and Littlefield (Totowa, N. J., 1981). I am grateful to the editors for comments and criticism and to the publisher for permission to reprint the essay here. A section of chapter 12 first appeared in *The New Republic* (January 3 and 10, 1981). Some of the essays collected in my book *Radical Principles* (New York, 1980), first published in the magazine *Dissent,* are early and tentative statements of the theory presented here. I was helped in reformulating them by Brian Barry's critical review of *Radical Principles* in *Ethics* (January 1982). The two lines from W. H. Auden's "In Time of War" are reprinted from *The English Auden: Poems, Essays, and Dramatic Writings, 1927–1939,* edited by Edward Mendelson (New York, 1978); copyright © 1977 by Edward Mendelson, William Meredith, and Monroe K. Spears, Executors of the Estate of W.H. Auden; with the kind permission of the publisher, Random House, Inc.

Mary Olivier, my secretary at the Institute for Advanced Study, typed the manuscript and then retyped it, again and again, with unfailing accuracy and unflagging patience.

Finally, Martin Kessler and Phoebe Hoss of Basic Books provided the kind of encouragement and editorial advice that, in a perfectly just society, all authors will receive.

SPHERES OF
JUSTICE

Pluralism:

   - In the widest sense; the world is
   totally made up of plural forces.
      └ every department

1

Complex Equality

Pluralism

Distributive justice is a large idea. It draws the entire world of goods within the reach of philosophical reflection. Nothing can be omitted; no feature of our common life can escape scrutiny. Human society is a distributive community. That's not all it is, but it is importantly that: we come together to share, divide, and exchange. We also come together to make the things that are shared, divided, and exchanged; but that very making—work itself—is distributed among us in a division of labor. My place in the economy, my standing in the political order, my reputation among my fellows, my material holdings: all these come to me from other men and women. It can be said that I have what I have rightly or wrongly, justly or unjustly; but given the range of distributions and the number of participants, such judgments are never easy.

The idea of distributive justice has as much to do with being and doing as with having, as much to do with production as with consumption, as much to do with identity and status as with land, capital, or personal possessions. Different political arrangements enforce, and different ideologies justify, different distributions of membership, power, honor, ritual eminence, divine grace, kinship and love, knowledge, wealth, physical security, work and leisure, rewards and punishments, and a host of goods more narrowly and materially conceived—food, shelter, clothing, transportation, medical care, commodities of every sort, and all the odd things (paintings, rare books, postage stamps) that human beings collect. And this multiplicity of goods is matched by a multiplicity of distributive procedures, agents, and criteria. There are such things as simple distributive systems—slave galleys, monasteries, insane asylums, kindergartens (though each of these, looked at closely, might show unexpected complexities); but no full-fledged human society has ever avoided the multiplicity. We must study it all, the goods and the distributions, in many different times and places.

There is, however, no single point of access to this world of distributive arrangements and ideologies. There has never been a universal medium of exchange. Since the decline of the barter economy, money has been the most common medium. But the old maxim according to which there are some things that money can't buy is not only normatively but also factually true. What should and should not be up for sale is something men and women always have to decide and have decided in many different ways. Throughout history, the market has been one of the most important mechanisms for the distribution of social goods; but it has never been, it nowhere is today, a complete distributive system.

Similarly, there has never been either a single decision point from which all distributions are controlled or a single set of agents making decisions. No state power has ever been so pervasive as to regulate all the patterns of sharing, dividing, and exchanging out of which a society takes shape. Things slip away from the state's grasp; new patterns are worked out—familial networks, black markets, bureaucratic alliances, clandestine political and religious organizations. State officials can tax, conscript, allocate, regulate, appoint, reward, punish, but they cannot capture the full range of goods or substitute themselves for every other agent of distribution. Nor can anyone else do that: there are market coups and cornerings, but there has never been a fully successful distributive conspiracy.

And finally, there has never been a single criterion, or a single set of interconnected criteria, for all distributions. Desert, qualification, birth and blood, friendship, need, free exchange, political loyalty, democratic decision: each has had its place, along with many others, uneasily coexisting, invoked by competing groups, confused with one another.

In the matter of distributive justice, history displays a great variety of arrangements and ideologies. But the first impulse of the philosopher is to resist the displays of history, the world of appearances, and to search for some underlying unity: a short list of basic goods, quickly abstracted to a single good; a single distributive criterion or an interconnected set; and the philosopher himself standing, symbolically at least, at a single decision point. I shall argue that to search for unity is to misunderstand the subject matter of distributive justice. Nevertheless, in some sense the philosophical impulse is unavoidable. Even if we choose pluralism, as I shall do, that choice still requires a coherent defense. There must be principles that justify the choice and set limits to it, for pluralism does not require us to endorse every proposed distributive criteria or to accept every would-be agent. Conceivably, there is a single principle and a single legitimate kind of pluralism. But this would still be a pluralism that encompassed a wide range of distributions. By contrast, the deepest assumption of most of the philosophers who have written about justice, from Plato onward, is that there is one, and only one, distributive system that philosophy can rightly encompass.

Today this system is commonly described as the one that ideally rational men and women would choose if they were forced to choose impartially, knowing nothing of their own situation, barred from making particularist claims, confronting an abstract set of goods.[1] If these constraints on knowing and claiming are suitably shaped, and if the goods are suitably defined, it is probably true that a singular conclusion can be produced. Rational men and women, constrained this way or that, will choose one, and only one, distributive system. But the force of that singular conclusion is not easy to measure. It is surely doubtful that those same men and women, if they were transformed into ordinary people, with a firm sense of their own identity, with their own goods in their hands, caught up in everyday troubles, would reiterate their hypothetical choice or even recognize it as their own. The problem is not, most importantly, with the particularism of interest, which philosophers have always assumed they could safely—that is, uncontroversially—set aside. Ordinary people can do that too, for the sake, say, of the public interest. The greater problem is with the particularism of history, culture, and membership. Even if they are committed to impartiality, the question most likely to arise in the minds of the members of a political community is not, What would rational individuals choose under universalizing conditions of such-and-such a sort? But rather, What would individuals like us choose, who are situated as we are, who share a culture and are determined to go on sharing it? And this is a question that is readily transformed into, What choices have we already made in the course of our common life? What understandings do we (really) share?

Justice is a human construction, and it is doubtful that it can be made in only one way. At any rate, I shall begin by doubting, and more than doubting, this standard philosophical assumption. The questions posed by the theory of distributive justice admit of a range of answers, and there is room within the range for cultural diversity and political choice. It's not only a matter of implementing some singular principle or set of principles in different historical settings. No one would deny that there is a range of morally permissible implementations. I want to argue for more than this: that the principles of justice are themselves pluralistic in form; that different social goods ought to be distributed for different reasons, in accordance with different procedures, by different agents; and that all these differences derive from different understandings of the social goods themselves—the inevitable product of historical and cultural particularism.

A Theory of Goods

Theories of distributive justice focus on a social process commonly described as if it had this form:

People distribute goods to (other) people.

Here, "distribute" means give, allocate, exchange, and so on, and the focus is on the individuals who stand at either end of these actions: not on producers and consumers, but on distributive agents and recipients of goods. We are as always interested in ourselves, but, in this case, in a special and limited version of ourselves, as people who give and take. What is our nature? What are our rights? What do we need, want, deserve? What are we entitled to? What would we accept under ideal conditions? Answers to these questions are turned into distributive principles, which are supposed to control the movement of goods. The goods, defined by abstraction, are taken to be movable in any direction.

But this is too simple an understanding of what actually happens, and it forces us too quickly to make large assertions about human nature and moral agency—assertions unlikely, ever, to command general agreement. I want to propose a more precise and complex description of the central process:

People conceive and create goods, which they then distribute among themselves.

Here, the conception and creation precede and control the distribution. Goods don't just appear in the hands of distributive agents who

6

do with them as they like or give them out in accordance with some general principle.[2] Rather, goods with their meanings—because of their meanings—are the crucial medium of social relations; they come into people's minds before they come into their hands; distributions are patterned in accordance with shared conceptions of what the goods are and what they are for. Distributive agents are constrained by the goods they hold; one might almost say that goods distribute themselves among people.

> Things are in the saddle
> And ride mankind.[3]

But these are always particular things and particular groups of men and women. And, of course, we make the things—even the saddle. I don't want to deny the importance of human agency, only to shift our attention from distribution itself to conception and creation: the naming of the goods, and the giving of meaning, and the collective making. What we need to explain and limit the pluralism of distributive possibilities is a theory of goods. For our immediate purposes, that theory can be summed up in six propositions.

1. All the goods with which distributive justice is concerned are social goods. They are not and they cannot be idiosyncratically valued. I am not sure that there are any other kinds of goods; I mean to leave the question open. Some domestic objects are cherished for private and sentimental reasons, but only in cultures where sentiment regularly attaches to such objects. A beautiful sunset, the smell of new-mown hay, the excitement of an urban vista: these perhaps are privately valued goods, though they are also, and more obviously, the objects of cultural assessment. Even new inventions are not valued in accordance with the ideas of their inventors; they are subject to a wider process of conception and creation. God's goods, to be sure, are exempt from this rule—as in the first chapter of Genesis: "and God saw every thing that He had made, and, behold, it was very good" (1:31). That evaluation doesn't require the agreement of mankind (who might be doubtful), or of a majority of men and women, or of any group of men and women meeting under ideal conditions (though Adam and Eve in Eden would probably endorse it). But I can't think of any other exemptions. Goods in the world have shared meanings because conception and creation are social processes. For the same reason, goods have different meanings in different societies. The same "thing" is valued for different reasons, or it is valued here and disvalued there. John Stuart Mill once complained that "people like in crowds," but I know of no other way to like or to dislike social goods.[4] A solitary person could hardly understand the meaning of the

goods or figure out the reasons for taking them as likable or dislikable. Once people like in crowds, it becomes possible for individuals to break away, pointing to latent or subversive meanings, aiming at alternative values—including the values, for example, of notoriety and eccentricity. An easy eccentricity has sometimes been one of the privileges of the aristocracy: it is a social good like any other.

2. Men and women take on concrete identities because of the way they conceive and create, and then possess and employ social goods. "The line between what is me and mine," wrote William James, "is very hard to draw."[5] Distributions can not be understood as the acts of men and women who do not yet have particular goods in their minds or in their hands. In fact, people already stand in a relation to a set of goods; they have a history of transactions, not only with one another but also with the moral and material world in which they live. Without such a history, which begins at birth, they wouldn't be men and women in any recognizable sense, and they wouldn't have the first notion of how to go about the business of giving, allocating, and exchanging goods.

3. There is no single set of primary or basic goods conceivable across all moral and material worlds—or, any such set would have to be conceived in terms so abstract that they would be of little use in thinking about particular distributions. Even the range of necessities, if we take into account moral as well as physical necessities, is very wide, and the rank orderings are very different. A single necessary good, and one that is always necessary—food, for example—carries different meanings in different places. Bread is the staff of life, the body of Christ, the symbol of the Sabbath, the means of hospitality, and so on. Conceivably, there is a limited sense in which the first of these is primary, so that if there were twenty people in the world and just enough bread to feed the twenty, the primacy of bread-as-staff-of-life would yield a sufficient distributive principle. But that is the only circumstance in which it would do so; and even there, we can't be sure. If the religious uses of bread were to conflict with its nutritional uses—if the gods demanded that bread be baked and burned rather than eaten—it is by no means clear which use would be primary. How, then, is bread to be incorporated into the universal list? The question is even harder to answer, the conventional answers less plausible, as we pass from necessities to opportunities, powers, reputations, and so on. These can be incorporated only if they are abstracted from every particular meaning—hence, for all practical purposes, rendered meaningless.

4. But it is the meaning of goods that determines their movement. Distributive criteria and arrangements are intrinsic not to the

8

good-in-itself but to the social good. If we understand what it is, what it means to those for whom it is a good, we understand how, by whom, and for what reasons it ought to be distributed. All distributions are just or unjust relative to the social meanings of the goods at stake. This is in obvious ways a principle of legitimation, but it is also a critical principle.* When medieval Christians, for example, condemned the sin of simony, they were claiming that the meaning of a particular social good, ecclesiastical office, excluded its sale and purchase. Given the Christian understanding of office, it followed—I am inclined to say, it necessarily followed—that office holders should be chosen for their knowledge and piety and not for their wealth. There are presumably things that money can buy, but not this thing. Similarly, the words *prostitution* and *bribery*, like *simony*, describe the sale and purchase of goods that, given certain understandings of their meaning, ought never to be sold or purchased.

5. Social meanings are historical in character; and so distributions, and just and unjust distributions, change over time. To be sure, certain key goods have what we might think of as characteristic normative structures, reiterated across the lines (but not all the lines) of time and space. It is because of this reiteration that the British philosopher Bernard Williams is able to argue that goods should always be distributed for "relevant reasons"—where relevance seems to connect to essential rather than to social meanings.[7] The idea that offices, for example, should go to qualified candidates—though not the only idea that has been held about offices—is plainly visible in very different societies where simony and nepotism, under different names, have similarly been thought sinful or unjust. (But there has been a wide divergence of views about what sorts of position and place are properly called "offices.") Again, punishment has been widely understood as a negative good that ought to go to people who are judged to deserve it on the basis of a verdict, not of a political decision. (But what constitutes a verdict? Who is to deliver it? How, in short, is justice to be done to accused men and women? About these questions there has been significant disagreement.) These examples invite empirical investigation.

---

*Aren't social meanings, as Marx said, nothing other than "the ideas of the ruling class," "the dominant material relationships grasped as ideas"?[6] I don't think that they are ever only that or simply that, though the members of the ruling class and the intellectuals they patronize may well be in a position to exploit and distort social meanings in their own interests. When they do that, however, they are likely to encounter resistance, rooted (intellectually) in those same meanings. A people's culture is always a joint, even if it isn't an entirely cooperative, production; and it is always a complex production. The common understanding of particular goods incorporates principles, procedures, conceptions of agency, that the rulers would not choose if they were choosing *right now*—and so provides the terms of social criticism. The appeal to what I shall call "internal" principles against the usurpations of powerful men and women is the ordinary form of critical discourse.

There is no merely intuitive or speculative procedure for seizing upon relevant reasons.

6. When meanings are distinct, distributions must be autonomous. Every social good or set of goods constitutes, as it were, a distributive sphere within which only certain criteria and arrangements are appropriate. Money is inappropriate in the sphere of ecclesiastical office; it is an intrusion from another sphere. And piety should make for no advantage in the marketplace, as the marketplace has commonly been understood. Whatever can rightly be sold ought to be sold to pious men and women and also to profane, heretical, and sinful men and women (else no one would do much business). The market is open to all comers; the church is not. In no society, of course, are social meanings entirely distinct. What happens in one distributive sphere affects what happens in the others; we can look, at most, for relative autonomy. But relative autonomy, like social meaning, is a critical principle—indeed, as I shall be arguing throughout this book, a radical principle. It is radical even though it doesn't point to a single standard against which all distributions are to be measured. There is no single standard. But there are standards (roughly knowable even when they are also controversial) for every social good and every distributive sphere in every particular society; and these standards are often violated, the goods usurped, the spheres invaded, by powerful men and women.

Dominance and Monopoly

In fact, the violations are systematic. Autonomy is a matter of social meaning and shared values, but it is more likely to make for occasional reformation and rebellion than for everyday enforcement. For all the complexity of their distributive arrangements, most societies are organized on what we might think of as a social version of the gold standard: one good or one set of goods is dominant and determinative of value in all the spheres of distribution. And that good or set of goods is commonly monopolized, its value upheld by the strength and cohesion of its owners. I call a good dominant if the individuals who have it, because they have it, can command a wide range of other goods. It is monopolized whenever a single man or woman, a monarch in the world of value—or a group of men and women, oligarchs—successfully hold it against all rivals. Dominance describes a way of using social goods that isn't limited by their intrinsic meanings or that shapes those meanings in its own image. Monopoly describes a way of owning or controlling social goods in order to exploit their dominance. When goods are scarce and widely needed, like water in the desert, monopoly itself will make them dominant. Mostly, however, dominance is a more elaborate social creation, the work of many hands, mixing reality and symbol. Physical strength, familial reputation, religious or political office, landed wealth, capital, technical knowledge: each of these, in different historical periods, has been dominant; and each of them has been monopolized by some group of men and women. And then all good things come to those who have the one best thing. Possess that one, and the others come in train. Or, to change the metaphor, a dominant good is converted into another good, into many others, in accordance with what often appears to be a natural process but is in fact magical, a kind of social alchemy.

No social good ever entirely dominates the range of goods; no monopoly is ever perfect. I mean to describe tendencies only, but crucial tendencies. For we can characterize whole societies in terms of the patterns of conversion that are established within them. Some characterizations are simple: in a capitalist society, capital is dominant and readily converted into prestige and power; in a technocracy, technical knowledge plays the same part. But it isn't difficult to imagine, or to find, more complex social arrangements. Indeed, capitalism and technocracy are more complex than their names imply, even if the names do convey real information about the most important forms of sharing, dividing, and exchanging. Monopolistic control of a dominant good makes a ruling class, whose members stand atop the distributive system—much as philosophers, claiming to have the wisdom they love, might like to do. But since dominance is always incomplete and monopoly imperfect, the rule of every ruling class is unstable. It is continually challenged by other groups in the name of alternative patterns of conversion.

Distribution is what social conflict is all about. Marx's heavy emphasis on productive processes should not conceal from us the simple truth that the struggle for control of the means of production is a distributive struggle. Land and capital are at stake, and these are goods that can be shared, divided, exchanged, and endlessly converted. But land and capital are not the only dominant goods; it is possible (it has historically been possible) to come to them by way of other goods—military or political power, religious office and charisma, and so on. History reveals no single dominant good and no naturally dominant good, but only different kinds of magic and competing bands of magicians.

The claim to monopolize a dominant good—when worked up for public purposes—constitutes an ideology. Its standard form is to connect legitimate possession with some set of personal qualities through the medium of a philosophical principle. So aristocracy, or the rule of the best, is the principle of those who lay claim to breeding and intelligence: they are commonly the monopolists of landed wealth and familial reputation. Divine supremacy is the principle of those who claim to know the word of God: they are the monopolists of grace and office. Meritocracy, or the career open to talents, is the principle of those who claim to be talented: they are most often the monopolists of education. Free exchange is the principle of those who are ready, or who tell us they are ready, to put their money at risk: they are the monopolists of movable wealth. These groups—and others, too, similarly marked off by their principles and possessions—compete with one another, struggling for supremacy. One group wins, and then a different one; or coalitions are worked out, and supremacy is uneasily shared. There is no final victory, nor should there be. But that is not to say that the claims of the different groups are necessarily wrong, or that the principles they invoke are of no value as distributive criteria; the principles are often exactly right within the limits of a particular sphere. Ideologies are readily corrupted, but their corruption is not the most interesting thing about them.

It is in the study of these struggles that I have sought the guiding thread of my own argument. The struggles have, I think, a paradigmatic form. Some group of men and women—class, caste, strata, estate, alliance, or social formation—comes to enjoy a monopoly or a near monopoly of some dominant good; or, a coalition of groups comes to enjoy, and so on. This dominant good is more or less systematically converted into all sorts of other things—opportunities, powers, and reputations. So wealth is seized by the strong, honor by the wellborn, office by the well educated. Perhaps the ideology that justifies the seizure is widely believed to be true. But resentment and resistance are (almost) as pervasive as belief. There are always some people, and after a time there are a great many, who think the seizure is not justice but usurpation. The ruling group does not possess, or does not uniquely possess, the qualities it claims; the conversion process violates the common understanding of the goods at stake. Social conflict is intermittent, or it is endemic; at some point, counterclaims are put forward. Though these are of many different sorts, three general sorts are especially important:

Complex Equality

1. The claim that the dominant good, whatever it is, should be redistributed so that it can be equally or at least more widely shared: this amounts to saying that monopoly is unjust.
2. The claim that the way should be opened for the autonomous distribution of all social goods: this amounts to saying that dominance is unjust.
3. The claim that some new good, monopolized by some new group, should replace the currently dominant good: this amounts to saying that the existing pattern of dominance and monopoly is unjust.

The third claim is, in Marx's view, the model of every revolutionary ideology—except, perhaps, the proletarian or last ideology. Thus, the French Revolution in Marxist theory: the dominance of noble birth and blood and of feudal landholding is ended, and bourgeois wealth is established in its stead. The original situation is reproduced with different subjects and objects (this is never unimportant), and then the class war is immediately renewed. It is not my purpose here to endorse or to criticize Marx's view. I suspect, in fact, that there is something of all three claims in every revolutionary ideology, but that, too, is not a position that I shall try to defend here. Whatever its sociological significance, the third claim is not philosophically interesting—unless one believes that there is a naturally dominant good, such that its possessors could legitimately claim to rule the rest of us. In a sense, Marx believed exactly that. The means of production is the dominant good throughout history, and Marxism is a historicist doctrine insofar as it suggests that whoever controls the prevailing means legitimately rules.[8] After the communist revolution, we shall all control the means of production: at that point, the third claim collapses into the first. Meanwhile, Marx's model is a program for ongoing distributive struggle. It will matter, of course, who wins at this or that moment, but we won't know why or how it matters if we attend only to the successive assertions of dominance and monopoly.

Simple Equality

It is with the first two claims that I shall be concerned, and ultimately with the second alone, for that one seems to me to capture best the plurality of social meanings and the real complexity of distributive systems. But the first is the more common among philosophers; it matches

13

their own search for unity and singularity; and I shall need to explain its difficulties at some length.

Men and women who make the first claim challenge the monopoly but not the dominance of a particular social good. This is also a challenge to monopoly in general; for if wealth, for example, is dominant and widely shared, no other good can possibly be monopolized. Imagine a society in which everything is up for sale and every citizen has as much money as every other. I shall call this the "regime of simple equality." Equality is multiplied through the conversion process, until it extends across the full range of social goods. The regime of simple equality won't last for long, because the further progress of conversion, free exchange in the market, is certain to bring inequalities in its train. If one wanted to sustain simple equality over time, one would require a "monetary law" like the agrarian laws of ancient times or the Hebrew sabbatical, providing for a periodic return to the original condition. Only a centralized and activist state would be strong enough to force such a return; and it isn't clear that state officials would actually be able or willing to do that, if money were the dominant good. In any case, the original condition is unstable in another way. It's not only that monopoly will reappear, but also that dominance will disappear.

In practice, breaking the monopoly of money neutralizes its dominance. Other goods come into play, and inequality takes on new forms. Consider again the regime of simple equality. Everything is up for sale, and everyone has the same amount of money. So everyone has, say, an equal ability to buy an education for his children. Some do that, and others don't. It turns out to be a good investment: other social goods are, increasingly, offered for sale only to people with educational certificates. Soon everyone invests in education; or, more likely, the purchase is universalized through the tax system. But then the school is turned into a competitive world within which money is no longer dominant. Natural talent or family upbringing or skill in writing examinations is dominant instead, and educational success and certification are monopolized by some new group. Let's call them (what they call themselves) the "group of the talented." Eventually the members of this group claim that the good they control should be dominant outside the school: offices, titles, prerogatives, wealth too, should all be possessed by themselves. This is the career open to talents, equal opportunity, and so on. This is what fairness requires; talent will out; and in any case, talented men and women will enlarge the resources available to everyone else. So Michael Young's meritocracy is born, with all its attendant inequalities.[9]

What should we do now? It is possible to set limits to the new conversion patterns, to recognize but constrain the monopoly power of the talented. I take this to be the purpose of John Rawls's difference principle, according to which inequalities are justified only if they are designed to bring, and actually do bring, the greatest possible benefit to the least advantaged social class.[10] More specifically, the difference principle is a constraint imposed on talented men and women, once the monopoly of wealth has been broken. It works in this way: Imagine a surgeon who claims more than his equal share of wealth on the basis of the skills he has learned and the certificates he has won in the harsh competitive struggles of college and medical school. We will grant the claim if, and only if, granting it is beneficial in the stipulated ways. At the same time, we will act to limit and regulate the sale of surgery—that is, the direct conversion of surgical skill into wealth.

This regulation will necessarily be the work of the state, just as monetary laws and agrarian laws are the work of the state. Simple equality would require continual state intervention to break up or constrain incipient monopolies and to repress new forms of dominance. But then state power itself will become the central object of competitive struggles. Groups of men and women will seek to monopolize and then to use the state in order to consolidate their control of other social goods. Or, the state will be monopolized by its own agents in accordance with the iron law of oligarchy. Politics is always the most direct path to dominance, and political power (rather than the means of production) is probably the most important, and certainly the most dangerous, good in human history.* Hence the need to constrain the agents of constraint, to establish constitutional checks and balances. These are limits imposed on political monopoly, and they are all the more important once the various social and economic monopolies have been broken.

One way of limiting political power is to distribute it widely. This may not work, given the well-canvassed dangers of majority tyranny; but these dangers are probably less acute than they are often made out to be. The greater danger of democratic government is that it will be

---

*I should note here what will become more clear as I go along, that political power is a special sort of good. It has a twofold character. First, it is like the other things that men and women make, value, exchange, and share: sometimes dominant, sometimes not; sometimes widely held, sometimes the possession of a very few. And, second, it is unlike all the other things because, however it is had and whoever has it, political power is the regulative agency for social goods generally. It is used to defend the boundaries of all the distributive spheres, including its own, and to enforce the common understandings of what goods are and what they are for. (But it can also be used, obviously, to invade the different spheres and to override those understandings.) In this second sense, we might say, indeed, that political power is always dominant—at the boundaries, but not within them. The central problem of political life is to maintain that crucial distinction between "at" and "in." But this is a problem that cannot be solved given the imperatives of simple equality.

weak to cope with re-emerging monopolies in society at large, with the social strength of plutocrats, bureaucrats, technocrats, meritocrats, and so on. In theory, political power is the dominant good in a democracy, and it is convertible in any way the citizens choose. But in practice, again, breaking the monopoly of power neutralizes its dominance. Political power cannot be widely shared without being subjected to the pull of all the other goods that the citizens already have or hope to have. Hence democracy is, as Marx recognized, essentially a reflective system, mirroring the prevailing and emerging distribution of social goods.[11] Democratic decision making will be shaped by the cultural conceptions that determine or underwrite the new monopolies. To prevail against these monopolies, power will have to be centralized, perhaps itself monopolized. Once again, the state must be very powerful if it is to fulfill the purposes assigned to it by the difference principle or by any similarly interventionist rule.

Still, the regime of simple equality might work. One can imagine a more or less stable tension between emerging monopolies and political constraints, between the claim to privilege put forward by the talented, say, and the enforcement of the difference principle, and then between the agents of enforcement and the democratic constitution. But I suspect that difficulties will recur, and that at many points in time the only remedy for private privilege will be statism, and the only escape from statism will be private privilege. We will mobilize power to check monopoly, then look for some way of checking the power we have mobilized. But there is no way that doesn't open opportunities for strategically placed men and women to seize and exploit important social goods.

These problems derive from treating monopoly, and not dominance, as the central issue in distributive justice. It is not difficult, of course, to understand why philosophers (and political activists, too) have focused on monopoly. The distributive struggles of the modern age begin with a war against the aristocracy's singular hold on land, office, and honor. This seems an especially pernicious monopoly because it rests upon birth and blood, with which the individual has nothing to do, rather than upon wealth, or power, or education, all of which—at least in principle—can be earned. And when every man and woman becomes, as it were, a smallholder in the sphere of birth and blood, an important victory is indeed won. Birthright ceases to be a dominant good; henceforth, it purchases very little; wealth, power, and education come to the fore. With regard to these latter goods, however, simple equality cannot be sustained at all, or it can only be sustained subject to the vicissitudes I have just described.

Complex Equality

Within their own spheres, as they are currently understood, these three tend to generate natural monopolies that can be repressed only if state power is itself dominant and if it is monopolized by officials committed to the repression. But there is, I think, another path to another kind of equality.

Tyranny and Complex Equality

I want to argue that we should focus on the reduction of dominance—not, or not primarily, on the break-up or the constraint of monopoly. We should consider what it might mean to narrow the range within which particular goods are convertible and to vindicate the autonomy of distributive spheres. But this line of argument, though it is not uncommon historically, has never fully emerged in philosophical writing. Philosophers have tended to criticize (or to justify) existing or emerging monopolies of wealth, power, and education. Or, they have criticized (or justified) particular conversions—of wealth into education or of office into wealth. And all this, most often, in the name of some radically simplified distributive system. The critique of dominance will suggest instead a way of reshaping and then living with the actual complexity of distributions.

Imagine now a society in which different social goods are monopolistically held—as they are in fact and always will be, barring continual state intervention—but in which no particular good is generally convertible. As I go along, I shall try to define the precise limits on convertibility, but for now the general description will suffice. This is a complex egalitarian society. Though there will be many small inequalities, inequality will not be multiplied through the conversion process. Nor will it be summed across different goods, because the autonomy of distributions will tend to produce a variety of local monopolies, held by different groups of men and women. I don't want to claim that complex equality would necessarily be more stable than simple equality, but I am inclined to think that it would open the way for more diffused and particularized forms of social conflict. And the resistance to convertibility would be maintained, in large degree, by ordinary men and women within their own spheres of competence and control, without large-scale state action.

This is, I think, an attractive picture, but I have not yet explained just why it is attractive. The argument for complex equality begins from our understanding—I mean, our actual, concrete, positive, and particular understanding—of the various social goods. And then it moves on to an account of the way we relate to one another through those goods. Simple equality is a simple distributive condition, so that if I have fourteen hats and you have fourteen hats, we are equal. And it is all to the good if hats are dominant, for then our equality is extended through all the spheres of social life. On the view that I shall take here, however, we simply have the same number of hats, and it is unlikely that hats will be dominant for long. Equality is a complex relation of persons, mediated by the goods we make, share, and divide among ourselves; it is not an identity of possessions. It requires then, a diversity of distributive criteria that mirrors the diversity of social goods.

The argument for complex equality has been beautifully put by Pascal in one of his *Pensées*.

> The nature of tyranny is to desire power over the whole world and outside its own sphere.
> There are different companies—the strong, the handsome, the intelligent, the devout—and each man reigns in his own, not elsewhere. But sometimes they meet, and the strong and the handsome fight for mastery—foolishly, for their mastery is of different kinds. They misunderstand one another, and make the mistake of each aiming at universal dominion. Nothing can win this, not even strength, for it is powerless in the kingdom of the wise. . . .
> *Tyranny.* The following statements, therefore, are false and tyrannical: "Because I am handsome, so I should command respect." "I am strong, therefore men should love me. . . ." "I am . . . et cetera."
> Tyranny is the wish to obtain by one means what can only be had by another. We owe different duties to different qualities: love is the proper response to charm, fear to strength, and belief to learning.[12]

Marx made a similar argument in his early manuscripts; perhaps he had this *pensée* in mind:

> Let us assume man to be man, and his relation to the world to be a human one. Then love can only be exchanged for love, trust for trust, etc. If you wish to enjoy art you must be an artistically cultivated person; if you wish to influence other people, you must be a person who really has a stimulating and encouraging effect upon others. . . . If you love without evoking love in return, i.e., if you are not able, by the manifestation of yourself as a loving person, to make yourself a beloved person—then your love is impotent and a misfortune.[13]

These are not easy arguments, and most of my book is simply an exposition of their meaning. But here I shall attempt something more simple and schematic: a translation of the arguments into the terms I have already been using.

The first claim of Pascal and Marx is that personal qualities and social goods have their own spheres of operation, where they work their effects freely, spontaneously, and legitimately. There are ready or natural conversions that follow from, and are intuitively plausible because of, the social meaning of particular goods. The appeal is to our ordinary understanding and, at the same time, against our common acquiesence in illegitimate conversion patterns. Or, it is an appeal from our acquiesence to our resentment. There is something wrong, Pascal suggests, with the conversion of strength into belief. In political terms, Pascal means that no ruler can rightly command my opinions merely because of the power he wields. Nor can he, Marx adds, rightly claim to influence my actions: if a ruler wants to do that, he must be persuasive, helpful, encouraging, and so on. These arguments depend for their force on some shared understanding of knowledge, influence, and power. Social goods have social meanings, and we find our way to distributive justice through an interpretation of those meanings. We search for principles internal to each distributive sphere.

The second claim is that the disregard of these principles is tyranny. To convert one good into another, when there is no intrinsic connection between the two, is to invade the sphere where another company of men and women properly rules. Monopoly is not inappropriate within the spheres. There is nothing wrong, for example, with the grip that persuasive and helpful men and women (politicians) establish on political power. But the use of political power to gain access to other goods is a tyrannical use. Thus, an old description of tyranny is generalized: princes become tyrants, according to medieval writers, when they seize the property or invade the family of their subjects.[14] In political life—but more widely, too—the dominance of goods makes for the domination of people.

The regime of complex equality is the opposite of tyranny. It establishes a set of relationships such that domination is impossible. In formal terms, complex equality means that no citizen's standing in one sphere or with regard to one social good can be undercut by his standing in some other sphere, with regard to some other good. Thus, citizen X may be chosen over citizen Y for political office, and then the two of them will be unequal in the sphere of politics. But they will not be unequal generally so long as X's office gives him no advantages over Y in any other sphere—superior medical care, access to better schools for his children, entrepreneurial opportunities, and so on. So long as office is not a dominant good, is not generally convertible, office holders will stand, or at least can stand, in a relation of equality to the men and women they govern.

But what if dominance were eliminated, the autonomy of the spheres established—and the same people were successful in one sphere after another, triumphant in every company, piling up goods without the need for illegitimate conversions? This would certainly make for an inegalitarian society, but it would also suggest in the strongest way that a society of equals was not a lively possibility. I doubt that any egalitarian argument could survive in the face of such evidence. Here is a person whom we have freely chosen (without reference to his family ties or personal wealth) as our political representative. He is also a bold and inventive entrepreneur. When he was younger, he studied science, scored amazingly high grades in every exam, and made important discoveries. In war, he is surpassingly brave and wins the highest honors. Himself compassionate and compelling, he is loved by all who know him. Are there such people? Maybe so, but I have my doubts. We tell stories like the one I have just told, but the stories are fictions, the conversion of power or money or academic talent into legendary fame. In any case, there aren't enough such people to constitute a ruling class and dominate the rest of us. Nor can they be successful in every distributive sphere, for there are some spheres to which the idea of success doesn't pertain. Nor are their children likely, under conditions of complex equality, to inherit their success. By and large, the most accomplished politicians, entrepreneurs, scientists, soldiers, and lovers will be different people; and so long as the goods they possess don't bring other goods in train, we have no reason to fear their accomplishments.

The critique of dominance and domination points toward an open-ended distributive principle. *No social good* x *should be distributed to men and women who possess some other good* y *merely because they possess* y *and without regard to the meaning of* x. This is a principle that has probably been reiterated, at one time or another, for every y that has ever been dominant. But it has not often been stated in general terms. Pascal and Marx have suggested the application of the principle against all possible y's, and I shall attempt to work out that application. I shall be looking, then, not at the members of Pascal's companies—the strong or the weak, the handsome or the plain—but at the goods they share and divide. The purpose of the principle is to focus our attention; it doesn't determine the shares or the division. The principle directs us to study the meaning of social goods, to examine the different distributive spheres from the inside.

Three Distributive Principles

The theory that results is unlikely to be elegant. No account of the meaning of a social good, or of the boundaries of the sphere within which it legitimately operates, will be uncontroversial. Nor is there any neat procedure for generating or testing different accounts. At best, the arguments will be rough, reflecting the diverse and conflict-ridden character of the social life that we seek simultaneously to understand and to regulate—but not to regulate until we understand. I shall set aside, then, all claims made on behalf of any single distributive criterion, for no such criterion can possibly match the diversity of social goods. Three criteria, however, appear to meet the requirements of the open-ended principle and have often been defended as the beginning and end of distributive justice, so I must say something about each of them. Free exchange, desert, and need: all three have real force, but none of them has force across the range of distributions. They are part of the story, not the whole of it.

Free Exchange

Free exchange is obviously open-ended; it guarantees no particular distributive outcome. At no point in any exchange process plausibly called "free" will it be possible to predict the particular division of social goods that will obtain at some later point.[15] (It may be possible, however, to predict the general structure of the division.) In theory at least, free exchange creates a market within which all goods are convertible into all other goods through the neutral medium of money. There are no dominant goods and no monopolies. Hence the successive divisions that obtain will directly reflect the social meanings of the goods that are divided. For each bargain, trade, sale, and purchase will have been agreed to voluntarily by men and women who know what that meaning is, who are indeed its makers. Every exchange is a revelation of social meaning. By definition, then, no x will ever fall into the hands of someone who possesses y, merely because he possesses y and without regard to what x actually means to some other member of society. The market is radically pluralistic in its operations and its outcomes, infinitely sensitive to the meanings that individuals attach to goods. What possible restraints can be imposed on free exchange, then, in the name of pluralism?

But everyday life in the market, the actual experience of free exchange, is very different from what the theory suggests. Money, supposedly the neutral medium, is in practice a dominant good, and it is monopolized by people who possess a special talent for bargaining and trading—the green thumb of bourgeois society. Then other people demand a redistribution of money and the establishment of the regime of simple equality, and the search begins for some way to sustain that regime. But even if we focus on the first untroubled moment of simple equality—free exchange on the basis of equal shares—we will still need to set limits on what can be exchanged for what. For free exchange leaves distributions entirely in the hands of individuals, and social meanings are not subject, or are not always subject, to the interpretative decisions of individual men and women.

Consider an easy example, the case of political power. We can conceive of political power as a set of goods of varying value, votes, influence, offices, and so on. Any of these can be traded on the market and accumulated by individuals willing to sacrifice other goods. Even if the sacrifices are real, however, the result is a form of tyranny—petty tyranny, given the conditions of simple equality. Because I am willing to do without my hat, I shall vote twice; and you who value the vote less than you value my hat, will not vote at all. I suspect that the result is tyrannical even with regard to the two of us, who have reached a voluntary agreement. It is certainly tyrannical with regard to all the other citizens who must now submit to my disproportionate power. It is not the case that votes can't be bargained for; on one interpretation, that's what democratic politics is all about. And democratic politicians have certainly been known to buy votes, or to try to buy them, by promising public expenditures that benefit particular groups of voters. But this is done in public, with public funds, and subject to public approval. Private trading is ruled out by virtue of what politics, or democratic politics, is—that is, by virtue of what we did when we constituted the political community and of what we still think about what we did.

Free exchange is not a general criterion, but we will be able to specify the boundaries within which it operates only through a careful analysis of particular social goods. And having worked through such an analysis, we will come up at best with a philosophically authoritative set of boundaries and not necessarily with the set that ought to be politically authoritative. For money seeps across all boundaries—this is the primary form of illegal immigration; and just where one ought to try to stop it is a question of expediency as well as of principle. Failure to stop it at some reasonable point has consequences throughout the range of distributions, but consideration of these belongs in a later chapter.

Desert

Like free exchange, desert seems both open-ended and pluralistic. One might imagine a single neutral agency dispensing rewards and punishments, infinitely sensitive to all the forms of individual desert. Then the distributive process would indeed be centralized, but the results would still be unpredictable and various. There would be no dominant good. No x would ever be distributed without regard to its social meaning; for, without attention to what x is, it is conceptually impossible to say that x is deserved. All the different companies of men and women would receive their appropriate reward. How this would work in practice, however, is not easy to figure out. It might make sense to say of this charming man, for example, that he deserves to be loved. It makes no sense to say that he deserves to be loved by this (or any) particular woman. If he loves her while she remains impervious to his (real) charms, that is his misfortune. I doubt that we would want the situation corrected by some outside agency. The love of particular men and women, on our understanding of it, can only be distributed by themselves, and they are rarely guided in these matters by considerations of desert.

The case is exactly the same with influence. Here, let's say, is a woman widely thought to be stimulating and encouraging to others. Perhaps she deserves to be an influential member of our community. But she doesn't deserve that I be influenced by her or that I follow her lead. Nor would we want my followership, as it were, assigned to her by any agency capable of making such assignments. She may go to great lengths to stimulate and encourage me, and do all the things that are commonly called stimulating or encouraging. But if I (perversely) refuse to be stimulated or encouraged, I am not denying her anything that she deserves. The same argument holds by extension for politicians and ordinary citizens. Citizens can't trade their votes for hats; they can't individually decide to cross the boundary that separates the sphere of politics from the marketplace. But within the sphere of politics, they do make individual decisions; and they are rarely guided, again, by considerations of desert. It's not clear that offices can be deserved—another issue that I must postpone; but even if they can be, it would violate our understanding of democratic politics were they simply distributed to deserving men and women by some central agency.

Similarly, however we draw the boundaries of the sphere within which free exchange operates, desert will play no role within those boundaries. I am skillful at bargaining and trading, let's say, and so accumulate a large number of beautiful pictures. If we assume, as painters mostly do, that pictures are appropriately traded in the market, then there is nothing wrong with my having the pictures. My title is legitimate. But it would be odd to say that I deserve to have them simply because I am good at bargaining and trading. Desert seems to require an especially close connection between particular goods and particular persons, whereas justice only sometimes requires a connection of that sort. Still, we might insist that only artistically cultivated people, who deserve to have pictures, should actually have them. It's not difficult to imagine a distributive mechanism. The state could buy all the pictures that were offered for sale (but artists would have to be licensed, so that there wouldn't be an endless number of pictures), evaluate them, and then distribute them to artistically cultivated men and women, the better pictures to the more cultivated. The state does something like this, sometimes, with regard to things that people need—medical care, for example—but not with regard to things that people deserve. There are practical difficulties here, but I suspect a deeper reason for this difference. Desert does not have the urgency of need, and it does not involve having (owning and consuming) in the same way. Hence, we are willing to tolerate the separation of owners of paintings and artistically cultivated people, or we are unwilling to require the kinds of interference in the market that would be necessary to end the separation. Of course, public provision is always possible alongside the market, and so we might argue that artistically cultivated people deserve not pictures but museums. Perhaps they do, but they don't deserve that the rest of us contribute money or appropriate public funds for the purchase of pictures and the construction of buildings. They will have to persuade us that art is worth the money; they will have to stimulate and encourage our own artistic cultivation. And if they fail to do that, their own love of art may well turn out to be "impotent and a misfortune."

Even if we were to assign the distribution of love, influence, offices, works of art, and so on, to some omnipotent arbiters of desert, how would we select them? How could anyone deserve such a position? Only God, who knows what secrets lurk in the hearts of men, would be able to make the necessary distributions. If human beings had to do the work, the distributive mechanism would be seized early on by some band of aristocrats (so they would call themselves) with a fixed conception of what is best and most deserving, and insensitive to the diverse excellences of their fellow citizens. And then desert would cease to be a pluralist criterion; we would find ourselves face to face with a new set (of an old sort) of tyrants. We do, of course, choose people as arbiters of desert—to serve on juries, for example, or to award prizes; it will be worth considering later what the prerogatives of a juror are. But it is important to stress here that he operates within a narrow range. Desert is a strong claim, but it calls for difficult judgments; and only under very special conditions does it yield specific distributions.

Need

Finally, the criterion of need. "To each according to his needs" is generally taken as the distributive half of Marx's famous maxim: we are to distribute the wealth of the community so as to meet the necessities of its members.[16] A plausible proposal, but a radically incomplete one. In fact, the first half of the maxim is also a distributive proposal, and it doesn't fit the rule of the second half. "From each according to his ability" suggests that jobs should be distributed (or that men and women should be conscripted to work) on the basis of individual qualifications. But individuals don't in any obvious sense need the jobs for which they are qualified. Perhaps such jobs are scarce, and there are a large number of qualified candidates: which candidates need them most? If their material needs are already taken care of, perhaps they don't need to work at all. Or if, in some non-material sense, they all need to work, then that need won't distinguish among them, at least not to the naked eye. It would in any case be odd to ask a search committee looking, say, for a hospital director to make its choice on the basis of the needs of the candidates rather than on those of the staff and the patients of the hospital. But the latter set of needs, even if it isn't the subject of political disagreement, won't yield a single distributive decision.

Nor will need work for many other goods. Marx's maxim doesn't help at all with regard to the distribution of political power, honor and fame, sailboats, rare books, beautiful objects of every sort. These are not things that anyone, strictly speaking, needs. Even if we take a loose view and define the verb to need the way children do, as the strongest form of the verb to want, we still won't have an adequate distributive criterion. The sorts of things that I have listed cannot be distributed equally to those with equal wants because some of them are generally, and some of them are necessarily, scarce, and some of them can't be possessed at all unless other people, for reasons of their own, agree on who is to possess them.

Need generates a particular distributive sphere, within which it is itself the appropriate distributive principle. In a poor society, a high proportion of social wealth will be drawn into this sphere. But given the great variety of goods that arises out of any common life, even when it is lived at a very low material level, other distributive criteria will always be operating alongside of need, and it will always be necessary to worry about the boundaries that mark them off from one another. Within its sphere, certainly, need meets the general distributive rule about x and y. Needed goods distributed to needy people in proportion to their neediness are obviously not dominated by any other goods. It's not having y, but only lacking x that is relevant. But we can now see, I think, that every criterion that has any force at all meets the general rule within its own sphere, and not elsewhere. This is the effect of the rule: different goods to different companies of men and women for different reasons and in accordance with different procedures. And to get all this right, or to get it roughly right, is to map out the entire social world.

Hierarchies and Caste Societies

Or, rather, it is to map out a particular social world. For the analysis that I propose is imminent and phenomenological in character. It will yield not an ideal map or a master plan but, rather, a map and a plan appropriate to the people for whom it is drawn, whose common life it reflects. The goal, of course, is a reflection of a special kind, which picks up those deeper understandings of social goods which are not necessarily mirrored in the everyday practice of dominance and monopoly. But what if there are no such understandings? I have been assuming all along that social meanings call for the autonomy, or the relative autonomy, of distributive spheres; and so they do much of the time. But it's not impossible to imagine a society where dominance and monopoly are not violations but enactments of meaning, where social goods are conceived in hierarchical terms. In feudal Europe, for example, clothing was not a commodity (as it is today) but a badge of rank. Rank dominated dress. The meaning of clothing was shaped in the image of the feudal order. Dressing in finery to which one wasn't entitled was a kind of lie; it made a false statement about who one was. When a

Complex Equality

king or a prime minister dressed as a commoner in order to learn something about the opinions of his subjects, this was a kind of politic deceit. On the other hand, the difficulties of enforcing the clothing code (the sumptuary laws) suggests that there was all along an alternative sense of what clothing meant. At some point, at least, one can begin to recognize the boundaries of a distinct sphere within which people dress in accordance with what they can afford or what they are willing to spend or how they want to look. The sumptuary laws may still be enforced, but now one can make—and ordinary men and women do, in fact, make—egalitarian arguments against them.

Can we imagine a society in which all goods are hierarchically conceived? Perhaps the caste system of ancient India had this form (though that is a far-reaching claim, and it would be prudent to doubt its truth: for one thing, political power seems always to have escaped the laws of caste). We think of castes as rigidly segregated groups, of the caste system as a "plural society," a world of boundaries.[17] But the system is constituted by an extraordinary integration of meanings. Prestige, wealth, knowledge, office, occupation, food, clothing, even the social good of conversation: all are subject to the intellectual as well as to the physical discipline of hierarchy. And the hierarchy is itself determined by the single value of ritual purity. A certain kind of collective mobility is possible, for castes or subcastes can cultivate the outward marks of purity and (within severe limits) raise their position in the social scale. And the system as a whole rests upon a religious doctrine that promises equality of opportunity, not in this life but across the lives of the soul. The individual's status here and now "is the result of his conduct in his last incarnation . . . and if unsatisfactory can be remedied by acquiring merit in his present life which will raise his status in the next."[18] We should not assume that men and women are ever entirely content with radical inequality. Nevertheless, distributions here and now are part of a single system, largely unchallenged, in which purity is dominant over other goods—and birth and blood are dominant over purity. Social meanings overlap and cohere.

The more perfect the coherence, the less possible it is even to think about complex equality. All goods are like crowns and thrones in a hereditary monarchy. There is no room, and there are no criteria, for autonomous distributions. In fact, however, even hereditary monarchies are rarely so simply constructed. The social understanding of royal power commonly involves some notion of divine grace, or magical gift, or human insight; and these criteria for office holding are potentially independent of birth and blood. So it is for most social goods: they are only imperfectly integrated into larger systems; they are understood, at least sometimes, in their own terms. The theory of goods explicates understandings of this sort (where they exist), and the theory of complex equality exploits them. We say, for example, that it is tyrannical for a man without grace or gift or insight to sit upon the throne. And this is only the first and most obvious kind of tyranny. We can search for many other kinds.

Tyranny is always specific in character: a particular boundary crossing, a particular violation of social meaning. Complex equality requires the defense of boundaries; it works by differentiating goods just as hierarchy works by differentiating people. But we can only talk of a *regime* of complex equality when there are many boundaries to defend; and what the right number is cannot be specified. There is no right number. Simple equality is easier: one dominant good widely distributed makes an egalitarian society. But complexity is hard: how many goods must be autonomously conceived before the relations they mediate can become the relations of equal men and women? There is no certain answer and hence no ideal regime. But as soon as we start to distinguish meanings and mark out distributive spheres, we are launched on an egalitarian enterprise.

The Setting of the Argument

The political community is the appropriate setting for this enterprise. It is not, to be sure, a self-contained distributive world: only the world is a self-contained distributive world, and contemporary science fiction invites us to speculate about a time when even that won't be true. Social goods are shared, divided, and exchanged across political frontiers. Monopoly and dominance operate almost as easily beyond the frontiers as within them. Things are moved, and people move themselves, back and forth across the lines. Nevertheless, the political community is probably the closest we can come to a world of common meanings. Language, history, and culture come together (come more closely together here than anywhere else) to produce a collective consciousness. National character, conceived as a fixed and permanent mental set, is obviously a myth; but the sharing of sensibilities and intuitions among the members of a historical community is a fact of life. Sometimes political and historical communities don't coincide, and there may well be a growing number of states in the world today where sensibilities and intuitions aren't readily shared; the sharing takes place in smaller units. And then, perhaps, we should look for some way to adjust distributive decisions to the requirements of those units. But this adjustment must itself be worked out politically, and its precise character will depend upon understandings shared among the citizens about the value of cultural diversity, local autonomy, and so on. It is to these understandings that we must appeal when we make our arguments—all of us, not philosophers alone; for in matters of morality, argument simply is the appeal to common meanings.

Politics, moreover, establishes its own bonds of commonality. In a world of independent states, political power is a local monopoly. These men and women, we can say, under whatever constraints, shape their own destiny. Or they struggle as best they can to shape their own destiny. And if their destiny is only partially in their own hands, the struggle is entirely so. They are the ones whose decision it is to tighten or loosen distributive criteria, to centralize or decentralize procedures, to intervene or refuse to intervene in this or that distributive sphere. Probably, some set of leaders make the actual decisions, but the citizens should be able to recognize the leaders as their own. If the leaders are cruel or stupid or endlessly venal, as they often are, the citizens or some of the citizens will try to replace them, fighting over the distribution of political power. The fight will be shaped by the institutional structures of the community—that is, by the outcomes of previous fights. Politics present is the product of politics past. It establishes an unavoidable setting for the consideration of distributive justice.

There is one last reason for adopting the view of the political community as setting, a reason that I shall elaborate on at some length in the next chapter. The community is itself a good—conceivably the most important good—that gets distributed. But it is a good that can only be distributed by taking people in, where all the senses of that latter phrase are relevant: they must be physically admitted and politically received. Hence membership cannot be handed out by some external agency; its value depends upon an internal decision. Were there no communities capable of making such decisions, there would in this case be no good worth distributing.

The only plausible alternative to the political community is humanity itself, the society of nations, the entire globe. But were we to take the globe as our setting, we would have to imagine what does not yet exist: a community that included all men and women everywhere. We would have to invent a set of common meanings for these people, avoiding if we could the stipulation of our own values. And we would have to ask the members of this hypothetical community (or their hypothetical representatives) to agree among themselves on what distributive arrangements and patterns of conversion are to count as just. Ideal contractualism or undistorted communication, which represents one approach—not my own—to justice in particular communities, may well be the only approach for the globe as a whole.[19] But whatever the hypothetical agreement, it could not be enforced without breaking the political monopolies of existing states and centralizing power at the global level. Hence the agreement (or the enforcement) would make not for complex but for simple equality—if power was dominant and widely shared—or simply for tyranny—if power was seized, as it probably would be, by a set of international bureaucrats. In the first case, the people of the world would have to live with the difficulties I have described: the continual reappearance of local privilege, the continual reassertion of global statism. In the second case, they would have to live with difficulties that are considerably worse. I will have a little more to say about these difficulties later. For now I take them to be reasons enough to limit myself to cities, countries, and states that have, over long periods of time, shaped their own internal life.

With regard to membership, however, important questions arise between and among such communities, and I shall try to focus on them and to draw into the light all those occasions when ordinary citizens focus on them. In a limited way, the theory of complex equality can be extended from particular communities to the society of nations, and the extension has this advantage: it will not run roughshod over local understandings and decisions. Just for that reason, it also will not yield a uniform system of distributions across the globe, and it will only begin to address the problems raised by mass poverty in many parts of the globe. I don't think the beginning unimportant; in any case, I can't move beyond it. To do that would require a different theory, which would take as its subject not the common life of citizens but the more distanced relations of states: a different theory, a different book, another time.

2

Membership

Members and Strangers

The idea of distributive justice presupposes a bounded world within which distributions takes place: a group of people committed to dividing, exchanging, and sharing social goods, first of all among themselves. That world, as I have already argued, is the political community, whose members distribute power to one another and avoid, if they possibly can, sharing it with anyone else. When we think about distributive justice, we think about independent cities or countries capable of arranging their own patterns of division and exchange, justly or unjustly. We assume an established group and a fixed population, and so we miss the first and most important distributive question: How is that group constituted?

I don't mean, How *was* it constituted? I am concerned here not with the historical origins of the different groups, but with the decisions they make in the present about their present and future populations. The primary good that we distribute to one another is membership in some human community. And what we do with regard to membership structures all our other distributive choices: it determines with whom we make those choices, from whom we require obedience and collect taxes, to whom we allocate goods and services.

Men and women without membership anywhere are stateless persons. That condition doesn't preclude every sort of distributive relation: markets, for example, are commonly open to all comers. But non-members are vulnerable and unprotected in the marketplace. Although they participate freely in the exchange of goods, they have no part in those goods that are shared. They are cut off from the communal provision of security and welfare. Even those aspects of security and welfare that are, like public health, collectively distributed are not guaranteed to non-members: for they have no guaranteed place in the collectivity and are always liable to expulsion. Statelessness is a condition of infinite danger.

But membership and non-membership are not the only—or, for our purposes, the most important—set of possibilities. It is also possible to be a member of a poor or a rich country, to live in a densely crowded or a largely empty country, to be the subject of an authoritarian regime or the citizen of a democracy. Since human beings are highly mobile, large numbers of men and women regularly attempt to change their residence and their membership, moving from unfavored to favored environments. Affluent and free countries are, like élite universities, besieged by applicants. They have to decide on their own size and character. More precisely, as citizens of such a country, we have to decide: Whom should we admit? Ought we to have open admissions? Can we choose among applicants? What are the appropriate criteria for distributing membership?

The plural pronouns that I have used in asking these questions suggest the conventional answer to them: we who are already members do the choosing, in accordance with our own understanding of what membership means in our community and of what sort of a community we want to have. Membership as a social good is constituted by our understanding; its value is fixed by our work and conversation; and then we are in charge (who else could be in charge?) of its distribution. But we don't distribute it among ourselves; it is already ours. We give it out to strangers. Hence the choice is also governed by our relationships with strangers—not only by our understanding of those relationships but also by the actual contacts, connections, alliances we have established and the effects we have had beyond our borders. But I shall focus first on strangers in the literal sense, men and women whom we meet, so to speak, for the first time. We don't know who they are or what they think, yet we recognize them as men and women. Like us but not of us: when we decide on membership, we have to consider them as well as ourselves.

I won't try to recount here the history of Western ideas about strangers. In a number of ancient languages, Latin among them, strangers and enemies were named by a single word. We have come only slowly, through a long process of trial and error, to distinguish the two and to acknowledge that, in certain circumstances, strangers (but not enemies) might be entitled to our hospitality, assistance, and good will. This acknowledgment can be formalized as the principle of mutual aid, which suggests the duties that we owe, as John Rawls has written, "not only to definite individuals, say to those cooperating together in some social arrangement, but to persons generally."[1] Mutual aid extends across political (and also cultural, religious, and linguistic) frontiers. The philosophical grounds of the principle are hard to specify (its history provides its practical ground). I doubt that Rawls is right to argue that we can establish it simply by imagining "what a society would be like if this duty were rejected"[2]—for rejection is not an issue within any particular society; the issue arises only among people who don't share, or don't know themselves to share, a common life. People who do share a common life have much stronger duties.

It is the absence of any cooperative arrangements that sets the context for mutual aid: two strangers meet at sea or in the desert or, as in the Good Samaritan story, by the side of the road. What precisely they owe one another is by no means clear, but we commonly say of such cases that positive assistance is required if (1) it is needed or urgently needed by one of the parties; and (2) if the risks and costs of giving it are relatively low for the other party. Given these conditions, I ought to stop and help the injured stranger, wherever I meet him, whatever his membership or my own. This is our morality; conceivably his, too. It is, moreover, an obligation that can be read out in roughly the same form at the collective level. Groups of people ought to help necessitous strangers whom they somehow discover in their midst or on their path. But the limit on risks and costs in these cases is sharply drawn. I need not take the injured stranger into my home, except briefly, and I certainly need not care for him or even associate with him for the rest of my life. My life cannot be shaped and determined by such chance encounters. Governor John Winthrop, arguing against free immigration to the new Puritan commonwealth of Massachusetts, insisted that this right of refusal applies also to collective mutual aid: "As for hospitality, that rule does not bind further than for some present occasion, not for continual residence."[3] Whether Winthrop's view can be defended is a question that I shall come to only gradually. Here I only want to point to mutual aid as a (possible) external principle for the distribution of membership, a principle that doesn't depend upon the prevailing view of membership within a particular society. The force of the principle is uncertain, in part because of its own vagueness, in part because it sometimes comes up against the internal force of social meanings. And these meanings can be specified, and are specified, through the decision-making processes of the political community.

We might opt for a world without particular meanings and without political communities: where no one was a member or where everyone "belonged" to a single global state. These are the two forms of simple equality with regard to membership. If all human beings were strangers to one another, if all our meetings were like meetings at sea or in the desert or by the side of the road, then there would be no membership to distribute. Admissions policy would never be an issue. Where and how we lived, and with whom we lived, would depend upon our individual desires and then upon our partnerships and affairs. Justice would be nothing more than non-coercion, good faith, and Good Samaritanism—a matter entirely of external principles. If, by contrast, all human beings were members of a global state, membership would already have been distributed, equally; and there would be nothing more to do. The first of these arrangements suggests a kind of global libertarianism; the second, a kind of global socialism. These are the two conditions under which the distribution of membership would never arise. Either there would be no such status to distribute, or it would simply come (to everyone) with birth. But neither of these arrangements is likely to be realized in the foreseeable future; and there are impressive arguments, which I will come to later, against both of them. In any case, so long as members and strangers are, as they are at present, two distinct groups, admissions decisions have to be made, men and women taken in or refused. Given the indeterminate requirements of mutual aid, these decisions are not constrained by any widely accepted standard. That's why the admissions policies of countries are rarely criticized, except in terms suggesting that the only relevant criteria are those of charity, not justice. It is certainly possible that a deeper criticism would lead one to deny the member/stranger distinction. But I shall try, nevertheless, to defend that distinction and then to describe the internal and the external principles that govern the distribution of membership.

The argument will require a careful review of both immigration and naturalization policy. But it is worth noting first, briefly, that there are certain similarities between strangers in political space (immigrants) and descendants in time (children). People enter a country by being born to parents already there as well as, and more often than, by crossing the frontier. Both these processes can be controlled. In the first case, however, unless we practice a selective infanticide, we will be dealing with unborn and hence unknown individuals. Subsidies for large families and programs of birth control determine only the size of the population, not the characteristics of its inhabitants. We might, of course, award the right to give birth differentially to different groups of parents, establishing ethnic quotas (like country-of-origin quotas in immigration policy) or class or intelligence quotas, or allowing right-to-give-birth certificates to be traded on the market. These are ways of regulating who has children and of shaping the character of the future population. They are, however, indirect and inefficient ways, even with regard to ethnicity, unless the state also regulates intermarriage and assimilation. Even well short of that, the policy would require very high, and surely unacceptable, levels of coercion: the dominance of political power over kinship and love. So the major public policy issue is the size of the population only—its growth, stability, or decline. To how many people do we distribute membership? The larger and philosophically more interesting questions—To what sorts of people?, and To what particular people?—are most clearly confronted when we turn to the problems involved in admitting or excluding strangers.

Analogies: Neighborhoods, Clubs, and Families

Admissions policies are shaped partly by arguments about economic and political conditions in the host country, partly by arguments about the character and "destiny" of the host country, and partly by arguments about the character of countries (political communities) in general. The last of these is the most important, in theory at least; for our understanding of countries in general will determine whether particular countries have the right they conventionally claim: to distribute membership for (their own) particular reasons. But few of us have any direct experience of what a country is or of what it means to be a member. We often have strong feelings about our country, but we have only dim perceptions of it. As a political community (rather than a place), it is, after all, invisible; we actually see only its symbols, offices, and representatives. I suspect that we understand it best when we compare it to other, smaller associations whose compass we can more easily grasp. For we are all members of formal and informal groups of many different sorts; we know their workings intimately. And all these groups have, and necessarily have, admissions policies. Even if we have never served as state officials, even if we have never emigrated from one country to another, we have all had the experience of accepting or rejecting strangers, and we have all had the experience of being accepted or rejected. I want to draw upon this experience. My argument will be worked through a series of rough comparisons, in the course of which the special meaning of political membership will, I think, become increasingly apparent.

Consider, then, three possible analogues for the political community: we can think of countries as neighborhoods, clubs, or families. The list is obviously not exhaustive, but it will serve to illuminate certain key features of admission and exclusion. Schools, bureaucracies, and companies, though they have some of the characteristics of clubs, distribute social and economic status as well as membership; I will take them up separately. Many domestic associations are parasitic for their memberships, relying on the procedures of other associations: unions depend upon the hiring policies of companies; parent-teacher organizations depend upon the openness of neighborhoods or upon the selectiveness of private schools. Political parties are generally like clubs; religious congregations are often designed to resemble families. What should countries be like?

The neighborhood is an enormously complex human association, but we have a certain understanding of what it is like—an understanding at least partially reflected (though also increasingly challenged) in contemporary American law. It is an association without an organized or legally enforceable admissions policy. Strangers can be welcomed or not welcomed; they cannot be admitted or excluded. Of course, being welcomed or not welcomed is sometimes effectively the same thing as being admitted or excluded, but the distinction is theoretically important. In principle, individuals and families move into a neighborhood for reasons of their own; they choose but are not chosen. Or, rather, in the absence of legal controls, the market controls their movements. Whether they move is determined not only by their own choice but also by their ability to find a job and a place to live (or, in a society different from our own, to find a factory commune or a cooperative apartment house ready to take them in). Ideally, the market works independently of the existing composition of the neighborhood. The state upholds this independence by refusing to enforce restrictive covenants and by acting to prevent or minimize discrimination in employment. There are no institutional arrangements capable of maintaining "ethnic purity"—though zoning laws sometimes maintain class segregation.[4]* With reference to any formal criteria, the neighborhood is a random association, "not a selection, but rather a specimen of life as a whole. . . . By the very indifference of space," as Bernard Bosanquet has written, "we are liable to the direct impact of all possible factors."[6]

It was a common argument in classical political economy that national territory should be as "indifferent" as local space. The same writers who defended free trade in the nineteenth century also defended unrestricted immigration. They argued for perfect freedom of contract, without any political restraint. International society, they thought, should take shape as a world of neighborhoods, with individuals moving freely about, seeking private advancement. In their view, as Henry Sidgwick reported it in the 1890s, the only business of state officials is "to maintain order over [a] particular territory . . . but not in any way to determine who is to inhabit this territory, or to restrict the enjoyment of its natural advantages to any particular portion of the human race."[7] Natural advantages (like markets) are open to all comers, within the limits of private property rights; and if they are used up or devalued by overcrowding, people presumably will move on, into the jurisdiction of new sets of officials.

Sidgwick thought that this is possibly the "ideal of the future," but he offered three arguments against a world of neighborhoods in the present. First of all, such a world would not allow for patriotic sentiment, and so the "casual aggregates" that would probably result from the free movement of individuals would "lack internal cohesion." Neighbors would be strangers to one another. Second, free movement might interfere with efforts "to raise the standard of living among the poorer classes" of a particular country, since such efforts could not be undertaken with equal energy and success everywhere in the world. And, third, the promotion of moral and intellectual culture and the efficient working of political institutions might be "defeated" by the continual creation of heterogeneous populations.[8] Sidgwick presented these three arguments as a series of utilitarian considerations that weigh against the benefits of labor mobility and contractual freedom. But they seem to me to have a rather different character. The last two arguments draw their force from the first, but only if the first is conceived in non-utilitarian terms. It is only if patriotic sentiment has some moral basis, only if communal cohesion makes for obligations and shared meanings, only if there are members as well as strangers, that state offi-

*The use of zoning laws to bar from neighborhoods (boroughs, villages, towns) certain sorts of people—namely, those who don't live in conventional families—is a new feature of our political history, and I shall not try to comment on it here.[5]

cials would have any reason to worry especially about the welfare of their own people (and of *all* their own people) and the success of their own culture and politics. For it is at least dubious that the average standard of living of the poorer classes throughout the world would decline under conditions of perfect labor mobility. Nor is there firm evidence that culture cannot thrive in cosmopolitan environments, nor that it is impossible to govern casual aggregations of people. As for the last of these, political theorists long ago discovered that certain sorts of regimes—namely, authoritarian regimes—thrive in the absence of communal cohesion. That perfect mobility makes for authoritarianism might suggest a utilitarian argument against mobility; but such an argument would work only if individual men and women, free to come and go, expressed a desire for some other form of government. And that they might not do.

Perfect labor mobility, however, is probably a mirage, for it is almost certain to be resisted at the local level. Human beings, as I have said, move about a great deal, but not because they love to move. They are, most of them, inclined to stay where they are unless their life is very difficult there. They experience a tension between love of place and the discomforts of a particular place. While some of them leave their homes and become foreigners in new lands, others stay where they are and resent the foreigners in their own land. Hence, if states ever become large neighborhoods, it is likely that neighborhoods will become little states. Their members will organize to defend the local politics and culture against strangers. Historically, neighborhoods have turned into closed or parochial communities (leaving aside cases of legal coercion) whenever the state was open: in the cosmopolitan cities of multinational empires, for example, where state officials don't foster any particular identity but permit different groups to build their own institutional structures (as in ancient Alexandria), or in the receiving centers of mass immigration movements (early twentieth century New York) where the country is an open but also an alien world—or, alternatively, a world full of aliens. The case is similar where the state doesn't exist at all or in areas where it doesn't function. Where welfare monies are raised and spent locally, for example, as in a seventeenth-century English parish, the local people will seek to exclude newcomers who are likely welfare recipients. It is only the nationalization of welfare (or the nationalization of culture and politics) that opens the neighborhood communities to whoever chooses to come in.

Neighborhoods can be open only if countries are at least potentially closed. Only if the state makes a selection among would-be members

Membership

and guarantees the loyalty, security, and welfare of the individuals it
selects, can local communities take shape as "indifferent" associations,
determined solely by personal preference and market capacity. Since
individual choice is most dependent upon local mobility, this would
seem to be the preferred arrangement in a society like our own. The
politics and the culture of a modern democracy probably require the
kind of largeness, and also the kind of boundedness, that states provide.
I don't mean to deny the value of sectional cultures and ethnic communities; I mean only to suggest the rigidities that would be forced upon
both in the absence of inclusive and protective states. To tear down
the walls of the state is not, as Sidgwick worriedly suggested, to create
a world without walls, but rather to create a thousand petty fortresses.

The fortresses, too, could be torn down: all that is necessary is a
global state sufficiently powerful to overwhelm the local communities.
Then the result would be the world of the political economists, as Sidgwick described it—a world of radically deracinated men and women.
Neighborhoods might maintain some cohesive culture for a generation
or two on a voluntary basis, but people would move in, people would
move out; soon the cohesion would be gone. The distinctiveness of cultures and groups depends upon closure and, without it, cannot be conceived as a stable feature of human life. If this distinctiveness is a value,
as most people (though some of them are global pluralists, and others
only local loyalists) seem to believe, then closure must be permitted
somewhere. At some level of political organization, something like the
sovereign state must take shape and claim the authority to make its
own admissions policy, to control and sometimes restrain the flow of
immigrants.

But this right to control immigration does not include or entail the
right to control emigration. The political community can shape its own
population in the one way, not in the other: this is a distinction that
gets reiterated in different forms throughout the account of membership. The restraint of entry serves to defend the liberty and welfare,
the politics and culture of a group of people committed to one another
and to their common life. But the restraint of exit replaces commitment with coercion. So far as the coerced members are concerned,
there is no longer a community worth defending. A state can, perhaps,
banish individual citizens or expel aliens living within its borders (if
there is some place ready to receive them). Except in times of national
emergency, when everyone is bound to work for the survival of the community, states cannot prevent such people from getting up and leaving.
The fact that individuals can rightly leave their own country, however,

doesn't generate a right to enter another (any other). Immigration and emigration are morally asymmetrical.[9] Here the appropriate analogy is with the club, for it is a feature of clubs in domestic society—as I have just suggested it is of states in international society—that they can regulate admissions but cannot bar withdrawals.

Like clubs, countries have admissions committees. In the United States, Congress functions as such a committee, though it rarely makes individual selections. Instead, it establishes general qualifications, categories for admission and exclusion, and numerical quotas (limits). Then admissible individuals are taken in, with varying degrees of administrative discretion, mostly on a first-come, first-served basis. This procedure seems eminently defensible, though that does not mean that any particular set of qualifications and categories ought to be defended. To say that states have a right to act in certain areas is not to say that anything they do in those areas is right. One can argue about particular admissions standards by appealing, for example, to the condition and character of the host country and to the shared understandings of those who are already members. Such arguments have to be judged morally and politically as well as factually. The claim of American advocates of restricted immigration (in 1920, say) that they were defending a homogeneous white and Protestant country, can plausibly be called unjust as well as inaccurate: as if non-white and non-Protestant citizens were invisible men and women, who didn't have to be counted in the national census![10] Earlier Americans, seeking the benefits of economic and geographic expansion, had created a pluralist society; and the moral realities of that society ought to have guided the legislators of the 1920s. If we follow the logic of the club analogy, however, we have to say that the earlier decision might have been different, and the United States might have taken shape as a homogeneous community, an Anglo-Saxon nation-state (assuming what happened in any case: the virtual extermination of the Indians who, understanding correctly the dangers of invasion, struggled as best they could to keep foreigners out of their native lands). Decisions of this sort are subject to constraint, but what the constraints are I am not yet ready to say. It is important first to insist that the distribution of membership in American society, and in any ongoing society, is a matter of political decision. The labor market may be given free rein, as it was for many decades in the United States, but that does not happen by an act of nature or of God; it depends upon choices that are ultimately political. What kind of community do the citizens want to create? With what other men and women do they want to share and exchange social goods?

Membership

These are exactly the questions that club members answer when they make membership decisions, though usually with reference to a less extensive community and to a more limited range of social goods. In clubs, only the founders choose themselves (or one another); all other members have been chosen by those who were members before them. Individuals may be able to give good reasons why they should be selected, but no one on the outside has a right to be inside. The members decide freely on their future associates, and the decisions they make are authoritative and final. Only when clubs split into factions and fight over property can the state intervene and make its own decision about who the members are. When states split, however, no legal appeal is possible; there is no superior body. Hence, we might imagine states as perfect clubs, with sovereign power over their own selection processes.*

But if this description is accurate in regard to the law, it is not an accurate account of the moral life of contemporary political communities. Clearly, citizens often believe themselves morally bound to open the doors of their country—not to anyone who wants to come in, perhaps, but to a particular group of outsiders, recognized as national or ethnic "relatives." In this sense, states are like families rather than clubs, for it is a feature of families that their members are morally connected to people they have not chosen, who live outside the household. In time of trouble, the household is also a refuge. Sometimes, under the auspices of the state, we take in fellow citizens to whom we are not related, as English country families took in London children during the blitz; but our more spontaneous beneficence is directed at our own kith and kin. The state recognizes what we can call the "kinship principle" when it gives priority in immigration to the relatives of citizens. That is current policy in the United States, and it seems especially appropriate in a political community largely formed by the admission of immigrants. It is a way of acknowledging that labor mobility has a social price: since laborers are men and women with families, one cannot admit them for the sake of their labor without accepting some commitment to their aged parents, say, or to their sickly brothers and sisters.

In communities differently formed, where the state represents a nation largely in place, another sort of commitment commonly develops, along lines determined by the principle of nationality. In time of trouble, the state is a refuge for members of the nation, whether or not

---

*Winthrop made the point clearly: "If we here be a corporation established by free consent, if the place of our habitation be our own, then no man hath right to come into us . . . without our consent."[11] I will come back to the question of "place" later (page 43).

they are residents and citizens. Perhaps the border of the political community was drawn years ago so as to leave their villages and towns on the wrong side; perhaps they are the children or grandchildren of emigrants. They have no legal membership rights, but if they are persecuted in the land where they live, they look to their homeland not only with hope but also with expectation. I am inclined to say that such expectations are legitimate. Greeks driven from Turkey, Turks from Greece, after the wars and revolutions of the early twentieth century, had to be taken in by the states that bore their collective names. What else are such states for? They don't only preside over a piece of territory and a random collection of inhabitants; they are also the political expression of a common life and (most often) of a national "family" that is never entirely enclosed within their legal boundaries. After the Second World War, millions of Germans, expelled by Poland and Czechoslovakia, were received and cared for by the two Germanies. Even if these states had been free of all responsibility in the expulsions, they would still have had a special obligation to the refugees. Most states recognize obligations of this sort in practice; some do so in law.

Territory

We might, then, think of countries as national clubs or families. But countries are also territorial states. Although clubs and families own property, they neither require nor (except in feudal systems) possess jurisdiction over territory. Leaving children aside, they do not control the physical location of their members. The state does control physical location—if only for the sake of clubs and families and the individual men and women who make them up; and with this control there come certain obligations. We can best examine these if we consider once again the asymmetry of immigration and emigration.

The nationality principle has one significant limit, commonly accepted in theory, if not always in practice. Though the recognition of national affinity is a reason for permitting immigration, nonrecognition is not a reason for expulsion. This is a major issue in the modern world, for many newly independent states find themselves in control of territory into which alien groups have been admitted under the auspices of the old imperial regime. Sometimes these people are forced to leave, the victims of a popular hostility that the new government cannot restrain. More often the government itself fosters such hostility, and takes positive action to drive out the "alien elements," invoking when it does so some version of the club or the family analogy. Here, however, neither analogy applies: for though no "alien" has a right to be a member of a club or a family, it is possible, I think, to describe a kind of territorial or locational right.

Hobbes made the argument in classical form when he listed those rights that are given up and those that are retained when the social contract is signed. The retained rights include self-defense and then "the use of fire, water, free air, *and place to live in,* and . . . all things necessary for life." (italics mine)[12] The right is not, indeed, to a particular place, but it is enforceable against the state, which exists to protect it; the state's claim to territorial jurisdiction derives ultimately from this individual right to place. Hence the right has a collective as well as an individual form, and these two can come into conflict. But it can't be said that the first always or necessarily supercedes the second, for the first came into existence for the sake of the second. The state owes something to its inhabitants simply, without reference to their collective or national identity. And the first place to which the inhabitants are entitled is surely the place where they and their families have lived and made a life. The attachments and expectations they have formed argue against a forced transfer to another country. If they can't have this particular piece of land (or house or apartment), then some other must be found for them within the same general "place." Initially, at least, the sphere of membership is given: the men and women who determine what membership means, and who shape the admissions policies of the political community, are simply the men and women who are already there. New states and governments must make their peace with the old inhabitants of the land they rule. And countries are likely to take shape as closed territories dominated, perhaps, by particular nations (clubs or families), but always including aliens of one sort or another—whose expulsion would be unjust.

This common arrangement raises one important possibility: that many of the inhabitants of a particular country won't be allowed full membership (citizenship) because of their nationality. I will consider that possibility, and argue for its rejection, when I turn to the specific problems of naturalization. But one might avoid such problems entirely, at least at the level of the state, by opting for a radically different arrangement. Consider once again the neighborhood analogy: perhaps we should deny to national states, as we deny to churches and political parties, the collective right of territorial jurisdiction. Perhaps we should insist upon open countries and permit closure only in non-territorial groups. Open neighborhoods together with closed clubs and families: that is the structure of domestic society. Why can't it, why shouldn't it be extended to the global society?

An extension of this sort was actually proposed by the Austrian socialist writer Otto Bauer, with reference to the old multinational empires of Central and Eastern Europe. Bauer would have organized nations into autonomous corporations permitted to tax their members for educational and cultural purposes, but denied any territorial dominion. Individuals would be free to move about in political space, within the empire, carrying their national memberships with them, much as individuals move about today in liberal and secular states, carrying their religious memberships and partisan affiliations. Like churches and parties, the corporations could admit or reject new members in accordance with whatever standards their old members thought appropriate.[13]

The major difficulty here is that all the national communities that Bauer wanted to preserve came into existence, and were sustained over the centuries, on the basis of geographical coexistence. It isn't any misunderstanding of their histories that leads nations newly freed from imperial rule to seek a firm territorial status. Nations look for countries because in some deep sense they already have countries: the link between people and land is a crucial feature of national identity. Their leaders understand, moreover, that because so many critical issues (including issues of distributive justice, such as welfare, education, and so on) can best be resolved within geographical units, the focus of political life can never be established elsewhere. "Autonomous" corporations will always be adjuncts, and probably parasitic adjuncts, of territorial states; and to give up the state is to give up any effective self-determination. That's why borders, and the movements of individuals and groups across borders, are bitterly disputed as soon as imperial rule recedes and nations begin the process of "liberation." And, once again, to reverse this process or to repress its effects would require massive coercion on a global scale. There is no easy way to avoid the country (and the proliferation of countries) as we currently know it. Hence the theory of justice must allow for the territorial state, specifying the rights of its inhabitants and recognizing the collective right of admission and refusal.

The argument cannot stop here, however, for the control of territory opens the state to the claim of necessity. Territory is a social good in a double sense. It is living space, earth and water, mineral resources and potential wealth, a resource for the destitute and the hungry. And it is protected living space, with borders and police, a resource for the persecuted and the stateless. These two resources are different, and we might conclude differently with regard to the kinds of claim that can be made on each. But the issue at stake should first be put in general terms. Can a political community exclude destitute and hungry, persecuted and stateless—in a word, necessitous—men and women simply because they are foreigners? Are citizens bound to take in strangers? Let us assume that the citizens have no formal obligations; they are bound by nothing more stringent than the principle of mutual aid. The principle must be applied, however, not to individuals directly but to the citizens as a group, for immigration is a matter of political decision. Individuals participate in the decision making, if the state is democratic; but they decide not for themselves but for the community generally. And this fact has moral implications. It replaces immediacy with distance and the personal expense of time and energy with impersonal bureaucratic costs. Despite John Winthrop's claim, mutual aid is more coercive for political communities than it is for individuals because a wide range of benevolent actions is open to the community which will only marginally affect its present members considered as a body or even, with possible exceptions, one by one or family by family or club by club. (But benevolence will, perhaps, affect the children or grandchildren or great-grandchildren of the present members—in ways not easy to measure or even to make out. I'm not sure to what extent considerations of this sort can be used to narrow the range of required actions.) These actions probably include the admission of strangers, for admission to a country does not entail the kinds of intimacy that could hardly be avoided in the case of clubs and families. Might not admission, then, be morally imperative, at least for *these* strangers, who have no other place to go?

Some such argument, turning mutual aid into a more stringent charge on communities than it can ever be on individuals, probably underlies the common claim that exclusion rights depend upon the territorial extent and the population density of particular countries. Thus, Sidgwick wrote that he "cannot concede to a state possessing large tracts of unoccupied land an absolute right of excluding alien elements."[14] Perhaps, in his view, the citizens can make some selection among necessitous strangers, but they cannot refuse entirely to take strangers in so long as their state has (a great deal of) available space. A much stronger argument might be made from the other side, so to speak, if we consider the necessitous strangers not as objects of beneficent action but as desperate men and women, capable of acting on their own behalf. In *Leviathan,* Hobbes argued that such people, if they cannot earn a living in their own countries, have a right to move into "countries not sufficiently inhabited: where nevertheless they are not to exterminate those they find there, but constrain them to inhabit closer together and not range a great deal of ground to snatch what they find."[15] Here the "Samaritans" are not themselves active but acted upon and (as we shall see in a moment) charged only with nonresistance.

"White Australia" and the Claim of Necessity

The Hobbesian argument is clearly a defense of European colonization—and also of the subsequent "constraint" of native hunters and gatherers. But it has a wider application. Sidgwick, writing in 1891, probably had in mind the states the colonists had created: the United States, where agitation for the exclusion of immigrants had been at least a sporadic feature of political life all through the nineteenth century; and Australia, then just beginning the great debate over immigration that culminated in the "White Australia" policy. Years later, an Austrialian minister of immigration defended that policy in terms that should by now be familiar: "We seek to create a homogeneous nation. Can anyone reasonably object to that? Is not this the elementary right of every government, to decide the composition of the nation? It is just the same prerogative as the head of a family exercises as to who is to live in his own house."[16] But the Australian "family" held a vast territory of which it occupied (and I shall assume, without further factual reference, still occupies) only a small part. The right of white Australians to the great empty spaces of the subcontinent rested on nothing more than the claim they had staked, and enforced against the aboriginal population, before anyone else. That does not seem a right that one would readily defend in the face of necessitous men and women, clamoring for entry. If, driven by famine in the densely populated lands of Southeast Asia, thousands of people were to fight their way into an Australia otherwise closed to them, I doubt that we would want to charge the invaders with aggression. Hobbes's charge might make more sense: "Seeing every man, not only by Right, but also by necessity of Nature, is supposed to endeavor all he can, to obtain that which is necessary for his conservation; he that shall oppose himself against it, for things superfluous, is guilty of the war that thereupon is to follow."[17]

But Hobbes's conception of "things superfluous" is extraordinarily wide. He meant, superfluous to life itself, to the bare requirements of physical survival. The argument is more plausible, I think, if we adopt a more narrow conception, shaped to the needs of particular historical communities. We must consider "ways of life" just as, in the case of individuals, we must consider "life plans." Now let us suppose that the great majority of Australians could maintain their present way of life, subject only to marginal shifts, given a successful invasion of the sort I have imagined. Some individuals would be more drastically affected, for they have come to "need" hundreds or even thousands of empty miles for the life they have chosen. But such needs cannot be given moral priority over the claims of necessitous strangers. Space on that scale is a luxury, as time on that scale is a luxury in more conventional Good Samaritan arguments; and it is subject to a kind of moral encroachment. Assuming, then, that there actually is superfluous land, the claim of necessity would force a political community like that of White Australia to confront a radical choice. Its members could yield land for the sake of homogeneity, or they could give up homogeneity (agree to the creation of a multiracial society) for the sake of the land. And those would be their only choices. White Australia could survive only as Little Australia.

I have put the argument in these forceful terms in order to suggest that the collective version of mutual aid might require a limited and complex redistribution of membership and/or territory. Farther than this we cannot go. We cannot describe the littleness of Little Australia without attending to the concrete meaning of "things superfluous." To argue, for example, that living space should be distributed in equal amounts to every inhabitant of the globe would be to allow the individual version of the right to a place in the world to override the collective version. Indeed, it would deny that national clubs and families can ever acquire a firm title to a particular piece of territory. A high birthrate in a neighboring land would immediately annul the title and require territorial redistribution.

The same difficulty arises with regard to wealth and resources. These, too, can be superfluous, far beyond what the inhabitants of a particular state require for a decent life (even as they themselves define the meaning of a decent life). Are those inhabitants morally bound to admit immigrants from poorer countries for as long as superfluous resources exist? Or are they bound even longer than that, beyond the limits of mutual aid, until a policy of open admissions ceases to attract and benefit the poorest people in the world? Sidgwick seems to have opted for the first of these possibilities; he proposed a primitive and parochial version of Rawls's difference principle: immigration can be restricted as soon as failure to do so would "interfere materially . . . with the efforts of the government to maintain an adequately high standard of life among the members of the community generally—especially the poorer classes."[18] But the community might well decide to cut off immigration even before that, if it were willing to export (some of) its superfluous wealth. Its members would face a choice similar to that of the Australians: they could share their wealth with necessitous strangers outside their country or with necessitous strangers inside their country. But just how much of their wealth do they have to share? Once again, there must be some limit, short (and probably considerably short) of simple equality, else communal wealth would be subject to indefinite drainage. The very phrase "communal wealth" would lose its meaning if all resources and all products were globally common. Or, rather, there would be only one community, a world state, whose redistributive processes would tend over time to annul the historical particularity of the national clubs and families.

If we stop short of simple equality, there will continue to be many communities, with different histories, ways of life, climates, political structures, and economies. Some places in the world will still be more desirable than others, either to individual men and women with particular tastes and aspirations, or more generally. Some places will still be uncomfortable for at least some of their inhabitants. Hence immigration will remain an issue even after the claims of distributive justice have been met on a global scale—assuming, still, that global society is and ought to be pluralist in form and that the claims are fixed by some version of collective mutual aid. The different communities will still have to make admissions decisions and will still have a right to make them. If we cannot guarantee the full extent of the territorial or material base on which a group of people build a common life, we can still say that the common life, at least, is their own and that their comrades and associates are theirs to recognize or choose.

Refugees

There is, however, one group of needy outsiders whose claims cannot be met by yielding territory or exporting wealth; they can be met only by taking people in. This is the group of refugees whose need is for membership itself, a non-exportable good. The liberty that makes certain countries possible homes for men and women whose politics or religion isn't tolerated where they live is also non-exportable: at least we have found no way of exporting it. These goods can be shared only within the protected space of a particular state. At the same time, admitting refugees doesn't necessarily decrease the amount of liberty the members enjoy within that space. The victims of political or religious persecution, then, make the most forceful claim for admission. If you don't take me in, they say, I shall be killed, persecuted, brutally oppressed by the rulers of my own country. What can we reply?

Toward some refugees, we may well have obligations of the same sort that we have toward fellow nationals. This is obviously the case with regard to any group of people whom we have helped turn into refugees. The injury we have done them makes for an affinity between us: thus Vietnamese refugees had, in a moral sense, been effectively Americanized even before they arrived on these shores. But we can also be bound to help men and women persecuted or oppressed by someone else—if they are persecuted or oppressed because they are like us. Ideological as well as ethnic affinity can generate bonds across political lines, especially, for example, when we claim to embody certain principles in our communal life and encourage men and women elsewhere to defend those principles. In a liberal state, affinities of this latter sort may be highly attenuated and still morally coercive. Nineteenth-century political refugees in England were generally not English liberals. They were heretics and oppositionists of all sorts, at war with the autocracies of Central and Eastern Europe. It was chiefly because of their enemies that the English recognized in them a kind of kin. Or, consider the thousands of men and women who fled Hungary after the failed revolution of 1956. It is hard to deny them a similar recognition, given the structure of the Cold War, the character of Western propaganda, the sympathy already expressed with East European "freedom fighters." These refugees probably had to be taken in by countries like Britain and the United States. The repression of political comrades, like the persecution of co-religionists, seems to generate an obligation to help, at least to provide a refuge for the most exposed and endangered people. Perhaps every victim of authoritarianism and bigotry is the moral comrade of a liberal citizen: that is an argument I would like to make. But that would press affinity too hard, and it is in any case unnecessary. So long as the number of victims is small, mutual aid will generate similar practical results; and when the number increases, and we are forced to choose among the victims, we will look, rightfully, for some more direct connection with our own way of life.

If, on the other hand, there is no connection at all with particular victims, antipathy rather than affinity, there can't be a requirement to choose them over other people equally in need.* Britain and the United States could hardly have been required, for example, to offer refuge to Stalinists fleeing Hungary in 1956, had the revolution triumphed. Once again, communities must have boundaries; and however these are determined with regard to territory and resources, they depend with regard to population on a sense of relatedness and mutuality. Refugees must appeal to that sense. One wishes them success; but in particular cases, with reference to a particular state, they may well have no right to be successful.

Since ideological (far more than ethnic) affinity is a matter of mutual recognition, there is a lot of room here for political choice—and thus, for exclusion as well as admission. Hence it might be said that my argument doesn't reach to the desperation of the refugee. Nor does it suggest any way of dealing with the vast numbers of refugees generated by twentieth-century politics. On the one hand, everyone must have a place to live, and a place where a reasonably secure life is possible. On the other hand, this is not a right that can be enforced against particular host states. (The right can't be enforced in practice until there is an international authority capable of enforcing it; and were there such an authority, it would certainly do better to intervene against the states whose brutal policies had driven their own citizens into exile, and so enable them all to go home.) The cruelty of this dilemma is mitigated to some degree by the principle of asylum. Any refugee who has actually made his escape, who is not seeking but has found at least a temporary refuge, can claim asylum—a right recognized today, for example, in British law; and then he cannot be deported so long as the only available country to which he might be sent "is one to which he is unwilling to go owing to well-founded fear of being persecuted for reasons of race, religion, nationality . . . or political opinion."[20] Though he is a stranger, and newly come, the rule against expulsion applies to him as if he had already made a life where he is: for there is no other place where he can make a life.

But this principle was designed for the sake of individuals, consid-

*Compare Bruce Ackerman's claim that "the *only* reason for restricting immigration is to protect the ongoing process of liberal conversation itself" (the italics are Ackerman's).[19] People publicly committed to the destruction of "liberal conversation" can rightfully be excluded—or perhaps Ackerman would say that they can be excluded only if their numbers or the strength of their commitment poses a real threat. In any case, the principle stated in this way applies only to liberal states. But surely other sorts of political communities also have a right to protect their members' shared sense of what they are about.

ered one by one, where their numbers are so small that they cannot have any significant impact upon the character of the political community. What happens when the numbers are not small? Consider the case of the millions of Russians captured or enslaved by the Nazis in the Second World War and overrun by Allied armies in the final offensives of the war. All these people were returned, many of them forcibly returned, to the Soviet Union, where they were immediately shot or sent on to die in labor camps.[21] Those of them who foresaw their fate pleaded for asylum in the West, but for expediential reasons (having to do with war and diplomacy, not with nationality and the problems of assimilation), asylum was denied them. Surely, they should not have been forcibly returned—not once it was known that they would be murdered; and that means that the Western allies should have been ready to take them in, negotiating among themselves, I suppose, about appropriate numbers. There was no other choice: at the extreme, the claim of asylum is virtually undeniable. I assume that there are in fact limits on our collective liability, but I don't know how to specify them.

This last example suggests that the moral conduct of liberal and humane states can be determined by the immoral conduct of authoritarian and brutal states. But if that is true, why stop with asylum? Why be concerned only with men and women actually on our territory who ask to remain, and not with men and women oppressed in their own countries who ask to come in? Why mark off the lucky or the aggressive, who have somehow managed to make their way across our borders, from all the others? Once again, I don't have an adequate answer to these questions. We seem bound to grant asylum for two reasons: because its denial would require us to use force against helpless and desperate people, and because the numbers likely to be involved, except in unusual cases, are small and the people easily absorbed (so we would be using force for "things superfluous"). But if we offered a refuge to everyone in the world who could plausibly say that he needed it, we might be overwhelmed. The call "Give me . . . your huddled masses yearning to breathe free" is generous and noble; actually to take in large numbers of refugees is often morally necessary; but the right to restrain the flow remains a feature of communal self-determination. The principle of mutual aid can only modify and not transform admissions policies rooted in a particular community's understanding of itself.

Alienage and Naturalization

The members of a political community have a collective right to shape the resident population—a right subject always to the double control that I have described: the meaning of membership to the current members and the principle of mutual aid. Given these two, particular countries at particular times are likely to include among their residents men and women who are in different ways alien. These people may be members in their turn of minority or pariah groups, or they may be refugees or immigrants newly arrived. Let us assume that they are rightfully where they are. Can they claim citizenship and political rights within the community where they now live? Does citizenship go with residence? In fact, there is a second admissions process, called "naturalization," and the criteria appropriate to this second process must still be determined. I should stress that what is at stake here is citizenship and not (except in the legal sense of the term) nationality. The national club or family is a community different from the state, for reasons I have already sketched. Hence it is possible, say, for an Algerian immigrant to France to become a French citizen (a French "national") without becoming a Frenchman. But if he is not a Frenchman, but only a resident in France, has he any right to French citizenship?

One might insist, as I shall ultimately do, that the same standards apply to naturalization as to immigration, that every immigrant and every resident is a citizen, too—or, at least, a potential citizen. That is why territorial admission is so serious a matter. The members must be prepared to accept, as their own equals in a world of shared obligations, the men and women they admit; the immigrants must be prepared to share the obligations. But things can be differently arranged. Often the state controls naturalization strictly, immigration only loosely. Immigrants become resident aliens and, except by special dispensation, nothing more. Why are they admitted? To free the citizens from hard and unpleasant work. Then the state is like a family with live-in servants.

That is not an attractive image, for a family with live-in servants is—inevitably, I think—a little tyranny. The principles that rule in the household are those of kinship and love. They establish the underlying pattern of mutuality and obligation, of authority and obedience. The servants have no proper place in that pattern, but they have to be assimilated to it. Thus, in the pre-modern literature on family life, servants are commonly described as children of a special sort: children, because they are subject to command; of a special sort, because they are not allowed to grow up. Parental authority is asserted outside its sphere, over adult men and women who are not, and can never be, full members of the family. When this assertion is no longer possible, when servants come to be seen as hired workers, the great household begins its slow decline. The pattern of living-in is gradually reversed; erstwhile servants seek households of their own.

The Athenian Metics

It is not possible to trace a similar history at the level of the political community. Live-in servants have not disappeared from the modern world. As "guest workers" they play an important role in its most advanced economies. But before considering the status of guest workers, I want to turn to an older example and consider the status of resident aliens (metics) in ancient Athens. The Athenian polis was almost literally a family with live-in servants. Citizenship was an inheritance passed on from parents to children (and only passed on if both parents were citizens: after 450 B.C., Athens lived by the law of double endogamy). Hence a great deal of the city's work was done by residents who could not hope to become citizens. Some of these people were slaves; but I shall not focus on them, since the injustice of slavery is not disputed these days, at least not openly. The case of the metics is harder and more interesting.

"We throw open our city to the world," said Pericles in his Funeral Oration, "and never exclude foreigners from any opportunity." So the metics came willingly to Athens, drawn by economic opportunity, perhaps also by the city's "air of freedom." Most of them never rose above the rank of laborer or "mechanic," but some prospered: in fourth-century Athens, metics were represented among the wealthiest merchants. Athenian freedom, however, they shared only in its negative forms. Though they were required to join in the defense of the city, they had no political rights at all; nor did their descendants. Nor did they share in the most basic of welfare rights: "Foreigners were excluded from the distribution of corn."[22] As usual, these exclusions both expressed and enforced the low standing of the metics in Athenian society. In the surviving literature, metics are commonly treated with contempt—though a few favorable references in the plays of Aristophanes suggest the existence of alternative views.[23]

Aristotle, though himself a metic, provides the classic defense of exclusion, apparently responding to critics who argued that co-residence and shared labor were a sufficient basis for political membership. "A citizen does not become such," he wrote, "merely by inhabiting a place." Labor, even necessary labor, is no better as a criterion: "you must not posit as citizens all those [human beings] without whom you could not have a city."[24] Citizenship required a certain "excellence" that was not available to everyone. I doubt that Aristotle really believed this excellence to be transmitted by birth. For him, the existence of members and non-members as hereditary castes was probably a matter of convenience. Someone had to do the hard work of the city, and it was best if the workers were clearly marked out and taught their place from birth. Labor itself, the everyday necessity of economic life, put the excellence of citizenship beyond their reach. Ideally, the band of citizens was an aristocracy of the leisured (in fact, it included "mechanics" just as the metics included men of leisure); and its members were aristocrats because they were leisured, not because of birth and blood or any inner gift. Politics took most of their time, though Aristotle would not have said that they ruled over slaves and aliens. Rather, they took turns ruling one another. The others were simply their passive subjects, the "material condition" of their excellence, with whom they had no political relations at all.

In Aristotle's view, slaves and aliens lived in the realm of necessity; their fate was determined by the conditions of economic life. Citizens, by contrast, lived in the realm of choice; their fate was determined in the political arena by their own collective decisions. But the distinction is a false one. In fact, citizens made all sorts of decisions that were authoritative for the slaves and aliens in their midst—decisions having to do with war, public expenditure, the improvement of trade, the distribution of corn, and so on. Economic conditions were subject to political control, though the extent of that control was always frighteningly limited. Hence slaves and aliens were indeed ruled; their lives were shaped politically as well as economically. They, too, stood within the arena, simply by virtue of being inhabitants of the protected space of the city-state; but they had no voice there. They could not hold public office or attend the assembly or serve on a jury; they had no officers or political organizations of their own and were never consulted about impending decisions. If we take them to be, despite Aristotle, men and women capable of rational deliberation, then we have to say that they were the subjects of a band of citizen-tyrants, governed without consent. Indeed, this seems to have been at least the implicit view of other Greek writers. Thus Isocrates's critique of oligarchy: when some citi-

Membership

zens monopolize political power, they become "tyrants" and turn their fellows into "metics."[25] If that's true, then the actual metics must always have lived with tyranny.

But Isocrates would not have made that last point; nor do we have any record of metics who made it. Slavery was a much debated issue in ancient Athens, but "no vestige survives of any controversy over the *metoikia.*"[26] Some of the sophists may have had their doubts, but the ideology that distinguished metics from citizens seems to have been widely accepted among metics and citizens alike. The dominance of birth and blood over political membership was part of the common understanding of the age. Athenian metics were themselves hereditary citizens of the cities from which they had come; and though this status offered them no practical protection, it helped, perhaps, to balance their low standing in the city where they lived and worked. They, too, if they were Greeks, were of citizen blood; and their relation with the Athenians could plausibly be described (as it was described by Lycias, another metic, and more ready than Aristotle to acknowledge his status) in contractual terms: good behavior in exchange for fair treatment.[27]

This view hardly applies, however, to the children of the first metic generation; no contractualist argument can justify the creation of a caste of resident aliens. The only justification of the *metoikia* lies in the conception of citizenship as something that the Athenians literally could not distribute given what they thought it was. All they could offer to aliens was fair treatment, and that was all the aliens could think to ask of them. There is considerable evidence for this view, but there is evidence against it, too. Individual metics were occasionally enfranchised, though perhaps corruptly. Metics played a part in the restoration of democracy in 403 B.C. after the government of the Thirty Tyrants; and they were eventually rewarded, despite strong opposition, with a grant of citizenship.[28] Aristotle made it an argument against large cities that "resident aliens readily assume a share in the exercise of political rights"—which suggests that there was no conceptual barrier to the extension of citizenship.[29] In any case, there is certainly no such barrier in contemporary democratic communities, and it is time now to consider our own metics. The question that apparently gave the Greeks no trouble is both practically and theoretically troubling today. Can states run their economies with live-in servants, guest workers, excluded from the company of citizens?

Guest Workers

I will not attempt a full description of the experience of contemporary guest workers. Laws and practices differ from one European country to another and are constantly changing; the situation is complex and unstable. All that is necessary here is a schematic sketch (based chiefly on the legal situation in the early 1970s) designed to highlight those features of the experience that are morally and politically controversial.[30]

Consider, then, a country like Switzerland or Sweden or West Germany, a capitalist democracy and welfare state, with strong trade unions and a fairly affluent population. The managers of the economy find it increasingly difficult to attract workers to a set of jobs that have come to be regarded as exhausting, dangerous, and degrading. But these jobs are also socially necessary; someone must be found to do them. Domestically, there are only two alternatives, neither of them palatable. The constraints imposed on the labor market by the unions and the welfare state might be broken, and then the most vulnerable segment of the local working class driven to accept jobs hitherto thought undesirable. But this would require a difficult and dangerous political campaign. Or, the wages and working conditions of the undesirable jobs might be dramatically improved so as to attract workers even within the constraints of the local market. But this would raise costs throughout the economy and, what is probably more important, challenge the existing social hierarchy. Rather than adopt either of these drastic measures, the economic managers, with the help of their government, shift the jobs from the domestic to the international labor market, making them available to workers in poorer countries who find them less undesirable. The government opens recruiting offices in a number of economically backward countries and draws up regulations to govern the admission of guest workers.

It is crucial that the workers who are admitted should be "guests," not immigrants seeking a new home and a new citizenship. For if the workers came as future citizens, they would join the domestic labor force, temporarily occupying its lower ranks, but benefiting from its unions and welfare programs and in time reproducing the original dilemma. Moreover, as they advanced, they would come into direct competition with local workers, some of whom they would outdo. Hence the regulations that govern their admission are designed to bar them from the protection of citizenship. They are brought in for a fixed time period, on contract to a particular employer; if they lose their jobs, they have to leave; they have to leave in any case when their visas expire. They are either prevented or discouraged from bringing dependents along with them, and they are housed in barracks, segregated by sex, on the outskirts of the cities where they work. Mostly they are young men or women in their twenties or thirties; finished with education, not yet infirm, they are a minor drain on local welfare services (unemployment insurance is not available to them since they are not permitted to be unemployed in the countries to which they have come). Neither citizens nor potential citizens, they have no political rights. The civil liberties of speech, assembly, association—otherwise strongly defended—are commonly denied to them, sometimes explicitly by state officials, sometimes implicitly by the threat of dismissal and deportation.

Gradually, as it becomes clear that foreign workers are a long-term requirement of the local economy, these conditions are somewhat mitigated. For certain jobs, workers are given longer visas, allowed to bring in their families, and admitted to many of the benefits of the welfare state. But their position remains precarious. Residence is tied to employment, and the authorities make it a rule that any guest worker who cannot support himself and his family without repeated recourse to state welfare programs, can be deported. In time of recession, many of the guests are forced to leave. In good times, however, the number who choose to come, and who find ways to remain, is high; soon some 10 percent to 15 percent of the industrial labor force is made up of foreigners. Frightened by this influx, various cities and towns establish residence quotas for guest workers (defending their neighborhoods against an open state). Bound to their jobs, the guests are in any case narrowly restricted in choosing a place to live.

Their existence is harsh and their wages low by European standards, less so by their own standards. What is most difficult is their homelessness: they work long and hard in a foreign country where they are not encouraged to settle down, where they are always strangers. For those workers who come alone, life in the great European cities is like a self-imposed prison term. They are deprived of normal social, sexual, and cultural activities (of political activity, too, if that is possible in their home country) for a fixed period of time. During that time, they live narrowly, saving money and sending it home. Money is the only return that the host countries make to their guests; and though much of it is exported rather than spent locally, the workers are still very cheaply had. The costs of raising and educating them where they work, and of paying them what the domestic labor market requires, would be much higher than the amounts remitted to their home countries. So the relation of guests and hosts seems to be a bargain all around: for the harshness of the working days and years is temporary, and the money sent home counts there in a way it could never count in a European city.

But what are we to make of the host country as a political community? Defenders of the guest-worker system claim that the country is now a neighborhood economically, but politically still a club or a family. As a place to live, it is open to anyone who can find work; as a forum or assembly, as a nation or a people, it is closed except to those who meet the requirements set by the present members. The system is a perfect synthesis of labor mobility and patriotic solidarity. But this account somehow misses what is actually going on. The state-as-neighborhood, an "indifferent" association governed only by the laws of the market, and the state-as-club-or-family, with authority relations and police, do not simply coexist, like two distinct moments in historical or abstract time. The market for guest workers, while free from the particular political constraints of the domestic labor market, is not free from all political constraints. State power plays a crucial role in its creation and then in the enforcement of its rules. Without the denial of political rights and civil liberties and the everpresent threat of deportation, the system would not work. Hence guest workers can't be described merely in terms of their mobility, as men and women free to come and go. While they are guests, they are also subjects. They are ruled, like the Athenian metics, by a band of citizen-tyrants.

But don't they agree to be ruled? Isn't the contractualist argument effective here, with men and women who actually come in on contracts and stay only for so many months or years? Certainly they come knowing roughly what to expect, and they often come back knowing exactly what to expect. But this kind of consent, given at a single moment in time, while it is sufficient to legitimize market transactions, is not sufficient for democratic politics. Political power is precisely the ability to make decisions over periods of time, to change the rules, to cope with emergencies; it can't be exercised democratically without the ongoing consent of its subjects. And its subjects include every man and woman who lives within the territory over which those decisions are enforced. The whole point of calling guest workers "guests," however, is to suggest that they don't (really) live where they work. Though they are treated like indentured servants, they are not in fact indentured. They can quit their jobs, buy train or airline tickets, and go home; they are citizens elsewhere. If they come voluntarily, to work and not to settle, and if they can leave whenever they want, why should they be granted political rights while they stay? Ongoing consent, it might be argued, is required only from permanent residents. Aside from the explicit provisions of their contracts, guest workers have no more rights than tourists have.

In the usual sense of the word, however, guest workers are not "guests," and they certainly are not tourists. They are workers, above all; and they come (and generally stay for as long as they are allowed) because they need the work, not because they expect to enjoy the visit. They are not on vacation; they do not spend their days as they please. State officials are not polite and helpful, giving directions to the museums, enforcing the traffic and currency laws. These guests experience the state as a pervasive and frightening power that shapes their lives and regulates their every move—and never asks for their opinion. Departure is only a formal option; deportation, a continuous practical threat. As a group, they constitute a disenfranchised class. They are typically an exploited or oppressed class as well, and they are exploited or oppressed at least in part because they are disenfranchised, incapable of organizing effectively for self-defense. Their material condition is unlikely to be improved except by altering their political status. Indeed, the purpose of their status is to prevent them from improving their condition; for if they could do that, they would soon be like domestic workers, unwilling to take on hard and degrading work or accept low rates of pay.

And yet the company of citizens from which they are excluded is not an endogamous company. Compared with Athens, every European country is radically heterogeneous in character, and they all have naturalization procedures in place. Guest workers, then, are excluded from the company of men and women that includes other people exactly like themselves. They are locked into an inferior position that is also an anomalous position; they are outcasts in a society that has no caste norms, metics in a society where metics have no comprehensible, protected, and dignified place. That is why the government of guest workers looks very much like tyranny: it is the exercise of power outside its sphere, over men and women who resemble citizens in every respect that counts in the host country, but are nevertheless barred from citizenship.

The relevant principle here is not mutual aid but political justice. The guests don't need citizenship—at least not in the same sense in which they might be said to need their jobs. Nor are they injured, helpless, destitute; they are able-bodied and earning money. Nor are they standing, even figuratively, by the side of the road; they are living among the citizens. They do socially necessary work, and they are deeply enmeshed in the legal system of the country to which they have come. Participants in economy and law, they ought to be able to regard themselves as potential or future participants in politics as well. And they must be possessed of those basic civil liberties whose exercise is so much preparation for voting and office holding. They must be set on the road to citizenship. They may choose not to become citizens, to return home or stay on as resident aliens. Many—perhaps most—will choose to return because of their emotional ties to their national family and their native land. But unless they have that choice, their other choices cannot be taken as so many signs of their acquiescence to the economy and law of the countries where they work. And if they do have that choice, the local economy and law are likely to look different: a firmer recognition of the guests' civil liberties and some enhancement of their opportunities for collective bargaining would be difficult to avoid once they were seen as potential citizens.

I should add that something of the same sort might be obtained in another way. The host countries might undertake to negotiate formal treaties with the home countries, setting out in authoritative form a list of "guest rights"—the same rights, roughly, that the workers might win for themselves as union members and political activists. The treaty could include a proviso stipulating its periodic renegotiation, so that the list of rights could be adapted to changing social and economic conditions. Then, even when they were not living at home, the original citizenship of the guests would work for them (as it never worked for the Athenian metics); and they would, in some sense, be represented in local decision making. In one way or another, they ought to be able to enjoy the protection of citizenship or potential citizenship.

Leaving aside such international arrangements, the principle of political justice is this: that the processes of self-determination through which a democratic state shapes its internal life, must be open, and equally open, to all those men and women who live within its territory, work in the local economy, and are subject to local law.* Hence, second admissions (naturalization) depend on first admissions (immigration) and are subject only to certain constraints of time and qualification,

---

*It has been suggested to me that this argument doesn't plausibly apply to privileged guests: technical advisors, visiting professors, and so on. I concede the point, though I'm not sure just how to describe the category "guest workers" so as to exclude these others. But the others are not very important, and it is in the nature of their privileged positions that they are able to call upon the protection of their home states if they ever need it. They enjoy a kind of extra-territoriality.

never to the ultimate constraint of closure. When second admissions are closed, the political community collapses into a world of members and strangers, with no political boundaries between the two, where the strangers are subjects of the members. Among themselves, perhaps, the members are equal; but it is not their equality but their tyranny that determines the character of the state. Political justice is a bar to permanent alienage—either for particular individuals or for a class of changing individuals. At least, this is true in a democracy. In an oligarchy, as Isocrates wrote, even the citizens are really resident aliens, and so the issue of political rights doesn't arise in the same way. But as soon as some residents are citizens in fact, all must be so. No democratic state can tolerate the establishment of a fixed status between citizen and foreigner (though there can be stages in the transition from one of these political identities to the other). Men and women are either subject to the state's authority, or they are not; and if they are subject, they must be given a say, and ultimately an equal say, in what that authority does. Democratic citizens, then, have a choice: if they want to bring in new workers, they must be prepared to enlarge their own membership; if they are unwilling to accept new members, they must find ways within the limits of the domestic labor market to get socially necessary work done. And those are their only choices. Their right to choose derives from the existence in this particular territory of a community of citizens; and it is not compatible with the destruction of the community or its transformation into yet another local tyranny.

Membership and Justice

The distribution of membership is not pervasively subject to the constraints of justice. Across a considerable range of the decisions that are made, states are simply free to take in strangers (or not)—much as they are free, leaving aside the claims of the needy, to share their wealth with foreign friends, to honor the achievements of foreign artists, scholars, and scientists, to choose their trading partners, and to enter into collective security arrangements with foreign states. But the right to choose an admissions policy is more basic than any of these, for it is not merely a matter of acting in the world, exercising sovereignty, and pursuing national interests. At stake here is the shape of the community that acts in the world, exercises sovereignty, and so on. Admission and exclusion are at the core of communal independence. They suggest the deepest meaning of self-determination. Without them, there could not be *communities of character,* historically stable, ongoing associations of men and women with some special commitment to one another and some special sense of their common life.[31]

But self-determination in the sphere of membership is not absolute. It is a right exercised, most often, by national clubs or families, but it is held in principle by territorial states. Hence it is subject both to internal decisions by the members themselves (*all* the members, including those who hold membership simply by right of place) and to the external principle of mutual aid. Immigration, then, is both a matter of political choice and moral constraint. Naturalization, by contrast, is entirely constrained: every new immigrant, every refugee taken in, every resident and worker must be offered the opportunities of citizenship. If the community is so radically divided that a single citizenship is impossible, then its territory must be divided, too, before the rights of admission and exclusion can be exercised. For these rights are to be exercised only by the community as a whole (even if, in practice, some national majority dominates the decision making) and only with regard to foreigners, not by some members with regard to others. No community can be half-metic, half-citizen and claim that its admissions policies are acts of self-determination or that its politics is democratic.

The determination of aliens and guests by an exclusive band of citizens (or of slaves by masters, or women by men, or blacks by whites, or conquered peoples by their conquerors) is not communal freedom but oppression. The citizens are free, of course, to set up a club, make membership as exclusive as they like, write a constitution, and govern one another. But they can't claim territorial jurisdiction and rule over the people with whom they share the territory. To do this is to act outside their sphere, beyond their rights. It is a form of tyranny. Indeed, the rule of citizens over non-citizens, of members over strangers, is probably the most common form of tyranny in human history. I won't say much more than this about the special problems of non-citizens and strangers: henceforth, whether I am talking about the distribution of security and welfare or about hard work or power itself, I shall assume that all the eligible men and women hold a single political status. This assumption doesn't exclude other sorts of inequality further down the road, but it does exclude the piling up of inequalities that is characteristic of divided societies. The denial of membership is always the first of a long train of abuses. There is no way to break the train, so we must deny the rightfulness of the denial. The theory of distributive justice begins, then, with an account of membership rights. It must vindicate at one and the same time the (limited) right of closure, without which there could be no communities at all, and the political inclusiveness of the existing communities. For it is only as members somewhere that men and women can hope to share in all the other social goods—security, wealth, honor, office, and power—that communal life makes possible.

3

Security and Welfare

Membership and Need

Membership is important because of what the members of a political community owe to one another and to no one else, or to no one else in the same degree. And the first thing they owe is the communal provision of security and welfare. This claim might be reversed: communal provision is important because it teaches us the value of membership. If we did not provide for one another, if we recognized no distinction between members and strangers, we would have no reason to form and maintain political communities. "How shall men love their country," Rousseau asked, "if it is nothing more for them than for strangers, and bestows on them only that which it can refuse to none?"[1] Rousseau believed that citizens ought to love their country and therefore that their country ought to give them particular reasons to do so. Membership (like kinship) is a special relation. It's not enough to say, as Edmund Burke did, that "to make us love our country, our country ought to be lovely."[2] The crucial thing is that it be lovely for us—though we always hope that it will be lovely for others (we also love its reflected loveliness).

Political community for the sake of provision, provision for the sake of community: the process works both ways, and that is perhaps its crucial feature. Philosophers and political theorists have been too quick to turn it into a simple calculation. Indeed, we are rationalists of everyday life; we come together, we sign the social contract or reiterate the signing of it, in order to provide for our needs. And we value the contract insofar as those needs are met. But one of our needs is community itself: culture, religion, and politics. It is only under the aegis of these three that all the other things we need become *socially recognized needs*, take on historical and determinate form. The social contract is an agreement to reach decisions together about what goods are necessary to our common life, and then to provide those goods for one another. The signers owe one another more than mutual aid, for that they owe or can owe to anyone. They owe mutual provision of all those things for the sake of which they have separated themselves from mankind as a whole and joined forces in a particular community. *Amour social* is one of those things; but though it is a distributed good—often unevenly distributed—it arises only in the course of other distributions (and of the political choices that the other distributions require). Mutual provision breeds mutuality. So the common life is simultaneously the prerequisite of provision and one of its products.

Men and women come together because they literally cannot live apart. But they can live together in many different ways. Their survival and then their well-being require a common effort: against the wrath of the gods, the hostility of other people, the indifference and malevolence of nature (famine, flood, fire, and disease), the brief transit of a human life. Not army camps alone, as David Hume wrote, but temples, storehouses, irrigation works, and burial grounds are the true mothers of cities.[3] As the list suggests, origins are not singular in character. Cities differ from one another, partly because of the natural environments in which they are built and the immediate dangers their builders encounter, partly because of the conceptions of social goods that the builders hold. They recognize but also create one another's needs and so give a particular shape to what I will call the "sphere of security and welfare." The sphere itself is as old as the oldest human community. Indeed, one might say that the original community is a sphere of security and welfare, a system of communal provision, distorted, no doubt, by gross inequalities of strength and cunning. But the system has, in any case, no natural form. Different experiences and different conceptions lead to different patterns of provision. Though there are some goods that are needed absolutely, there is no good such that once we see it, we know how it stands vis-à-vis all other goods and how much of it we owe to one another. The nature of a need is not self-evident.

Communal provision is both general and particular. It is general whenever public funds are spent so as to benefit all or most of the members without any distribution to individuals. It is particular whenever

goods are actually handed over to all or any of the members.* Water,
for example, is one of "the bare requirements of civil life," and the
building of reservoirs is a form of general provision.⁴ But the delivery
of water to one rather than to another neighborhood (where, say, the
wealthier citizens live) is particular. The securing of the food supply
is general; the distribution of food to widows and orphans is particular.
Public health is most often general, the care of the sick, most often
particular. Sometimes the criteria for general and particular provision
will differ radically. The building of temples and the organization of
religious services is an example of general provision designed to meet
the needs of the community as a whole, but communion with the gods
may be allowed only to particularly meritorious members (or it may
be sought privately in secret or in nonconformist sects). The system
of justice is a general good, meeting common needs; but the actual distribution of rewards and punishments may serve the particular needs
of a ruling class, or it may be organized, as we commonly think it should
be, to give to individuals what they individually deserve. Simone Weil
has argued that, with regard to justice, need operates at both the general and the particular levels, since criminals need to be punished.⁵ But
that is an idiosyncratic use of the word *need*. More likely, the punishment of criminals is something only the rest of us need. But need does
operate both generally and particularly for other goods: health care is
an obvious example that I will later consider in some detail.

Despite the inherent forcefulness of the word, needs are elusive. People don't just have needs, they have ideas about their needs; they have
priorities, they have degrees of need; and these priorities and degrees
are related not only to their human nature but also to their history and
culture. Since resources are always scarce, hard choices have to be
made. I suspect that these can only be political choices. They are subject to a certain philosophical elucidation, but the idea of need and
the commitment to communal provision do not by themselves yield
any clear determination of priorities or degrees. Clearly we can't meet,
and we don't have to meet, every need to the same degree or any need

*I don't mean to reiterate here the technical distinction that economists make between public
and private goods. General provision is always public, at least on the less stringent definitions
of that term (which specify only that public goods are those that can't be provided to some and
not to other members of the community). So are most forms of particular provision, for even
goods delivered to individuals generate non-exclusive benefits for the community as a whole.
Scholarships to orphans, for example, are private to the orphans, public to the community of
citizens within which the orphans will one day work and vote. But public goods of this latter
sort, which depend upon prior distributions to particular persons or groups, have been controversial in many societies; and I have designed my categories so as to enable me to examine them
closely.

to the ultimate degree. The ancient Athenians, for example, provided public baths and gymnasiums for the citizens but never provided anything remotely resembling unemployment insurance or social security. They made a choice about how to spend public funds, a choice shaped presumably by their understanding of what the common life required. It would be hard to argue that they made a mistake. I suppose there are notions of need that would yield such a conclusion, but these would not be notions acceptable to—they might not even be comprehensible to—the Athenians themselves.

The question of degree suggests even more clearly the importance of political choice and the irrelevance of any merely philosophical stipulation. Needs are not only elusive; they are also expansive. In the phrase of the contemporary philosopher Charles Fried, needs are voracious; they eat up resources.[6] But it would be wrong to suggest that therefore need cannot be a distributive principle. It is, rather, a principle subject to political limitation; and the limits (within limits) can be arbitrary, fixed by some temporary coalition of interests or majority of voters. Consider the case of physical security in a modern American city. We could provide absolute security, eliminate every source of violence except domestic violence, if we put a street light every ten yards and stationed a policeman every thirty yards throughout the city. But that would be very expensive, and so we settle for something less. How much less can only be decided politically.* One can imagine the sorts of things that would figure in the debates. Above all, I think, there would be a certain understanding—more or less widely shared, controversial only at the margins—of what constitutes "enough" security or of what level of insecurity is simply intolerable. The decision would also be affected by other factors: alternate needs, the state of the economy, the agitation of the policemen's union, and so on. But whatever decision is ultimately reached, for whatever reasons, security is provided because the citizens need it. And because, at some level, they all need it, the criterion of need remains a critical standard (as we shall see) even though it cannot determine priority and degree.

---

*And should be decided politically: that is what democratic political arrangements are for. Any philosophical effort to stipulate in detail the rights or the entitlements of individuals would radically constrain the scope of democratic decision making. I have argued this point elsewhere.[7]

Communal Provision

There has never been a political community that did not provide, or try to provide, or claim to provide, for the needs of its members as its members understood those needs. And there has never been a political community that did not engage its collective strength—its capacity to direct, regulate, pressure, and coerce—in this project. The modes of organization, the levels of taxation, the timing and reach of conscription: these have always been a focus of political controversy. But the use of political power has not, until very recently, been controversial. The building of fortresses, dams, and irrigation works; the mobilization of armies; the securing of the food supply and of trade generally—all these require coercion. The state is a tool that cannot be made without iron. And coercion, in turn, requires agents of coercion. Communal provision is always mediated by a set of officials (priests, soldiers, and bureaucrats) who introduce characteristic distortions into the process, siphoning off money and labor for their own purposes or using provision as a form of control. But these distortions are not my immediate concern. I want to stress instead the sense in which every political community is in principle a "welfare state." Every set of officials is at least putatively committed to the provision of security and welfare; every set of members is committed to bear the necessary burdens (and actually does bear them). The first commitment has to do with the duties of office; the second, with the dues of membership. Without some shared sense of the duty and the dues there would be no political community at all and no security or welfare—and the life of mankind "solitary, poor, nasty, brutish, and short."

But how much security and welfare is required? Of what sorts? Distributed how? Paid for how? These are the serious issues, and they can be resolved in many different ways. Since every resolution will be appropriate or inappropriate to a particular community, it will be best to turn now to some concrete examples. I have chosen two, from different historical periods, with very different general and particular distributive commitments. The two represent the two strands of our own cultural tradition, Hellenic and Hebraic; but I have not looked for anything like extreme points on the range of possibilities. Rather, I have chosen two communities that are, like our own, relatively democratic and generally respectful of private property. Neither of them, so far as I know, has ever figured significantly in histories of the welfare state; and yet the citizens of both understood well the meaning of communal provision.

Athens in the Fifth and Fourth Centuries

"The Hellenistic city-states were highly sensitive to what may be called the general welfare, that is, they were quite willing to take measures which looked to the benefit of the citizenry as a whole; to social welfare . . . in particular the benefit of the poor as such, they were, on the contrary, largely indifferent."[8] This comment by the contemporary classicist Louis Cohn-Haft occurs in the course of a study of the "public physicians" of ancient Greece, a minor institution but a useful starting point for my own account. In Athens, in the fifth century B.C. (and during the later Hellenistic period in many Greek cities), a small number of doctors were elected to public office, much as generals were elected, and paid a stipend from public funds. It's not clear what their duties were; the surviving evidence is fragmentary. They apparently charged fees for their services much as other doctors did, though it seems likely that "as stipendiaries of the whole citizen body [they] would be under considerable social pressure not to refuse a sick person who could not pay a fee." The purpose of the election and the stipend seems to have been to assure the presence of qualified doctors in the city—in time of plague, for example. The provision was general, not particular; and the city apparently took little interest in the further distribution of medical care. It did honor public physicians who "gave themselves ungrudgingly to all who claimed to need them"; but this suggests that the giving was not a requirement of the office; the doctors were paid for something else.[9]

This was the common pattern at Athens, but the range of general provision was very wide. It began with defense: the fleet, the army, the walls down to Piraeus, were all the work of the citizens themselves under the direction of their magistrates and generals. Or, perhaps it began with food: the Assembly was required, at fixed intervals, to consider an agenda item that had a fixed form—"corn and the defense of the country." Actual distributions of corn occurred only rarely; but the import trade was closely watched, and the internal market regulated, by an impressive array of officials: ten commissioners of trade, ten superintendents of the markets, ten inspectors of weights and measures, thirty-five "corn guardians" who enforced a just price, and—in moments of crisis—a group of corn buyers "who sought supplies wherever it could find them, raised public subscriptions for the necessary funds, introduced price reductions and rationing."[10] All of these officials were chosen by lot from among the citizens. Or, perhaps it began with religion: the major public buildings of Athens were temples, built with public money; priests were public officials who offered sacrifices on the city's behalf. Or, perhaps it began, as in Locke's account of the origins of the state, with justice: Athens was policed by a band of state slaves (eighteen hundred Scythian archers); the city's courts were intricately organized and always busy. And beyond all this, the city provided a variety of other goods. Five commissioners supervised the building and repair of the roads. A board of ten enforced a rather minimal set of public health measures: "they ensure that the dung collectors do not deposit dung within ten *stados* of the walls."[11] As I have already noted, the city provided baths and gymnasiums, probably more for social than for hygienic reasons. The burial of corpses found lying on the streets was a public charge. So were the funerals of the war dead, like the one at which Pericles spoke in 431. Finally, the great drama festivals were publicly organized and paid for, through a special kind of taxation, by wealthy citizens. Is this last an expense for security and welfare? We might think of it as a central feature of the religious and political education of the Athenian people. By contrast, there was no public expenditure for schools or teachers at any level: no subsidies for reading and writing or for philosophy.

Alongside all this, the particular distributions authorized by the Athenian Assembly—with one central exception—came to very little. "There is a law," Aristotle reported, "that anyone with property of less than three *minae* who suffers from a physical disability which prevents his undertaking any employment should come before the Council, and if his claim is approved he should receive two *obols* a day subsistence from public funds."[12] These (very small) pensions could be challenged by any citizen, and then the pensioner had to defend himself before a jury. One of the surviving orations of Lycias was written for a crippled pensioner. "All fortune, good and bad," Lycias had the pensioner tell the jury, "is to be shared in common by the community as a whole."[13] This was hardly an accurate description of the city's practices. But the citizens did recognize their obligations to orphans and also to the widows of fallen soldiers. Beyond that, particular provision was left to the families of those who needed it. The city took an interest but only at a distance: a law of Solon required fathers to teach their sons a trade and sons to maintain their parents in old age.

The central exception, of course, was the distribution of public funds to all those citizens who held an office, served on the Council, attended the Assembly, or sat on a jury. Here a particular distribution served a general purpose: the maintenance of a vigorous democracy. The monies paid out were designed to make it possible for artisans and farmers to miss a day's work. Public spirit was still required, for the amounts were small, less than the daily earnings even of an unskilled laborer. But the yearly total was considerable, coming to something like half of the internal revenue of the city in the fifth century and more than that at many points in the fourth.[14] Since the revenue of the city was not raised from taxes on land or income (but from taxes on imports, court fines, rents, the income of the silver mines, and so on), it can't be said that these payments were redistributive. But they did distribute public funds so as to balance somewhat the inequalities of Athenian society. This was particularly the case with regard to payments to elderly citizens who would not have been working anyway. Professor M. I. Finley is inclined to attribute to this distributive effect the virtual absence of civil strife or class war throughout the history of democratic Athens.[15] Perhaps this was an intended result, but it seems more likely that what lay behind the payments was a certain conception of citizenship. To make it possible for each and every citizen to participate in political life, the citizens as a body were prepared to lay out large sums. Obviously, this appropriation benefited the poorest citizens the most, but of poverty itself the city took no direct notice.

A Medieval Jewish Community

I shall not refer here to any particular Jewish community but shall try to describe a typical community in Christian Europe during the high Middle Ages. I am concerned primarily to produce a list of goods generally or particularly provided; and the list doesn't vary significantly from one place to another. Jewish communities under Islamic rule, especially as these have been reconstructed in the remarkable books of Professor S. D. Goitein, undertook essentially the same sort of provision though under somewhat different circumstances.[16] In contrast to Athens, all these were autonomous but not sovereign communities. In Europe, they possessed full powers of taxation, though much of the money they raised had to be passed on to the secular—that is, Christian—king, prince, or lord, either in payment of his taxes or as bribes, subsidies, "loans," and so on. This can be thought of as the price of protection. In the Egyptian cities studied by Goitein, the largest part of the communal funds was raised through charitable appeals, but the standardized form of the gifts suggests that social pressure worked very much like political power. It was hardly possible to live in the Jewish community without contributing; and short of conversion to Christianity, a Jew had no alternative; there was no place else to go.

In principle, these were democratic communities, governed by an assembly of male members, meeting in the synagogue. External pressures tended to produce oligarchy or, more precisely, plutocracy—the rule of the heads of the wealthiest families, who were best able to deal with avaricious kings. But the rule of the wealthy was continually challenged by more ordinary members of the religious community, and was balanced by the authority of the rabbinic courts. The rabbis played a crucial role in the apportionment of taxes, a matter of ongoing and frequently bitter controversy. The rich preferred a *per capita* tax, though in moments of crisis they could hardly avoid contributing what was necessary to their own, as well as the community's, survival. The rabbis seem generally to have favored proportional (a few of them even raised the possibility of progressive) taxation.[17]

As one might expect in communities whose members were at best precariously established, subject to intermittent persecution and constant harassment, a high proportion of public funds was distributed to individuals in trouble. But though it was established early on that the poor of one's own community took precedence over "foreign" Jews, the larger solidarity of a persecuted people is revealed in the very strong commitment to the "ransom of captives"—an absolute obligation on any community to which an appeal was made, and a significant drain on communal resources. "The redemption of captives," wrote Maimonides, "has precedence over the feeding and clothing of the poor."[18] This priority derived from the immediate physical danger in which the captive found himself, but it probably also had to do with the fact that his danger was religious as well as physical. Forced conversion or slavery to a non-Jewish owner were threats to which the organized Jewish communities were especially sensitive; for these were above all religious communities, and their conceptions of public life and of the needs of individual men and women were alike shaped through centuries of religious discussion.

The major forms of general provision—excluding protection money—were religious in character, though these included services that we now think of as secular. The synagogue and its officials, the courts and their officials, were paid for out of public funds. The courts administered Talmudic law, and their jurisdiction was wide (though it did not extend to capital crimes). Economic dealings were closely regulated, especially dealings with non-Jews since these could have implications for the community as a whole. The pervasive sumptuary laws were also designed with non-Jews in mind, so as not to excite envy and resentment. The community provided public baths, more for religious than for hygienic reasons, and supervised the work of the slaughterers. Kosher meat was taxed (in the Egyptian communities, too), so this was both a form of provision and a source of revenue. There was also some effort made to keep the streets clear of rubbish and to avoid overcrowding in Jewish neighborhoods. Toward the end of the medieval period, many communities established hospitals and paid communal midwives and physicians.

Particular distributions commonly took the form of a dole: regular weekly or twice-weekly distributions of food; less frequent distributions of clothing; special allocations for sick people, stranded travelers, widows and orphans, and so on—all this on a remarkable scale given the size and resources of the communities. Maimonides had written that the highest form of charity was the gift or loan or partnership designed to make the recipient self-supporting. These words were often quoted but, as Goitein has argued, they did not shape the structure of social services in the Jewish community. Perhaps the poor were too numerous, the situation of the community itself too precarious, for anything more than relief. Goitein has calculated that among the Jews of Old Cairo, "there was one relief recipient to every four contributors to the charities."[19] The contributors of money also contributed their time and energy: from their ranks came a host of minor officials involved in the endless work of collection and distribution. Hence, the dole was a large and continuous drain, accepted as a religious obligation, with no end in sight until the coming of the messiah. This was divine justice with a touch of Jewish irony: "You must help the poor in proportion to their needs, but you are not obligated to make them rich."[20]

Beyond the dole, there were additional forms of particular provision, most importantly for educational purposes. In fifteenth-century Spain, some sixty years before the expulsion, a remarkable effort was made to establish something like universal and compulsory public education. The Valladolid synod of 1432 established special taxes on meat and wine, and on weddings, circumcisions, and burials, and ordered

> that every community of fifteen householders [or more] shall be obliged to maintain a qualified elementary teacher to instruct their children in Scripture. . . . The parents shall be obliged to send their children to that teacher, and each shall pay him in accordance with their means. If this revenue should prove inadequate, the community shall be obliged to supplement it.

More advanced schools were required in every community of forty or more householders. The chief rabbi of Castile was authorized to divert money from wealthy to impoverished communities in order to subsidize struggling schools.[21] This was a program considerably more ambitious than anything attempted earlier on. But throughout the Jewish communities a great deal of attention was paid to education: the school fees of poor children were commonly paid; and there were greater or lesser public subsidies, as well as additional charitable support, for religious schools and academies. Jews went to school the way Greeks went to the theater or the assembly—as neither group could have done had these institutions been left entirely to private enterprise.

Together, the Jews and the Greeks suggest not only the range of communal activity but also, and more important, the way in which this activity is structured by collective values and political choices. In any political community where the members have something to say about their government, some such pattern will be worked out: a set of general and particular provisions designed to sustain and enhance a common culture. The point would hardly have to be made were it not for contemporary advocates of a minimal or libertarian state, who argue that all such matters (except for defense) should be left to the voluntary efforts of individuals.[22] But individuals left to themselves, if that is a practical possibility, will necessarily seek out other individuals for the sake of collective provision. They need too much from one another—not only material goods, which might be provided through a system of free exchange, but material goods that have, so to speak, a moral and cultural shape. Certainly one can find examples—there are many—of states that failed to provide either the material goods or the morality or that provided them so badly, and did so much else, that ordinary men and women yearned for nothing so much as deliverance from their impositions. Having won deliverance, however, these same men and women don't set out simply to maintain it but go on to elaborate a pattern of provision suited to their own needs (their own conception of their needs). The arguments for a minimal state have never recommended themselves to any significant portion of mankind. Indeed, what is most common in the history of popular struggles is the demand not for deliverance but for performance: that the state actually serve the purposes it claims to serve, and that it do so for all its members. The political community grows by invasion as previously excluded groups, one after another—plebians, slaves, women, minorities of all sorts—demand their share of security and welfare.

Fair Shares

What is their rightful share? There are, in fact, two different questions here. The first concerns the range of goods that ought to be shared, the boundaries of the sphere of security and welfare: that is the subject of the next section. The second concerns the distributive principles appropriate within the sphere, which I shall try now to tease out of the Greek and Jewish examples.

We can best begin with the Talmudic maxim that the poor must (the imperative is important) be helped in proportion to their needs. That is common sense, I suppose, but it has an important negative thrust: not in proportion to any personal quality—physical attractiveness, say, or religious orthodoxy. One of the persistent efforts of Jewish communal organization, never entirely successful, was the elimination of beggary. The beggar is rewarded for his skill in telling a story, for his pathos, often—in Jewish lore—for his audacity; and he is rewarded in accordance with the kindness, the self-importance, the *noblesse oblige* of his benefactor, but never simply in proportion to his needs. But if we tighten the link between need and provision, we can free the distributive process from all these extraneous factors. When we give out food, we will attend directly to the purpose of the giving: the relief of hunger. Hungry men and women don't have to stage a performance, or pass an exam, or win an election.

This is the inner logic, the social and moral logic of provision. Once the community undertakes to provide some needed good, it must provide it to all the members who need it in proportion to their needs. The actual distribution will be limited by the available resources; but all other criteria, beyond need itself, are experienced as distortions and not as limitations of the distributive process. And the available resources of the community are simply the past and present product, the accumulated wealth of its members—not some "surplus" of that wealth. It is commonly argued that the welfare state "rests on the availability of some form of economic surplus."[23] But what can that mean? We can't subtract from the total social product the maintenance costs of men and machines, the price of social survival, and then finance the welfare state out of what is left, for we will already have financed the welfare state out of what we have subtracted. Surely the price of social survival includes state expenditures for military security, say, and public health, and education. Socially recognized needs are the first charge against the social product; there is no real surplus until they have been met. What the surplus finances is the production and exchange of commodities outside the sphere of need. Men and women who appropriate vast sums of money for themselves, while needs are still unmet, act like tyrants, dominating and distorting the distribution of security and welfare.

I should stress again that needs are not merely physical phenomena. Even the need for food takes different forms under different cultural conditions. Thus the general distributions of food before religious holidays in the Jewish communities: a ritual and not a physical need was being served. It was important not only that the poor should eat but also that they should eat the right sorts of food, for otherwise they would be cut off from the community—but they were helped in the first place only because they were members of the community. Similarly, if disability is a reason for providing a pension, then every disabled citizen is entitled to that pension; but it still remains to work out what constitutes disability. In Athens this was accomplished, characteristically, through litigation. One can readily imagine alternative means but not, given the initial recognition of disability, alternative reasons. In fact, Lycias's pensioner felt bound to tell the jury that he was really a good fellow: I don't mean to suggest that the inner logic of provision is always or immediately understood. But the crucial charge against the pensioner was that he wasn't seriously disabled, and his crucial response was that he indeed fell within the category of disabled citizens as it had always been understood.

Education raises harder questions of cultural definition, and so may serve to complicate our understanding of both the possiblities and the limits of distributive justice in the sphere of security and welfare. Ignorance is obviously a more ambiguous notion than hunger or disability, for it is always relative to some body of socially valued knowledge. The education that children need is relative to the life we expect or want them to have. Children are educated for some reason, and they are educated particularly, not generally ("general education" is a modern idea designed to meet the specific requirements of our own society). In the medieval Jewish communities, the purpose of education was to enable adult men to participate actively in religious services and in discussions of religious doctrine. Since women were religiously passive, the community undertook no commitment to their education. In every other area of particular provision—food, clothing, medical care—women were helped exactly as men were helped, in proportion to their needs. But women did not need an education, for they were in fact less than full members of the (religious) community. Their primary place was not the synagogue but the household. Male dominance was most immediately expressed in the synagogue services (as it was among the Athenians in the Assembly debates) and then converted into the concrete coinage of subsidized schooling.

That dominance was occasionally challenged by writers who pointed to the importance of religious observance in the household, or to the religious significance of childrearing, or (less often) to the contributions women might make to religious knowledge.[24] The argument necessarily focused on religion, and its success depended upon some moral or intellectual enhancement of the role of women in religious life. Because there were tensions within the Jewish tradition, there was something to argue about. It was at most a marginal enhancement that was aimed at, however; and so far as I know the synagogue was never actually described as a tyranny of men. Educational equality waited upon the development of alternative communities within which women might more readily claim to be members: thus the contemporary arguments for equality that invoke, as I shall do, the idea of an inclusive citizenship.

The Jewish communities did aim at including all men, however, and so faced the problem of organizing an educational system that cut across class lines. This might be achieved in a variety of ways. The community could organize charity schools for the poor, like the special schools for orphans in Old Cairo. Or it could pay the fees of poor children attending schools established and largely paid for by the better-off: this was the most common practice among medieval Jews. Or it could provide an education for everyone through the tax system and bar any additional charges even for those children whose parents could afford to pay more than their taxes. There is some pressure, I think, to move from the first to the second of these arrangements and then to some version of the third. For any social designation of the poor as "charity cases" is likely to produce discriminatory treatment within the schools themselves. Or, it is likely to be experienced by the children (or by their parents) as so degrading that it inhibits their participation in school activities (or their support for those activities). These effects may not be common to all cultures, but they are obviously widespread. Among medieval Jews, there was a great reluctance to accept public charity and some stigma attached to those who did so. Indeed, it can be one of the purposes of communal provision to stigmatize the poor and teach them their proper place—in, but not wholly of, the community. But except in some rigidly hierarchical society, that will never be its formal or publicly proclaimed purpose, and it will never be its only purpose. And if the publicly proclaimed purpose is, for example, to educate (male) children to read and discuss Scripture, then a common education commonly provided would seem to be the best arrangement.

Goitein notes a movement in this direction in the communities he has studied, but thinks the reasons were largely financial.[25] Perhaps the rabbis of Spain had grasped the value of the common school: hence the element of compulsion in the scheme they devised. In any case, whenever the purpose of communal provision is to open the way to communal participation, it will make sense to recommend a form of provision that is the same for all the members. And it might well be said that, in democratic regimes, all provision has this purpose. The Athenian decision to pay every citizen who attended the Assembly the same (small) amount of money probably derives from some recognition of this fact. It would not have been difficult to devise a means test. But the citizens were not paid in proportion to their means, or to their needs as individuals, because it was not as individuals but as citizens that they were paid, and as citizens they were equal to one another. On the other hand, the Athenians barred from public office those citizens to whom disability pensions were paid.[26] That probably reflects a peculiar view of disability, but it may also be taken to symbolize the degrading effects that sometimes (though not always) follow when communal provision takes the form of public charity.

The Extent of Provision

Distributive justice in the sphere of welfare and security has a twofold meaning: it refers, first, to the recognition of need and, second, to the recognition of membership. Goods must be provided to needy members because of their neediness, but they must also be provided in such a way as to sustain their membership. It's not the case, however, that members have a claim on any specific set of goods. Welfare rights are fixed only when a community adopts some program of mutual provision. There are strong arguments to be made that, under given historical conditions, such-and-such a program should be adopted. But these are not arguments about individual rights; they are arguments about the character of a particular political community. No one's rights were violated because the Athenians did not allocate public funds for the education of children. Perhaps they believed, and perhaps they were right, that the public life of the city was education enough.

The right that members can legitimately claim is of a more general sort. It undoubtedly includes some version of the Hobbesian right to life, some claim on communal resources for bare subsistence. No community can allow its members to starve to death when there is food available to feed them; no government can stand passively by at such a time—not if it claims to be a government of or by or for the community. The indifference of Britain's rulers during the Irish potato famine in the 1840s is a sure sign that Ireland was a colony, a conquered land, no real part of Great Britain.[27] This is not to justify the indifference—one has obligations to colonies and to conquered peoples—but only to suggest that the Irish would have been better served by a government, virtually any government, of their own. Perhaps Burke came closest to describing the fundamental right that is at stake here when he wrote: "Government is a contrivance of human wisdom to provide for human wants. Men have a right that these wants should be provided for by this wisdom."[28] It only has to be said that the wisdom in question is the wisdom not of a ruling class, as Burke seems to have thought, but of the community as a whole. Only its culture, its character, its common understandings can define the "wants" that are to be provided for. But culture, character, and common understandings are not givens; they don't operate automatically; at any particular moment, the citizens must argue about the extent of mutual provision.

They argue about the meaning of the social contract, the original and reiterated conception of the sphere of security and welfare. This is not a hypothetical or an ideal contract of the sort John Rawls has described. Rational men and women in the original position, deprived of all particular knowledge of their social standing and cultural understanding, would probably opt, as Rawls has argued, for an equal distribution of whatever goods they were told they needed.[29] But this formula doesn't help very much in determining what choices people will make, or what choices they should make, once they know who and where they are. In a world of particular cultures, competing conceptions of the good, scarce resources, elusive and expansive needs, there isn't going to be a single formula, universally applicable. There isn't going to be a single, universally approved path that carries us from a notion like, say, "fair shares" to a comprehensive list of the goods to which that notion applies. Fair shares of what?

Justice, tranquility, defense, welfare, and liberty: that is the list provided by the United States Constitution. One could construe it as an exhaustive list, but the terms are vague; they provide at best a starting point for public debate. The standard appeal in that debate is to a larger idea: the Burkeian general right, which takes on determinate force only under determinate conditions and requires different sorts of provision in different times and places. The idea is simply that we have come together, shaped a community, in order to cope with difficulties and dangers that we could not cope with alone. And so whenever we find ourselves confronted with difficulties and dangers of that sort, we look for communal assistance. As the balance of individual and collective capacity changes, so the kinds of assistance that are looked for change, too.

The history of public health in the West might usefully be told in these terms. Some minimal provision is very old, as the Greek and Jewish examples suggest; the measures adopted were a function of the community's sense of danger and the extent of its medical knowledge. Over the years, living arrangements on a larger scale bred new dangers, and scientific advance generated a new sense of danger and a new awareness of the possibilities of coping. And then groups of citizens pressed for a wider program of communal provision, exploiting the new science to reduce the risks of urban life. That, they might rightly say, is what the community is for. A similar argument can be made in the case of social security. The very success of general provision in the field of public health has greatly extended the span of a normal human life and then also the span of years during which men and women are unable to support themselves, during which they are physically but most often not socially, politically, or morally incapacitated. Once again, support for the disabled is one of the oldest and most common forms of particular provision. But now it is required on a much larger scale than ever before. Families are overwhelmed by the costs of old age and look for help to the political community. Exactly what ought to be done will be a matter of dispute. Words like *health, danger, science,* even *old age,* have very different meanings in different cultures; no external specification is possible. But this is not to say that it won't be clear enough to the people involved that something—some particular set of things—ought to be done.

Perhaps these examples are too easy. Disease is a general threat; old age, a general prospect. Not so unemployment and poverty, which probably lie beyond the ken of many well-to-do people. The poor can always be isolated, locked into ghettos, blamed and punished for their own misfortune. At this point, it might be said, provision can no longer be defended by invoking anything like the "meaning" of the social contract. But let us look more closely at the easy cases; for, in fact, they involve all the difficulties of the difficult ones. Public health and social security invite us to think of the political community, in T. H. Marshall's phrase, as a "mutual benefit club."[30] All provision is reciprocal; the members take turns providing and being provided for, much as Aristotle's citizens take turns ruling and being ruled. This is a happy picture, and one that is readily understandable in contractualist terms. It is not only the case that rational agents, knowing nothing of their specific situation, would agree to these two forms of provision; the real agents, the ordinary citizens, of every modern democracy have in fact agreed to them. The two are, or so it appears, equally in the interests of hypothetical and of actual people. Coercion is only necessary in practice because some minority of actual people don't understand, or don't consistently understand, their real interests. Only the reckless and the improvident need to be forced to contribute—and it can always be said of them that they joined in the social contract precisely in order to protect themselves against their own recklessness and improvidence. In fact, however, the reasons for coercion go much deeper than this; the political community is something more than a mutual benefit club; and the extent of communal provision in any given case—what it is and what it should be—is determined by conceptions of need that are more problematic than the argument thus far suggests.

Consider again the case of public health. No communal provision is possible here without the constraint of a wide range of activities profitable to individual members of the community but threatening to some larger number. Even something so simple, for example, as the provision of uncontaminated milk to large urban populations requires extensive public control; and control is a political achievement, the result (in the United States) of bitter struggles, over many years, in one city after another.[31] When the farmers or the middlemen of the dairy industry defended free enterprise, they were certainly acting rationally in their own interests. The same thing can be said of other entrepreneurs who defend themselves against the constraints of inspection, regulation, and enforcement. Public activities of these sorts may be of the highest value to the rest of us; they are not of the highest value to all of us. Though I have taken public health as an example of general provision, it is provided only at the expense of some members of the community. Moreover, it benefits most the most vulnerable of the others: thus, the special importance of the building code for those who live in crowded tenements, and of anti-pollution laws for those who live in the immediate vicinity of factory smokestacks or water drains. Social security, too, benefits the most vulnerable members, even if, for reasons I have already suggested, the actual payments are the same for everyone. For the well-to-do can, or many of them think they can, help themselves even in time of trouble and would much prefer not to be forced to help anyone else. The truth is that every serious effort at communal provision (insofar as the income of the community derives from the wealth of its members) is redistributive in character.[32] The benefits it provides are not, strictly speaking, mutual.

Once again, rational agents ignorant of their own social standing would agree to such a redistribution. But they would agree too easily, and their agreement doesn't help us understand what sort of a redistribution is required: How much? For what purposes? In practice, redistribution is a political matter, and the coercion it involves is foreshadowed by the conflicts that rage over its character and extent. Every particular measure is pushed through by some coalition of particular interests. But the ultimate appeal in these conflicts is not to the particular interests, not even to a public interest conceived as their sum, but to collective values, shared understandings of membership, health, food and shelter, work and leisure. The conflicts themselves are often focused, at least overtly, on questions of fact; the understandings are assumed. Thus the entrepreneurs of the dairy industry denied as long as they could the connection between contaminated milk and tuberculosis. But once that connection was established, it was difficult for them to deny that milk should be inspected: *caveat emptor* was not, in such a case, a plausible doctrine. Similarly, in the debates over old-age pensions in Great Britain, politicians mostly agreed on the traditional British value of self-help but disagreed sharply about whether self-help was still possible through the established working-class friendly societies. These were real mutual-benefit clubs organized on a strictly voluntary basis, but they seemed about to be overwhelmed by the growing numbers of the aged. It became increasingly apparent that the members simply did not have the resources to protect themselves and one another from poverty in old age. And few British politicians were prepared to say that they should be left unprotected.[33]

Here, then, is a more precise account of the social contract: it is an agreement to redistribute the resources of the members in accordance with some shared understanding of their needs, subject to ongoing political determination in detail. The contract is a moral bond. It connects the strong and the weak, the lucky and the unlucky, the rich and the poor, creating a union that transcends all differences of interest, drawing its strength from history, culture, religion, language, and so on. Arguments about communal provision are, at the deepest level, interpretations of that union. The closer and more inclusive it is, the wider the recognition of needs, the greater the number of social goods that are drawn into the sphere of security and welfare.[34] I don't doubt that many political communities have redistributed resources on very different principles, not in accordance with the needs of the members generally but in accordance with the power of the wellborn or the wealthy. But that, as Rousseau suggested in his *Discourse on Inequality*, makes a fraud of the social contract.[35] In any community, where resources are taken away from the poor and given to the rich, the rights of the poor are being violated. The wisdom of the community is not engaged in providing for their wants. Political debate about the nature of those wants will have to be repressed, else the fraud will quickly be exposed. When all the members share in the business of interpreting the social contract, the result will be a more or less extensive system of communal provision. If all states are in principle welfare states, democracies are most likely to be welfare states in practice. Even the imitation of democracy breeds welfarism, as in the "people's democracies," where the state protects the people against every disaster except those that it inflicts on them itself.

So democratic citizens argue among themselves and opt for many different sorts of security and welfare, extending far beyond my "easy" examples of public health and old-age pensions. The category of socially recognized needs is open-ended. For the people's sense of what they need encompasses not only life itself but also the good life, and the appropriate balance between these two is itself a matter of dispute. The Athenian drama and the Jewish academies were both financed with money that could have been spent on housing, say, or on medicine. But drama and education were taken by Greeks and Jews to be not merely enhancements of the common life but vital aspects of communal welfare. I want to stress again that these are not judgments that can easily be called incorrect.

An American Welfare State

What sort of communal provision is appropriate in a society like our own? It's not my purpose here to anticipate the outcomes of democratic debate or to stipulate in detail the extent or the forms of provision. But it can be argued, I think, that the citizens of a modern industrial democracy owe a great deal to one another, and the argument will provide a useful opportunity to test the critical force of the principles I have defended up until now: that every political community must attend to the needs of its members as they collectively understand those needs; that the goods that are distributed must be distributed in proportion to need; and that the distribution must recognize and uphold the underlying equality of membership. These are very general principles; they are meant to apply to a wide range of communities—to any community, in fact, where the members are each other's equals (before God or the law), or where it can plausibly be said that, however they are treated in fact, they ought to be each other's equals. The principles probably don't apply to a community organized hierarchically, as in traditional India, where the fruits of the harvest are distributed not according to need but according to caste—or rather, as Louis Dumont has written, where "the needs of each are conceived to be different, depending on [his] caste." Everyone is guaranteed a share, so Dumont's Indian village is still a welfare state, "a sort of cooperative where the main aim is to ensure the subsistence of everyone in accordance with his social function," but not a welfare state or a cooperative whose principles we can readily understand.[36] (But Dumont does not tell us how food is supposed to be distributed in time of scarcity. If the subsistence standard is the same for everyone, then we are back in a familiar world.)

Clearly, the three principles apply to the citizens of the United States; and they have considerable force here because of the affluence of the community and the expansive understanding of individual need. On the other hand, the United States currently maintains one of the shabbier systems of communal provision in the Western world. This is so for a variety of reasons: the community of citizens is loosely organized; various ethnic and religious groups run welfare programs of their own; the ideology of self-reliance and entrepreneural opportunity is widely accepted; and the movements of the left, particularly the labor movement, are relatively weak.[37] Democratic decision making reflects these realities, and there is nothing in principle wrong with that. Nevertheless, the established pattern of provision doesn't measure up to the internal requirements of the sphere of security and welfare, and the common understandings of the citizens point toward a more elaborate pattern. One might also argue that American citizens should work to build a stronger and more intensely experienced political community. But this argument, though it would have distributive consequences, is not, properly speaking, an argument about distributive justice. The question is, What do the citizens owe one another, given the community they actually inhabit?

Consider the example of criminal justice. The actual distribution of punishments is an issue I will take up in a later chapter. But the autonomy of punishment, the certainty that people are being punished for the right reasons (whatever those are), depends upon the distribution of resources within the legal system. If accused men and women are to receive their rightful share of justice, they must first have a rightful share of legal aid. Hence the institution of the public defender and the assigned counsel: just as the hungry must be fed, so the accused must be defended; and they must be defended in proportion to their needs. But no impartial observer of the American legal system today can doubt that the resources necessary to meet this standard are not generally available.[38] The rich and the poor are treated differently in American courts, though it is the public commitment of the courts to treat them the same. The argument for a more generous provision follows from that commitment. If justice is to be provided at all, it must be provided equally for all accused citizens without regard to their wealth (or their race, religion, political partisanship, and so on). I don't mean to underestimate the practical difficulties here; but this, again, is the inner logic of provision, and it makes for an illuminating example of complex equality. For the inner logic of reward and punishment is different, requiring, as I shall argue later, that distributions be proportional to desert and not to need. Punishment is a negative good that ought to be monopolized by those who have acted badly—and who have been found guilty of acting badly (after a resourceful defense).

Legal aid raises no theoretical problems because the institutional structures for providing it already exist, and what is at stake is only the readiness of the community to live up to the logic of its own institutions. I want to turn now to an area where American institutions are relatively underdeveloped, and where communal commitment is problematic, the subject of continuing political debate: the area of medical care. But here the argument for a more extensive provision must move more slowly. It isn't enough to summon up a "right to treatment." I shall have to recount something of the history of medical care as a social good.

The Case of Medical Care

Until recent times, the practice of medicine was mostly a matter of free enterprise. Doctors made their diagnosis, gave their advice, healed or didn't heal their patients, for a fee. Perhaps the private character of the economic relationship was connected to the intimate character of the professional relationship. More likely, I think, it had to do with the relative marginality of medicine itself. Doctors could, in fact, do very little for their patients; and the common attitude in the face of disease (as in the face of poverty) was a stoical fatalism. Or, popular remedies were developed that were not much less effective, sometimes more effective, than those prescribed by established physicians. Folk medicine sometimes produced a kind of communal provision at the local level, but it was equally likely to generate new practitioners, charging fees in their turn. Faith healing followed a similar pattern.

Leaving these two aside, we can say that the distribution of medical care has historically rested in the hands of the medical profession, a guild of physicians that dates at least from the time of Hippocrates in the fifth century B.C. The guild has functioned to exclude unconventional practitioners and to regulate the number of physicians in any given community. A genuinely free market has never been in the interest of its members. But it is in the interest of the members to sell their services to individual patients; and thus, by and large, the well-to-do have been well cared for (in accordance with the current understanding of good care) and the poor hardly cared for at all. In a few urban communities—in the medieval Jewish communities, for example—medical services were more widely available. But they were virtually unknown for most people most of the time. Doctors were the servants of the rich, often attached to noble houses and royal courts. With regard to this practical outcome, however, the profession has always had a collective bad conscience. For the distributive logic of the practice of medicine seems to be this: that care should be proportionate to illness and not to wealth. Hence, there have always been doctors, like those honored in ancient Greece, who served the poor on the side, as it were, even while they earned their living from paying patients. Most doctors, present in an emergency, still feel bound to help the victim without regard to his material status. It is a matter of professional Good Samaritanism that the call "Is there a doctor in the house?" should not go unanswered if there is a doctor to answer it. In ordinary times, however, there was little call for medical help, largely because there was little faith in its actual helpfulness. And so the bad conscience of the profession was not echoed by any political demand for the replacement of free enterprise by communal provision.

In Europe during the Middle Ages, the cure of souls was public, the cure of bodies private. Today, in most European countries, the situation is reversed. The reversal is best explained in terms of a major shift in the common understanding of souls and bodies: we have lost confidence in the cure of souls, and we have come increasingly to believe, even to be obsessed with, the cure of bodies. Descartes's famous declaration that the "preservation of health" was the "chief of all goods" may be taken to symbolize the shift—or to herald it, for in the history of popular attitudes, Descartes's *Discourse on Method* came very early.[39] Then, as eternity receded in the popular consciousness, longevity moved to the fore. Among medieval Christians, eternity was a socially recognized need; and every effort was made to see that it was widely and equally distributed, that every Christian had an equal chance at salvation and eternal life: hence, a church in every parish, regular services, catechism for the young, compulsory communion, and so on. Among modern citizens, longevity is a socially recognized need; and increasingly every effort is made to see that it is widely and equally distributed, that every citizen has an equal chance at a long and healthy life: hence doctors and hospitals in every district, regular check-ups, health education for the young, compulsory vaccination, and so on.

Parallel to the shift in attitudes, and following naturally from it, was a shift in institutions: from the church to the clinic and the hospital. But the shift has been gradual: a slow development of communal interest in medical care, a slow erosion of interest in religious care. The first major form of medical provision came in the area of prevention, not of treatment, probably because the former involved no interference with the prerogatives of the guild of physicians. But the beginnings of provision in the area of treatment were roughly simultaneous with the great public health campaigns of the late nineteenth century, and the two undoubtedly reflect the same sensitivity to questions of physical survival. The licensing of physicians, the establishment of state medical schools and urban clinics, the filtering of tax money into the great voluntary hospitals: these measures involved, perhaps, only marginal interference with the profession—some of them, in fact, reinforced its guildlike character; but they already represent an important public commitment.[40] Indeed, they represent a commitment that ultimately can be fulfilled only by turning physicians, or some substantial number of them, into public physicians (as a smaller number once turned themselves into court physicians) and by abolishing or constraining the market in medical care. But before I defend that transformation, I want to stress the unavoidability of the commitment from which it follows.

What has happened in the modern world is simply that disease itself, even when it is endemic rather than epidemic, has come to be seen as a plague. And since the plague can be dealt with, it *must* be dealt with. People will not endure what they no longer believe they have to endure. Dealing with tuberculosis, cancer, or heart failure, however, requires a common effort. Medical research is expensive, and the treatment of many particular diseases lies far beyond the resources of ordinary citizens. So the community must step in, and any democratic community will in fact step in, more or less vigorously, more or less effectively, depending on the outcome of particular political battles. Thus, the role of the American government (or governments, for much of the activity is at the state and local levels): subsidizing research, training doctors, providing hospitals and equipment, regulating voluntary insurance schemes, underwriting the treatment of the very old. All this represents "the contrivance of human wisdom to provide for human wants." And all that is required to make it morally necessary is the development of a "want" so widely and deeply felt that it can plausibly be said that it is the want not of this or that person alone but of the community generally—a "human want" even though culturally shaped and stressed.*

But once communal provision begins, it is subject to further moral constraints: it must provide what is "wanted" equally to all the members of the community; and it must do so in ways that respect their membership. Now, even the pattern of medical provision in the United States, though it stops far short of a national health service, is intended to provide minimally decent care to all who need it. Once public funds are committed, public officials can hardly intend anything less. At the

---

*Arguing against Bernard Williams's claim that the only proper criterion for the distribution of medical care is medical need,[41] Robert Nozick asks why it doesn't then follow "that the only proper criterion for the distribution of barbering services is barbering need"?[42] Perhaps it does follow if one attends only to the "internal goal" of the activity, conceived in universal terms. But it doesn't follow if one attends to the social meaning of the activity, the place of the good it distributes in the life of a particular group of people. One can conceive of a society in which haircuts took on such central cultural significance that communal provision would be morally required, but it is something more than an interesting fact that no such society has ever existed. I have been helped in thinking about these issues by an article of Thomas Scanlon's; I adopt here his "conventionalist" alternative.[43]

same time, however, no political decision has yet been made to challenge directly the system of free enterprise in medical care. And so long as that system exists, wealth will be dominant in (this part of) the sphere of security and welfare; individuals will be cared for in proportion to their ability to pay and not to their need for care. In fact, the situation is more complex than that formula suggests, for communal provision already encroaches upon the free market, and the very sick and the very old sometimes receive exactly the treatment they should receive. But it is clear that poverty remains a significant bar to adequate and consistent treatment. Perhaps the most telling statistic about contemporary American medicine is the correlation of visits to doctors and hospitals with social class rather than with degree or incidence of illness. Middle- and upper-class Americans are considerably more likely to have a private physician and to see him often, and considerably less likely to be seriously ill, than are their poorer fellow citizens.[44] Were medical care a luxury, these discrepancies would not matter much; but as soon as medical care becomes a socially recognized need, and as soon as the community invests in its provision, they matter a great deal. For then deprivation is a double loss—to one's health and to one's social standing. Doctors and hospitals have become such massively important features of contemporary life that to be cut off from the help they provide is not only dangerous but also degrading.

But any fully developed system of medical provision will require the constraint of the guild of physicians. Indeed, this is more generally true: the provision of security and welfare requires the constraint of those men and women who had previously controlled the goods in question and sold them on the market (assuming, what is by no means always true, that the market predates communal provision). For what we do when we declare this or that good to be a needed good is to block or constrain its free exchange. We also block any other distributive procedure that doesn't attend to need—popular election, meritocratic competition, personal or familial preference, and so on. But the market is, at least in the United States today, the chief rival of the sphere of security and welfare; and it is most importantly the market that is pre-empted by the welfare state. Needed goods cannot be left to the whim, or distributed in the interest, of some powerful group of owners or practitioners.

Most often, ownership is abolished, and practitioners are effectively conscripted or, at least, "signed up" in the public service. They serve for the sake of the social need and not, or not simply, for their own sakes: thus, priests for the sake of eternal life, soldiers for the sake of national defense, public school teachers for the sake of their pupils' education. Priests act wrongly if they sell salvation; soldiers, if they set up as mercenaries; teachers, if they cater to the children of the wealthy. Sometimes the conscription is only partial, as when lawyers are required to be officers of the court, serving the cause of justice even while they also serve their clients and themselves. Sometimes the conscription is occasional and temporary, as when lawyers are required to act as "assigned counsels" for defendants unable to pay. In these cases, a special effort is made to respect the personal character of the lawyer-client relationship. I would look for a similar effort in any fully developed national health service. But I see no reason to respect the doctor's market freedom. Needed goods are not commodities. Or, more precisely, they can be bought and sold only insofar as they are available above and beyond whatever level of provision is fixed by democratic decision making (and only insofar as the buying and selling doesn't distort distributions below that level).

It might be argued, however, that the refusal thus far to finance a national health service constitutes a political decision by the American people about the level of communal care (and about the relative importance of other goods): a minimal standard for everyone—namely, the standard of the urban clinics; and free enterprise beyond that. That would seem to me an inadequate standard, but it would not necessarily be an unjust decision. It is not, however, the decision the American people have made. The common appreciation of the importance of medical care has carried them well beyond that. In fact, federal, state, and local governments now subsidize different levels of care for different classes of citizens. This might be all right, too, if the classification were connected to the purposes of the care—if, for example, soldiers and defense workers were given special treatment in time of war. But the poor, the middle class, and the rich make an indefensible triage. So long as communal funds are spent, as they currently are, to finance research, build hospitals, and pay the fees of doctors in private practice, the services that these expenditures underwrite must be equally available to all citizens.

This, then, is the argument for an expanded American welfare state. It follows from the three principles with which I began, and it suggests that the tendency of those principles is to free security and welfare from the prevailing patterns of dominance. Though a variety of institutional arrangements is possible, the three principles would seem to favor provision in kind; they suggest an important argument against current proposals to distribute money instead of education, legal aid, or medical care. The negative income tax, for example, is a plan to increase the purchasing power of the poor—a modified version of simple equality.[45] This plan would not, however, abolish the dominance of wealth in the sphere of need. Short of a radical equalization, men and women with greater purchasing power could still, and surely would, bid up the price of needed services. So the community would be investing, though now only indirectly, in individual welfare but without fitting provision to the shape of need. Even with equal incomes, health care delivered through the market would not be responsive to need; nor would the market provide adequately for medical research. This is not an argument against the negative income tax, however, for it may be the case that money itself, in a market economy, is one of the things that people need. And then it too, perhaps, should be provided in kind.

I want to stress again that no *a priori* stipulation of what needs ought to be recognized is possible; nor is there any *a priori* way of determining appropriate levels of provision. Our attitudes toward medical care have a history; they have been different; they will be different again. The forms of communal provision have changed in the past and will continue to change. But they don't change automatically as attitudes change. The old order has its clients; there is a lethargy in institutions as in individuals. Moreover, popular attitudes are rarely so clear as they are in the case of medical care. So change is always a matter of political argument, organization, and struggle. All that the philosopher can do is to describe the basic structure of the arguments and the constraints they entail. Hence the three principles, which can be summed up in a revised version of Marx's famous maxim: From each according to his ability (or his resources); to each according to his socially recognized needs. This, I think, is the deepest meaning of the social contract. It only remains to work out the details—but in everyday life, the details are everything.

A Note on Charity and Dependency

The long-term effect of communal provision is to constrict the range not only of buying and selling but also of charitable giving. At least this is true in Judeo-Christian communities, where charity has traditionally been a major supplement to taxes and tithes and a major source of poor relief. In the West today, it seems to be a general rule that the more developed the welfare state, the less room there is, and the less motivation there is, for charitable giving.[46] This is not an unanticipated or even an unwanted result. The argument against charity is very much like the argument against beggary. For begging is a kind of performance extracted from the poor by the charitable, and the performance is unseemly—an especially painful example of the power of money outside its sphere. "Charity wounds him who receives," writes Marcel Mauss in his classic anthropological essay *The Gift*, "and our whole moral effort is directed towards suppressing the unconscious harmful patronage of the rich almoner."[47] Charity can also be a way of buying influence and esteem, though this is more likely with acts of religious, educational, or cultural foundation than it is with ordinary poor relief. Acts of this sort may be objectionable, too; since it can plausibly be argued that priests and believers, teachers and pupils, and citizens generally—not wealthy men and women—should make the crucial decisions in the areas of religion, education, and culture. But I want to focus here only on the immediate use of wealth to help those in need: the classic meaning of Jewish and Christian charity.

Private charity breeds personal dependence, and then it breeds the familiar vices of dependence: deference, passivity, and humility on the one hand; arrogance on the other. If communal provision is to respect membership, it must aim at overcoming these vices. But the mere replacement of private charity by a public dole does not have this effect. It may be necessary nonetheless, for the community is more likely to maintain a steady, consistent, and impersonal program of relief and so to help the poor in proportion to their needs. Relief by itself, however, does not produce independence: the old patterns survive; the poor are still deferential, passive, and humble, while public officials take on the arrogance of their private predecessors. Hence, the importance of programs like those that Maimonides recommended, that aim at setting up the poor on their own: rehabilitation, retraining, subsidizing small businesses, and so on. Work itself is one of the things that men and women need, and that the community must help provide whenever they are unable to provide it for themselves and for one another.

But this, too, requires centralized planning and administration and invites the interventions of planners and administrators. It is also important that any program of communal provision leave room for various forms of local self-help and voluntary association. The goal is participation in communal activities, the concrete realization of membership. But it's not the case that, first, one overcomes poverty and then, that having been achieved, the formerly poor join the political and cultural life of the rest of the community; rather, the struggle against poverty (and against every other sort of neediness) is one of those activities in which many citizens, poor and not so poor and well-to-do alike, ought to participate. And this means that there is a place, even in a community aiming at a (complex) equality of members, for what Richard Titmuss has called "the gift relationship."[48]

The Examples of Blood and Money

Titmuss studied the ways in which a number of countries collect blood for hospital use, and focused chiefly on two different ways —purchase and voluntary donation. His book is a defense of donation, both because it is more efficient (it produces better blood), and because it expresses and enhances a spirit of communal altruism. The argument is rich and rewarding, but it would be even more so had Titmuss developed a second comparison—for which, however, he could have found no practical examples. One can imagine another form of provision, namely, a tax on blood, a requirement that everyone contribute so many pints a year. This would greatly improve the supply since it would increase the number of donors and enable medical authorities to choose among them, collecting blood only from the healthiest citizens, much as we conscript only the able-bodied for military service. Titmuss would still want to say, I expect, that the gift relation is better, and not only because a tax on blood would represent—at least within our cultural world—too great an attack on bodily integrity. For it is his purpose to argue that there is a virtue in private giving, and he would rightly doubt that this virtue can be duplicated by public taking, even when the taking is mandated by a democratic decision.

But this argument might hold also for money, at least when the amounts are small and the capacity to contribute is widely shared. The gift of blood does not represent an exercise of power by those men and women able to give; nor does it make for deference and dependency among those in need. Donors act out of a desire to help, and they do help, and undoubtedly they feel some pride in having helped. But none of this generates any special self-importance, for the help is widely available. So equality redeems charity. Now, what if the great majority of citizens were equally, or more or less equally, capable of contributing money (to a "community chest," say) for the sake of their neediest fellows? No doubt, taxation would still be necessary, not only for services like defense, internal security, and public health, where provision is general, but for many forms of particular provision, too. But there is an argument to be made, very much like Titmuss's argument about blood, that private giving should be encouraged. The act of giving is good in itself; it builds a sense of solidarity and communal competence. And now the connected activities of organizing fund-raising campaigns and deciding how to spend the money will involve ordinary citizens in work that parallels and supplements the work of officials and generally increases the level of participation.

And if the argument applies to money, it applies also, and even more importantly, to time and energy. These two are the most valuable gifts that citizens can make to one another. The professionalization of "social work" has tended to displace those amateur officials who presided over communal provision in the Greek and Jewish communities, and now some modern substitute is sorely needed. Thus, a recent study of social work in the welfare state: "a mobilization of altruistic capacities is essential if real help is to be offered to those most in need"—where "real help" means communal integration as much as provision and relief.[49] Bureaucracy is unavoidable given the size of contemporary political communities and the range of necessary services. But the stark dualism of professional caretakers and helpless wards can pose radical dangers for democratic government unless it is mediated by volunteers, organizers, representatives of the poor and the old, local friends and neighbors. One might think of the gift relationship as a kind of politics: like the vote, the petition, and the demonstration, the gift is a way of giving concrete meaning to the union of citizens. And as welfare generally aims at overcoming the dominance of money in the sphere of need, so the active participation of citizens in the business of welfare (and security, too) aims at making sure that the dominance of money is not simply replaced by the dominance of political power.

4

Money and Commodities

The Universal Pander

There are two questions with regard to money: What can it buy? and, How is it distributed? The two must be taken up in that order, for only after we have described the sphere within which money operates, and the scope of its operations, can we sensibly address its distribution. We must figure out how important money really is.

It is best to begin with the naïve view, which is also the common view, that money is all-important, the root of all evil, the source of all good. "Money answereth all things," as Ecclesiastes says. According to Marx, it is the universal pander, arranging scandalous couplings between people and goods, breaching every natural, every moral barrier. Marx might have discovered this by looking around in nineteenth-century Europe, but in fact he found it in a book, Shakespeare's *Timon of Athens*, where Timon, digging for buried gold, interrogates his object:

> Gold? yellow, glittering, precious gold? No, gods,
> I am no idle votarist: roots, you clear heavens!
> Thus much of this will make black, white; foul, fair;
> Wrong, right; base, noble; old, young; coward,
>   valiant.
> . . . .
>   Why this
> Will lug your priests and servants from your sides;
> Pluck stout men's pillows from below their heads:

This yellow slave
Will knit and break religions; bless th'accurst;
Make the hoar leprosy ador'd; place thieves,
And give them title, knee, and approbation,
With senators on the bench: this is it
That makes the wappen'd widow wed again;
She whom the spital-house and ulcerous sores
Would cast the gorge at, this embalms and spices
To the April day again. Come, damned earth,
Thou common whore of mankind, that putt'st odds
Among the rout of nations, I will make thee
Do thy right nature.[1]

Timon has been brought to a state of nihilistic despair, but this is never-theless the familiar language of moral criticism. We don't like to see priests corrupted, or stout men robbed of their comfort, or religions broken, or thieves admitted to rank and title. But why shouldn't the "wappen'd widow" be spiced to the April day again? Timon is moved here by an aesthetic, not a moral, scruple. The point, however, is the same: the widow is transformed by her money. So are we all, if only we are rich enough. "What I am and can do," wrote Marx, "is not at all determined by my individuality. I am ugly, but I can buy the most beautiful women for myself. Consequently, I am not ugly . . . I am stupid, but since money is the real mind of all things, how should its possessor be stupid?"[2]

This is the "right nature" of money—perhaps especially so in a capi-talist society, but more generally too. Marx, after all, was quoting Shakespeare, and Shakespeare put his words into the mouth of an Athe-nian gentleman. Wherever money is used, it panders between incom-patible things, it breaks into "the self-subsistent entities" of social life, it inverts individuality, "it forces contraries to embrace." But that, of course, is what money is for; that's why we use it. It is, in more neutral language, the universal medium of exchange—and a great convenience, too, for exchange is central to the life we share with other men and women. The simple egalitarianism of Shakespeare's plebeian rebel Jack Cade:

. . . there shall be no money![3]

has its echoes in contemporary radical and socialist thought, but I have difficulty imagining what sort of society it is meant to suggest. Contem-porary radicals certainly do not intend to re-establish a barter economy and pay workers in kind. Perhaps they mean to pay workers in labor/time chits exchangeable only at state stores. But these would soon be exchanged more widely, behind the backs of the police if necessary. And Timon would reappear, digging for buried chits.

What Shakespeare and Marx objected to is the universality of the medium, not the medium itself. Timon thinks that universality is of the nature of money, and perhaps he is right. Conceived abstractly, money is simply a representation of value. Hence, it's not implausible to hold that every valued thing, every social good, can be represented in monetary terms. It may be that a series of translations are necessary in order to get from this valued thing to that cash value. But there is no reason to think that the translations can not be made; indeed, they are made every day. Life itself has a value, and then eventually a price (different conceivably for different lives)—else how could we even think about insurance and compensation? At the same time, we also experience the universality of money as somehow degrading. Consider the definition of the cynic attributed to Oscar Wilde: "A man who knows the price of everything and the value of nothing." That definition is too absolute; it's not cynical to think that price and value will sometimes coincide. But often enough money fails to represent value; the translations are made, but as with good poetry, something is lost in the process. Hence we can buy and sell universally only if we disregard real values; while if we attend to values, there are things that cannot be bought and sold. Particular things: the abstract universality of money is undercut and circumscribed by the creation of values that can't easily be priced or that we don't want priced. Though these values are often in dispute, we can investigate what they are. It is an empirical matter. What monetary exchanges are blocked, banned, resented, conventionally deplored?

What Money Can't Buy

I have already referred to the sin of simony, which we might take as a paradigmatic example of a blocked exchange. God's offices are not for sale—not, at least, so long as God is conceived in a certain way. In a culture different from that of the Christian Middle Ages, the block might be broken: if the gods can be appeased by sacrifices, why can't they be bribed by glittering gold? In the church, however, this sort of bribery is ruled out. Not that it doesn't occur, but everyone knows that it ought not to occur. It is a clandestine trade; buyer and seller alike will lie about what they have done. Dishonesty is always a useful guide to the existence of moral standards. When people sneak across the boundary of the sphere of money, they advertise the existence of the boundary. It's there, roughly at the point where they begin to hide and dissemble. But sometimes it takes a fight to mark off a clear line, and until then trade is more or less open. Money is innocent until proven guilty.

Conscription in 1863

The Enrollment and Conscription Act of 1863 established the first military draft in American history. From colonial times, militia service had been compulsory, but that was a local and neighborly compulsion, and it was generally thought that no one was bound to fight far from home. The Mexican War, for example, was fought entirely with volunteers. But the Civil War was a struggle on a different scale; enormous armies were massed for battle; fire power was greater than ever before; casualties were high; and the need for men grew as the fighting dragged on. The War Department—and President Lincoln, too—thought that a national draft was the only way to win the war.[4] The draft was bound to be unpopular, given the localist traditions of American politics and the deep anti-statism of liberal thought (and the extent and depth of anti-war feeling). And, in fact, its enforcement was bitterly and often violently opposed. But it set a precedent. Compulsion was definitively lifted from the local to the national level where it has sat ever since; and service in the federal army, rather than the local militia, was established as the obligation of citizens. One provision of the 1863 act, however, set only a negative precedent—the exemption of any man whose name was drawn in the lottery if he was willing and able to put up three hundred dollars to pay a substitute.

Exemptions could be purchased for three hundred dollars. The practice was not entirely new. The local militias fined men who did not turn out for muster, and it was a matter of some resentment that well-to-do citizens often treated the fine as a tax in lieu of service (while impoverished citizens were threatened with debtor's prison).[5] But now the war and the bloodiness of the war sharpened the resentment. "Does [Lincoln] think that poor men are to give up their lives," asked one New Yorker, "and let rich men pay three hundred dollars in order to stay home?"[6] It's not clear what part such opinions played in the anti-draft riots that rocked Manhattan in July of 1863, after the first drawing of lots. In any case, it was an opinion reiterated across the country that poor men should not have to give up their lives; and though the law was enforced, nothing like it was ever re-enacted. Was the trade innocent in the militias, when little more was involved than a few hours of drilling and marching? Certainly, a Rousseauian political theorist would say No, and he could once have made a strong appeal to the republican convictions of ordinary Americans. But militia service was radically devalued in the years before the Civil War, and the Rousseauian punishments for non-attendance—ostracism or expulsion from the community—would have seemed excessive to most Americans. Perhaps the fine captured the meaning of the service. The case was different, however, when life itself was at stake.

It's not that three hundred dollars was too cheap a price, or that dangerous jobs could not be sold for more or less than that amount on the labor market. Rather, the state could not impose a dangerous job on some of its citizens and then exempt others for a price. That claim spoke to a deep sense of what it meant to be a citizen of the state—or better, of this state, the United States in 1863. One could make the claim good, I think, even against a majority of the citizens, for they might well misunderstand the logic of their own institutions or fail to apply consistently the principles they professed to hold. But in 1863 it was the resistance and resentment of masses of citizens that drew the line between what could be sold and what could not. The War Department had acted casually, and Congress had barely attended to the legislation. They meant, it was later said, only to provide an "incentive" for enlistment.[7] In fact, they counted on a double incentive: the danger of death was an incentive for some men to pay three hundred dollars to other men, for whom three hundred dollars was an incentive to accept the danger of death. It was a bad business in a republic, for it seemed to abolish the *public thing* and turn military service (even when the republic itself was at stake!) into a private transaction.

That the law was never re-enacted is not to say that similar effects have not been sought. Only the methods have been less direct and the results less efficiently achieved, as in the case of draft deferrals for college students or of bonuses for conscripts who re-enlist. But we acknowledge now the principle of equal treatment—because of the political struggles of 1863; and we know roughly where the boundary is that it marks out. So we can oppose even roundabout and clandestine crossings, re-enactments through legislative subterfuge of what cannot be re-enacted openly. The sale of exemptions is a blocked exchange; and there are many other sales similarly blocked, at least in principle.

Blocked Exchanges

Let me try to suggest the full set of blocked exchanges in the United States today. I will rely in part on the first chapter of Arthur Okun's *Equality and Efficiency,* where Okun draws a line between the sphere of money and what he calls "the domain of rights."[8] Rights, of course, are proof against sale and purchase, and Okun revealingly recasts the Bill of Rights as a series of blocked exchanges. But it's not only rights that stand outside the cash nexus. Whenever we ban the use of money, we do indeed establish a right—namely, that this particular good be distributed in some other way. But we must argue about the meaning of the good before we can say anything more about its rightful distribution. I want now to postpone most of the arguments and simply provide a list of things that cannot be had for money. The list repeats or anticipates other chapters, for it is a feature of the sphere of money that it abuts every other sphere; that's why it is so important to fix its boundaries. Blocked exchanges set limits on the dominance of wealth.

1. Human beings cannot be bought and sold. The sale of slaves, even of oneself as a slave, is ruled out. This is an example of what Okun calls "prohibitions on exchanges born of desperation."[9] There are many such prohibitions; but the others merely regulate the labor market, and I will list them separately. This one establishes what is and is not marketable: not persons or the liberty of persons, but only their labor power and the things they make. (Animals are marketable because we conceive them to be without personality, even though liberty is undoubtedly a value for some of them.) Personal liberty is not, however, proof against conscription or imprisonment; it is proof only against sale and purchase.

2. Political power and influence cannot be bought and sold. Citizens cannot sell their votes or officials their decisions. Bribery is an illegal transaction. It hasn't always been so; in many cultures gifts from clients and suitors are a normal part of the remuneration of office holders. But here the gift relationship will only work—that is, fit into a set of more or less coherent meanings—when "office" hasn't fully emerged as an autonomous good, and when the line between public and private is hazy and indistinct. It won't work in a republic, which draws the line sharply: Athens, for example, had an extraordinary set of rules designed to repress bribery; the more offices the citizens shared, the more elaborate the rules became.[10]

3. Criminal justice is not for sale. It is not only that judges and juries

cannot be bribed, but that the services of defense attorneys are a matter of communal provision—a necessary form of welfare given the adversary system.

4. Freedom of speech, press, religion, assembly: none of these require money payments; none of them are available at auction; they are simply guaranteed to every citizen. It's often said that the exercise of these freedoms costs money, but that's not strictly speaking the case: talk and worship are cheap; so is the meeting of citizens; so is publication in many of its forms. Quick access to large audiences is expensive, but that is another matter, not of freedom itself but of influence and power.

5. Marriage and procreation rights are not for sale. Citizens are limited to one spouse and cannot purchase a license for polygamy. And if limits are ever set on the number of children we can have, I assume that these won't take the form that I imagined in chapter 2: licenses to give birth that can be traded on the market.

6. The right to leave the political community is not for sale. The modern state has, to be sure, an investment in every citizen, and it might legitimately require that some part of that investment be repaid, in work or money, before permitting emigration. The Soviet Union has adopted a policy of this sort, chiefly as a mechanism to bar emigration altogether. Used differently, it seems fair enough, even if it then has differential effects on successful and unsuccessful citizens. But the citizens can claim, in their turn, that they never sought the health care and education that they received (as children, say) and owe nothing in return. That claim underestimates the benefits of citizenship, but nicely captures its consensual character. And so it is best to let them go, once they have fulfilled those obligations-in-kind (military service) that are fulfilled in any case by young men and women who aren't yet fully consenting citizens. No one can buy his way out of these.

7. And so, again, exemptions from military service, from jury duty, and from any other form of communally imposed work cannot be sold by the government or bought by citizens—for reasons I have already given.

8. Political offices cannot be bought; to buy them would be a kind of simony, for the political community is like a church in this sense, that its services matter a great deal to its members and wealth is no adequate sign of a capacity to deliver those services. Nor can professional standing be bought, insofar as this is regulated by the community, for doctors and lawyers are our secular priests; we need to be sure about their qualifications.

9. Basic welfare services like police protection or primary and second-

ary schooling are purchasable only at the margins. A minimum is guaranteed to every citizen and doesn't have to be paid for by individuals. If policemen dun shopkeepers for protection money, they are acting like gangsters, not like policemen. But shopkeepers can hire security guards and nightwatchmen for the sake of a higher level of protection than the political community is willing to pay for. Similarly, parents can hire private tutors for their children or send them to private schools. The market in services is subject to restraint only if it distorts the character, or lowers the value, of communal provision. (I should also note that some goods are partially provided, hence partially insulated from market control. The mechanism here is not the blocked but the subsidized exchange—as in the case of college and university education, many cultural activities, travel generally, and so on.)

10. Desperate exchanges, "trades of last resort," are barred, though the meaning of desperation is always open to dispute. The eight-hour day, minimum wage laws, health and safety regulations: all these set a floor, establish basic standards, below which workers cannot bid against one another for employment. Jobs can be auctioned off, but only within these limits. This is a restraint of market liberty for the sake of some communal conception of personal liberty, a reassertion, at lower levels of loss, of the ban on slavery.

11. Prizes and honors of many sorts, public and private, are not available for purchase. The Congressional Medal of Honor cannot be bought, nor can the Pulitzer Prize or the Most Valuable Player Award, or even the trophy given by a local Chamber of Commerce to the "businessman of the year." Celebrity is certainly for sale, though the price can be high, but a good name is not. Prestige, esteem, and status stand somewhere between these two. Money is implicated in their distribution; but even in our own society, it is only sometimes determinative.

12. Divine grace cannot be bought—and not only because God doesn't need the money. His servants and deputies often do need it. Still, the sale of indulgences is commonly thought to require reform, if not Reformation.

13. Love and friendship cannot be bought, not on our common understanding of what these two mean. Of course, one can buy all sorts of things—clothing, automobiles, gourmet foods, and so on—that make one a better candidate for love and friendship or more self-confident in the pursuit of lovers and friends. Advertisers commonly play on these possibilities, and they are real enough.

> For money has a power above
> The stars of fate, to manage love.[11]

But the direct purchase is blocked, not in the law but more deeply, in our shared morality and sensibility. Men and women marry for money, but this is not a "marriage of true minds." Sex is for sale, but the sale does not make for "a meaningful relationship." People who believe that sexual intercourse is morally tied to love and marriage are likely to favor a ban on prostitution—just as, in other cultures, people who believed that intercourse was a sacred ritual would have deplored the behavior of priestesses who tried to make a little money on the side. Sex can be sold only when it is understood in terms of pleasure and not exclusively in terms of married love or religious worship.

14. Finally, a long series of criminal sales are ruled out. Murder, Inc., cannot sell its services; blackmail is illegal; heroin cannot be sold, nor can stolen goods, or goods fraudulently described, or adulterated milk, or information thought vital to the security of the state. And arguments go on about unsafe cars, guns, inflammable shirts, drugs with uncertain side effects, and so on. All these are useful illustrations of the fact that the sphere of money and commodities is subject to continuous redefinition.

I think that this is an exhaustive list, though it is possible that I have omitted some crucial category. In any case, the list is long enough to suggest that if money answereth all things, it does so, as it were, behind the backs of many of the things and in spite of their social meanings. The market where exchanges of these sorts are free is a black market, and the men and women who frequent it are likely to do so sneakily and then to lie about what they are doing.

What Money Can Buy

What is the proper sphere of money? What social goods are rightly marketable? The obvious answer is also the right one; it points us to a range of goods that have probably always been marketable, whatever else has or has not been: all those objects, commodities, products, services, beyond what is communally provided, that individual men and women find useful or pleasing, the common stock of bazaars, emporiums, and trading posts. It includes, and probably always has included, luxuries as well as staples, goods that are beautiful as well as goods that are functional and durable. Commodities, even when they are primitive and simple, are above all commodious; they are a source of comfort, warmth, and security. Things are our anchors in the world.[12] But while we all need to be anchored, we don't all need the same anchor. We are differently attached; we have different tastes and desires; we surround ourselves, clothe ourselves, furnish our homes, with a great variety of things, and we use, enjoy, and display the things we have in a great variety of ways. Object relations are polymorphous in character. It is sometimes said that this polymorphousness is a modern perversion, but I suspect that it is a constant of human life. Archeological digs regularly turn up a profusion of goods (or bits and pieces of goods, the shards of commodities): decorated pots and vases; baskets; jewelry; mirrors; trimmed, embroidered, beaded, and feathered clothing; tapestries; scrolls—and coins, endless numbers of coins; for all these other things, once barter has been superseded, exchange for money. No doubt, every culture has its own characteristic set of commodities, determined by its mode of production, its social organization, and the range of its trade. But the number of commodities in every set is always large, and the standard way of sorting them out is market exchange.

Not the only way: gift giving is an important alternative, and I will come back to it later. But the market is standard, even though what counts as a commodity is not standard. And market relations reflect a certain moral understanding that applies to all those social goods that count as marketable (and doesn't apply to those that don't). Sometimes the understanding is implicit; in our own society, ever since the emancipation of the market from feudal constraints, the understanding has been explicit, its elaboration a central feature of our cultural life. Beyond whatever is communally provided, no one is entitled to this or that useful or pleasing object. Commodities don't come with proper names attached, like packages from a department store. The right way to possess such things is by making them, or growing them, or somehow providing them or their cash equivalents for others. Money is both the measure of equivalence and the means of exchange; these are the proper functions of money and (ideally) its only functions. It is in the market that money does its work, and the market is open to all comers.

In part, this view of money and commodities rests upon the sense that there is no more efficient distributive process, no better way of bringing individual men and women together with the particular things they take to be useful or pleasing. But at a deeper level, market morality (in, say, its Lockeian form) is a celebration of the wanting, making, owning, and exchanging of commodities. They are indeed widely wanted, and they have to be made if they are to be had. Even Locke's acorns—his example of a simple and primitive commodity—don't grow on trees; the metaphor doesn't apply: they are not readily and universally available. Things can be had only with effort; it is the effort that seems to supply the title or, at least, the original title; and once they are owned, they can also be exchanged.[13] So wanting, making, owning, and exchanging hang together; they are, so to speak, commodity's modes. Still, one can recognize these modes without celebrating them. Their conjunction is appropriate within the boundaries of the sphere of money and commodities, not elsewhere. The Lockeian celebration has tended to overspill the boundaries, turning market power into a kind of tyranny, distorting distributions in other spheres. This is a common perception, and I shall recur to it frequently. But commodities can outgrow their proper place in another way, which requires more immediate notice.

Ask again, What does money buy? The sociologist Lee Rainwater, studying the "social meanings of income," gives a radical and worrying reply: "Money buys membership in industrial society." Rainwater doesn't mean to tell us that immigration and naturalization officials can be bribed. His argument cuts deeper. The normal activities that enable individuals to see themselves and to be seen by others as full members, social persons, have increasingly become consumption activities; they require money.

> Thus money does not just buy food and clothing and housing and appliances, cars . . . and vacations. The purchase of all these commodities in turn allows the achievement and day-to-day living out of an identity as an at least "average American." . . . When people are not protected from this inexorable dynamic of money economies by some local cultural enclave, they cannot fail to define themselves most basically in terms of their access to all that money can buy.[14]

It's not just that individuals differentiate themselves by the choices they make within the sphere of money and commodities, or even that they are differentiated by their successes and failures in that sphere. Of course, the market is a setting for competition, and so it distributes certain sorts of esteem and dis-esteem (not all sorts). But Rainwater wants to say more than this. Unless we can spend money and deploy goods at levels beyond what is required for subsistence, unless we have some of the free time and convenience that money can buy, we suffer a loss more serious than poverty itself, a kind of status starvation, a sociological disinheritance. We become aliens in our own homeland—and often in our own homes. We can no longer play our parts as parents, friends, neighbors, associates, comrades, or citizens. It's not true everywhere; but in America today and in every society where the market is triumphant, commodities mediate membership. Unless we own a certain number of socially required things, we cannot be socially recognized and effective persons.

Rainwater provides a sociological account of the fetishism of commodities. He describes an advertiser's dream, for this is the central message of the modern advertisement: that commodities carry meanings far beyond their obvious use, and that we need them for the sake of standing and identity. One can always say of the advertiser that he is exaggerating, even lying about, the importance of this automobile, say, or that brand of Scotch. But what if, behind his particular lies, there is a larger truth? Commodities are symbols of belonging; standing and identity are distributed through the market, sold for cash on the line (but available also to speculators who can establish credit). On the other hand, in a democratic society, the most basic definitions and self-definitions can't be put up for purchase in this way. For citizenship entails what we might call "belongingness"—not merely the sense, but the practical reality, of being at home in (this part of) the social world. This is a condition that can be renounced but never traded; it is not alienable in the marketplace. Economic failure, whatever loss of esteem comes with it, should never have the effect of devaluing citizenship, in either the legal or the social sense. And if it does have that effect, we must seek for remedies.

The obvious remedy is to redistribute money itself (through a negative income tax, for example) independently of the communal provision of goods and services: as we provide medical care in kind for the sake of health and longevity, so we would provide money in kind for the sake of membership. Or, we might guarantee jobs and a minimal income, on the premise that money and commodities are more likely to contribute to a strong sense of identity, in our culture, if they have been earned. But we can't redistribute commodities directly, not if we are to allow individual men and women to choose for themselves the things they find useful or pleasing and to define themselves and shape and symbolize their identities over and above the membership they share. And we can't try to locate the particular things without which membership is devalued or lost and make them the objects of communal provision, for the market will quickly turn up new things. If it's not one thing, it will be another, and advertisers will tell us that *this* is what we need now, if we are to hold our heads high. But the redistribution of money or of jobs and income neutralizes the market. Henceforth, commodities have only their use value—or, symbolic values are radically individualized and can no longer play any significant public role.

These arrangements will be fully effective, however, only if the redistribution leaves everyone with the same amount of money, and that is not, for reasons I have already given, a stable condition. The market produces and reproduces inequalities; people end up with more or less, with different numbers and different kinds of possessions. There is no way to ensure that everyone is possessed of whatever set of things marks the "average American," for any such effort will simply raise the average. Here is a sad version of the pursuit of happiness: communal provision endlessly chasing consumer demand. Perhaps there is some point beyond which the fetishism of commodities will lose its grip. Perhaps, more modestly, there is some lower point at which individuals are safe against any radical loss of status. That last possibility suggests the value of partial redistributions in the sphere of money, even if the result is something well short of simple equality. But it also suggests that we must look outside that sphere and strengthen autonomous distributions elsewhere. There are, after all, activities more central to the meaning of membership than owning and using commodities.

Our purpose is to tame "the inexorable dynamic of a money economy," to make money harmless—or, at least, to make sure that the harms experienced in the sphere of money are not mortal, not to life and not to social standing either. But the market remains a competitive sphere, where risk is common, where the readiness to take risks is often a virtue, and where people win and lose. An exciting place: for even when money buys only what it should buy, it is still a very good thing to have. It answereth some things that nothing else can answer. And once we have blocked every wrongful exchange and controlled the sheer weight of money itself, we have no reason to worry about the answers the market provides. Individual men and women still have reason to worry, and so they will try to minimize their risks, or to share them or spread them out, or to buy themselves insurance. In the regime of complex equality, certain sorts of risks will regularly be shared, because the power to impose risks on others, to make authoritative decisions in factories and corporations, is not a marketable good. This is only one more example of a blocked exchange; I will take it up in detail later. Given the right blocks, there is no such thing as a maldistribution of consumer goods. It just doesn't matter, from the standpoint of complex equality, that you have a yacht and I don't, or that the sound system of her hi-fi set is greatly superior to his, or that we buy our rugs from Sears Roebuck and they get theirs from the Orient. People will focus on such matters, or not: that is a question of culture, not of distributive justice. So long as yachts and hi-fi sets and rugs have only use value and individualized symbolic value, their unequal distribution doesn't matter.[15]

The Marketplace

There is a stronger argument about the sphere of money, the common argument of the defenders of capitalism: that market outcomes matter a great deal because the market, if it is free, gives to each person exactly what he deserves. The market rewards us all in accordance with the contributions we make to one another's well-being.[16] The goods and services we provide are valued by potential consumers in such-and-such a way, and these values are aggregated by the market, which determines the price we receive. And that price is our desert, for it expresses the only worth our goods and services can have, the worth they actually have for other people. But this is to misunderstand the meaning of desert. Unless there are standards of worth independent of what people want (and are willing to buy) at this or that moment in time, there can be no deservingness at all. We would never know what a person deserved until we saw what he had gotten. And that can't be right.

Imagine a novelist who writes what he hopes will be a best seller. He studies his potential audience, designs his book to meet the current fashion. Perhaps he had to violate the canons of his art in order to do that, and perhaps he is a novelist for whom the violation was painful. He has stooped to conquer. Does he now deserve the fruits of his conquest? Does he deserve a conquest that bears fruit? His novel appears, let's say, during a depression when no one has money for books, and very few copies are sold; his reward is small. Has he gotten less than he deserves? (His fellow writers smile at his disappointment; perhaps that's what he deserves.) Years later, in better times, the book is reissued and does well. Has its author become more deserving? Surely desert can't hang on the state of the economy. There is too much luck involved here; talk of desert makes little sense. We would do better to say simply that the writer is entitled to his royalties, large or small.[17]

Money and Commodities

He is like any other entrepreneur; he has bet on the market. It's a chancy business, but he knew that when he made the bet. He has a right to what he gets—after he has paid the costs of communal provision (he lives not only in the market but also in the city). But he can't claim that he has gotten less than he deserves, and it doesn't matter if the rest of us think that he has gotten more. The market doesn't recognize desert. Initiative, enterprise, innovation, hard work, ruthless dealing, reckless gambling, the prostitution of talent: all these are sometimes rewarded, sometimes not.

But the rewards that the market provides, when it provides them, are appropriate to these sorts of effort. The man or woman who builds a better mousetrap, or opens a restaurant and sells delicious blintzes, or does a little teaching on the side, is looking to earn money. And why not? No one would want to feed blintzes to strangers, day after day, merely to win their gratitude. Here in the world of the petty bourgeoisie, it seems only right that an entrepreneur, able to provide timely goods and services, should reap the rewards he had in mind when he went to work.

This is, indeed, a kind of "rightness" that the community may see fit to enclose and restrain. The morality of the bazaar belongs in the bazaar. The market is a zone of the city, not the whole of the city. But it is a great mistake, I think, when people worried about the tyranny of the market seek its entire abolition. It is one thing to clear the Temple of traders, quite another to clear the streets. The latter move would require a radical shift in our understanding of what material things are for and of how we relate to them and to other people through them. But the shift is not accomplished by the abolition; commodity exchange is merely driven underground; or it takes place in state stores, as in parts of Eastern Europe today, drearily and inefficiently.

The liveliness of the open market reflects our sense of the great variety of desirable things; and so long as that is our sense, we have no reason not to relish the liveliness. Walt Whitman's argument in *Democratic Vistas* seems to me exactly right:

> For fear of mistake, I may as well distinctly specify, as cheerfully included in the model and standard of these Vistas, a practical, stirring, worldly, moneymaking, even materialistic character. It is undeniable that our farms, stores, offices, dry goods, coal and groceries, enginery, cash accounts, traders, earnings, markets, etc., should be attended to in earnest, and actively pursued, just as if they had a real and permanent existence.[18]

There is nothing degraded about buying and selling—nothing degraded in wanting to own that shirt (to wear it, to be seen in it), or in wanting to own this book (to read it, to mark it up), and nothing degraded in making such things available for a price, even if the price is such that I can't buy both the shirt and the book at the same time. But I want them both! That is another of the misfortunes with which the theory of distributive justice is not concerned.

The merchant panders to our desires. But so long as he isn't selling people or votes or political influence, so long as he hasn't cornered the market in wheat in a time of drought, so long as his cars aren't death traps, his shirts inflammable, this is a harmless pandering. He will try, of course, to sell us things we don't really want; he will show us the best side of his goods and conceal their dark side. We will have to be protected against fraud (as he will against theft). But the exchange is in principle a relation of mutual benefit; and neither the money that the merchant makes, nor the accumulation of things by this or that consumer, poses any threat to complex equality—not if the sphere of money and commodities is properly bounded.

But this argument may work only for the petty bourgeoisie, for the world of the bazaar and the street, for the corner grocery, the bookshop, the boutique, the restaurant (but not the chain of restaurants). What are we to think of the successful entrepreneur, who turns himself into a man of enormous wealth and power? I should stress that this sort of success is not the goal of every shopkeeper, not in the traditional bazaar, where long-term growth, a "rags-to-riches pattern of linear progress," doesn't figure in the economic culture, and not even in our own society, where it does.[19] There are rewards in making do, living comfortably, dealing over the years with familiar men and women. Entrepreneurial triumph is only one of the ends of business. But it is an end intensely sought; and while failure is not problematic (failed entrepreneurs are still citizens in good standing), success inevitably is. The problems are of two sorts: first, the extraction not only of wealth but of prestige and influence from the market; second, the deployment of power within it. I will take these up in order, looking first at the history of an enterprise and then at the politics of some commodities.

The World's Biggest Department Store

Consider, then, the case of Rowland Macy, and the Strauss brothers, and their famous store. Macy was a Yankee trader, a prototypical member of the petty bourgeoisie, who owned and ran a succession of dry goods businesses and failed in every one of them—until 1858 when he opened a store on Sixth Avenue and Fourteenth Street in Manhattan.[20] In the course of his failures, Macy had experimented with new advertising techniques and retail policies: cash on the line, fixed prices, a commitment not to be undersold. Other merchants were engaged in similar experiments, more or less successfully; but Macy's new store, for reasons not easy to grasp, achieved an extraordinary success. And as it grew, Macy diversified his stock, gradually creating an entirely new kind of enterprise. What we can think of as the invention of the department store took place at roughly the same time in a number of cities—Paris, London, Philadelphia, and New York; and it is probably true that the invention was (somehow) called for by common social and economic conditions.[21] But Rowland Macy rode the tide with considerable skill and great boldness, and he died in 1877 a wealthy man. Macy's only son was an alcoholic, who inherited his father's money but not his business. The store, after a short interlude, passed into the hands of Nathan and Isidor Strauss, who for some years had run a concession, selling chinaware, in the basement.

Thus far, there are no difficulties. Macy's success no doubt left other merchants floundering in its wake, weakened or even ruined. But we can't shield the others from the risks of the market (so long as there is a market); we can only shield them from the further risks of penury and personal degradation. In fact, the Japanese government does something more than this: "it has established limits on the construction of new department stores, discount houses, and shopping centers, thus slowing down the impact they have on small retail stores."[22] The policy is aimed at maintaining the stability of neighborhoods, and that may well be a wise policy; given a certain understanding of neighborhood as a distributed good and of the city as a cluster of differentiated zones, it may even be a morally necessary policy. In any case, it offers protection only to merchants who have dropped out of the larger competition. There is no help for Macy's rivals except insofar as they can help themselves. And so long as a success like that of Rowland Macy is contained within the sphere of money, the rest of us can only watch it with the same admiration (or envy) that we might feel for the author of a best seller.

There is, I suppose, a loose sense in which it might be said that successful entrepreneurs are monopolists of wealth: as a class, they uniquely enjoy its special prerogatives; the goods it can purchase are at their beck and call as they are at no one else's. Simple equality would make this sort of thing impossible, but simple equality cannot be sustained without eliminating buying and selling (and every other sort of exchange relation, too). And again, so long as money controls commodities and nothing else, why should we worry about its accumulation? The objections are aesthetic—as with Timon and the "wappen'd widow"—not moral. They have to do more with ostentation than with domination.

But the success of the Strauss family was not contained in this way. Isidor and Nathan and their younger brother Oscar moved easily into a wider world than Rowland Macy had ever known. Isidor was a friend and adviser of President Cleveland, took an active part in various campaigns for tariff reform, ran successfully for Congress in 1894. Nathan was active in New York politics, a member of Tammany, successively park commissioner and president of the board of health. Oscar was Secretary of Commerce and Labor in Theodore Roosevelt's cabinet and later held a number of ambassadorial appointments. The three together make a useful example, for these were not robber barons or union busters (Macy's cigar makers struck successfully for higher wages in 1895, and the store's printshop was fully organized sometime in the 1890s).[23] By all accounts they were decent and capable public servants. And yet it can hardly be doubted that they owed their political influence to their wealth and continuing business success. It might be said that they did not, after all, buy their influence but rather came by it because of the respect they had won in the market—respect as much for their intelligence as for their money. Moreover, Isidor Strauss did have to stand for election before he could serve in Congress. And he lost his fight for tariff reform. All that is true, and yet other men of similar intelligence did not play such a part in their country's politics. The problem is hard, for money talks in subtle and indirect ways, and sometimes, no doubt, the people for whom it talks are admirable people; success in the market does not come only to ruthless and self-serving entrepreneurs. Still, this is insidious talk in a democratic state, and it requires us to seek some way of limiting the accumulation of money (much as we must limit its weight). An enterprise like Macy's grows because men and women find it helpful; those same men and women may also, just conceivably, find it helpful to be governed by the owners of such an enterprise. But these must be two entirely separate decisions.

Washing Machines, Television Sets, Shoes, and Automobiles

In principle, stores like Macy's provide people with what they want, and then the stores succeed; or they don't, and then they fail. They are helpful, or not. Long before entrepreneurs become public servants, they are private servants who respond to the commands of the sovereign consumer. This is the myth of the market. But it isn't difficult to offer an alternative account of market relations. The market, according to the French social theorist André Gorz, "is a place where huge production and sales oligopolies . . . encounter a fragmented multiplicity of buyers who, because of their dispersed state, are totally powerless." Hence the consumer is not, and can never be, sovereign. "He is only able to choose between a variety of products, but he has no power to bring about the production of other articles, more suited to his needs, in place of those offered to him."[24] The crucial decisions are made by corporate owners and managers or by large-scale retailers: they determine the range of commodities within which the rest of us make our choices, and so the rest of us don't necessarily get the things we (really) want. Gorz concludes that these decisions should be collectivized. It's not enough that the market be limited; it must in effect be replaced by democratic politics.

Consider now some of Gorz's examples. Appliances designed for individuals, he argues, are incompatible with those designed for collective use. "The privately owned washing machine, for example, operates against the installation of public laundries." A decision must be made about which of these to foster. "Should emphasis be laid on the improvement of collective services or on the supply of individual equipment . . . ? Should there be a mediocre television receiver in every apartment, or a television room in every apartment house, with equipment of the highest possible quality?"[25] Gorz believes that these questions can be answered only by the "associated producers," who are also consumers—that is, by the democratic public as a whole. But this seems an odd way to locate decision-making power with regard to goods of this sort. If a collective decision is called for here, I should think it would best be made at the level of the apartment house or the city block. Let the residents decide what kinds of public room they want to pay for, and there will soon be different sorts of apartment house, different sorts of neighborhood, catering to different tastes. But decisions of this kind will figure on the market in exactly the same way as an individual decision does; they will merely have greater weight. If the weight is great enough, the right machines will be produced and sold. Established manufacturers and retailers may be unready or unable to deliver what is wanted, but then new manufacturers and retailers will come forward out of the world of inventors, craftsmen, machine shops, and specialty stores. The petty bourgeoisie is the reserve army of the entrepreneurial class. Its members are waiting, not for the decisions of the "associated producers," but for the call of the market. Monopoly in the strict sense—the exclusive control of productive means or retail outlets—would make it impossible to answer the call. But this sort of market power the state can rightly block. It does so in the name of free exchange, not of political democracy (and not of simple equality either: there is, again, no way to guarantee equal success to every entrepreneur).

Nor would democracy be well served if such matters as the choice of washing machines and television sets had to be debated in the assembly. Where would the debates stop? Gorz is full of questions: "Should everyone have four pairs of short-lived shoes a year, or one solid pair and two short-lived ones?"[26] One can imagine a wartime rationing system within which such decisions would have to be made collectively. Similarly, one can imagine a water shortage that led the political community to limit or even to ban the production of the domestic washing machine. But surely in the ordinary course of events this is the place for private or local choice and then for market response. And the market, as I have already suggested, does seem to generate both solid and shoddy shoes and larger and smaller washing machines.

But something more is at stake here. Gorz wants to suggest that the rising tide of private goods makes the lives of the poor harder and harder. As increasing numbers of consumers acquire their own washing machines, laundries are forced out of business (or their prices are pushed up, and they become a luxury service). Then everyone needs a washing machine. Similarly, as public forms of entertainment lose their hold, as neighborhood movie houses close, everyone needs a television set. As public transportation decays, everyone needs a car; and so on. The costs of poverty increase, and the poor are driven to the margins of society.[27] This is the same problem that Rainwater raises, and it requires the same sort of redistribution. In some cases, perhaps, subsidies are possible, as with bus and subway fares. More often, only additional income will serve the purposes of social membership and integration. It may be a mistake to tie membership so closely to private consumption; but if the two are tied, then members must also be consumers.

One might, however, stress the political rather than the economic aspects of membership. I suspect that Gorz really prefers the laundry room and the television room because he thinks of them as communal alternatives to bourgeois privatization—places where people will meet and talk, plan assignations, maybe even argue about politics. These are public goods in the sense that every tenant, whether or not he uses the rooms, will benefit from the heightened sociability, the more friendly atmosphere, of the apartment house as a whole. Yet they are the sorts of goods that tend to get lost in the individualistic shuffle of the market. They don't get lost because of the power of corporate managers and department store owners, or not primarily because of that, but rather because of the preferences of consumers, who make their choices, as it were, one by one, each one thinking only of himself (more accurately: of his home and family).[28] Would consumers choose differently if they voted as members of a group? I'm not sure, but certainly the market would accommodate them if they did. Those people who, like Gorz, favor collective over private consumption would have to make their case, and they would win or lose, or win in this neighborhood or apartment house and lose in that one. The strong point in Gorz's argument is the claim that there should be a forum where the case can be made. The market is not such a forum, but to say that is not to criticize the market; it is only to insist that it must stand alongside of, and not replace, the sphere of politics.

The point is most vividly made with reference to the automobile, conceivably the most important of modern commodities. Standing in what is now a central tradition of social criticism, Gorz is ready to renounce it: "The privately owned car upsets the whole urban structure . . . hampers the rational exploitation of public transport and militates against a great many forms of group and community leisure activity (notably by destroying the neighborhood as a living environment)."[29] He is probably right, but the car is also the symbol of individual freedom; and I doubt that any democratic public within living memory would have voted against it, even if the long-term consequences of its mass production and use had been known in advance. In this case, indeed, a communitywide decision is necessary, for the private car requires an enormous subsidy in the form of roads and their maintenance. Today we may be locked into that subsidy, without a great deal of room to maneuver. But we are not locked in merely because Henry Ford made more money selling automobiles than he could have made selling streetcars. An explanation of that sort misses a great deal of cultural as well as political and economic history. And it is, of course, still necessary to argue about the relative size of the subsidies for private cars and public transportation. That is properly a political, not a market, decision; so the citizens who make it have to be one another's equals, and their diverse interests—as producers and consumers, apartment dwellers and home owners, central city residents and suburbanites—have to be represented in the political process.

The Determination of Wages

Because votes cannot be traded, while money and goods and services can be, the equality of citizens will never be reproduced in the marketplace. The resources that people bring to the market are themselves determined, at least in principle, by the market. Men and women have to "make" money, and they do that by selling their labor power and their acquired skills. The price they get depends upon the availability of labor and the demand for particular commodities (they can't make money producing goods that nobody wants). We could abolish the market in labor in the same way as the market in commodities—by assigning jobs, by assigning shoes, through some political or administrative process. The argument against doing this is the same in both cases. Leaving aside questions of efficiency, it is an argument about how individuals relate to jobs and commodities, what these two mean in individual lives, how they are sought, used, enjoyed. I don't want to suggest any necessary similarity between the two. For most of us, our work, though it is instrumental to the possession of things, is more important than any set of possessions. But that means only that the assignment of work is even more likely than the assignment of things to be experienced as an act of tyranny.

The case would be different if work were assigned by birth and rank—and different for things, too; for in societies where work is hereditary and hierarchical, so is consumption. Men and women who are allowed to perform only certain sorts of jobs are usually allowed to use and display only certain sorts of commodities. But it is a crucial feature of individual identity, in the United States today, that though one does this, one could also do that; though one has this, one could also have that. We daydream about our options. As we get older, the daydreams tend to collapse, especially among the poor, who gradually come to realize that they lack not only the time but also the resources to exploit the opportunities of the market. And they lack those resources, so they are told, because of the market. The price of their freedom is also the cause of their loss. They were not born to be poor; they have simply failed to make money.

In fact, the more perfect the market, the smaller the inequalities of income will be, and the fewer the failures. If we assume a rough equality in mobility, information, and opportunities for training, it ought to be the case that the most attractive jobs will draw the most applicants, and so the wages they pay will fall; less attractive jobs will be shunned, and so those wages will rise. Special skills and combinations of skills will still have their premium; I don't mean to deny the earning power of talented (and very tall) basketball players or of movie stars. But many people will work to acquire the relevant skills or to put together the right combinations, and in many areas of economic life, the success rate will be high. So the gross inequalities that we see around us today could not be sustained. They derive more significantly from status hierarchies, organizational structures, and power relationships than from the free market.[30] (And they are sustained by inheritance, which I will come to a little later.) Try now to imagine a situation in which hierarchy, organization, and power were, not eliminated, but neutralized by equality, so that the specific inequalities of the market stand out. What sorts of income difference would persist? The remaining bundle of factors that make for differences is not easy to disentangle; its complexities are still debated among economists and sociologists, and I have no way of resolving the debate.[31] I intend only a rough and speculative sketch—based on a minimum of empirical evidence, for the conditions that I shall describe have been realized in only a few places and in incomplete form. Imagine, then, a democratically run farm or factory in a market society, a producers' commune. All the members are equal in status; the precise structure of their enterprise lies within their own control; power is collectively exercised through committees, assemblies, debates, and elections. How will the members pay one another? Will they establish differential pay for jobs requiring greater and lesser skill? For harder and easier jobs? For dirty and clean jobs? Or will they insist on equal pay?

The answers to these questions are likely to be similar to the answers to Gorz's questions: different for different factories and farms. This is the subject matter of factory and farm politics, just as public and private consumption is the subject matter of apartment house politics. And democratic decisions will go this way and that, depending on the prevailing ideology of the workers, the character of their enterprise, the course of the debates. Given the requirements of democratic decision making and its general ethos, we can expect that differentials will not be large. This has been the experience so far in factories owned or managed by workers. In Yugoslavia, for example, "the general trend of council-made wage schedules has been egalitarian."[32] A recent study of American experiments is similarly emphatic: "In each of the cases reported here, if the worker-owned enterprises did not make wages completely uniform, they at least equalized them significantly compared with capitalist-owned firms and even with the public bureaucracy."[33] The new distributive rules seem, moreover, to have no negative effects on productivity.

If the new rules did have negative effects, they would presumably be changed—at least, there would be strong reasons to change them. For the workers must still live within the constraints of the market. They can only distribute what they earn, and they have to recruit new members as needed, often for particular places requiring particular skills. Hence inequalities are certain to arise, within a particular factory if recruitment or work assignment requires differential pay, and if it does not, then between and among different factories. Some factories will be more successful than others, just as Macy's was more successful than other stores. Their members will have to decide whether to invest in expansion and further success or to distribute the profits—and if to distribute, whether to do so in the form of personal income or communal services. Other factories will flounder and fail, perhaps because they bet on the market and lost, perhaps because of internal dissension and mismanagement. And then the rest of us will have to decide whether to subsidize the failures—for the sake of a town's survival and prosperity, say—exactly as we do now with capitalist firms.

Income is determined, then, by a combination of political and market factors. I shall have to defend in chapter 12 the particular account of the political factors that I have just given. Here I want only to argue that this account reproduces, under the conditions of large-scale industry and agriculture, just those features of the petty-bourgeois economy that make its risks, and the inequalities that follow from those risks, defensible. Democratic decision making, like petty-bourgeois small holding, is a way of bringing the market home, connecting its opportunities and dangers to the actual effort, initiative, and luck of individuals (and groups of individuals). This is what complex equality requires: not that the market be abolished, but that no one be cut off from its possibilities because of his low status or political powerlessness.

I have followed in these last pages an argument first sketched out by R. H. Tawney in the years before the First World War. The argument is worth quoting at some length:

> When most men were small land-holders or small craftsmen . . . they took risks. But at the same time they took profits and surpluses. At the present day, the workman takes risks . . . but he has not got the prospect of exceptional gains, the opportunities for small speculation, the power to direct his own life, which makes the bearing of risks worthwhile.

Money and Commodities

Tawney didn't doubt that the bearing of risks is worthwhile. Not that masses of men and women must live always at the very edge of danger: against that sort of life, the community must provide protection. But protection has its limits; and beyond those limits, individuals and groups of individuals are on their own, free to seek out danger or avoid it if they can. If they were not free, neither individuals nor groups could possibly be what our culture (ideally) requires them to be—that is, active, energetic, creative, democratic, giving shape to their own public and private lives. Risk is "bracing," Tawney went on,

> *if it is voluntarily undertaken,* because in that case a man balances probable gains and losses and stakes his brains and character on success. But when the majority of persons are hired servants, they do not decide what risks they shall bear. It is decided for them by their masters. They gain nothing if the enterprise succeeds: they have neither the responsibility of effort nor the pride of achievement; they merely have the sufferings of failure. No wonder that, as long as this is so, they desire above all things security. . . . In such circumstances the plea that men should be allowed to take risks . . . is an attack not upon modern attempts at giving the wage-earner security, but upon the whole wage system.[34]

The *whole* wage system is, perhaps, an exaggeration. Though workers under the distributive rules that Tawney favored would not literally sell their labor power and their acquired skills, they would still present themselves, power and skills in hand, before the personnel director or the personnel committee of the local factory. The terms on which they were admitted to the cooperative and the income they received would still be determined in part by market forces—even if they were co-determined through a democratic political process. Tawney was not proposing the abolition of the labor market; he was trying, as I have been doing, to define the boundaries within which it properly operates.

Redistributions

One can conceive the market as a sphere without boundaries, an unzoned city—for money is insidious, and market relations are expansive. A radically *laissez-faire* economy would be like a totalitarian state, invading every other sphere, dominating every other distributive process.

It would transform every social good into a commodity. This is market imperialism. I suppose that it is less dangerous than state imperialism because it is easier to control. The blocked exchanges are so many controls, enforced not only by officials but also by ordinary men and women defending their interests and asserting their rights. The blocks don't always hold, however; and when market distributions can't be contained within their proper limits, we must look to the possibility of political redistributions.

I am not talking now about the redistributions out of which we finance the welfare state. These come from a pool of wealth, the "common wealth," to which everyone contributes according to his available resources. Out of this pool we pay for physical security, communal worship, civil liberties, schooling, medical care—whatever we take to be the entailments of membership. Private wealth comes later. Historically as well as sociologically, pooling and sharing are prior to buying and selling.[35] Later, conceivably, communal provision can encroach upon the market. This is the claim made by the leaders of every tax revolt from the French Poujadists of the 1950s to the advocates of California's Proposition 13: that the burdens of membership have grown too heavy and that they constrain the rightful enjoyments, unduly limit the risks and incentives, of the sphere of money and commodities.[36] These critics may be right, at least sometimes; certainly there are real conflicts here. And hard practical choices: for if the constraints and limits are too severe, productivity may fall, and then there will be less room for the social recognition of needs. But at some level of taxation, if not necessarily at prevailing levels, the political community can't be said to invade the sphere of money; it merely claims its own.

Market imperialism requires another sort of redistribution, which is not so much a matter of drawing a line as of redrawing it. What is at issue now is the dominance of money outside its sphere, the ability of wealthy men and women to trade in indulgences, purchase state offices, corrupt the courts, exercise political power. Commonly enough, the market has its occupied territories, and we can think of redistribution as a kind of moral irredentism, a process of boundary revision. Different principles guide the process at different points in time and space. For my immediate purposes, the most important principle has this (rough) form: the exercise of power belongs to the sphere of politics, while what goes on in the market should at least approximate an exchange between equals (a free exchange). These last words don't mean that every commodity will sell for a "just price" or that every worker will receive his "just reward."* Justice of that sort is alien to the market. But every exchange must be the result of a bargain, not of a command or an ultimatum. If the market is to work properly, "exchanges born of desperation" must be ruled out, for necessity, as Ben Franklin wrote, "never made a good bargain."[38] In a sense, the welfare state underwrites the sphere of money when it guarantees that men and women will never be forced to bargain without resources for the very means of life. When the state acts to facilitate union organization, it serves the same purpose. Workers who stand alone are liable to be forced into trades of last resort, driven by their poverty, or their lack of particular marketable skills, or their inability to move their families to accept the ultimatum of some local employer. Collective bargaining is more likely to be an exchange between equals. It doesn't guarantee a good bargain, any more than communal provision does, but it helps to sustain the integrity of the market.

But I am concerned now to sustain the integrity of the other distributive spheres—by depriving powerful entrepreneurs, for example, of the means of capturing political power or bending public officials to their will. When money carries with it the control, not of things only but of people, too, it ceases to be a private resource. It no longer buys goods and services on the market; it buys something else, somewhere else, where (given our democratic understanding of politics) buying and selling is ruled out. If we can't block the purchase, then we have to socialize the money, which is only to recognize that it has taken on a political character. The point at which that becomes necessary is open to dispute. It isn't a fixed point but changes with the relative strength and coherence of the political sphere.

It would be a mistake to imagine, however, that money has political effects only when it "talks" to candidates and officials, only when it is discreetly displayed or openly flaunted in the corridors of power. It also has political effects closer to home, in the market itself and in its firms and enterprises. Here, too, boundary revision is called for. When union negotiators first demanded the establishment of grievance machinery, for example, they argued that plant discipline had to be handled like criminal justice in the state, on a judicial or semi-judicial basis,

---

*Perhaps we should think of the just price as another form of blocked exchange: a price is fixed by some process other than bargaining, and exchange at any other price is ruled out. The range of goods controlled in this way varies greatly across cultures and historical periods, but food is the most commonly controlled good.[37] Among ourselves, the just price survives in the case of public utilities, most often privately owned, where rates are, or are supposed to be, fixed with reference not to what the market will bear but to some common understanding of a "fair" profit—and where standards of service are similarly controlled.

and not like the decision to buy and sell commodities, on the basis of entrepreneurial judgments (or the whim of particular entrepreneurs).[39] At stake was the government of the workplace, and government is not a market matter—not, at least, in a democratic society. Of course, the fight for grievance procedures was not only a dispute about boundaries; it was also a class struggle. The workers defended an enlarged political sphere because they were more likely to do well within it; they had an interest in drawing the lines in a certain way. But we can still say, as I would be inclined to do, that their claims were just. These are matters that admit not only of struggle but also of argument.

The argument can be carried one step further. Even within the adversary relation of owners and workers, with unions and grievance procedures in place, owners may still exercise an illegitimate kind of power. They make all sorts of decisions that severely constrain and shape the lives of their employees (and their fellow citizens, too). Might not the enormous capital investment represented by plants, furnaces, machines, and assembly lines be better regarded as a political than an economic good? To say this doesn't mean that it can't be shared among individuals in a variety of ways, but only that it shouldn't carry the conventional entailments of ownership. Beyond a certain scale, the means of production are not properly called commodities, any more than the irrigation system of the ancient Egyptians, the roads of the Romans or the Incas, the cathedrals of medieval Europe, or the weapons of a modern army are called commodities, for they generate a kind of power that lifts them out of the economic sphere. I will come back to these issues when I consider in detail the sphere of politics. Here I only want to stress that even this last redistribution would still leave, if not the capitalist market, then the market itself, intact.

Redistributions are of three sorts: first, of market power, as in the blocking of desperate exchanges and the fostering of trade unions; second, of money directly, through the tax system; third, of property rights and the entailments of ownership, as in the establishment of grievance procedures or the cooperative control of the means of production. All three redistributions redraw the line between politics and economics, and they do so in ways that strengthen the sphere of politics—the hand of citizens, that is, not necessarily the power of the state. (In Eastern Europe today, a similar kind of "moral irredentism" would strengthen the economic sphere and expand the reach of market relations.) But however strong their hand, citizens can't make just any decisions they please. The sphere of politics has its own boundaries; it abuts on other spheres and finds its limits in those abutments. Hence redistribution can never produce simple equality, not so long as money and commodities still exist, and there is some legitimate social space within which they can be exchanged—or, for that matter, given away.

Gifts and Inheritance

In the United States today, the gift is determined by the commodity. If I can own this object and exchange it for something else (within the sphere of money and commodities), then surely I can give it to whomever I please. If I can shape my identity through my possessions, then I can do so through my dispossessions. And, even more surely, what I can't possess, I can't give away. But it will be useful to think more carefully about the gift, for in its history we can learn a great deal about ourselves—and find, too, some interesting ways of being different. I will begin with one of the best known of anthropological accounts.

Gift Exchange in the Western Pacific

Bronislaw Malinowski's study of exchange relations among the Trobriand Islanders and their island neighbors is long and full of detail; I cannot begin to suggest its complexities.[40] I shall attempt only a brief review of its central focus, the *Kula*, a system of gift exchanges in which necklaces of red shell and bracelets of white shell travel in opposite directions, over many miles, around a circle of islands and gift partners. The necklaces and bracelets are ritual objects, stereotypical in form though various in value; the finest of them are very valuable indeed, the most valuable things that the islanders have, much sought after and greatly cherished. The two objects are exchanged for one another and for nothing else. But this isn't a "trade" in our sense of the word: necklaces and bracelets "can never be exchanged from hand to hand, with the equivalence between the two objects discussed, bargained about and computed."[41] The exchange has the form of a series of gifts. I give my *Kula* partner a necklace; and some time later, perhaps as much as a year later, he gives me a bracelet or a set of bracelets. Nor does the series end there. I pass on the bracelets to some other partner and receive another necklace, which I in turn give away. These objects are only temporary possessions; every several years, they move around the circle, the *Kula* ring, necklaces in a clockwise, bracelets in a counterclockwise, direction. "One transaction does not finish the *Kula* relationship, the rule being 'once in the *Kula*, always in the *Kula.*' "[42]

Every gift is a return, then, for some previous gift. The equivalence is left to the giver, though "he is expected to give back full and fair value." Indeed, "every movement of the *Kula* articles, every detail of the transaction, is . . . regulated by a set of traditional rules and conventions."[43] There is room for generosity and room for resentment, but the fundamental structure is fixed. We might better think of it as a system of alliances than as an economic system, though that distinction would be lost on the Trobriand Islanders. The *Kula* ring has its analogue in our social round, where friends exchange presents and invitations in what is necessarily a conventionalized pattern. The exchange is not a bargain; one can't buy one's way out of the obligations it entails; returns must be in kind. And the relation isn't terminated by the return: the presents and invitations go round and round, back and forth within a group of friends. The *Kula* ring looms larger in the life of its participants, however, than the social round does in ours. It is, as Marshall Sahlins has argued, the acting out of a social contract, and all other relationships and transactions take place in its shadow, or better, under the protection of the peace it establishes and guarantees.[44]

Among these is what Malinowski calls "trade, pure and simple" and what the islanders call *gimwali.* Here the trade is in commodities, not ritual objects; and it is entirely legitimate to bargain, to haggle, to seek private advantage. The *gimwali* is free; it can be carried on between any two strangers; and the striking of a bargain terminates the transaction. The islanders draw a sharp line between this sort of trade and the exchange of gifts. When criticizing bad conduct in the *Kula,* they will say that "it was done like a *gimwali.* "[45] At the same time, success in trade pure and simple will enhance one's status in the *Kula,* for the exchange of necklaces and bracelets is accompanied by other sorts of gift giving and by elaborate feastings, and so requires considerable resources. I suppose it is true of us, too, that success in buying and selling changes one's position in the social round. But we are more likely to spend our money on ourselves than on others. Among the islanders, by contrast, every form of production and accumulation is subordinated to the *Kula*—the freedom of "getting," to a highly conventionalized and morally coercive form of "spending."

The gift, then, is not determined by the commodity. The islanders have, indeed, a conception of ownership; and though it allows less freedom than our own conception does, it still leaves room for personal choice and private (or familial) use; but it does not extend to the *Kula* objects. These belong to the ring, not to the individual. They can't be held for too long (else one gets a reputation for being "slow" in the *Kula*). They can't be given to one's children rather than to one's partners. They can't be passed the wrong way round the circle or traded for other sorts of things. They move in a certain direction, on a certain schedule, to the accompaniment of certain rites and ceremonies. The gift, the islanders might say, is too important to be left to the whim of the giver.

The Gift in the Napoleonic Code

Among the Trobriand Islanders, gifts make friends, build trust, shape alliances, guarantee peace. The giver is a man of influence and prestige; and the more he can give away, the greater his largesse, the larger he will loom among his peers. But a very different view of the gift is dominant in many cultures, according to which it is less an enhancement of the status than a dissipation of the estate of the giver. There is only so much wealth, land and money and things, and every gift makes it less. But this wealth doesn't simply belong to the individual (and still less to his circle of friends); he is its legal owner only under certain descriptions and for certain purposes. Under other descriptions and for other purposes, it belongs to his family or, better, to his lineage. And then the political authorities step in to protect the interests of the next generation.

This view of wealth has its origins in tribal and feudal law; it has a long history which I shall not recount. During the French Revolution an effort was made to break up aristocratic estates and all great concentrations of wealth by guaranteeing equal legacies to heirs of equal rank. This guarantee found its place in the Napoleonic Code, though in modified form; and it obviously represents a severe restraint upon the testamentary power of individual owners. Even more important, I think, the Code aimed to regulate the power of the owner during his own lifetime by limiting his right to bestow his money as he pleased, to pleasing strangers or to relatives outside the direct line of descent. The legislators fixed a reserve, a percentage of the total estate (all the property that the individual had ever owned), that could not be given away and that had to pass by intestacy. "The reserve varied with the number and kinds of . . . heirs that survived—one-half of the estate if there were no children, three-fourths if there were three or fewer children, four-fifths if there were four, and so on." If the right amounts were not available for distribution, testamentary gifts were canceled, *inter vivos* gifts "reduced" or "returned."[46]

Here again, the gift does not follow the rules of the commodity. Individual owners can do what they like with their money so long as they spend it on themselves. They can eat gourmet foods prepared by gourmet chefs, vacation on the Riviera, risk their estate at blackjack or roulette. The law regulates their generosity to strangers, not their self-indulgence. The contrast seems odd, but it isn't incomprehensible. It would require a harshly coercive regime to police self-indulgence, while the control of gifts, or of large-scale gifts, looks easier (it has proven in fact to be very difficult). But there is a deeper distinction at work here. Getting and spending, in the ordinary sense of those words, belongs to the sphere of money and commodities, and it is governed by the principles of that sphere, which are principles of freedom. But the distribution of the family estate belongs to another sphere—the sphere of kinship—which is governed by principles of mutuality and obligation. The boundaries are as hard to draw here as anywhere else; in the United States today, they are drawn far more narrowly than in the Napoleonic Code. But our own conceptions of maintenance, alimony, and child care suggest the existence of a pool of familial wealth, rather like the pool of communal wealth, where free disbursement is not permitted. It might be argued that maintenance, say, is an obligation freely incurred when one marries and has children. But no agreement, no contract, no individual understanding sets the shape of the obligation. This is collectively, not individually, determined; and the determination reflects our collective understanding of what a family is.

More generally, however, from the founding of the republic on, Americans have been remarkably free to do what they like with their money. The family has been less central here than in Europe, probably because of the absence of a feudal past; and as a result, wealth has more readily passed out of familial control. In his *Principles of Political Economy,* first published in 1848, John Stuart Mill praised this feature of American life, quoting Charles Lyell's *Travels in North America:*

> Not only is it common for rich capitalists to leave by a will a portion of their fortune towards the endowment of national institutions, but individuals during their lifetime make magnificent grants of money for the same objects. There is here no compulsory law for the equal partition of property among children, as in France, and on the other hand, no custom of entail or primogeniture, as in England, so that the affluent feel themselves at liberty to share their wealth between their kindred and the public.[47]

But if philanthropy is uncontrolled, even encouraged by the state, gifts and bequests of other sorts and legacies to kin are still subject to the law—not as to their direction, so to speak, but as to their size. At the moment, this legal control doesn't amount to much, but the principle is established, and it is important to try to understand its moral basis and to attempt some conclusions about its proper practical extent.

Mill offered a utilitarian account of the limitations on bequest and inheritance. If we estimate a large fortune at its true value, he said, "that of the pleasures and advantages that can be purchased with it," then, "it must be apparent to everyone, that the difference to the possessor between a moderate independence and five times as much, is insignificant when weighed against the enjoyment that might be given . . . by some other disposal of the four-fifths."[48] But I doubt very much that this view of the marginal utility of wealth will persuade any potential owner of a large fortune. There is so much else, beyond moderate independence, that money can buy. Mill suggested a better reason for the policies he advocated when he summed up their intended effects: to make the "enormous fortunes which no one needs for any personal purpose but ostentation or improper power . . . less numerous."[49] Ostentation is surely unimportant; it is a common foible within the sphere of money and, short of sumptuary laws rigorously enforced, impossible to control. But improper power must be controlled if the integrity of the political sphere is to be upheld. Ideally, perhaps, enormous fortunes should be broken up before they can be transferred. But there may be grounds for permitting substantial (though not unlimited) accumulation within a single lifetime: the major political effects are often not felt until the next generation, whose members are raised to a habit of command. In any case, the chief purpose of limiting bequest and inheritance, as of every other form of redistribution, is to secure the boundaries of the different spheres. Once this is done, Mill's marginal utility argument will look more plausible, for there won't be all that much that an individual can do with his money. It still isn't that argument, however, that fixes the limits on transfers. The limits will have been fixed already with reference to the relative strength of the boundaries (and the success of other sorts of boundary defense). If we succeeded absolutely in barring the conversion of money into political power, for example, then we might not limit its accumulation or alienation at all. As things are, we have strong reasons to limit both of these—reasons that have less to do with the marginal utility of money than with its extramural effectiveness.

The right to give and the right to receive follow from the social meaning of money and commodities; but the rights prevail only so long as these two things, and only these, are given and received. "The ownership of a thing," as Mill said, "cannot be looked upon as complete without the power of bestowing it, at death or during life, at the owner's pleasure."[50] What can be owned can also be given away. The unilateral gift is a phenomenon unique to the sphere of money and commodities as it has taken shape in our own society. It doesn't figure in the *Kula* or in any other system of gift exchange. It is severely constrained, if not ruled out entirely, whenever ownership is vested in the family or the lineage. It is a special feature of our culture, opening the way to special sorts of generosity and public-spiritedness (and special sorts of whimsy and meanness, too). It isn't generous or public-spirited, however, to try to pass on a political office—or any position of power over others—to one's friends and relatives. Nor can professional standing or public honor be transferred at will, for such things lie within no one's gift. Simple equality would require a long list of further prohibitions; indeed, it would require a total ban on gifts. But surely the gift is one of the finer expressions of ownership as we know it. And so long as they act within their sphere, we have every reason to respect those men and women who give their money away to persons they love or to causes to which they are committed, even if they make distributive outcomes unpredictable and uneven. Love and commitment, like enterprise, have their risks and (sometimes) their windfalls, which it is no necessary part of a theory of distributive justice to deny or repress.

5

Office

Simple Equality in the Sphere of Office

According to the dictionary, an office is "a place of trust, authority, or service under constituted authority . . . an official position or employment." I propose a broader definition so as to encompass the expanded range of "constituted authority" in the modern world: an office is any position in which the political community as a whole takes an interest, choosing the person who holds it or regulating the procedures by which he is chosen. Control over appointments is crucial. The distribution of offices is not a matter of individual or small group discretion. Offices cannot be appropriated by private persons, passed down in families, or sold on the market. This is, of course, a stipulative definition, for social and economic positions of the sort that it covers have in the past been distributed in all these ways. In the societies that Weber called "patrimonial," even positions in the state bureaucracy were held as property by powerful individuals and handed on from father to son. No appointment was necessary; the son succeeded to his office as to his land; and though the ruler might claim the right to recognize, he could not dispute, the title. Today the market is the major alternative to the system of offices, and the holders of market power or their authorized representatives—personnel managers, plant foremen, and so on—are the major alternatives to the constituted authorities. But the distribution of position and place through the market is increasingly subject to political regulation.

The idea of office is very old. In the West, it developed most clearly within the Christian church and took on its special edge in the course of the long struggle to disengage the church from the privatized world of feudalism. Church leaders made two arguments: first, that ecclesiastical positions could not be owned by the incumbents or their feudal patrons and given out to friends and relatives; second, that they could not be traded or sold. Nepotism and simony were both of them sins, and sins likely to be committed so long as private individuals controlled the distribution of religious offices. Offices were to be distributed instead by the constituted authorities of the church, acting on God's behalf and for the sake of His service. God, we might say, was the first meritocrat, and piety and divine knowledge were the qualifications He required of His officials (also, no doubt, managerial capacity, skill in handling money, and political *savoir faire*). Discretion was not abolished but was relocated within an official hierarchy and subjected to a variety of constraints.[1]

From the church, the idea of office was taken over and secularized by the advocates of a civil service. Theirs, too, was a long struggle: first, against the personal discretion claimed by aristocrats and gentlemen; and then, against the partisan discretion claimed by radical democrats. Like the service of God, so the service of the political community was slowly turned into the work of qualified individuals, beyond the reach of powerful families or triumphant factions and parties. One might work out a democratic defense of factions and parties, and then of what came to be called the "spoils system," for here discretion in hiring seems to be mandated by a majority of the citizens: I shall pursue this line of argument later. But the fight for the spoils system was lost as soon as that name was established. Offices are too important to be conceived of as the spoils of victory. Or, victories are too transient, majorities too unstable, to shape the civil service of a modern state. Instead, the examination has become the crucial distributive mechanism—so that today, in a state like Massachusetts, for example, virtually the only state job for which there is no examination (leaving aside the governor and his cabinet and a number of advisory and regulatory commisions) is the job of "laborer," and even for it hiring procedures are closely supervised.[2] There are no spoils left. Jobs have steadily been turned into offices, for the sake of honesty and efficiency ("good government") and also for the sake of justice and equal opportunity.

The fight for the idea of office in church and state makes up two parts of a story that now has a third part: the gradual extension of the idea into civil society. Today membership in most professions has been made "official" insofar as the state controls licensing procedures and participates in the enforcement of standards for professional practice. Indeed, any employment for which academic certification is required is a kind of office, since the state also controls the accreditation of academic institutions and often runs them itself. In principle, at least, grades and degrees are not for sale. Perhaps it is the pressure of the market that forces employers to require (increasingly advanced) certificates; but in the process of academic selection, training, and examination, standards are brought to bear that are not simply market standards and in which state agents take an active interest.

The interest in this case doesn't have to do with God or the community as a whole, but has rather to do with all the individual clients, patients, consumers of goods and services who depend upon the competence of office holders. We are not inclined to expose helpless and needful people to officials selected by birth or arbitrarily patronized by some powerful individual. We are also not inclined to expose them to self-selected officials who have not come through some process, more or less elaborate, of training and testing. Since offices are relatively scarce, these processes must be fair to all candidates, and must be seen to be fair; and such fairness, too, requires that their design be taken out of the hands of private decision makers. More and more, this authority has been politicized, that is, made into a matter of public debate, subjected to governmental scrutiny and regulation. The process began with the professions, but it has recently been extended so as to impose constraints on many different sorts of selection procedure. Indeed, laws that fix "fair employment practices" and judicial decisions that require "affirmative action" programs have the effect of turning all the jobs to which they apply into something like offices.

In these last examples, justice is the main concern rather than efficiency or honest competence, though these two may be served as well. I think it is fair to say that the current thrust of both politics and political philosophy is toward the reconceptualization of every job as an office—for the sake of justice. This is certainly the implication of the latter (and least controversial) part of Rawls's second principle of justice: "Social and economic inequalities are to be arranged so that they are . . . attached to offices and positions open to all under conditions of fair equality of opportunity."[3] Any position for which people compete, and where the victory of one constitutes a social or economic advantage over the others, must be distributed "fairly," in accordance with advertised criteria and transparent procedures. It would be unjust if some private person, for reasons of his own or for no publicly known and approved reason at all, simply handed out offices and positions.

Offices must be won in open competition. The goal is a perfect meritocracy, the realization (at last!) of the French revolutionary slogan: the career open to talents. The revolutionaries of 1789 thought that nothing more was necessary to achieve this goal than the destruction of aristocratic monopoly and the abolition of every legal barrier to individual advancement. This was still the view of Durkheim a century later when he described the good society as one that required an "organic" division of labor, where "no obstacle, of whatever nature, prevents [individuals] from occupying the place in the social framework . . . compatible with their faculties."[4] In fact, however, this happy outcome requires the positive work of the state: administering exams, establishing criteria for training and certification, regulating search and selection procedures. Only the state can counter the particularizing effects of individual discretion, market power, and corporate privilege, and guarantee to every citizen an equal chance to measure up to universal standards.

So the old division of labor is replaced by a universal civil service, and a kind of simple equality is established. The sum of the available opportunities is divided by the number of interested citizens, and everyone is given the same chance of winning a place. That at any rate is the tendency of contemporary development, though there is obviously much that needs to be done if it is to reach its logical endpoint: a system incorporating every job the holding of which might conceivably constitute a social or economic advantage, and to which every citizen has exactly equal access. The picture is not unattractive, but it requires us to agree that all jobs are indeed offices, and that they must be distributed, if not for the same reasons, then for the same kinds of reason. These will necessarily be meritocratic reasons, for no others connect careers and talents. State officials will have to define the necessary merits and enforce their uniform application. Individual citizens will strive to acquire these merits and then to turn the acquisition into a new monopoly. Social inequalities, Durkheim wrote, will "exactly express natural inequalities."[5] No, they will express a particular set of natural and artificial inequalities associated with going to school, taking an examination, doing well in an interview, leading a disciplined life, and obeying orders. What can a universal civil service be but a vast and intricate hierarchy within which some mix of intellectual and bureaucratic virtues are dominant?

But there is another kind of simple equality aimed precisely at avoiding this outcome. It is less important, on this view, that every job be turned into an office than that every citizen be turned into an office holder, less important to democratize selection than to randomize distribution (by lottery or rotation, for example). This was the Greek view of the civil service, but in postclassical times it has most commonly been represented by a certain sort of populist radicalism which has its source in a deep resentment of office holders—priests, lawyers, doctors, and bureaucrats. Resentment can, no doubt, breed a complicated and subtle politics. The spontaneous and unreflective demand of populist radicals, however, has often been simple indeed: death to all office holders!

> Away with him! away with him! he speaks Latin![6]

Populist radicalism is anti-clerical, anti-professional, and anti-intellectual. In part, it takes this form because office holders are often lowborn men and women who—class renegades—serve the interests of the highborn. But the hostility is also connected to what Shakespeare's Hamlet calls "the insolence of office": that is, the special claims that office holders commonly make, that they are entitled to their offices and then to the authority and status that go with their offices, because they have been tested and certified in accordance with socially approved standards. Office is their achievement, and it marks them off as superior to their fellow citizens.

The more reflective forms of populism played an important part first in Protestant, then in democratic and socialist, thought. Luther's call for the priesthood of all believers has had its parallel for virtually every kind of office holding. Thus, the reiterated revolutionary effort to simplify the language of the law so that every citizen can be his own lawyer; or Rousseau's argument for a system of public schools where ordinary citizens take turns as teachers; or the Jacksonian demand for rotation in office; or Lenin's vision of a society in which "every literate person" is also a bureaucrat.[7] The crucial argument in all these examples is that office holding itself, and not merely the power to distribute offices, represents an unjustifiable monopoly. If office holders need not be killed, it is necessary at least to repudiate their claims to qualification and prerogative. Away with Latin, then, and with every other form of arcane knowledge that makes office holding mysterious and difficult.

Now social equality "exactly" expresses natural equality—the ability of every citizen to share in every aspect of social and political activity. Taken literally, however, this sharing is possible only in small, homogeneous, economically unsophisticated societies: ancient Athens is the prime example. In more complex societies, there is a characteristic difficulty, nicely expressed in the contemporary Chinese debate about the role of "experts" and "reds."[8] If one devalues knowledge, one falls back on ideology; for some kind of guiding principle, some standard reference for the regulation and evaluation of work, is necessary in the management of a modern economy. If talent and training are denied legitimacy even within their appropriate sphere, then ideological zeal is likely to rule illegitimately outside of its own. When office holding is universalized, it is also devalued, and the way is open for the tyranny of the political adviser and the commissar.

Rotation in office can coexist with a system of professional selection. The modern conscript army is an obvious example, and it is not difficult to imagine similar arrangements in many other areas of social life. As this example suggests, however, it is difficult to do away with selection entirely. The ancient Athenians elected their generals because they thought that this was a case where qualifications were necessary and a lottery inappropriate. And when Napoleon said that every private carried a marshal's baton in his knapsack, he did not mean that any private could be a marshal. Offices that require long training or special qualities of leadership cannot readily be universalized; scarce offices can only be shared among a limited number of people, and often the rotation of individuals into and out of them would be highly disruptive of both private life and economic activity. Not everyone can be a hospital director, even if the rigid hierarchy of the contemporary hospital is broken down. More important, not everyone can be a doctor. Not everyone can be chief engineer in the factory, even if the factory is democratically run. More important, again, not everyone can work in the most successful or pleasant factories.

Against the two forms of simple equality, I want to defend a more complicated set of social and economic arrangements. A universal civil service would merely replace the dominance of private power with the dominance of state power—and then with the dominance of talent or education or whatever quality state officials thought necessary for office holding. The problem here is to contain the universalization of office, to attend more particularly to the actual job and its social meaning, to draw a line (it will have to be drawn differently in different cultures) between those selection processes that the political community should control and those it should leave to private individuals and collegial bodies. Again, rotation in office will only work for some offices, not for others; and its extension beyond its bounds could only be a fraud, a mask for new sorts of domination. The problem here is not to break the monopoly of the qualified, but to set limits to their prerogatives. Whatever qualities we choose to require—the knowledge of Latin, or the ability to pass an exam, deliver a lecture, or make cost/benefit calculations—we must insist that these do not become the basis of tyrannical claims to power and privilege. Office holders should be held rigidly to the purposes of their office. As we require containment, so we require humility. Were these two properly understood and enforced, the distribution of office might loom less large in egalitarian thought than it currently does.

Meritocracy

But the processes by which individual men and women are selected for admission to medical school, say, or for employment in this or that factory, and then for all subsequent appointments and promotions, will always be important. They require careful and extended discussion. My own purpose is to defend a mixed system of selection, but I shall begin by focusing on the criteria and procedures that might apply in a universal civil service. I shall join, that is, the argument about meritocracy. This is the crucial argument in any political community where the idea of office has taken hold, as it has in the United States, not only in church and state but in civil society, too. Assume, then, that every job is an office, that distribution is in the hands, ultimately, of the political community as a whole, and that every member is entitled to "fair equality of opportunity." What should the distributive processes look like? I should stress at the start that there are positions and employments that don't properly fall within the range of political control; but it will be easier to see what these are once I have described the internal (social and moral) logic of the distribution of office.

The principle that underlies the idea of meritocracy in the minds of most of its supporters is simply this: that offices should be filled by the most qualified people because qualification is a special case of desert. People may or may not deserve their qualities, but they deserve those places for which their qualities fit them. The whole purpose of abolishing private discretion is to distribute offices according to desert (talent, merit, and so on.)[9] Actually, the case is more complicated than these formulations suggest. For many offices, only minimal qualification is required; a very large number of applicants can do the work perfectly well, and no additional training would enable them to do it better. Here fairness seems to require that the offices be distributed among qualified candidates on a "first come, first served" basis (or through a lottery); and then *desert* is surely too strong a term to describe the fit between the office holder and his place. But other offices are open-ended with regard to the training and skill they require, and for them it might make sense to say that, though a number of candidates are qualified, the most qualified deserves the office. Desert does not seem to be relative in the same way that qualification is, but Dryden's line:

> That he, who best deserves, alone may reign,[10]

suggests that there may be deserving individuals who don't in the final analysis deserve any particular office, just as there are qualified individuals who must give way to the most qualified.

But this line of argument misses an important difference between desert and qualification. Both terms, no doubt, are ambiguous in their meaning, and we often use them in ways that overlap. But I think I can draw a useful line between them by focusing on particular selection processes and particular social goods. *Desert* implies a very strict sort of entitlement, such that the title precedes and determines the selection, while *qualification* is a much looser idea. A prize, for example, can be deserved because it already belongs to the person who has given the best performance; it remains only to identify that person. Prize committees are like juries in that they look backward and aim at an objective decision. An office, by contrast, cannot be deserved because it belongs to the people who are served by it, and they or their agents are free (within limits I will specify later) to make any choice they please. Search committees are unlike juries in that their members look forward as well as back: they make predictions about the candidate's future performances, and they also express preferences about how the office should be filled.

Consideration for office falls between these two. I shall argue in the next section that all citizens, or all citizens with some minimal training or skill, have a right to be considered when offices are given out. But the competition for a particular office is a competition that no particular person deserves (or has a right) to win. Whatever an individual's qualifications, no injustice is done to him if he isn't chosen. This is not to say that no injustice can be done to him, but only that not choosing him is not itself unjust. If someone is chosen without reference to his qualifications, but for the sake of his aristocratic blood or because he had bribed the members of the search committee, we will say indeed that he doesn't deserve the office. All the other candidates have been treated unfairly. And conceivably we will say of a good choice that he does deserve it. In this latter case, however, it's likely that a number of other people deserve it, too, and that none of them *really* deserves it. Offices don't fit individuals the way verdicts do. Assuming an honest search, no one can complain that he has been unfairly treated—even if, from the standpoint of the office itself and the people who depend upon it, the wrong candidate was chosen. This is clearest in the case of elective office, but the argument applies to all offices except purely honorary ones, which are exactly like prizes. (It is probably because all offices are, in part, honorary that notions of desert sneak into our discussion of the various candidates.)

The contrast between prizes and offices, desert and qualification, may be sharpened if we consider two hypothetical but not atypical cases. (1) X has written what is commonly agreed to be the best novel of 1980; but a group of men and women committed to a more experimental mode than that in which X writes, persuade their fellow jury members to give the novel-of-the-year award to Y, who has written an inferior novel in the preferred mode. They agree about the relative merits of the two books but act so as to encourage experimental writing. That may or may not be a good thing to do, but they have treated X unfairly. (2) X is the most qualified candidate for a hospital directorship in the sense that he possesses to a greater degree than anyone else those managerial talents commonly agreed to be required in the office. But a group of men and women who want to turn the hospital in a certain direction persuade their fellows on the selection committee to choose Y, who shares their commitment. They may be right or wrong about what they want to do with the hospital, but they have not treated X unfairly.

Without the "common agreement" that I have stipulated, these two cases might look less different. If we make the ideas of desert and qualification controversial, as they are, then it might plausibly be said that the prize and the office should go to those individuals who best fit the definitions finally worked out. Still, the members of the jury ought to refrain from reading their private literary program into the definition of desert, while the members of the selection committee are not bound by any similar self-denying ordinance in their arguments about qualification. Hence there will be legitimate complaints about the awarding of a literary prize if the process has been overtly politicized—even if the politics is "literary." But, under similar circumstances, there are no legitimate complaints about the choice of an office holder (unless the choice is made on irrelevant political grounds, as when postmasters, for example, are chosen because of their party loyalty, not because of their views on how the post office should be run). The jury, because it looks backward, must reflect what is best in a shared tradition of literary criticism; the selection committee is part of an ongoing process of political or professional definition.

The distinction I have been trying to work out seems to fail, however, in all those cases where we distribute offices on the basis of examination scores. Surely the title "doctor," for example, belongs to all those individuals who achieve a certain score on the medical boards. The actual test merely determines who, and how many, these individuals are. And then it must be true that anyone who studies hard, works through the necessary material, and passes the examination, deserves to be a doctor: it would be unjust to deny him the title. But it would not be unjust to deny him an internship or a residency in a particular hospital. The hospital selection committee need not choose the applicant with the highest score; it looks not only back to his exams but forward to performances not yet performed. Nor is it unjust if men and women decline to consult him about their medical problems. His title merely qualifies him to seek a place and a practice; it doesn't entitle him to either one. The examination that yields the title is important but not all important, and it is only because the examination is not all important that we allow it the importance it has. If offices, with all their authority and prerogatives, could be deserved, we would be at the mercy of the deserving. Instead, we leave ourselves room for choice. As members of the hospital staff (responsible to a governing board that at least putatively represents the general community), we choose our colleagues; as individuals in the marketplace, we choose our professional consultants. In both cases, the choice belongs to the choosers in a way that verdicts can't belong to the members of a jury.

Even the title of "doctor," though it is like a prize in that it can be deserved, is unlike a prize in that it cannot be deserved once and for all. A prize is given for a performance, and because the performance cannot be unperformed, the prize cannot be taken away. A subsequent discovery of fraud might lead to the dishonoring of the winner; but so long as the performance stands, so does the honor, whatever happens afterward. Professional titles, by contrast, are subject to continuous public scrutiny, and reference to the examination score that provided the original entitlement is of no avail if subsequent performances don't measure up to publicly established standards. Disqualification, to be sure, involves a judicial or semi-judicial procedure, and we would be inclined to say that only "deserving" individuals can justly be disqualified. Once again, removal from a particular office is a different matter. The procedures can be and generally are political in character; desert is not a necessary consideration. For some offices, both judicial and political procedures are available: presidents, for example, can be impeached or defeated for re-election. They can only be impeached, supposedly, if they deserve to be; they can be defeated without regard to desert. The common rule is that both titles and particular offices are policed—the former with reference to questions of desert, the latter with reference to whatever questions are of interest to interested men and women.

If we were to regard all offices as prizes and distribute (and redistribute) both titles and particular places on the basis of desert, the resulting social structure would be a meritocracy. A distribution of this sort, under this name, is often advocated by people who intend, I think, to guarantee only consideration to the qualifed, not office to the deserving. But on the assumption that there are some people committed to the establishment of a strict meritocracy, it is worth pausing for a moment to consider the philosophical and the practical merits of that idea. There is no way to establish a meritocracy except by attending exclusively to the past record of the candidates. Hence the close connection between meritocracy and testing, for the test provides a simple and objective record. A universal civil service requires a universal civil service examination. No such thing has ever existed, but there is one example that comes close enough to be useful.

The Chinese Examination System

For some thirteen centuries, the Chinese government recruited its officials through an intricate system of examinations. The system extended only to the imperial service. Civil society was a world of *laissez faire:* there were no examinations for businessmen, doctors, engineers, astronomers, musicians, herbalists, specialists in occult prognostics, and so on. The sole reason for participating in what one scholar has called "the examination life" was to secure a state office.[11] But offices were by far the most important source of social prestige in post-feudal China. Though the power of money grew over the thirteen centuries of the examination system, and it was possible during much of that time to purchase offices, high status was overwhelmingly associated with high scores. China was ruled by a class of professionals, and each member of that class carried with him a certificate of merit.

From the emperor's point of view, the purpose of the examinations was, first, to break up the hereditary aristocracy and, second, to collect talent for the state. "The world's men of unusual ambitions have been trapped in my bag!" boasted the emperor T'ai-tsung (627–649) after watching a procession of new graduates.[12] But the trap would not work unless there was equality of opportunity, or something close to that, for the emperor's subjects. So the government struggled (always with inadequate resources) to produce, alongside the examinations, a system of local public schools and scholarships, and took all sorts of precautions to rule out cheating and favoritism. The school system was never completed; the precautions were never entirely effective. But peasant children, the Horatio Algers of old China, did work their way up the "ladder of success," and the grading of examinations was remarkably fair, at least until the decadence of the system in the nineteenth century. In a number of famous cases, examiners who tried to favor their relatives were put to death—a punishment for nepotism never equaled in the West. And the result was a degree of social mobility that has probably also never been equaled in the West, even in modern times. Highly placed and powerful families could not survive a generation or two of inept children.[13]

But was the Chinese system really meritocratic? Were offices held by those who "most deserved" to hold them? It would be difficult to construct a set of arrangements more likely to produce a meritocracy, and yet the history of the examinations serves only to suggest the meaninglessness of the term. During the earliest period (the Tang dynasty), the examinations were supplemented and sometimes superseded by an older system in which local officials were required to recommend meritorious men for government service. There were some sixty itemized "merits" that the officials were supposed to look for, "broadly related to moral character, literary training, administrative ability, and knowledge of military affairs."[14] But however detailed the list, the recommendations were inevitably subjective; too often officials simply pressed their friends and relatives upon the attention of their superiors. The bright and ambitious young men whom the emperor wanted were not the ones he got; the poor were rarely recommended. Slowly, over a period of time, the examination system emerged as the major, virtually the sole, avenue of bureaucratic selection and advancement. It was more objective and more fair. But then the sixty "merits" had to be dropped. The examinations could test only a much more limited range of talent and ability.

I cannot describe the subsequent evolution of the examinations in any detail here. They were designed originally to test the candidates' knowledge of the Confucian classics and, more important, their ability to think in a "Confucian" manner. The conditions of the test were always the special conditions of a mass examination, the tension multiplied by the stakes. Locked in a small compartment, with a small box of food, the candidates wrote elaborate essays and poems on the classical texts and also on contemporary problems of philosophy and government.[15] But a long process of routinization, generated by a kind of collaboration between the candidates and the examiners, led eventually to the suppression of the more speculative questions. Instead, examiners increasingly stressed memorization, philology, and calligraphy, and candidates paid more attention to old examination questions than to the meaning of the old books. What was tested, increasingly, was the ability to take a test. There can't be much doubt that that ability was accurately tested. But it's not clear what meaning we should attach to success. "Talent," wrote the satirical novelist Wu Ching-tzu, "is gained through preparation for examination. If Confucius were present, he would devote himself to preparation for examination. How else could one gain office?"[16] That is like saying that were Hobbes alive today, he would probably get tenure at Harvard. Yes, but would he write *Leviathan?*

The replacement of intellectual life by "examination life" is probably inevitable as soon as the examination becomes the chief means of social advance. And once that has happened, it is no longer certain that the emperor's bag is full of talent: "It is not that the examination system can uncover extraordinary talent," wrote a nineteenth-century critic, "but that extraordinary talent sometimes emerges out of the examination system."[17] But one might well make a similar argument even about the system in its earlier stages. There are, after all, a wide range of human abilities—many of them relevant to, say, provincial administration—that are untested by the study of the Confucian classics. There may even be a deep intuitive knowledge of Confucianism that can't be tested by writing an examination. All such tests are conventional in character, and it is only from within the convention that one can say that successful candidates deserve their degrees and that the subsequent rule of the degree holders constitutes a meritocracy.

In fact, successful candidates did not automatically assume an office. The examinations generated a pool of potential office holders, from which the Board of Civil Appointments, a permanent search committee, made selections, looking perhaps for some subset of the sixty "merits" or arguing about which "merits" were most necessary at a given time. Hence, it can't be said that those who passed the examination deserved to hold an office; only that they were entitled to be considered for a range of offices. Any other system would have been hopelessly rigid, leaving no room for judgments about abilities other than exam taking or, later, for judgments about performance on the job. But all such judgments were particularist and political in character; they had none of the objectivity of exam scores; and it must have been the case that individuals in some sense meritorious were passed over —sometimes intentionally, sometimes not. Similarly, meritorious individuals sometimes failed the examinations. I don't want to say, however, that these individuals deserved an office. That would be to substitute my own judgment for that of the responsible officials. And I have no special insight, any more than they did, into the general or universal meaning of merit.

In the sphere of office, committee work is crucial. More and more today, that work is subject to legal constraints aimed at ensuring fairness and something like objectivity: equal consideration to equally serious candidates. But few people advocate doing away with committees altogether, giving every candidate the same examination (they can never get the same interview), and making office holding automatic for candidates who get such-and-such a score. The committee is appropriate because of its representative character. What is at stake, after all, is not some abstract office but this place, at this moment in time, in this organization or agency, where these other people are already working, and where these issues are being debated. The committee reflects the time and place, speaks for the other people, and is itself an arena for the continuing debate. The choice that it makes, though constrained by certain universal criteria, is above all particularist in character. Candidates are not only fit or unfit in general terms; they also fit or don't fit the place they want to fill. That latter point is always a matter of judgment, and so requires that there be a group of judges, arguing among themselves. Some measures of fitness in the sense of "fitting in" are ruled out, as we shall see. But the list of relevant qualities is always long—like the sixty "merits"; and no one candidate possesses them all to the utmost. The particularity of the office is paralleled by the particularity of the candidates. They are individual men and women, with widely differing strengths and weaknesses. Even if one believed in choosing the one deserving or meritorious (or "best deserving" or most meritorious) person from out of the mass, there would be no way of identifying that person. The members of the selection committee would disagree about the appropriate balance of strengths and weaknesses, and they would disagree about the actual balance in any given individual. Here, too, they would begin by making judgments and end by taking a vote.

Advocates of meritocracy have in mind a simple but far-reaching goal: a place for every person and every person in the right place. Once God was thought to cooperate in this endeavor; now state action is required.

> Some must be great. Great offices will have
> Great talents. And God gives to every man
> The virtue, temper, understanding, taste,
> That lifts him into life, and lets him fall
> Just in the niche he was ordain'd to fill.[18]

But this is a mythic conception of social order and misses entirely our complex understanding of both persons and places. It suggests that, in principle, given full information, all selections should be unanimous, agreed to not only by the selection committee and the successful candidates, but also by the unsuccessful candidates—exactly like judicial decisions, where even convicted criminals ought to be able to acknowledge that they have gotten what they deserve. In practice, selections are not like that; nor are they conceivably like that, unless we imagine a world where we could not only predict but actually foresee the future performances of all the candidates, comparing factual with counterfactual knowledge of the years to come. Even then, I suspect that the arguments of search committees would be different from the arguments of juries, but the precise nature of the difference would be harder to make out.

The Meaning of Qualification

Strictly speaking, there is no such thing as a meritocracy. Particular choices always have to be made among possible "merits" or, more accurately, among the range of human qualities, and then among relatively qualified individuals. There is no way of avoiding these choices, for no individual has any claim on the office or any prior title to it; nor is there any single quality or objective ordering of qualities in accordance with which an impersonal selection might be made. To call a job an "office" is to say only that discretionary authority has been politicized, not that it has been abolished. Still, it is necessary to fix certain constraints even on the authority of representative committees and so to mark off the sphere of office from that of politics. Committees are constrained in two ways: they must give equal consideration to every qualified candidate, and they must take into account only relevant qualities. These two constraints overlap because the idea of relevance enters into our understanding of equal consideration. But I will take them up separately.

Citizenship is the first office, the crucial social and political "place" and the precondition of all the others. The boundaries of the political community are also the limits of the process of politicization. Non-citizens have no candidate rights; the procedural safeguards of equal consideration don't extend to them. Jobs don't have to be advertised in foreign journals; recruiters need not venture beyond the borders; deadlines need not be set with regard to the international mails. It may be foolish to exclude foreigners from consideration for certain offices (university professorships most clearly, where we might also feel bound to recognize membership in the "republic of letters"), but exclusion is no violation of their rights. The right to equal consideration, like the right to "fair shares" of welfare and security, arises only in the context of a shared political life. It is one of the things the members owe to one another.

Among citizens, equal consideration applies at every point of selection, not only among candidates for office, but also among candidates for training, and hence is a constraint not only on this particular selection committee but on every committee and on all those decisions that gradually narrow the pool of qualified candidates. Imagine a child of five able to set long-term goals for himself, to shape a project, to decide, say, that he wants to be a doctor. He should have roughly the same chance as any other child—similarly ambitious, similarly intelligent, similarly sensitive to the needs of others—to get the necessary education and win the desired place. I won't try to say here what educational arrangements this equality would require; that is the subject of another chapter. But I do want to stress that the equality will always be rough. The claim that every citizen should have exactly the same share of available opportunities doesn't make much sense, not only because of the unpredictable impact of particular schools and teachers on particular students, but also because of the inevitable placement of different individuals in different applicant pools. Simple equality can be promised only within a single pool at a single time and place. But applicant pools differ radically over time, and conceptions of office change. And so an individual who would have looked well qualified for a particular place last year is lost in the crowd this year; or his qualities are no longer those the selection committee has centrally in mind. Equal consideration does not mean that competitive conditions must be held constant for all individuals; only, whatever the conditions, the qualities of each individual must be attended to.

In fact, not qualities simply but qualifications are at issue here. Qualifications are pointed qualities or qualities relevant to a particular office. Relevance, of course, is always a matter of dispute, and the range of permissible disagreement is wide. But that range has limits; there are some things that shouldn't enter into the discussions of the selection committee. If there were no limits, the idea of equal consideration would collapse. For what we mean when we say that all candidates should be considered is that they all should have (roughly) the same chance to present their credentials and to make the best case they can on their own behalf. The case they try to make is that they can do the job and do it well. And in order to make that case, they have to be able to form some notion of what doing it well means, what skills it requires, what attitudes and values are appropriate, and so on. If they are accepted or rejected for reasons that have nothing to do with any of this, then it can't be said that their qualifications have been attended to. If we were not able to distinguish qualifications from qualities, then we would never know whether individuals have had a chance to qualify. Nor would it be possible for individuals, like my imaginary five-year-old, to set goals for themselves and to work in some rational way for their achievement.

But we do know, at least in general terms, what qualities are relevant, for relevant qualities are inherent in the practice, abstracted from the experience, of office holding. Selection committees are committed to look for those qualities—committed, that is, to look for qualified candidates, not only out of fairness to the candidates but also out of a concern for all those people who depend upon the service of qualified office holders. Their dependency has to be taken into account, too, though not necessarily their preferences about either qualities or candidates. The right to equal consideration works like any other right, setting limits on the enforcement of popular preferences. But within the range of relevant qualities, or within the range of legitimate debate about relevance, popular preferences should count; we should expect them to be represented on the selection committee.

The range of relevance is best understood by considering what lies beyond it: abilities that won't be used on the job, personal characteristics that won't affect performance, and political affiliations and group identifications beyond citizenship itself. We don't require candidates for office to jump through hoops, like Swift's Lilliputians. We don't rule out men and women with red hair or bad taste in movies or a passion for ice-skating. Rotarians, Seventh Day Adventists, Trotskyites, long-term members of the Vegetarian Party, immigrants from Norway, Bessarabia, the South Sea Islands, are none of them barred from office holding. But these are easy cases. In fact, all three categories—abilities, characteristics, and identifications—are problematic. It is clear, for example, that the Chinese examinations, particularly in their later phase, tested abilities that can at best have been only marginally relevant to the offices at stake. The same can surely be said of many civil service examinations today. These are merely conventional ways of reducing the size of the applicant pool; and if candidates have an equal chance to prepare for them, examinations are not necessarily objectionable. But insofar as their use precludes promotion up the ranks on the basis of experience and performance, it ought to be resisted. For what we want is the best possible performance on the job, not on the exam.

Greater difficulties are raised by a number of personal characteristics; I will take age as an example. For most offices, the age of the candidate tells us nothing at all about the kind of job he will do. But it does tell us, roughly, how long he will do it. Is that a relevant consideration? Surely people ought to be able to change not only their jobs but also their careers, retrain themselves, start again in middle age. Consistency in office seeking isn't always an admirable quality. And yet in organizations built on long-term commitment and in jobs requiring extensive on-the-job training, older candidates are likely to be at a disadvantage. Perhaps their maturity should be a balancing consideration—even if younger candidates complain that they have not had an equal chance to mature. The thought of trying to balance length of service against maturity in office suggests forcefully how far we are from judgments about desert and how committed we are to controversy about relevance.

The deepest and most divisive controversies focus on the importance of connection, affiliation, and membership. It was with reference to these that the idea of office, as I have described it, first took shape. The first quality to be declared irrelevant to office holding was family connection to the person making the appointment. Not that nepotism is uncommon in the sphere of office, but it is commonly regarded as a form of corruption. It is a (relatively minor) example of tyranny to say that because so-and-so is my relative, he should exercise the prerogatives of office. At the same time, the reiterated campaigns against nepotism suggest again how problematic the idea of relevance is and how difficult it is to apply.

What's Wrong with Nepotism?

The term referred originally to the practice of certain popes and bishops who assigned offices to their nephews (or illegitimate sons), seeking, like feudal office holders, to have heirs and not merely successors. Since it was one of the purposes of clerical celibacy to cut the church loose from the feudal system and to ensure a succession of qualified individuals, the practice was identified as sinful early on.[19] The identification was so strict (though it could rarely be enforced in the feudal period) that it came to rule out any appointment of relatives either by ecclesiastical officials or by lay patrons, even if they possessed all the relevant qualities. The same thing happened, many years later, in political life; and here the argument was commonly extended, though with a diminishing sense of "sin," from relatives to friends. Sometimes the ban on relatives has been given legal standing, as in Norway, for example, where it is against the law for two members of the same family to serve in the same cabinet. In academic life, too, university departments have often been barred from hiring the relatives (but not the friends) of current members. The root idea is that objective standards are unlikely to be brought to bear in such decisions. This is probably true; but, still, an absolute ban seems unfair. What is wanted is a hiring procedure that discounts family membership, not one that disqualifies all members.

Sometimes, however, membership can't be discounted. In certain political offices, for example, we expect officials to choose as their associates men and women upon whom they can depend, who are their friends or associates in some party or movement. And then, why not their relatives, if they are close to their relatives? Trust may well be surest when connections are of blood, and trustfulness is an important qualification for office. We might say, then, that the Norwegian law is more strict than is required by the principle of equal consideration. When President John F. Kennedy appointed his brother attorney general, it was without doubt an example of nepotism, but not of the sort that we need be concerned to ban. Robert Kennedy was qualified enough, and his closeness to his brother would probably help him in the work he had to do. This permissiveness, however, cannot be extended very far. We can see its difficulties if we consider the claim of racial, ethnic, and religious groups that they ought to be served exclusively by office holders chosen from among their own members. Here is a kind of collective nepotism, and its effect would be to narrow radically the scope of candidate rights.

It may be the case, again, that for certain offices (in certain parts of a city, say) men and women are needed who share the racial or ethnic identification of the residents, speak their language, are intimately familiar with their customs, and so on. Perhaps this is a matter of routine effectiveness or even—as with the police—of physical safety. And then selection committees will legitimately look for the necessary people. But we will want, I think, to limit the ways in which group membership counts as a qualification, much as we limit the ways in which blood relationship counts, and for similar reasons. The extension of trust or "friendship" beyond the family and of citizenship beyond race, ethnicity, and religion, is a significant political achievement; and one of its major purposes is precisely to secure the career open to talents—that is, the candidate rights of all citizens.

We might choose simply to stand by this achievement. But the question whether group membership ought to count as a qualification for office is complicated by the fact that it has so often counted as a disqualification. Because of their membership, and not for any reason having to do with their individual qualifications, men and women have been discriminated against in the distribution of offices. Hence it is said, for the sake of fairness and redress, we should now discriminate in their favor, even set aside a certain number of offices exclusively for them. This claim is so central to contemporary political debate that I shall need to take it up at some length. Nothing else tests so sharply the meaning of equal consideration.

The Reservation of Office

The crucial political issue is the justice of quotas or reserved offices, for which membership in some group is a necessary, though not presumably a sufficient qualification.[20] In principle, as I have already argued, all offices are reserved or potentially reserved to members of the political community. Further reservation is and should be controversial. I want to postpone for a moment the controversy about reservation as a form of redress and ask first whether it might be justifiable in itself, as a permanent feature of the distributive system. For it is sometimes taken as a sure sign of discrimination that the pattern of office holding within one group is different from the pattern within other groups.[21] Certain offices, say, are held disproportionately by the members of one race or by men and women with common ethnic origins or religious affiliations. If justice requires or necessarily constitutes a single reiterated pattern, then legislators and judges will have to be called in to establish the right proportions. Whatever distribution of offices prevails within the most prosperous or powerful group will have to be reiterated within every other group. The more perfect the reiteration, the more certain we can be that particular candidates are not suffering because of their membership.

That justice in this sense involves considerable coercion might be a small matter if the coercion were remedial and temporary in character and if the reiterated pattern turned out to be the natural product of equal consideration. Insofar as the groups that constitute our pluralist society are really different from one another, however, neither of these conditions is likely to hold. For the patterns of office holding are determined not only by the decisions of selection committees but also by a multitude of individual decisions: to train or not to train, to apply or not to apply for this or that job. And these individual decisions are shaped in turn by family life, socialization, neighborhood culture, and so on. A pluralist society, with different kinds of families and neighborhoods, will naturally produce a diversity of patterns. Justice as reiteration could only be an artificial order.

That is not yet an argument against reiteration, only a characterization of it. At many points in our social life, we interfere with natural—that is, uncoerced and spontaneous—processes. The distribution of offices to relatives is undoubtedly a natural process. In each case of interference, however, we have to think carefully about what is at stake. And the first thing at stake here is equal consideration for all citizens. When offices are reserved, the members of all those groups except the one for which the reservation is made are treated as if they were foreigners. Their qualifications are not attended to; they have no candidate rights. This sort of thing might be acceptable in a bi-national state, where the members of the two nations stand, in fact, as foreigners to one another. What is required between them is mutual accommodation, not justice in any positive sense; and accommodation may best be achieved in a federal system where both groups have some guaranteed representation.[22] Even a more loosely pluralist society may well require (for the sake of mutual accommodation) racially or ethnically "balanced" party tickets, say, or cabinets and courts that include representatives of all the major groups. I am not inclined to regard this sort of thing as a violation of equal consideration: being a "representative man" or a "representative woman" is, after all, a kind of qualification in politics. And so long as the arrangements are informal, they can always be overturned for the sake of outstanding candidates. But the theory of justice as reiteration would require that every set of office holders in the universal civil service correspond in its racial and ethnic composition to the American population as a whole. And that, in turn, would require large-scale denials of equal consideration. Equality would obviously be denied whenever the proportion of applicants from this or that group differed from its assigned representation. It would, indeed, be denied even if the proportion was exactly right, because applicants from each group would be compared only with their own "kind," on the assumption that qualifications distributed evenly across kinds, an assumption that for any given applicant pool is bound to be false.

But perhaps the United States ought to be a federation of groups rather than a community of citizens. And perhaps each group ought to have its own set of indigenous office holders. Only then, it might be argued, would the group as a whole be equal to all other groups. What is at stake, on this view, is not equal consideration for individuals but equal standing for races and religions: communal integrity, self-respect for the members as members. Equality of this sort is a common demand of national liberation movements. For it is a feature of imperialist rule that key offices in the state and economy are colonized by outsiders. As soon as independence is won, a struggle begins to take these offices back. That struggle is often waged in brutal and unjust ways, but it isn't in itself unjust for a newly liberated nation to seek to staff its bureaucracies and professions with its own nationals. In these circumstances, collective nepotism and the reservation of office may well be legitimate. But as this example suggests, reservation is possible only after boundaries have been drawn between members and strangers. In American society today, there are no such such boundaries. Individuals move freely across the vaguely and informally drawn line between ethnic or religious identification and non-identification; the line is in no way policed; the movements are not even recorded. It would be possible, of course, to change all this, but it is important to stress how radical a change would be required. Only if every American citizen had some clearcut racial, ethnic, or religious identification (or series of identifications, since the groups to which we belong have overlapping memberships), and only if these identifications were legally established and regularly checked, would it be possible to reserve to each group its own set of offices.*

The principle of equal consideration would then apply only within the federated groups. Equality is always relative; it requires us to compare the treatment of this individual to some set of others, not to all others. We can always change the distributive system simply by redrawing its boundaries. There is no single set of just boundaries (though there are unjust boundaries—that is, those that enclose people, as in a ghetto, against their will). Hence a federal arrangement, so long as it was established through some democratic process, would not be unjust. We would compare members to their fellow members and then groups to other groups, and our judgments about justice would depend upon how the comparisons turned out. But this would, I think, be an unwise arrangement for the United States today, inconsistent with our historical traditions and shared understandings—inconsistent, too, with contemporary living patterns, deeply and bitterly divisive. I am going to assume that advocates of reserved offices don't have anything like this in mind. They are focused on more immediate problems and, whatever they sometimes say, do not in fact intend that the remedies they propose should be generalized and made permanent.

The Case of American Blacks

At this point, it is important to be as concrete as possible. The immediate problems are those of American blacks, and they arise in the context of a painful history. In part, this is a history of economic and educational discrimination, so that the number of black men and women holding offices in American society has (until very recently at least) been lower than it should be, given the qualification levels of black candidates. More important, it is a history of slavery, repression, and degradation, so that black neighborhood culture and communal institutions do not support efforts to qualify in anything like the way they would have had they developed under conditions of freedom and racial equality. (We can say this without claiming that all cultures and communi-

---

*This fact is painfully visible in the case of the Indian untouchables, for whom the government has designed an elaborate system of reserved offices. In principle, India has abolished the caste system, but the untouchables can only be helped if they can be recognized, and proportionality in office holding can only be established if they can be counted. Hence the category "untouchable" had to be reintroduced in the 1961 census, and procedures had to be established by which individuals seeking reserved offices could prove their status. The result, as reported by Harold Isaacs, who is generally sympathetic to reservation, is a hardening of caste lines: "The policy of giving relief by caste groups has increased . . . caste immobility."[23]

ties, even under ideal conditions, would provide identical kinds of support.) The first of the problems of American blacks can be remedied by insisting on the practical details of equal consideration: fair employment practices, open search and selection procedures, extensive recruiting, serious efforts to discover talent even when it isn't conventionally displayed, and so on. But the second problem requires more radical and far-reaching treatment. For a time, it is said, blacks must be guaranteed a fixed share of offices, because only a significant number of office holders interacting with clients and constituents can create a stronger culture.

I want to stress that the argument I am now considering is not that the black community ought to be served—can only rightly be served—by black politicians, postmen, schoolteachers, doctors, and so on, and that all other communities ought similarly to be served by their own members. The force of the argument does not depend upon its generalizability. Or rather, the appropriate generalization is this: that any group similarly disadvantaged should be helped in similar ways. The argument is historically shaped and limited, adapted to particular conditions, temporary in character. The norm remains that of equal consideration for individual citizens, and that norm is to be restored as soon as blacks escape from the trap that their blackness has become in a society with a long history of racism.

But the difficulty with the remedy proposed is that it would require the denial of equal consideration to white candidates who are neither participants in, nor direct beneficiaries of, racist practices. An important and morally legitimate social purpose is to be served by violating the candidate rights of individuals.[24] But perhaps that description is too strong. Ronald Dworkin has argued that the right at issue is not a right to equal consideration when offices are distributed, but only a more general right to equal consideration when policies about office holding are worked out. So long as we count each citizen equally when we weigh the costs against the benefits of reserving offices, we violate no one's rights.[25] It is useful to set this claim against the claim of the meritocrats. If they suggest too close a connection between jobs and the qualities relevant to doing them, Dworkin suggests too loose a connection. He seems to deny that there are any significant limits on the qualities that might count as qualifications. In our culture, however, careers are supposed to be open to talents; and people chosen for an office will want to be assured that they were chosen because they really do possess, to a greater degree than other candidates, the talents that the search committee thinks necessary to the office. The other candidates will want to be assured that their talents were seriously considered. And all the rest of us will want to know that both assurances are true. That's why reserved offices in the United States today have been the subject not only of controversy but also of deception. Self-esteem and self-respect, mutual confidence and trust, are at stake as well as social and economic status.

Rights are also at stake—not natural or human rights but rights derived from the social meaning of offices and careers and vindicated in the course of long political struggles. Just as we could not adopt a system of preventive detention without violating the rights of innocent people, even if we weighed fairly the costs and benefits of the system as a whole, so we can't adopt a quota system without violating the rights of candidates. Dworkin's argument has a form that seems to me entirely appropriate in the case of public expenditures. So long as the general program of expenditure is democratically determined, a decision to invest heavily in this or that depressed area or to favor agriculture over industry raises no moral problems, even if individuals are, as they will be, advantaged and disadvantaged. But offices are careers and prison terms are lives, and these sorts of goods cannot be distributed the way money can; they cut too close to the core of individuality and personal integrity. Once the community undertakes to distribute them, it must attend closely to their social meaning. And that requires equal consideration for all equally serious candidates and (as I will argue in chapter 11) punishment only for criminals.

But if rights are at stake in these cases, rights can be overridden. They represent very strong barriers to certain sorts of intrusive or injurious treatment, but these are never absolute barriers. We break through them when we must, in time of crisis or great danger, when we think we have no alternative. Hence, any argument in favor of reserving offices must include a description of the current crisis and a detailed account of the inadequacy of alternative measures. Conceivably, such an argument can be made in the United States today, but I don't think it has yet been made. However starkly one paints the picture of black communal life, it seems clear that programs and policies that might plausibly be expected to alter the picture remain untried. Indeed, the reservation of office looks more like a first than a last resort—even though it comes after many years of doing nothing at all. The reason it has been turned to first is that, while it violates individual rights, it poses no threat to established hierarchies or to the class structure as a whole. For the purpose of reserving offices, as I have already argued, is to reiterate hierarchy, not to challenge or transform it. By contrast, the alternative measures, though they would violate no one's rights, would require a significant redistribution of wealth and resources (for the sake, say, of a national commitment to full employment). But this would be a redistribution in line with the social understandings that shape the welfare state and, though opposition would be strong, the redistribution of wealth is more likely than the reservation of office to have enduring results. In general, the struggle against a racist past is more likely to be won if it is fought in ways that build on, rather than challenge, understandings of the social world shared by the great majority of Americans, black and white alike.

The reservation of office has another feature that may help explain why it holds a favored position (among alternatives, to be sure, none of which are strongly supported by contemporary political élites). In principle, the men and women denied offices as a result of reservation will simply be the more marginal (white) applicants, given whatever understanding of qualification, and hence of marginality, particular selection committees adopt. The impact will be felt in all religions, ethnic groups, and social classes. In practice, however, the impact is certain to be less diffuse and therefore less threatening to powerful individuals and families. It will be felt, above all, by the next most disadvantaged group, by those men and women whose neighborhood culture and communal institutions provide not much more support than black candidates get from their own culture and institutions. Reservation won't fulfill the Biblical prophecy according to which the last shall be first; it will guarantee, at most, that the last shall be next to last. I don't think that there is any way to avoid this result, except by increasing the number of groups for which offices are reserved and turning the remedial program into something much more systematic and permanent. The victims of unequal consideration will come from the weakest or the next-weakest group. Unless one is prepared to give up the very idea of qualification, the costs cannot be distributed any further.*

---

*It is interesting that the policy of veteran's preference in civil service employment seems to have been widely accepted, though there has been some political opposition and a number of legal challenges. The range of the acceptance may have something to do with the range of the benefit: veterans come from all social classes and racial groups. Or perhaps it is commonly agreed that veterans have in fact lost years of schooling or job experience, while other members of their own age cohort moved ahead, so that a policy of preference re-establishes equality between the same groups that were made unequal by conscription. In practice, however, veterans are often helped at the expense of the weakest members of the next generation of candidates, who enjoy no advantage in training or experience. Even this is sometimes justified as a legitimate expression of national gratitude. But surely offices are the wrong currency with which to pay such debts. Educational benefits are better, since they are actually paid by the nation—that is, the body of taxed citizens—and not by an arbitrarily selected subgroup. If this is right, reparation rather than reservation might be a better way to compensate American blacks for the effects of past mistreatment.[26]

Professionalism and the Insolence of Office

What makes the distribution of office so important is that so much else is distributed along with office (or some offices): honor and status, power and prerogative, wealth and comfort. Office is a dominant good, carrying others in its train. The claim to dominance is "the insolence of office"; and if we could find some way to control that insolence, office holding would begin to take on its proper proportions. We need, then, to describe the internal character of the sphere of office—the activities, relationships, and rewards that legitimately go along with holding an office. What comes after qualification and selection?

An office is both a social function and a personal career. It requires the exercise of talents and skills for a purpose. The office holder makes a living from his performance, but his first reward is the performance itself, the actual work for which he has prepared, which he presumably wants to do, and which other men and women want to do as well. The work may be harried, intricate, exhausting, but it is nevertheless a great satisfaction. It is satisfying also to talk about it with colleagues, develop a jargon, keep secrets from laymen. "Shoptalk" is a more likely pleasure for people who work in offices than for those who work in shops. The crucial secret, of course, is that the work could easily be redistributed. A large number of men and women could do it as well, and enjoy it as much, as the current incumbents.

I don't mean to deny the value of expert knowledge—or the existence of experts. The mechanic who repairs my car knows things that I don't know and that are, moreover, mysterious to me. So does the doctor who looks after my body, and the lawyer who leads me through the labyrinth of the law. But, in principle, I can learn what they know; other people have learned it; and still other people have learned some of it. Even by myself and as I am, I know enough to question the advice I get from the experts I consult, and I can strengthen my hand by talking to my friends and reading a bit. The distribution of socially useful knowledge is not a seamless web, but there are no enormous gaps. Or rather, unless they are artificially maintained, the gaps will get filled in, by different sorts of people with different talents and skills and different conceptions of expertise.

Professionalism is one form of artificial maintenance. It is at the same time much more than that; it is an ethical code, a social bond, a pattern of mutual regulation and self-discipline. But surely the chief purpose of professional organization is to make a particular body of knowledge the exclusive possession of a particular body of men (more recently, of women, too).[27] This is an effort undertaken by the office holders on their own behalf. Their motives are, in part, material; they aim to limit their numbers so that they can command high fees and salaries. This is the second reward of office holding. But there is more than money at stake when groups of office holders lay claim to professional status. Status itself is at stake: the third reward. Professional men and women have an interest in specifying the nature of their own performances, shucking off tasks that seem to them below the level of their training and certification. They seek a place in a hierarchy and shape their work to the heights they hope to attain. New professions are then formed to fill out the hierarchy, each additional group seeking to isolate some performance or set of performances where competence can be certified and, to some degree at least, monopolized. But it is a feature of these newer professions, as T. H. Marshall has pointed out, that while there is an educational ladder leading into them, "there is no ladder leading out." The adjacent heights can be reached only "by a different road starting at a different level of the educational system."[28] Doctors and nurses offer a useful example of closely connected professionals with nontransferable certificates. Professionalism, then, is a way of drawing lines.

It is also a way of establishing power relationships. Professionals exercise power down the work hierarchy and also in their relations with clients. Properly speaking, they issue commands to their subordinates, but only hypothetical imperatives to clients. If you want to get well, they say, do this and this. But the greater the distance they are able to establish, the greater the secrets at their command, the less hypothetical their imperatives are. Contemptuous of our ignorance, they simply tell us what to do. There are, of course, men and women who resist the temptation to move from authoritative knowledge to authoritarian conduct, but the temptation and the opportunity are always there: this is the fourth reward of office.

The expansion of office and the rise of professionalism go hand in hand; for as soon as we set out to ensure the appointment of qualified people, we invite the inflation of specialized knowledge and expertise. That is one very good reason for containing the expansion and denying the universality of the civil service, but it is also a reason for setting limits to the dominance of official (and professional) status and its wide-ranging convertibility. We do want qualified people to serve as bureaucrats, doctors, engineers, teachers, and so on, but we don't want these people to rule over us. We can find ways to pay them their due short of bearing with their insolence.

But what is their due? Each of the four rewards of office has its appropriate and inappropriate forms. To some extent, these are determined politically—the product of ideological arguments and common understandings; and one can only insist that established office holders, members of this or that profession, have no exclusive rights in the process of determination. But it ought to be possible to suggest some general guidelines, derived from the social understanding of office itself. The first reward is the pleasure of performance, and there is no doubt that qualified office holders are entitled to all the pleasure they can derive from the work they do. But they are not entitled to shape their performances so as to heighten their pleasure (or their income, status, or power) at other people's expense. They serve communal purposes, and so their work is subject to the control of the citizens of the community. We exercise that control whenever we specify the qualifications for a particular office or the standards of competent or ethical conduct. There is no *a priori* reason, then, to accede to any particular segregation of specialized skills and techniques. For it is always possible that the community would be better served by requiring office holders to move back and forth across the existing lines of specialization. Consider, for example, a recent proposal for the replacement of fee-for-service physicians by "functional health teams":

> Members of the team should be prepared to adapt their skills to consumer needs rather than to shift the consumer to another health worker as a professional expediency. The physician should be prepared and willing to assume "nursing" roles when warranted and conversely the nurse to provide treatment if appropriate.[29]

That may or may not be a good idea, but the proposal makes a useful point. Conventional performances often fail to serve the purpose of the office; they may even represent a conspiracy against the purpose of the office. So the performer must be bent to his proper task.

And then he must be given his proper financial reward. But what the size of the reward should be, we have no easy way to determine. The labor market doesn't work well here, chiefly because of the dominance of office, but also because of the social character of the work that officials do and the need for certification and licensing. The holders of high office, especially, have been able to limit the size of the applicant pool from which their peers and successors are chosen and so to push up their collective income. Undoubtedly, the pool for some offices has real limits, even given a realistic set of qualifications. But it is plainly not the market alone, or not the free market, that is at work in setting the wages of office.[30] Sometimes office holders simply hold us up. Then we have every right to resist—and to look for some political counterpart to professional power. Where important work is at stake, as Tawney has argued, "no decent man can stand out for his price. A general does not haggle with his government for the precise pecuniary equivalent of his contribution to victory. A sentry who gives the alarm to a sleeping battalion does not spend the next day collecting the capital value of the lives he has saved."[31] Indeed, this is too optimistic: the domestic equivalents of the general and the sentry often enough won't fight at all or even sound the alarm until they have won their "price." But we have no reason to accede to their demand; nor is there any evidence that a resolute refusal to accede would result in vacant offices or unqualified office holders. Military offices are an interesting example here, for they appear to attract qualified individuals whenever their social prestige is high, without regard to the salaries offered, which are generally lower than the same individuals could command on the market. But they prefer—it's not unreasonable—another sort of command.

The argument is sometimes made that offices, especially professional offices, must be well paid so that the incumbents can "pursue the life of the mind."[32] But the life of the mind is, as lives go, relatively inexpensive; and in any case, the wages of office are rarely spent on its requirements. Once we have understood the complex processes by which office holders are selected, and recognized the intrinsic rewards of office, I can see no argument against holding down income differentials between offices and other sorts of employment. And, in fact, that is the steady tendency of democratic decision making. The classic example is the resolution of the Paris commune of 1871 that "the public service should be done at workmen's wages."[33] But the tendency is visible in all democratic states and most clearly with regard to offices in the state bureaucracy. In 1911, for example, the income of higher civil servants in Great Britain was 17.8 times as high as the income per head of the employed population; in 1956, it was only 8.9 times as high. The comparable figures for the United States (for 1900 and 1958) were 7.8 and 4.1; for Norway (1910 and 1957), they were 5.3 and 2.1.[34] The trend is general for all offices and all professions, with the exception of doctors in the United States, where we seem to have followed George Bernard Shaw's advice: "If you are going to have doctors, you had better have doctors well-off."[35] But the establishment of a national health service would probably reduce differentials here, too.

"Honor," wrote Adam Smith, "makes a great part of the reward of all honorable professions. In point of pecuniary gain, all things considered, they are generally under-recompensed."[36] I doubt that last point, but the first is certainly true, and it is true for all office holders, up and down whatever status hierarchy exists. But honor is a reward that ought to be measured out by performance and not by place; only when it is so measured can we properly speak of it as something that people deserve. When it is deserved, it is the highest reward of office. To do a job well, and to be known to do it well: surely this is what men and women most want from their work. By contrast, to insist upon honor without regard to performance is one of the most common forms of official insolence. "If lawyers dispensed true justice, and physicians possessed the true art of healing, they would not need square bonnets [the symbol of their office]," wrote Pascal, who thought justice and healing beyond the capacity of man-without-God.[37] But at least we can ask that lawyers and doctors come as close as they can to our ideals of justice and healing, and we can refuse to pay tribute to their bonnets.

The power of office holders is harder to limit (and I shall consider it only briefly here and come back to it when I discuss the sphere of politics). Office is an important reason for exercising authority, but the rule of professionals and bureaucrats, even of qualified professionals and bureaucrats, is not attractive. They will use their offices whenever they can to extend their power beyond what their qualifications warrant or their function requires. That's why it is so important that the men and women who are subjected to the authority of office holders have a voice in determining the nature of the function. In part, this determination is informal, worked out in the daily encounters between office holders and clients. It ought to be one of the chief purposes of public education to prepare people for these encounters, to make citizens more knowledgeable and offices less mysterious. But it is also necessary to act in other ways to fill in the gaps in the distribution of knowledge and power: to discourage the segregation of specialties and specialists, to impose more cooperative patterns of work, and to supplement the self-regulation of professionals with one or another sort of communal supervision (review boards, for example). This last is most important, and especially so at local levels where popular participation is most realistic. Here the argument about welfare bureaucrats can be generalized to all office holders: they can only do their job properly if they don't do it alone. Indeed, they have no right to do it alone, despite the fact that their competence has been certified by the constituted authorities who presumably represent the body of clients and consumers. For clients and consumers have a more immediate interest, and their collective judgments of the performance of office holders are crucial to the ongoing work. The point is to subject not "experts" to "reds" but office holders to citizens. Only then will it be clear to everyone that office is a form of service and not yet another occasion for tyranny.

The Containment of Office

There are two reasons for the expansion of office. The first has to do with the political control of activities and employments vital to the well-being of the community; the second has to do with "fair equality of opportunity." Both are good reasons, but neither separately nor together do they require a universal civil service. What they do require is the elimination or curtailment of private (individual and group) discretion with regard to certain sorts of jobs. Democratic politics takes the place of private discretion. Its mandate may be exercised directly by bureaucrats or judges, or indirectly by committees of citizens acting in accordance with publicly established rules; but the critical reference is to the political community as a whole, and effective power lies with the state. Any system that even comes close to a universal civil service is bound to be a centralized operation. The inevitable tendency of all efforts to achieve political control and equality of opportunity is to reinforce and enhance centralized power. As in the other areas of social life, the attempt to defeat tyranny raises the specter of new tyrannies.

But not all jobs need be turned into offices. I have said that offices belong to the people who are served by them: elective and state administrative offices to the people as a whole; professional and corporate offices to clients and consumers who can only be represented politically through the state apparatus. But there are clearly jobs to which this description doesn't usefully apply or where its application would cost far more than it could conceivably be worth; and there are jobs that seem to belong to smaller groups of people, where the relevant politics is the politics of the group, not of the state. If we look at some examples, we will quickly see, I think, that a powerful argument can be made against the idea of office and in favor of decentralized search and selection procedures.

Office

The World of the Petty Bourgeoisie

I have already argued for the value of entrepreneurial activity. Small stores, industrial shops, and the trade in services constitute together a world of work and exchange that is socially valuable: the source, occasionally, of economic innovation; the staple of neighborhood life. In the United States, most jobs in the petty bourgeois sector are exempt from affirmative action and fair employment practices laws; effective regulation just isn't possible. But it is possible to eliminate the sector entirely (or at least to drive it underground), as has been done in the so-called socialist states—and this in the name of equality. For it is obvious that jobs in stores, shops, and services are not distributed "fairly." Nor can eager candidates qualify for the available opportunities through some impersonal procedure. The petty-bourgeois economy is a personalist world, where favors are constantly being exchanged and jobs given out to friends and relatives. Nepotism is not merely approved; it often appears to be morally required. Within the limits of this morality, discretion reigns supreme: the discretion of owners, families, tightly knit unions, local political bosses, and so on.

And yet, interference by the constituted authorities seems to me not only undesirable but illegitimate. Partly, this is a matter of scale. Considered *en masse,* entrepreneurial activity is very important; but the individual enterprises are not very important, and the community has no reason to seek control over them. (Or, it should seek only minimal control—as, for example, in the establishment of a minimum wage.) But one must also attend to the forms of petty-bourgeois life, where jobs are located within a particular kind of social network: close quarters, daily routines, local connections, personal service, familial cooperation. It is no accident that a succession of newly arrived immigrant groups have been able to move into this economic world and to prosper there. For they can help one another in ways that cease to be possible once they enter the impersonal world of office holding.

Workers' Control

Imagine now that some substantial part of the American economy is made up of democratically run companies and factories. I mean to defend workers' control later, in chapter 12. But I shall anticipate that argument (again) in order to ask what sorts of hiring procedures would be appropriate in, say, a factory commune. Should the democratically elected personnel manager or search committee be required to live up to the standards of "fair equality of opportunity"? It is probably inaccurate to speak here of "hiring procedures." Once a commune has been established, what is really at stake is the admission of new members. And qualification in the strict sense—the ability to do the job or to learn to do the job—seems only the first requirement for admission. The present members are free, if they like, to set additional requirements, having to do with the sense they have of their common life. But are they free to favor their relatives, friends, members of this or that ethnic group, men and women with particular political commitments?

In a society with a long history of racism, it would make sense to rule out racial criteria, hence to impose a minimal set of fair employment practices. But beyond this, the admissions process is properly left in the hands of the members. Presumably their commune will be located within some federal structure, and they will operate within a framework of rules: safety regulations, quality standards, and so on. But if they cannot choose their co-workers, it is difficult to see in what sense they can be said to "control" their workplace. And if they do have control, then one can assume that there will be different sorts of workplace, run on different principles, including those of ethnic, religious, and political homogeneity. And it may well happen that at a given time, in a given place, the most successful factory will be run largely by Italians, say, or by Mormons. I don't see anything wrong with that, so long as success isn't convertible outside its proper sphere.

Political Patronage

There are many government jobs, especially at local levels, that do not require any great skill and that commonly turn over at a fairly rapid rate. These are offices by definition, since they can be given out only by the constituted authorities. A lottery among the men and women who hold whatever minimal qualifications are called for would seem an obvious distributive procedure. This is the way we assign places on juries, for example; and it would certainly be appropriate, too, for local councils, commissions, review boards, courthouse jobs of various sorts, and so on. But given the authority of the elective principle in the United States, there appears to be nothing illegitimate about a patronage system—that is, a distribution by elected officials, conceived now as victorious political leaders, to their associates and followers. This is, indeed, to turn offices into "spoils"; but so long as these are not offices for which people might prepare themselves by months or years of training, and so long as experienced office holders are not arbitrarily displaced, no one is treated unfairly by the transformation. And it isn't implausible to argue that for certain sorts of government work, political activity is itself an important qualification.

Indeed, successful political activity is the crucial qualification for the highest offices: we don't distribute the jobs we call "representative" on anything like meritocratic grounds—or, at least, the merits at issue are not the sort that we could evaluate through an examination system. Here the distributive process is entirely politicized; and though the ideal voter should, perhaps, conduct himself like the member of a search committee, the actual body of voters is not constrained in the same way search committees are. We might trace a continuum of increasing freedom of choice from juries to committees to electorates. And then elected officials are, quite plausibly, allowed to draw some of their supporters after them into office, exercising the same discretion that was exercised when they themselves were chosen.

A patronage system serves to generate loyalty, commitment, and participation, and it may well be a necessary feature of any genuinely localist or decentralized democracy. A universal civil service is probably as incompatible with town democracy as with factory democracy. Or, local government, like small business, works best when there is room allowed for friendship and the exchange of favors. Once again, this is a question partly of scale, partly of the character of the jobs at stake. I don't mean to deny the importance of an impersonal, politically neutral bureaucracy, but that importance will be greater or less for different sorts of public activity. There is a range of activity for which partisan discretion seems, if not wholly appropriate, at least not inappropriate. One might even make it a matter of general agreement and expectation that certain jobs would "rotate" among political activists, depending on their success or failure on election day.

What these three examples suggest is that the establishment of a universal civil service would require a war not only against the pluralism and complexity of any human society, but quite specifically against democratic pluralism and complexity. But wouldn't that be a just war, a campaign for "fair equality of opportunity?" I have tried to argue that equality of opportunity is a standard for the distribution of some jobs, not of all jobs. It is most appropriate in centralized, professionalized, and bureaucratic systems, and its enforcement probably tends to generate such systems. Here communal control and individual qualification are necessary, and the crucial principle is "fairness." And here we must endure the rule of majorities and then of state officials, and the authority of qualified men and women. But there are clearly desirable jobs that fall outside these systems, that are justly (or not unjustly) controlled by private individuals or groups, and that do not have to be distributed "fairly." The existence of such jobs opens the way to a kind of success for which people don't need to qualify—indeed, can't qualify—and so sets limits on the authority of the qualified. There are areas of social and economic life where their writ doesn't run. The precise boundaries of these areas will always be problematic, but their reality isn't at all. We mark them off from the civil service, because the pattern of human relationships within them is better than it would be if they were not marked off—better, that is, given some particular understanding of what good human relationships are.

This, then, is complex equality in the sphere of office. It requires the career open to talents but sets limits on the prerogatives of the talented. If individual men and women are to plan their lives, to shape careers for themselves, there is no way to avoid the competition for office with all its triumphs and defeats. But one can reduce the frenzy of the competition by lowering the stakes. Offices are at stake, and nothing more. It was a personal tragedy when a candidate failed the Chinese civil service examinations. For him, everything was at stake: all China kowtowed to the successful candidate. But that would be for us a misconception of the value of office and the merits of office holders. Men and women committed to complex equality will cultivate a more realistic sense of what those merits are and of how they operate within the sphere of office. And they will recognize the autonomy of other spheres, where other forms of competition and cooperation, other forms of aggrandizement, honor, and service, legitimately prevail.

6

Hard Work

Equality and Hardness

It is not a question here of demanding or strenuous work. In that sense of the word, we can work hard in almost any office and at almost any job. I can work hard writing this book, and sometimes do. A task or a cause that seems to us worth the hard work it entails is clearly a good thing. For all our natural laziness, we go looking for it. But *hard* has another sense—as in "hard winter" and "hard heart"—where it means harsh, unpleasant, cruel, difficult to endure. Thus the account in Exodus of Israel's oppression, "And the Egyptians embittered their lives with hard labor" (1:14). Here the word describes jobs that are like prison sentences, work that people don't look for and wouldn't choose if they had even minimally attractive alternatives. This kind of work is a negative good, and it commonly carries other negative goods in its train: poverty, insecurity, ill health, physical danger, dishonor and degradation. And yet it is socially necessary work; it needs to be done, and that means that someone must be found to do it.

The conventional solution to this problem has the form of a simple equation: the negative good is matched by the negative status of the people into whose hands it is thrust. Hard work is distributed to degraded people. Citizens are set free; the work is imposed on slaves, resident aliens, "guest workers"—outsiders all. Alternatively, the insiders who do the work are turned into "inside" aliens, like the Indian untouchables or the American blacks after emancipation. In many societies, women have been the most important group of "inside" aliens, doing the work that men disdained and freeing the men not only for more rewarding economic activities but also for citizenship and politics. Indeed, the household work that women traditionally have done —cooking, cleaning, caring for the sick and the old—makes up a substantial part of the hard work of the economy today, for which aliens are recruited (and women prominently among them).

The idea in all these cases is a cruel one: negative people for a negative good. The work should be done by men and women whose qualities it is presumed to fit. Because of their race or sex, or presumed intelligence, or social status, they deserve to do it, or they don't deserve not to do it, or they somehow qualify for it. It's not the work of citizens, free men, white men, and so on. But what sort of desert, what sort of qualification is this? It would be hard to say what the hard workers of this or any other society have done to deserve the danger and degradation their work commonly entails; or how they, and they alone, have qualified for it. What secrets have we learned about their moral character? When convicts do hard labor, we can at least argue that they deserve their punishment. But even they are not state slaves; their degradation is (most often) limited and temporary, and it is by no means clear that the most oppressive sorts of work should be assigned to them. And if not to them, surely to no one else. Indeed, if convicts are driven to hard labor, then ordinary men and women should probably be protected from it, so as to make it clear that they are not convicts and have never been found guilty by a jury of their peers. And if even convicts shouldn't be forced to endure the oppression (imprisonment being oppression enough), then it is *a fortiori* true that no one else should endure it.

Nor can it be imposed on outsiders. I have already argued that the people who do this sort of work are so closely tied into the everyday life of the political community that they can't rightly be denied membership. Hard work is a naturalization process, and it brings membership to those who endure the hardship. At the same time, there is something attractive about a community whose members resist hard work (and whose new members are naturalized into the resistance). They have a certain sense of themselves and their careers that rules out the acceptance of oppression; they refuse to be degraded and have the strength to sustain the refusal. Neither the sense of self nor the personal strength are all that common in human history. They represent a significant achievement of modern democracy, closely connected to economic growth, certainly, but also to the success or the partial success of complex equality in the sphere of welfare. It is sometimes said to be an argument against the welfare state that its members are unwilling to take on certain sorts of jobs. But surely that is a sign of success. When we design a system of communal provision, one of our aims is to free people from the immediate constraints of physical need. So long as they are unfree, they are available for every sort of hard work, abased, as it were, by anticipation. Hungry, powerless, always insecure, they constitute "the reserve army of the proletariat." Once they have alternatives, they will rally and say No. Still, the work needs to be done. Who is to do it?

It is an old dream that no one will have to do it. We will solve the problem by abolishing the work, replacing men and women with machines wherever men and women find it unpleasant to be. Thus Oscar Wilde in his fine essay "The Soul of Man Under Socialism":

> All unintellectual labor, all monotonous, dull labor, all labor that deals with dreadful things and involves unpleasant conditions, must be done by machinery. Machinery must work for us in the coal mines and do all sanitary services, and be a stoker of steamers, and clean the streets, and run messages on wet days and do anything that is tedious and distressing.[1]

But that was always an unrealistic solution, for a great deal of hard work is required in the human services, where automation was never in prospect. Even where it was and still is in prospect, the invention and installation of the necessary machines is a much slower business than we once thought it would be. And machines as often replace people doing work they like to do as people doing "tedious and distressing" work. Technology is not morally discriminating in its effects.

If we set automation aside, the most common egalitarian argument is that the work should be shared, rotated (like political offices) among the citizens. Everyone should do it—except convicts, of course, who now have to be excluded so as to make sure that the work carries no stigma. This is another example of simple equality. It has its beginning, I think, in the dangerous work of war. As we conscript young men for war, so, it's been said, we should conscript men and women generally for all those necessary jobs that are unlikely to attract volunteers. An army of citizens will replace the reserve army of the proletariat. This is an attractive proposal, and I shall want to give it its due. It can't be defended, however, across the range of hardness—not even across the range of danger. Hence I will have to consider more complex distributions. Negative goods have to be dispersed not only among individuals but also among distributive spheres. Some we can share in the same way that we share the costs of the welfare state; some, if market conditions are roughly egalitarian, we can buy and sell; some require political arguments and democratic decision making. But all these forms have one thing in common: the distribution goes against the grain of the (negative) good. Except in the case of punishment, it just isn't possible to fit the distribution to the social meaning of the good, because there is no race or sex or caste and no conceivable set of individuals who can properly be singled out as society's hard workers. No one qualifies—there is no Pascalian company—and so all of us, in different ways and on different occasions, have to be available.

Dangerous Work

Soldiering is a special kind of hard work. In many societies, in fact, it is not conceived to be hard work at all. It is the normal occupation of young men, their social function, into which they are not so much drafted as ritually initiated, and where they find the rewards of camaraderie, excitement, and glory. It would be as odd, in these cases, to talk about conscripts as to talk about volunteers; neither category is relevant. Sometimes whole age cohorts go off to battle, doing what they are expected to do and what their members (most of them, at any rate) want to do. Sometimes, fighting is the special privilege of the élite, and compared with it, everything else is hard work, more or less degrading. Young men are energetic, combative, eager to show off; fighting for them is or can be a form of play, and only the rich can afford to play all the time. John Ruskin had a wonderfully romantic account of "consensual war," which aristocratic young men fight in much the same spirit as they might play football. Only the risks are greater, the excitement at a higher pitch, the contest more "beautiful."[2]

We might attempt a more down-to-earth romanticism: young men are soldiers in the same way that the French socialist writer Fourier thought children should be garbagemen. In both cases, passion is harnessed to social function. Children like to play in the dirt, Fourier thought, and so they are more ready than anyone else to collect and dispose of garbage. He proposed to organize his utopian community so as to exploit their readiness.[3] But I suspect that he would have found doing this more difficult than he anticipated. For it is hardly an accurate description of what garbagemen do to say that they *play* with the garbage. Similarly, the account of war as the natural activity of young men or the sport of aristocrats fits only a small number of wars, or it fits only certain sorts of engagements in war; and it doesn't fit modern warfare at all. Mostly soldiers have little opportunity for play; nor would their officers be happy with their playfulness. What soldiers do is, in the strictest sense, hard work. Indeed, we might take trench warfare in the First World War, or jungle warfare in the Second, as the first archetype of hardness.

Even when its true character is understood, however, soldiering is not a radically degraded activity. Rank-and-file soldiers are often recruited from the lowest classes, or from outcasts or foreigners, and they are often regarded with contempt by ordinary citizens. But the perceived value of their work is subject to sudden inflation, and there is always the chance that they will one day appear as the saviors of the country they defend. Soldiering is socially necessary, at least sometimes; and when it is, the necessity is visible and dramatic. At those times, soldiering is also dangerous, and it is dangerous in a way that makes a special mark on our imaginations. The danger is not natural but human; the soldier inhabits a world where other people—his enemies and ours, too—are trying to kill him. And he must try to kill them. He runs the risk of killing and being killed. For these reasons, I think, this is the first form of hard work that citizens are required, or require each other, to share. Conscription has other purposes too—above all, to produce the vast numbers of troops needed for modern warfare. But its moral purpose is to universalize or randomize the risks of war over a given generation of young men.

When the risks are of a different sort, however, the same purpose seems less pressing. Consider the case of coal mining. "The rate of accidents among miners is so high," wrote George Orwell in *The Road to Wigan Pier*, ". . . that casualties are taken for granted as they would be in a minor war."[4] It isn't easy, however, to imagine this sort of work being shared. Mining may not be highly skilled work, but it is certainly very difficult, and it's best done by men who have done it for a long time. It requires something more than "basic training." "At a pitch," wrote Orwell, "I could be a tolerable road-sweeper, or . . . a tenth-rate farm hand. But by no conceivable amount of effort or training could I become a coal-miner; the work would kill me in a few weeks."[5] Nor does it make much sense to break in upon the solidarity of the miners. Work in the pits breeds a strong bond, a tight community that is not welcoming to transients. That community is the great strength of the miners. A deep sense of place and clan and generations of class struggle have made for staying power. Miners are probably the least mobile of modern industrial populations. A conscript army of mineworkers, even if it were possible, would not be an attractive alternative to the social life the miners have designed for themselves.

But there is a deeper reason why the conscription of ordinary citizens for coal mining has never been urged by a political movement or become the subject of public discussion. The risks that miners live with are not imposed by a public enemy, and they don't involve the special terrors of killing and being killed. To some extent, indeed, the risks are imposed by negligent or profiteering owners, and then they are a political matter. But the obvious remedy is to nationalize the mines or regulate their operations; there seems no need to conscript miners. It makes sense to seek a similar remedy for the risks imposed by nature. In ancient Athens, the men who worked the silver mines were state slaves, permanently in the service of the city. Miners today are free citizens, but we might think of them, however the mines are owned, as citizens in the service of the nation. And then we might treat them as if they were conscripts, not sharing their risks, but sharing the costs of the remedy: research into mine safety, health care designed for their immediate needs, early retirement, decent pensions, and so on. The same argument plausibly applies to other dangerous activities, whenever they are socially necessary—not to mountain climbing, then, but to construction work on bridges, tall buildings, deep sea oil rigs, and so on. In all these cases, the casualty statistics may resemble those of a war; but the everyday experience is different, and so is our understanding of the work.

Grueling Work

Peacetime conscription raises still different issues. There remains a certain risk of war, which varies for each cohort of conscripts depending upon the political situation when they come of age. Mostly, however, what is being shared is the burden of service: the time spent, the difficult training, the harsh discipline. One could, of course, pay people to serve, recruit volunteers, opening up possibilities for advancement and encouraging soldiers to view the army as a career rather than the interruption of a career. This is an alternative that I will consider later. But I should note here an important political argument against it, which holds that citizen-soldiers are less likely than professionals or mercenaries to become the instruments of domestic oppression. The argument applies, however, only to soldiering (and to police work); while what is most interesting about peacetime conscription is that it invites the assimilation of soldiering to many other forms of hardness. If the army is manned, why shouldn't the roads be built, the sugar cane cut, the lettuce picked by conscripts?

Among political theorists, Rousseau made the strongest positive response to this question, drawing on a moral argument that is central to his theory as a whole. Men (and we would add, women too) must share in socially necessary work, as they share in politics and war, if they are ever to be the citizens of a self-governing community. If political participation and military service are required, so is the *corvée,* or labor service, else society divides into masters and servants, the two groups caught alike in the trap of hierarchy and dependency. We know that the republic is in decay, Rousseau argued, when its citizens "would rather serve with their money than with their persons."

> When it is necessary to march out to war, they pay troops and stay at home: when it is necessary to meet in council, they name deputies and stay at home. . . . In a country that is truly free, the citizens do everything with their own arms and nothing by means of money. . . . I am far from taking the common view: I hold enforced labor to be less opposed to liberty than taxes.[6]

The common view is that men and women are free only when they choose their own work. Taxes are the price of the choice, and the commutation of labor services into taxes is everywhere regarded as a victory for the common people. Rousseau's view is indeed radical, but it is undercut by an uncharacteristic vagueness. He never tells us how much of the community's work is to be shared among the citizens. Over what range of jobs will the *corvée* extend? We can imagine it extended so as to include every sort of hard work. Then the citizens would have to be organized into something like Trotsky's industrial army; there would be little room left for individual choice; and the command structure of the army would reproduce in new forms the old patterns of hierarchy and dependency. Rousseau almost certainly intended something more modest; he probably had in mind the sorts of work for which the *corvée* was historically used, like the building of the king's highways. A partial commitment, then, leaving more than enough time for the smallholders and craftsmen who inhabit Rousseau's ideal republic to pursue their own affairs: we can think of it as a symbolic commitment (though the work they share would be real work).

If this is right, then the choice of symbols is very important, and we must be clear about its purpose. Road building was a good choice for Rousseau because it was the typical form of forced labor under the old regime: men of noble birth were in principle exempt; the bourgeoisie was in practice exempt; the work was imposed on the poorest and weakest of the king's subjects, and so it was experienced as the most degrading kind of work. Were the citizens as a body to take it upon themselves, they would free the poor not only from the physical labor but also from its stigma—from aristocratic disdain and the bourgeois imitation of aristocratic disdain. That's not to say that work on the roads would cease to be a negative good for most of the people who did it, whether they were conscripts or volunteers. Back-breaking, grueling, and oppressive, it suggests the second archetype of hardness. But even a full-time commitment to it would cease to entail the disrespect of one's fellows. And then the other entailments might gradually be cut off, too; for the citizens might be ready to pay for the roads they needed, and the workers might be ready to demand more pay. All this might happen—but, in fact, we have evidence of a far more radical transformation in attitudes toward physical labor that actually did happen, and that happened, too, in something like a Rousseauian community.

The Israeli Kibbutz

From its beginning, Zionism presupposed the creation of a Jewish working class, and one or another form of Marxist ideology, exalting the power of the workers, was always a significant tendency within the movement. But there was, from the beginning again, another tendency, philosophically and politically more original, which exalted not the power of the workers but the dignity of the work, and which aimed to create not a class but a community. The kibbutz, or collective settlement, the product of this second tendency, represents an experiment in the transvaluation of values: the dignifying of work through the sharing of work. The creed of the early settlers was a "religion of labor" in which one took communion by working in the fields. And the hardest work was the most uplifting, spiritually, and socially, too.[7]

The first collectives were established in the early 1900s. By the 1950s, when Melford Spiro published his classic study *Kibbutz: Venture in Utopia*, the transvaluation of values was so successful that it was no longer necessary to require the members to share the physical labor of the collective. Everyone who could work wanted to work; a callused hand was a badge of honor. Only jobs with inconvenient hours

Hard Work

(dairyman, nightwatchman) had to be rotated among the members. High school teachers, on the other hand, had to be conscripted, for teaching was far less honored than work in the fields—an amazing fact, given the culture of European Jews.[8] (Less amazing, kitchen work posed problems, too, which I will come back to in a moment.)

It was crucial to the success of the kibbutz, I think, that each collective settlement was also a political community. It wasn't only the work that was shared, but decisions about the work. Hence the workers were free in that all-important sense that Rousseau calls "moral liberty": the burdens they lived with were self-imposed. Anyone who did not want to accept them could leave; anyone who refused to accept them could be expelled. But the members would always know that the shape of their workday and the allocation of tasks over time were matters of communal decision; and in these decisions they had, and would have, a significant voice. That's why the sharing could be total. In the case of a republican *corvée*, in a larger community and a more complex and differentiated economy, where the workers could participate only indirectly in decision making, a partial sharing would be more appropriate. But there is another contrast suggested by the kibbutz experience: between the close integration of work and politics possible in a residential community and the more partial integration possible in various on-the-job settings. Workers' control or self-management provides, as we shall see, an alternative to the *corvée*. The political reorganization of work can sometimes be a substitute for the sharing of work—though it is a central feature of the kibbutz, and a key to its moral character, that there the two go together.

The kibbutz is founded on a radical effort to transform a negative into a positive good. I have called that effort a success, and so, by and large, it is. But there is one area where it has not been successful. "Certain jobs are regarded as so distasteful," wrote Spiro, "that they are filled by a permanent rotation system . . . the most notable instance is work in the [communal] kitchen and dining room, cooking, dishwashing, and serving."[9] In the kibbutz that Spiro studied, women were drafted for a year at a time, men for two or three months, to do kitchen work. Now, sexual differentiation in work need not be problematic if it is freely chosen (either by individuals or by an assembly in which men and women have an equal voice) and if the different jobs are equally respected. The second of these conditions, however, didn't hold in this case. One might plausibly say that, with regard to food, the kitchen is as important as the fields. But kibbutz members were generally disdainful of bourgeois "graciousness" in eating; they had a

173

Rousseauian uneasiness with anything that smacked of luxury. Hence, Spiro reported, "little effort [was] made to improve the preparation of the food that [was] available."[10] (Food was rationed in Israel in the early 1950s.) Kitchen work might have been more respected if its products were more individuated and highly valued—and so one might hope for an improvement in its relative status as the hard edges of kibbutz ideology soften. But cleaning up after a meal may just be distasteful, however tasty the meal itself. And other sorts of cleaning up may be distasteful, too. Here, perhaps, kibbutz ideology comes up against a negative good that can't be transformed. Adam's curse would be no curse at all were there not some irreducible hardness in the hard work we have to do. And even in the kibbutz apparently, the curse is borne by some more than by others.

Dirty Work

In principle, there is no such thing as intrinsically degrading work; degradation is a cultural phenomenon. It is probably true in practice, however, that a set of activities having to do with dirt, waste, and garbage has been the object of disdain and avoidance in just about every human society. (Fourier's children haven't yet learned the mores of their elders.) The precise list will vary from one time and place to another, but the set is more or less common. In India, for example, it includes the butchering of cows and the tanning of cowhide—jobs that have a rather different standing in Western cultures. But otherwise the characteristic occupations of the Indian untouchables suggest what we can think of as the third archetype of hard work: they are the scavengers and sweepers, the carriers of waste and night soil. No doubt the untouchables are peculiarly degraded, but it is difficult to believe that the work they do will ever be attractive or widely esteemed. Bernard Shaw was perfectly right to say that "if all dustmen were dukes nobody would object to the dust,"[11] but it isn't easy to figure out how to produce such a happy arrangement. If all dustmen were dukes, they would find some new group, under another name, to do their dusting. Hence the question, in a society of equals, who will do the dirty work? has a special force. And the necessary answer is that, at least in some partial and symbolic sense, we will all have to do it. Then we will have an end to dukes, if not yet to dustmen. This is what Gandhi was getting at when he required his followers—himself, too—to clean the latrines of their ashram.[12] Here was a symbolic way of purging Hindu society of untouchability, but it also made a practical point: people should clean up their own dirt. Otherwise, the men and women who do it not only for themselves but for everyone else, too, will never be equal members of the political community.

What is required, then, is a kind of domestic *corvée*, not only in households—though it is especially important there—but also in communes, factories, offices, and schools. In all these places, we could hardly do better than to follow Walt Whitman's injunction (the poetry is weak but the argument right):

> For every man to see to it that he really do
>   something, for every woman too,
> . . . .
> To invent a little—something ingenious—to
>   aid the washing, cooking, cleaning,
> And hold it no disgrace to take a hand
>   at them themselves.[13]

There would probably be less dirt to clean up if everyone knew in advance of making it that he couldn't leave the cleaning to someone else. But some people—patients in a hospital, for example—can't help but leave it to someone else, and certain sorts of cleaning are best organized on a large scale. Work of this sort might be done as part of a national service program. Indeed, war and waste seem the ideal subjects of national service: the first, because of the special risks involved; the second, because of the dishonor. Perhaps the work should be done by the young, not because they will enjoy it, but because it isn't without educational value. Perhaps each citizen should be allowed to choose when in the course of his life he will take his turn. But it is certainly appropriate that the cleaning of city streets, say, or of national parks should be the (part-time) work of the citizens.

It is not an appropriate goal for social policy, however, that all the dirty work that needs to be done should be shared among all the citizens. That would require an extraordinary degree of state control over everyone's life, and it would interfere radically with other kinds of work, some of it also necessary, some of it only useful. I have argued for a partial and symbolic sharing: the purpose is to break the link between dirty work and disrespect. In one sense, the break has already been accomplished, or substantially accomplished, through a long process of cultural transformation that begins with the early modern attack on feudal hierarchy. Before God, Puritan preachers taught, all human callings, all useful work, is equal.[14] Today we are likely to rank jobs as more or less desirable, not as more or less respectable. Most of us would deny that any socially useful work can be or should be debasing. And yet we still impose on hard-working fellow citizens patterns of behavior, routines of distancing, that place them in a kind of pale: deferential movements, peremptory commands, refusals of recognition. When a garbageman feels stigmatized by the work he does, writes a contemporary sociologist, the stigma shows in his eyes. He enters "into collusion with us to avoid contaminating us with his lowly self." He looks away; and we do, too. "Our eyes do not meet. He becomes a non-person."[15] One way to break the collusion, and perhaps the best way, is to make sure that every citizen has a working knowledge of the working days of his hardest working fellows. Once that is done, it is possible to consider other mechanisms, including market mechanisms, for organizing the hard work of society.

So long as there is a reserve army, a class of degraded men and women driven by their poverty and their impoverished sense of their own value, the market will never be effective. Under such conditions, the hardest work is also the lowest paid, even though nobody wants to do it. But given a certain level of communal provision and a certain level of self-valuation, the work won't be done unless it is very well paid indeed (or unless the working conditions are very good). The citizens will find that if they want to hire their fellows as scavengers and sweepers, the rates will be high—much higher, in fact, than for more prestigious or pleasant work. This is a direct consequence of the fact that they are hiring *fellow* citizens. It is sometimes claimed that under conditions of genuine fellowship, no one would agree to be a scavenger or a sweeper. In that case, the work would have to be shared. But the claim is probably false. "We are so accustomed," as Shaw has written, "to see dirty work done by dirty and poorly paid people that we have come to think that it is disgraceful to do it, and that unless a dirty and disgraced class existed, it would not be done at all."[16] If sufficient money or leisure were offered, Shaw rightly insisted, people would come forward.

His own preference was for rewards that take the form of leisure or "liberty"—which will always be, he argued, the strongest incentive and the best compensation for work that carries with it little intrinsic satisfaction:

Hard Work

> In a picture gallery you will find a nicely dressed lady sitting at a table with nothing to do but to tell anyone who asks what is the price of any particular picture, and take an order for it if one is given. She has many pleasant chats with journalists and artists; and if she is bored she can read a novel. . . . But the gallery has to be scrubbed and dusted each day; and its windows have to be kept clean. It is clear that the lady's job is a much softer one than the charwoman's. To balance them you must either let them take their turns at the desk and at the scrubbing on alternate days or weeks; or else, as a first-class scrubber and duster and cleaner might make a very bad business lady, and a very attractive business lady might make a very bad scrubber, you must let the charwoman go home and have the rest of the day to herself earlier than the lady at the desk.[17]

The contrast between the "first-rate" charwoman and the "very attractive" business lady nicely combines the prejudices of class and sex. If we set aside those prejudices, the periodic exchange of work is less difficult to imagine. The lady, after all, will have to share in the scrubbing, dusting, and cleaning at home (unless she has, as Shaw probably expected her to have, a charwoman there, too). And what is the charwoman to do with her leisure? Perhaps she will paint pictures or read books about art. But then, though the exchange is easy, it may well be resisted by the charwoman herself. One of the attractions of Shaw's proposal is that it establishes hard work as an opportunity for people who want to protect their time. So they will clean or scrub or collect garbage for the sake of their leisure, and avoid if they can any more engaging, competitive, or time-consuming employment. Under the right conditions, the market provides a kind of sanctuary from the pressures of the market. The price of the sanctuary is so many hours a day of hard work—for some people, at least, a price worth paying.

The major alternative to Shaw's proposal is the reorganization of the work so as to change, not its physical requirements (for I'm assuming that they are not changeable), but its moral character. The history of garbage collecting in the city of San Francisco offers a nice example of this sort of transformation, which I want to dwell on briefly both for its own sake and because it connects in useful ways with my earlier discussion of office and with the arguments still to come about honor and power.

The San Francisco Scavengers

For the past sixty years, roughly half of the garbage of the city of San Francisco has been collected and disposed of by the Sunset Scavenger Company, a cooperative owned by its workers, the men who drive the trucks and carry the cans. In 1978 the sociologist Stewart Perry published a study of Sunset, a fine piece of urban ethnography and a valuable speculation on "dirty work and the pride of ownership"—it is my sole source in the paragraphs that follow. The cooperative is democratically run, its officers elected from the ranks and paid no more than the other workers. Forced by the Internal Revenue Service in the 1930s to adopt bylaws in which they are referred to as "stockholders," the members nevertheless insisted that they were, and would remain, faithful to the program of the original organizers "who intended to form and carry on a cooperative . . . where every member was a worker and actually engaged in the common work and where every member did his share of the work and expected every other member to work and do his utmost to increase the collective earnings."[18] Indeed, earnings have increased (more than those of manual workers generally); the company has grown; its elected officers have shown considerable entrepreneurial talent. Perry believes that the cooperative provides better-than-average service to the citizens of San Francisco and, what is more important here, better-than-average working conditions to its own members. That doesn't mean that the work is physically easier; rather, cooperation has made it more pleasant—has even made it a source of pride.*

In one sense, the work is in fact easier: the accident rate among Sunset members is significantly lower than the industry average. Garbage collecting is a dangerous activity. In the United States today, no other occupation has a higher risk of injury (though coal miners are subject to more serious injury). The explanation of these statistics is not clear. Garbage collecting is strenuous work, but no more so than many other jobs that turn out to have better safety records. Perry suggests that there may be a connection between safety and self-valuation. "The 'hidden injuries' of the status system may be linked to the apparent injuries that public health and safety experts can document."[20] The first "accident" of garbage collecting is the internalization of disrespect, and then other accidents follow. Men who don't value themselves don't take proper care of themselves. If this view is right, the better record of Sunset may be connected to the shared decision making and the sense of ownership.

---

*Perry's book, then, is an argument against Oscar Wilde's pessimism. "To sweep a slushy crossing," wrote Wilde, "is a disgusting occupation. To sweep it with mental, moral, or physical dignity seems to me to be impossible. To sweep it with joy would be appalling."[19] Perry's work suggests that Wilde underestimates the chances for dignity, if not for joy. It makes a difference how the worker stands to his work, his fellow workers, his fellow citizens. But I don't want to forget Wilde's point that what the worker does also makes a difference: there is no way to turn sweeping or scavenging into an attractive or intellectually stimulating occupation.

Hard Work

Membership in the Sunset Scavenger Company is distributed by a vote of the current members and then by the purchase of shares (it has generally not been difficult to borrow the necessary money, and the shares have steadily increased in value). The founders of the company were Italian-Americans, and so are the bulk of the members today; about half of them are related to other members; a fair number of sons have followed their fathers into the business. The success of the cooperative may owe something to the easiness of the members with one another. In any case, and whatever one wants to say about the work, they have made membership into a good thing. They don't distribute the good they have created, however, in accordance with "fair equality of opportunity." In New York City, because of a powerful union, garbage collecting is also a widely desired job, and there the job has been turned into an office. Candidates must qualify for the work by taking a civil service exam.[21] It would be interesting to know something about the self-valuation of the men who pass the exam and are hired as public employees. They probably earn more than the members of the Sunset cooperative, but they don't have the same security; they don't own their jobs. And they don't share risks and opportunities; they don't manage their own company. The New Yorkers call themselves "sanitationmen"; the San Franciscans, "scavengers": who has the greater pride? If the advantage lies, as I think it does, with the members of Sunset, then it is closely connected to the character of Sunset: a company of companions, who choose their own fellows. There is no way to qualify for the work except to appeal to the current members of the company. No doubt the members look for men who can do the necessary work and do it well, but they also look, presumably, for good companions.

But I don't want to underestimate the value of unionization, for this can be another form of self-management and another way of making the market work. There can't be any doubt that unions have been effective in winning better wages and working conditions for their members; sometimes they have even succeeded in breaking the link between income differentials and the status hierarchy (the New York garbage collectors are a prime example). Perhaps the general rule should be that wherever work can't be unionized or run cooperatively, it should be shared by the citizens—not symbolically and partially, but generally. Indeed, when union or cooperative work is available to everyone (when there is no reserve army), other work just won't get done unless people do it for themselves. This is clearly the case with domestic cooking and cleaning, an area where jobs are increasingly filled by new immigrants, not by citizens. "Mighty few young black women are doin' domestic work [today]," Studs Terkel was told by a very old black woman, a servant all her life. "And I'm glad. That's why I want my kids to go to school. This one lady told me, 'All you people are gettin' like that.' I said, 'I'm glad.' There's no more gettin' on their knees."[22] This is the sort of work that is largely dependent on its (degraded) moral character. Change the character, and the work may well become un-doable, not only from the perspective of the worker but from that of the employer, too. "When domestic servants are treated as human beings," wrote Shaw, "it is not worthwhile to keep them."[23]

This is not true of garbage collectors or of coal miners, though the demand for human treatment will certainly make every kind of dirty and dangerous work more expensive than it was before. It is an interesting question whether it is true for soldiers. One can, as I've said, recruit soldiers through the labor market; in the absence of a reserve army, the inducements would have to match or surpass those of other forms of hard work. Given the discipline necessary to military efficiency, however, unionization is difficult, self-management impossible. And that may well be the best argument for a conscript service even in peacetime. Conscription is a way of sharing the discipline and, perhaps more important, of bringing political controls to bear on its harshness. Some men and women enjoy the harshness, but I doubt that there are enough of them to defend the country. And while the army is an attractive career for those who hope to become officers, it isn't attractive—or in a community of citizens, it shouldn't be—for those who will fill the lower ranks. Soldiering has far more prestige than garbage collecting; but compared with a private in the army, the San Francisco scavengers and the New York sanitation workers look to me like free men.

What is most attractive in the experience of the Sunset company (as of the Israeli kibbutz) is the way in which hard work is connected to other activities—in this case, the meetings of the "stockholders," the debates over policy, the election of officers and new members. The company has also expanded into land-fill and salvage operations, providing new and diversified employment (including managerial jobs) for some of the members; though all of them, whatever they do now, have spent years riding the trucks and carrying the cans. Throughout most of the economy, the division of labor has developed very differently, continually separating out rather than integrating the hardest sorts of work. This is especially true in the area of the human services, in the care we provide for the sick and the old. Much of that work is still done in the home, where it is connected with a range of other jobs, and its difficulties are relieved by the relationships it sustains. Increasingly, however, it is institutional work; and within the great caretaking institutions—hospitals, mental asylums, old-age homes—the hardest work, the dirty work, the most intimate service and supervision, is relegated to the most subordinate employees. Doctors and nurses, defending their place in the social hierarchy, shift it onto the shoulders of aides, orderlies, and attendants—who do for strangers, day in and day out, what we can only just conceive of doing in emergencies for the people we love.

Perhaps the aides, orderlies, and attendants win the gratitude of their patients or of the families of their patients. That's not a reward I would want to underestimate, but gratitude is most often and most visibly the reward of doctors and nurses, the healers rather than merely the caretakers of the sick. The resentment of the caretakers is well known. W. H. Auden was clearly thinking of the patients, not the hospital staff, when he wrote:

> . . . the hospitals alone remind us
> of the equality of man.[24]

Orderlies and attendants have to cope for long hours with conditions that their institutional superiors see only intermittently, and that the general public doesn't see at all and doesn't want to see. Often they look after men and women whom the rest of the world has given up on (and when the world gives up, it turns away). Underpaid and overworked, at the bottom of the status system, they are nevertheless the last comforters of humanity—though I suspect that unless they have a calling for the work, they give as little comfort as they get. And sometimes they are guilty of those petty cruelties that make their jobs a little easier, and that their superiors, they firmly believe, would be as quick to commit in their place.

"There is a whole series of problems here," Everett Hughes has written, "which cannot be solved by some miracle of changing the social selection of those who enter the job."[25] In fact, if caretaking were shared—if young men and women from different social backgrounds took their turns as orderlies and attendants—the internal life of hospitals, asylums, and old-age homes would certainly be changed for the better. Perhaps this sort of thing is best organized locally rather than nationally, so as to establish a connection between caretaking and neighborliness; it might even be possible, with a little invention, to reduce somewhat the rigid impersonality of institutional settings. But such efforts will be supplementary at best. Most of the work will have to be done by people who have chosen it as a career, and the choice will not be easy to motivate in a society of equal citizens. Already, we must recruit foreigners to do a great deal of the hard and dirty work of our caretaking institutions. If we wish to avoid that sort of recruitment (and the oppression it commonly entails), we must, again, transform the work. "I have a notion," says Hughes, "that . . . 'dirty work' can be more easily endured when it is part of a good role, a role that is full of rewards to one's self. A nurse might do some things with better grace than a person who is not allowed to call herself a nurse, but is dubbed 'subprofessional' or 'non-professional.' "[26] That is exactly right. National service might be effective because, for a time at least, the role of neighbor or citizen would cover the necessary work. But over a longer period, the work can be covered only by an enhanced sense of institutional or professional place.

This enhancement is unlikely without far-reaching changes in our institutions and professions; it depends, then, on the outcome of long and prolonged political struggle, the balance of social forces, the organization of interests, and so on. But we might also think of it in terms more susceptible to philosophical discussion. What is necessary is what the Chinese call "the rectification of names." In one sense, names are historical and cultural givens; in another, they are subject to the play of social and political power. The process by which office holders and professionals hold onto the title and prestige of a particular place, while shunting off its less agreeable duties, is an example—perhaps the crucial example—of a power play. But unless one is a radical nominalist, it leaves the question of names still to be settled. "Who will be called a 'nurse' when the nurse's tasks are re-shuffled? Will it be the teacher and supervisor? The bedside comforter? Or will it be those who give more humble services?"[27] Surely we ought to give the name, and all that goes with the name, to the person who does the "nursing"—who (as the dictionary says) "waits upon and attends to" the sick. I don't mean to make any claims about the essence of nursing; nor do I intend a purely linguistic argument. My reference, once again, is to common understandings, and these are always subject to dispute. Still, it seems fair to say that there is a range of valued activities that include "humble services" and that are valued, at least in part, because they include such services. The hardness of the work is connected to the glory, and we should never be too quick to allow their separation, even in the name of efficiency or technological advance.

There is no easy or elegant solution, and no fully satisfying solution, to the problem of hard work. Positive goods have, perhaps, their appropriate destination; negative goods do not. "To escape facing this fact," wrote Shaw, "we may plead that some people have such very queer tastes that it is almost impossible to mention an occupation that you will not find somebody with a craze for. . . . The saying that God never made a job but he made a man or woman to do it is true up to a certain point."[28] But that plea doesn't take us very far. The truth is that hard work is unattractive work for most of the men and women who find themselves doing it. When they were growing up, they dreamed of doing something else. And as they age, the work gets more and more difficult. Thus, a fifty-year-old garbage collector to Studs Terkel: "the alleys are longer and the cans larger. Getting old."[29]

We can share (and partially transform) hard work through some sort of national service; we can reward it with money or leisure; we can make it more rewarding by connecting it to other sorts of activity—political, managerial, and professional in character. We can conscript, rotate, cooperate, and compensate; we can reorganize the work and rectify its names. We can do all these things, but we will not have abolished hard work; nor will we have abolished the class of hard workers. The first kind of abolitionism is, as I have already argued, impossible; the second would merely double hardness with coercion. The measures that I have proposed are at best partial and incomplete. They have an end appropriate to a negative good: a distribution of hard work that doesn't corrupt the distributive spheres with which it overlaps, carrying poverty into the sphere of money, degradation into the sphere of honor, weakness and resignation into the sphere of power. To rule out negative dominance: that is the purpose of collective bargaining, cooperative management, professional conflict, the rectification of names—the politics of hard work. The outcomes of this politics are indeterminate, certain to be different in different times and places, conditioned by previously established hierarchies and social understandings. But they will also be conditioned by the solidarity, the skillfulness, and the energy of the workers themselves.

7

Free Time

The Meaning of Leisure

Unlike money, office, education, and political power, free time is not a dangerous good. It does not easily convert into other goods; it can not be used to dominate other distributions. Aristocrats, oligarchs, and their capitalist imitators certainly enjoy a great many hours of free time, but the enjoyment is largely designed, as Thorstein Veblen argued at the end of the nineteenth century, for the display rather than the acquisition of wealth and power. Hence I shall deal briefly with such people and their pleasures; the conventional forms of upper-class idleness make only a small part of my subject.

Veblen's account of "honorific leisure" suggests, indeed, that it can be a trying and hectic business (though it is never hard work). For it's not enough merely to loaf; one must pile up "serviceable evidence of an unproductive expenditure of time."[1] What is crucial is simultaneously to do nothing useful and to make it known to the world that one is doing nothing useful. The bustle of a multitude of servants is a great help. But it is a problem that the permissible activity of aristocrats and oligarchs leaves behind no material products. Hence the "serviceable evidence" takes the form of conversational wit, exquisite manners, foreign travel, lavish entertainment, "quasi-scholarly and quasi-artistic accomplishments." It is a mistake, I think, to assume that high culture is dependent upon this sort of thing—though idle men and women often dabble in art and literature or patronize artists and writers. "All intellectual improvement arises from leisure," wrote Sam-

184

Free Time

uel Johnson,[2] but it wasn't this sort of leisure that he had in mind (nor does his life provide evidence for his proposition.) In any case, upper-class idleness will not be available under conditions of complex equality. The required concentration of social goods is unlikely to occur; the servants will be hard to find, or they won't bustle appropriately; uselessness will have a lower social value. Still, it is a good thing to be idle, to loaf away the time, at least sometimes; and the freedom to do that—in the concrete form of vacations, holidays, weekends, after-work hours—is a central issue of distributive justice.

For most people, leisure is simply the opposite of work; idleness, its essence. The etymological root of the Greek *schole,* as of the Hebrew *shabbat,* is the verb "to cease" or "to stop."[3] Presumably, it is work that is stopped, and the result is quiet, peace, rest (also enjoyment, play, celebration). But there is an alternative understanding of leisure that requires at least a brief description here. Free time is not only "vacant" time; it is also time at one's command. That lovely phrase "one's own sweet time" doesn't always mean that one has nothing to do, but rather that there is nothing that one has to do. We might say, then, that the opposite of leisure isn't work simply but necessary work, work under the constraint of nature or the market or, most important, the foreman or the boss. So there is a leisurely way of working (at one's own pace), and there are forms of work compatible with a life of leisure. "For leisure does not mean idleness," wrote T. H. Marshall in an essay on professionalism. "It means the freedom to choose your activities according to your own preferences and your own standards of what is best."[4] Professionals once eagerly claimed this freedom; it made them gentlemen, for though they earned their living working, they worked in a leisurely way. It's not difficult to imagine a setting in which this same freedom would make, not for gentility, but for citizenship. Consider, for example, the Greek artisan, whose aim in life, it has been said, was "to preserve his full personal liberty and freedom of action, to work when he felt inclined and when his duties as a citizen permitted him, to harmonize his work with all the other occupations that filled [his days], to participate in the government, to take his seat in the courts, to join in the games and festivals."[5] The picture is certainly idealized, but it is important to note that the ideal is that of a working man all of whose time is free time, who does not need a "vacation with pay" in order to enjoy a moment of leisure.

Aristotle argued that only the philosopher could rightly be said to live a leisured life, for philosophy was the only human activity pursued without the constraint of some further end.[6] Every other occupation, including politics, was tied to a purpose and was ultimately unfree, but philosophy was an end in itself. The artisan was a slave not only to the market where he sold his products, but to the products themselves. I suppose that the books we currently attribute to Aristotle were, by contrast, not products at all but mere by-products of philosophical contemplation. They were not written to make money or to win tenure or even eternal fame. Ideally, philosophy has no issue; at least, it is not pursued for the sake of its issue. One can see here the source (or perhaps it is already a reflection) of the aristocratic disdain for productive work. But it is both an unnecessary and a self-serving restriction on the meaning of leisure to make nonproductivity its central feature. That the philosopher's thoughts do not taint the idea of leisure, but the artisan's table or vase or statue do, is a thought likely to appeal only to philosophers. From a moral standpoint, it seems more important that human activity be directed from within than that it have no outside end or material outcome. And if we focus on self-direction, a wide variety of purposive activities can be brought within the compass of a life of leisure. Intellectual work is certainly one of these, not because it is useless—one can never be certain about that—but because intellectuals are commonly able to design, to their own specifications, the work they do. But other sorts of work can also be designed (planned, scheduled, organized) by the workers themselves, either individually or collectively; and then it isn't implausible to describe the work as "free activity" and the time as "free time."

Human beings also need a "cessation from rest," Marx once wrote, criticizing Adam Smith's description of rest as the ideal human condition, identical with freedom and happiness. "Certainly the measure of work seems externally given by the goal to be attained and by the obstacles to its attainment," he went on. "But Smith has no conception that this overcoming of obstacles is itself an exercise of freedom." Marx meant that it can sometimes be an exercise of freedom—whenever "the external goals, ceasing to appear merely as necessities of nature, become goals that the individual chooses for himself."[7] In part, what is at stake here is the control of work, the distribution of power in the workplace and in the economy at large—an issue I will come back to in a later chapter. But Marx also wanted to hint at some grand transformation in the way mankind relates to nature, an escape from the realm of necessity, a transcendence of the old distinction between work and play. Then one won't have to talk, as I have been doing, of work carried on at a leisurely pace or incorporated into a life of leisure, for work will simply be leisure and leisure will be work: free, productive activity, the "species life" of mankind.

For Marx, it is the great failing of bourgeois civilization that most men and women experience this sort of activity, if they experience it at all, only in spare and scattered moments, as a hobby, not as their life's work. In communist society, by contrast, everyone's work will be his hobby, everyone's vocation his avocation. But this vision, glorious as it is, is not a proper subject for the theory of justice. If it is ever realized, justice will no longer be problematic. Our concern is with the distribution of free time in the age before the transformation, escape, and transcendence have taken place—that is, here and now, when the rhythm of work and rest is still crucial to human well-being, and when some people, at least, will have no species life at all if they have no break from their usual occupations. However work is organized, however leisurely it is—and these are crucial questions—men and women still need leisure in the more narrow and conventional sense of a "cessation from work."

Two Forms of Rest

In a grimmer mood, Marx wrote that work will always remain a realm of necessity. The free development of human powers lies beyond that realm: "Its primary requisite is shortening the work day."[8] We might add, "and the work week, the work year, the work life." All these have been central issues in the distributive struggles, the class wars, of the last century. Marx's chapter on the working day in the first volume of *Capital* is a brilliant account of these struggles. So far as justice is concerned, however, it is marked by a pervasive (and characteristic) dualism. On the one hand, Marx insists that there is no argument from justice to the proper length of the working day:

> The capitalist maintains his rights as a purchaser when he tries to make the working day as long as possible . . . the laborer maintains his right as seller when he wishes to reduce the working day to one of definite normal duration. There is here, therefore, an antimony, right against right, both equally bearing the seal of the law of exchanges. Between equal rights force decides.[9]

On the other hand, Marx also insists—and this with rather more feeling—that force can decide wrongly:

In its blind unrestrainable passion, its were-wolf hunger for surplus labor, capital oversteps not only the moral, but even the merely physical . . . bounds of the working day. It usurps the time for growth, development, and healthy maintenance of the body.[10]

Physical bounds there surely are, though these are frighteningly minimal: "the few hours of repose without which labor-power absolutely refuses its services again."[11] If careful or inventive or maximally productive work is wanted, the bounds are more severe; a few hours won't be enough. Indeed, productivity increases with rest, at least up to a point; and rational capitalists, precisely because of their "were-wolf hunger," ought to find just that point. But this is a matter of prudence or efficiency, not of justice. Moral limits are much harder to specify, for they will vary from one culture to another, depending on the common understanding of a decent human life. But every understanding of which we have any historical record includes rest as well as work, and Marx had no difficulty exposing the hypocrisy of English apologists for the twelve-hour day and the seven-day week—"and that in a country of Sabbatarians!" In fact, set against the long history of work and rest, England in the 1840s and 1850s seems a hellish aberration. Though the rhythm and periodicity of work has been radically different among, say, peasants, artisans, and industrial workers, and though the length of particular working days shows great variation, the working year does seem to have had a normative shape—at least, a shape reiterated under a wide variety of cultural conditions. Calculations for ancient Rome, medieval Europe, and rural China before the revolution, for example, suggest something like a 2:1 ratio of days of work to days of rest.[12] And that is roughly where we are today (figuring a five-day week, a two-week vacation, and four to seven legal holidays).

The purposes of rest vary more radically. Marx's description is typical of nineteenth-century liberals and romantics: "time for education, for intellectual development, for the fulfilling of social functions and for social intercourse, for the free play of . . . bodily and mental activity."[13] Politics, which played such an important part in the free time of the Greek artisan, is not even mentioned; nor are religious observances. Nor is there much sense here of what any child could have explained to Marx, the value of doing nothing, of "passing" the time—unless "free play" is meant to include random thoughts, stargazing, and fantasy. We might incorporate Aristotle's definition of leisure and say that purposelessness, the state of being without fixed goals, is one (though only one) of leisure's characteristic purposes.

But however these purposes are described, they will not single out any particular group of men and women as more or less entitled to free time. There is no way of qualifying for leisure. It is indeed possible to qualify for certain sorts of leisurely work, as in the case of the professions. Similarly, one can win a fellowship that sets time free for research or writing. Society has an interest in seeing to it that classes in philosophy, say, are taught by qualified persons, but it has no interest in who thinks philosophical or unphilosophical thoughts. The free play of bodies and minds is . . . free. The quality of loafing is not judged. Hence, leisure, as it is conceived in a particular time and place, seems to belong to all the inhabitants of that time and place. No principle of selection or exclusion is available. The ancient association of wealth and power with idleness is only another form of tyranny. Because I am powerful and command obedience, I shall rest (and you shall work). It would be more appropriate to say that the reward of power is its exercise, and that power's justification is its conscientious or effective exercise—and this is a form of work, one of whose purposes is that others can rest. Thus, Shakespeare's Henry V, repeating the common self-defense of kings:

> . . . gross brain little wots
> What watch the king keeps to maintain the peace,
> Whose hours the peasant best advantages.[14]

And no one knows who among the peasants really does "best."

But the argument thus far, though it rules out working days like those described by Marx, doesn't require that everyone have exactly the same amount of free time. In fact, considerable variation is possible and even desirable given the many different kinds of work that people do. In his *Intelligent Woman's Guide,* Shaw wrote emphatically that justice demands "the equal distribution of . . . leisure or liberty among the whole population."[15] This is simple equality in the sphere of leisure; we would fix the length of the working day by adding up hours of work and dividing by numbers of people. But Shaw's assertion of equality is immediately followed by a wonderfully complex discussion of the different sorts of work and workers. I have already quoted his argument that the people who do society's sweeping and scrubbing should be compensated with additional free time. Nor is he averse to putting his own claim: "In my own case, in spite . . . of the fact that an author's work can as a rule quite well be divided into limited daily periods, I am usually obliged to work myself to a complete standstill and then go away for many weeks to recuperate."[16] That sounds reasonable enough, but we must look more closely now at the ways in which such patterns might justly be accommodated.

A Short History of Vacations

In the year 1960, an average of a million and a half Americans, 2.4 percent of the workforce, were on vacation every day.[17] It is an extraordinary figure, and undoubtedly it had at that point never been higher. Vacations have indeed a short history—for ordinary men and women, very short: as late as the 1920s, Sebastian de Grazia reports, only a small number of wage earners could boast of paid vacations.[18] The arrangement is far more common today, a central feature of every union contract; and the practice of "going away"—if not for many weeks, at least for a week or two—has also begun to spread across class lines. In fact, vacations have become the norm, so that we are encouraged to think of weekends as short vacations and of the years after retirement as a very long one. And yet the idea is new. The use of the word *vacation* to mean a private holiday dates only from the 1870s; the verb *to vacation,* from the late 1890s.

It all started as a bourgeois imitation of the aristocrat's retreat from court and city to country estate. Since few bourgeois men and women owned country estates, they retreated instead to seaside or mountain resorts. At the beginning, ideas about relaxation and pleasure were masked by ideas about the health-restoring qualities of fresh air and mineral or salt water: thus eighteenth-century Bath and Brighton, where one went to eat and talk and promenade and also, sometimes, "to take the waters." But the escape from city and town was soon popular for its own sake, and the entrepreneurial response slowly multiplied the number of resorts and cheapened the available amusements. The invention of the railroad made a similar escape possible for nineteenth-century workers, but they had no time for anything more than the "excursion"—to the sea and back in a single day. The great expansion of popular leisure began only after the First World War: more time, more places to go, more money, cheap lodgings, and the first projects in communal provision, public beaches, state parks, and so on.

What is crucial about the vacation is its individualist (or familial) character, greatly enhanced, obviously, by the arrival of the automobile. Everyone plans his own vacation, goes where he wants to go, does what he wants to do. In fact, of course, vacation behavior is highly patterned (by social class especially), and the escape it represents is generally from one set of routines to another.[19] But the experience is clearly one of freedom: a break from work, travel to some place new and different, the possibility of pleasure and excitement. It is indeed a problem that people vacation in crowds—and, increasingly, as the size of the crowds grows, it is a distributive problem, where space rather than time is the good in short supply. But we will misunderstand the value of vacations if we fail to stress that they are individually chosen and individually designed. No two vacations are quite alike.

They are, however, designed to the size of the individual (or familial) purse. Vacations are commodities: people have to buy them—with pay forgone and money spent; and their choices are limited by their buying power. I don't want to overemphasize this point, for it is also true that people fight for their vacations; they organize unions, bargain with their employers, go on strike for "time off," shorter work days, early retirement, and so on. No history of vacations would be complete without an account of these fights, but they are not the central feature of contemporary distributions. We might indeed conceive of time off in terms directly relative to those of work, so that individuals could choose, as Shaw suggests, hard and dirty work and long vacations or leisurely work and shorter vacations. But for most workers, right now, time is probably less important in determining the shape and value of their vacations than the money they are able to spend.

If wages and salaries were roughly equal, there would appear to be nothing wrong with making vacations purchasable. Money is an appropriate vehicle for individual design because it imposes the right sorts of choice: between work and its pay, on the one hand, and the expenses of this or that sort of leisure activity (or inactivity), on the other. We can assume that people with similar resources would make different choices, and the result would be a complex and highly particularized distribution. Some of them, for example, might take few or no vacations, preferring to earn more money and surround themselves with beautiful objects rather than escape to beautiful surroundings. Others might prefer many short vacations; still others, a long stint of work and a long rest. There is room here for collective as well as individual decision making (in unions and cooperative settlements, for example). But the decisive decisions must come at the individual level, for that is what vacations are. They bear the mark of their liberal and bourgeois origins.

Under conditions of complex equality, wages and salaries won't be equal; they will only be a great deal less unequal than they are today. In the petty-bourgeois world, men and women will still risk their money—and their time, too—and then find themselves with more or less of both than other people have. Factory communes will do well or not so well and then have more or less money and time to distribute among their members. And even for someone like Shaw, the exact length of his "many weeks" of rest and the conditions under which he spends them will probably depend as much upon the success of his plays as upon the requirements of his muse. On the other hand, as soon as vacations become—as they have become in the United States today—a central feature of social life and culture, some form of communal provision is required. It is necessary not only to make sure that the distribution isn't radically dominated by wealth and power, but also to guarantee a range of choice and sustain the reality of individual design. Hence, for example, the preservation of wildlife and wilderness, without which certain sorts of vacation (widely thought to be valuable) cease to be possible. And hence, too, the expenditure of tax money on parks, beaches, campsites, and so on, to make sure that there are places to go for all those people who want to "go away." Though the choices they make—where to go, how to lodge, what equipment to take along—won't be identically constrained for every individual or every family, a certain range of choice must be universally available.

But all this assumes the centrality of the vacation, and it is important to stress now that the vacation is an artifact of a particular time and place. It isn't the only form of leisure; it was literally unknown throughout most of human history, and the major alternative form survives even in the United States today. This is the public holiday. When ancient Romans or medieval Christians or Chinese peasants took time off from work, it was not to go away by themselves or with their families but to participate in communal celebrations. A third of their year, sometimes more, was taken up with civil commemorations, religious festivals, saint's days, and so on. These were their holidays, in origin, holy days, and they stand to our vacations as public health to individual treatment or mass transit to the private car. They were provided for everyone, in the same form, at the same time, and they were enjoyed together. We still have holidays of this sort, though they are in radical decline; and in thinking about them it will be well to focus on one of the most important of the survivals.

The Idea of the Sabbath

According to the Deuteronomic account, the Sabbath was instituted in commemoration of the escape from Egypt. Slaves work without cease or at the behest of their masters, and so the Israelites thought it the first mark of a free people that its members enjoy a fixed day of rest. Indeed, the divine command as reported in Deuteronomy has the slaves of the Israelites as its primary object: "that thy man-servant and thy maid-servant may rest as well as thou" (5:14). Egyptian oppression was not to be repeated even though slavery itself was not abolished. The Sabbath is a collective good. It is, as Martin Buber says, "the common property of all"—that means, of all who share in the common life. "Even the slave admitted into the household community, even the *ger*, the stranger [resident alien], admitted into the national community, must be permitted to share in the divine rest."[20] Domestic animals are included, too—"thine ox, . . . thine ass, . . . thy cattle,"—since animals presumably can enjoy a rest (though they can't take a vacation).

Max Weber argued that the strangers or resident aliens were required to rest in order to deny them any competitive advantage.[21] There is no reason for saying this—no evidence in the sources—beyond the conviction, not always associated with Weber, that economic motives must in principle be paramount. But it is true that, even in a pre-capitalist economy, it would be difficult to guarantee rest to everyone without imposing it on everyone. Public holidays require coercion. The absolute ban on work of any sort is unique, I think, to the Jewish Sabbath; but without some general sense of obligation and some enforcement mechanism, there could be no holidays at all. That is why, as obligation and enforcement have declined, holidays have ceased to be public occasions, have been attached to weekends, have become undifferentiated pieces of individual vacations. One can see here an argument for "blue laws," which can be justified much as taxation is justified: both have the form of a charge on productive or wage-earning time for the sake of communal provision.

Sabbath rest is more egalitarian than the vacation because it can't be purchased: it is one more thing that money can't buy. It is enjoined for everyone, enjoyed by everyone.* This equality has interesting spillover effects. Insofar as the celebration came to require certain sorts of food and clothing, Jewish communities felt themselves bound to provide these for all their members. Thus, Nehemiah, speaking to the Jews who had returned with him from Babylonia to Jerusalem: "This day is holy to the Lord, your God. . . . Go, eat of the richest food and drink of the most delicious wines, and send portions to those who have nothing provided." (8:9–10). Not to send portions would be to oppress the

---

*According to Jewish folklore, even the wicked in hell are permitted to rest on the Sabbath. Thus limits are set on punishment as well as on work by particular conceptions of "necessary" rest. One might say that the infliction of pain on the Sabbath would represent "cruel and unusual punishment."[22]

poor, for it would exclude them from a common celebration; it is a kind of banishment that they have done nothing to deserve. And then, as the Sabbath rest was shared, so it came to be argued that the work of preparing for the Sabbath should also be shared. How could people rest if they hadn't first worked? "Even if one is a person of very high rank and does not as a rule attend to the marketing or to other household chores," wrote Maimonides, thinking first of all of the rabbis and sages, "he should nevertheless himself perform one of these tasks in preparation for the Sabbath. . . . Indeed, the more one does in way of such preparations, the more praiseworthy he is."[23] So the universalism of the seventh day was extended at least to the sixth.

It might be said, however, that this is only another case where equality and the loss of liberty go together. Certainly, the Sabbath is impossible without the general commandment to rest—or, rather, what survives without the commandment, on a voluntary basis, is something less than the full Sabbath. On the other hand, the historical experience of the Sabbath is not an experience of unfreedom. The overwhelming sense conveyed in Jewish literature, secular as well as religious, is that the day was eagerly looked forward to and joyfully welcomed—precisely as a day of release, a day of expansiveness and leisure. It was designed, as Leo Baeck has written, "to provide the soul with a broad and lofty space," and so it seems to have done.[24] No doubt this sense of spaciousness will be lost on men and women who stand outside the community of believers but are still submitted, in one degree or another, to its rules. But it isn't their experience that is determining here. Holidays are for members, and members can be free—the evidence is clear—within the confines of the law. At least, they can be free when the law is a covenant, a social contract, even though the covenant is never individually designed.

Would people choose private vacations over public holidays? It isn't easy to imagine a situation in which the choice would present itself in such sharp and simple terms. In any community where holidays are possible, holidays will already exist. They will be part of the common life that makes the community, and they will shape and give meaning to the individual lives of the members. The history of the word *vacation* suggests how far we have come from such a common life. In ancient Rome, the days on which there were no religious festivals or public games were called *dies vacantes*, "empty days." The holidays, by contrast, were full—full of obligation but also of celebration, full of things to do, feasting and dancing, rituals and plays. This was when time ripened to produce the social goods of shared solemnity and revelry. Who would give up days like that? But we have lost that sense of fullness; and the days we crave are the empty ones, which we can fill by ourselves, as we please, alone or with our families. Sometimes we experience the fear of emptiness—the fear of retirement, for example, conceived now as an indefinite succession of empty days.* But the fullness that many retired people long for, the only one they know, is the fullness of work, not of rest. Vacations, I suspect, require the contrast of work; it is a crucial part of the satisfaction they give. Are holidays the same? That was Prince Hal's view, in Shakespeare's *Henry IV, Part I:*

> If all the year were playing holidays,
> To sport would be as tedious as to work;
> But when they seldom come, they wish'd for come.[26]

Hal's view is certainly the common one, and it seems to fit our own experience. But according to the ancient rabbis, the Sabbath is a foretaste of eternity. The messianic kingdom, which will come, as the old phrase has it, in the fullness of days, is a Sabbath (but not a vacation) without end.[27]

I should note, nevertheless, that each of the great revolutions has involved an attack on the traditional holidays, the Sabbaths, saints' days, and festivals—an attack undertaken partly for the sake of increased productivity, partly for the sake of a general effort to abolish traditional life styles and priestly hierarchies. The Chinese communists provide the most recent example: "There have been too many religious festivals," one of them wrote in 1958. "Because of superstitions and festivals, production has been discontinued more than 100 days annually, and in some areas 138 days. . . . The reactionary class [has] used these evil customs and rituals to enslave the people."[28] Conceivably, there is a point here, but the enslavement isn't obvious, and the abolition of the festivals has been bitterly resisted. With some sense, perhaps, of the reasons for that resistance, the communists have tried to substitute new holidays for the old ones—May Day, Red Army Day, and so on—and to develop new ceremonies and celebrations. For them, as for the French revolutionaries before them, the choice is not be-

---

*Or the fear of unemployment: in our culture, at least, the unemployed are unlikely to experience their time as full or free. They may take a brief vacation when they are first laid off, but after that their leisure will be a burden; unemployment makes for dead time.[25] We conceive of vacations as something earned through useful work—a "deserved" rest. Hence unemployment is threatening not only to our material welfare but also to our sense of ourselves as respectable members of a society within which a certain pattern of work and rest is established. A strong sense of citizenship might make unemployment less threatening: then citizens without work could "work" within a political movement aimed at reforming the economy or the welfare state. I return to these questions in chapters 11 and 12.

tween public and private leisure, but between two different kinds of public leisure. But that choice may well be misconceived. One can't pull holidays out of an ideological hat. In many villages, report two students of the new China, "the three major [revolutionary] holidays involve little else besides time off from work."[29] For all its commitment to collectivism, then, China may yet drift inexorably toward the distribution of free time first adopted by the European bourgeoisie. But if new communities do develop there or elsewhere, then new sorts of public celebration will develop with them. The help of vanguard bureaucrats won't be necessary. The members will find their own ways to express their fellow feeling and to act out the politics and culture they share.

Holidays and vacations are two different ways of distributing free time. Each has its own internal logic—or, more exactly, vacations have a single logic, while every holiday has a particular sub-logic, which we can read out of its history and rituals. One can imagine a mix of holidays and vacations: something like what we have known for the past century. And while the mix seems unstable, it does permit, as long as it lasts, some policy choices. It would be foolish, however, to suggest that these choices are constrained by the theory of justice. The United Nations' International Covenant on Economic, Social, and Cultural Rights includes in its (very long) list of rights "periodic holidays with pay"—that is, vacations.[30] But this is not to define human rights; it is simply to advocate a particular set of social arrangements, which isn't necessarily the best set or the best for every society and culture. The right that requires protection is of another sort entirely: not to be excluded from the forms of rest central to one's own time and place, to enjoy vacations (though not the same vacations) if vacations are central, to participate in the festivals that give shape to a common life wherever there is a common life. Free time has no single just or morally necessary structure. What is morally necessary is that its structure, whatever it is, not be distorted by what Marx called the "usurpations" of capital, or by the failure of communal provision when provision is called for, or by the exclusion of slaves, aliens, and pariahs. Freed from these distortions, free time will be experienced and enjoyed by the members of a free society in all the different ways they can collectively or individually invent.

8

Education

The Importance of Schools

Every human society educates its children, its new and future members. Education expresses what is, perhaps, our deepest wish: to continue, to go on, to persist in the face of time. It is a program for social survival. And so it is always relative to the society for which it is designed. The purpose of education, according to Aristotle, is to reproduce in each generation the "type of character" that will sustain the constitution: a particular character for a particular constitution.[1] But there are difficulties here. The members of society are unlikely to agree about what the constitution, in Aristotle's broad sense, actually is, or what it is becoming, or what it should be. Nor are they likely to agree about what character type will best sustain it or how that type might best be produced. In fact, the constitution will probably require more than one character type; the schools will not only have to train their students, they will also have to sort them out; and that is bound to be a controversial business.

Education is not, then, merely relative—or, its relativity doesn't tell us all we need to know about either its normative function or its actual effects. If it were true that the schools always served to reproduce society as it is—the established hierarchies, the prevailing ideologies, the existing workforce—and did nothing more, it would make no sense to talk about a just distribution of educational goods. Distribution here would parallel distribution elsewhere; there would be no independent sphere and no internal logic. Something like this may well be true when

197

there are no schools—when parents educate their own children or apprentice them in their future trades. Then social reproduction is direct and unmediated; the sorting-out process is carried on within the family with no need for communal intervention; and there exists no body of knowledge or intellectual discipline distinct from family chronicles and trade mysteries in terms of which the constitution can be interpreted, evaluated, argued about. But schools, teachers, and ideas create and fill an intermediate space. They provide a context, not the only one, but by far the most important one, for the development of critical understanding and for the production, as well as the reproduction, of social critics. This is a fact of life in all complex societies; even Marxist professors acknowledge (and conservative statesmen worry about) the relative autonomy of the schools.[2] But social criticism is the result of autonomy and doesn't help to explain it. What is most important is that schools, teachers, and ideas constitute a new set of social goods, conceived independently of other goods, and requiring, in turn, an independent set of distributive processes.

Teaching positions, student places, authority in the schools, grades and promotions, different sorts and levels of knowledge—all these have to be distributed, and the distributive patterns cannot simply mirror the patterns of the economy and the political order, because the goods in question are different goods. Of course, education is always supportive of some particular form of adult life, and the appeal from school to society, from a conception of educational justice to a conception of social justice, is always legitimate. But in making this appeal, we must also attend to the special character of the school, the teacher-student relationship, intellectual discipline generally. Relative autonomy is a function of what the educational process is and of the social goods that it involves as soon as it ceases to be direct and unmediated.

I want to stress the verb of being: what the educational process *is*. Justice has to do not only with the effects but also with the experience of education. The schools fill an intermediate space between family and society, and they also fill an intermediate time between infancy and adulthood. This is, no doubt, a space and a time for training and preparation, rehearsals, initiation ceremonies, "commencements," and so on; but the two also constitute a here-and-now that has its own importance. Education distributes to individuals not only their futures but their presents as well. Whenever there is space and time enough for such distributions, the educational process takes on a characteristic normative structure. I don't mean to describe anything like its "essence"; I simply want to suggest the most common conception of what it should be like. This is a conception that one finds in many different societies and the only one with which I shall be concerned. The adult world is represented, and its knowledge, traditions, and rituals are interpreted, by a corps of teachers who confront their students in a more or less enclosed community—what John Dewey called a "special social environment."[3] The students are granted a partial moratorium from the demands of society and economy. The teachers, too, are protected from the immediate forms of external pressure. They teach the truths they understand, and the same truths, to all the students in front of them, and respond to questions as best they can, without regard to the students' social origins.

That's not, I suppose, the way things always, or even usually, work in practice. It is all too easy to provide a list of tyrannical intrusions on the educational community, to describe the precariousness of academic freedom, the dependence of teachers on patrons and officials, the privileges that upper-class students routinely command, and all the expectations, prejudices, habits of deference and authority that students and teachers alike carry with them into the schoolroom. But I shall assume the reality of the norm, for the most interesting and the hardest distributive questions arise only after that assumption has been made. Which children is it who are admitted into the enclosed communities? Who goes to school? And to what sort of school? (What is the strength of the enclosure?) To study what? For how long? With what other students?

I'm not going to say much about the distribution of teaching positions. Teaching is commonly conceived as an office, and so it is necessary to look for qualified people and to open to all citizens an equal chance to qualify. And teaching is a particular office; it calls for particular qualifications, whose precise character have to be debated by town councils, governing boards, and search committees. I should stress, however, that my general assumption—that schools constitute a special environment and have a certain normative structure—militates against the practice of leaving education to the old men and women of the larger community or rotating ordinary citizens through the faculties.[4] For all such practices undercut the mediating character of the educational process and tend to reproduce the more direct "passing on" of folk memories, traditions, and skills. Strictly speaking, the existence of schools is tied up with the existence of intellectual disciplines and so of a corps of men and women qualified in those disciplines.

The Aztec "House of the Young Men"

Consider for a moment—it is an exotic but not atypical example—the educational system of the Aztec Indians. In ancient Mexico, there were two sorts of school. One was called simply the "house of the young men" and was attended by the mass of male children. It offered instruction in "the bearing of arms, arts and crafts, history and tradition, and ordinary religious observance"; and it seems to have been presided over by ordinary citizens, chosen from among the more experienced warriors, who "carried on in special quarters instruction given in a simpler day by the old men of the clan."[5] A very different sort of education was provided for the children of the élite (and for some selected children of plebeian families)—more austere, more rigorous, and more intellectual, too. In special schools attached to monasteries and temples, "all the knowledge of time and the country was taught: reading and writing in the pictographic characters, divination, chronology, poetry, and rhetoric." Now the teachers came from the priestly class, "chosen without any regard to their family, but only to their morals, their practices, their knowledge of doctrine and the purity of their lives."[6] We don't know how the children were chosen; in principle, at least, similar qualities were probably required, for it was from these schools that the priests themselves came. Though an élite education demanded sacrifice and self-discipline, it seems likely that school places were eagerly sought, particularly by ambitious plebes. In any case, I assume the existence of schools of this second kind; without them, distributive questions hardly arise.

One could argue that the "house of the young men" was also an intermediate institution. Aztec girls, unless they were trained as priestesses, mostly stayed at home and learned the womanly arts from the old women of the family. But these are two examples of the same thing: social reproduction in its direct form. The girls would henceforth remain at home, while the boys would band together to fight endless wars with neighboring cities and tribes. Nor would the selection of a few old women to teach the traditional folkways in a "house of the young women" have constituted an autonomous educational process. For that we must have teachers trained and tested in the "knowledge of doctrine." Assume now that there are such teachers. Whom should they teach?

Education

Basic Schooling: Autonomy and Equality

The mass of children can be divided, for purposes of education, in a number of ways. The simplest and most common division, of which most educational programs well into modern times have been nothing but variations, has this form: mediated education for the few, direct education for the many. This is the way men and women in their conventional roles—rulers and ruled, priests and laymen, upper classes and plebeian classes—have historically been distinguished. And, I suppose, reproduced, though it is important to say again that mediated education is always likely to turn out skeptics and adventurers alongside its more standard products. In any case, schools have mostly been élite institutions, dominated by birth and blood, or wealth, or gender, or hierarchical rank, and dominating in turn, over religious and political office. But this fact has little to do with their internal character; and, indeed, there is no easy way of enforcing the necessary distinctions from within the educational community. Here, let's say, is a body of doctrine having to do with government. To whom should it be taught? The established rulers claim the doctrine for themselves and their children. But unless children are naturally divided into rulers and ruled, it would seem, from the standpoint of the teachers, that the doctrine should be taught to anyone who presents himself and is capable of learning it. "If there were one class in the state," wrote Aristotle, "surpassing all others as much as gods and heroes are supposed to surpass mankind," then the teachers might plausibly direct their attention to that class alone. "But that is a difficult assumption to make, and we have nothing in actual life like the gulf between kings and subjects which the writer Scylax describes as existing in India."[7] Except in Scylax's India, then, no children can rightly be excluded from the enclosed community where the doctrine of government is taught. The same thing is true of other doctrines; nor does it require a philosopher to understand this.

Hillel on the Roof

An old Jewish folktale describes the great Talmudic sage as an impoverished young man who wanted to study at one of the Jerusalem academies. He earned money by chopping wood, but barely enough money to keep himself alive, let alone pay the admission fees for the lectures. One cold winter night, when he had no money at all, Hillel climbed to the roof of the school building and listened through the skylight. Exhausted, he fell asleep and was soon covered with snow. The next morning, the assembled scholars saw the sleeping figure blocking the light. When they realized what he had been doing, they immediately admitted him to the academy, waiving the fees. It didn't matter that he was ill dressed, pennyless, a recent immigrant from Babylonia, his family unknown. He was so obviously a student.[8]

The story depends for its force upon a set of assumptions about how schooling should be distributed. It is not a complete set; one couldn't derive an educational system from this sort of folk wisdom. But here is an understanding of the community of teachers and students that has no place for social distinctions. If the teachers see a likely student, they take him in. At least, that is the way legendary, and therefore ideal, teachers behave; they ask none of the conventional questions about wealth and status. One could almost certainly find legends, and actual biographies, similar to the Hillel story in other cultures. Many Chinese officials, for example, began their careers as poor farm boys taken in by a village teacher.[9] Is that the way teachers were supposed to behave? I don't know the answer in the case of China, but we are still inclined today, I think, to accept the moral of the Hillel story. "To serve educational needs, without regard to the vulgar irrelevancies of class and income," wrote R. H. Tawney, "is a part of the teacher's honor."[10] When schools are exclusive, it is because they have been captured by a social élite, not because they are schools.

But it is only the democratic state (or church or synagogue) that insists upon *inclusive* schools, where future citizens can be prepared for political (or religious) life. Now distribution is determined by what the school is for and not simply by what it is, by the social meaning of war or work or worship—or of citizenship, which commonly includes all of these. I don't mean that democracy requires democratic schools; Athens got along well enough without them. But if there is a body of knowledge that citizens must grasp, or think they must grasp, so as to play their parts, then they have to go to school; and then all of them have to go to school. Thus Aristotle, in opposition to the practices of his own city: "the system of education in a state must . . . be one and the same for all, and the provision of this system must be a matter of public action."[11] This is a simple equality in the sphere of education; and while simplicity is soon lost—for no educational system can ever be "the same for all"—it nevertheless fixes the policies of the democratic school. The simple equality of students is relative to the simple equality of citizens: one person/one vote, one child/one place in the educational system. We can think of educational equality as a form of welfare provision, where all children, conceived as future citizens, have the same need to know, and where the ideal of membership is best served if they are all taught the same things. Their education cannot be allowed to hang on the social standing or the economic capacity of their parents. (It remains a question whether it should hang on the moral and political convictions of their parents, for democratic citizens may well disagree about what their children need to know; I shall come back to this point.)

Simple equality is connected to need: all future citizens need an education. Seen from within the school, of course, need is by no means the sole criterion for the distribution of knowledge. Interest and capacity are at least as important—as the Hillel story suggests. Indeed, the teacher-student relationship seems to rest, above all, on these latter two. Teachers look for students, students look for teachers, who share their interests; and then they work together until the students have learned what they wanted to know or have gone as far as they can. Nevertheless, democratic need is by no means a political imposition on the schools. Advocates of democracy rightly claim that all children have an interest in the government of the state and a capacity to understand it. They meet the crucial requirements. But it is also true that children don't take an interest to the same degree, and that they don't have the same capacity to understand. Hence, as soon as they are inside the school, they can hardly help but begin to distinguish themselves.

How a school responds to these distinctions depends very much on its purposes and its curriculum. If the teachers are committed to the basic disciplines necessary for democratic politics, they will try to establish a shared knowledge among their students and to raise them to something like the same level. The aim is not to repress differences but rather to postpone them, so that children learn to be citizens first—workers, managers, merchants, and professionals only afterward. Everyone studies the subjects that citizens need to know. Schooling ceases to be the monopoly of the few; it no longer automatically commands rank and office.[12] For there is no privileged access to citizenship, no way of getting more of it, or getting it faster, by doing better at school. Schooling guarantees nothing and exchanges for very little, but it provides the common currency of political and social life. Isn't this a plausible account at least of basic education? Teaching children to read is, after all, an egalitarian business, even if teaching literary criticism (say) is not. The goal of the reading teacher is not to provide equal chances but to achieve equal results. Like the democratic theorist, he assumes that all his students have an interest and are able to learn. He doesn't try to make it equally possible for students to read; he tries to engage them in reading and *teach them to read.* Perhaps they should have equal chances to become literary critics, to hold professorships, publish articles, attack other people's books, but reading they should have simply; they should be readers (even if reading buys no privileges). Here the democratic commitment of the larger community is not so much reflected as matched and enhanced by the democratic practice of the school, once children are in school.

The Japanese Example

The match is all the more likely under contemporary conditions, the more autonomous a school is within the larger community. For the pressure to enlarge upon the natural distinctions that already exist among the students, to search out and mark off the future leaders of the country, comes almost entirely from the outside. In a valuable study of the development of educational equality in Japan in the years since the Second World War, William Cummings has argued that schools can provide a genuinely common education only if they are protected from corporate and governmental intrusion. Conversely, if they are protected, schools are likely to have egalitarian effects even in a capitalist society.[13] Assume, as I have been doing, the existence of more or less enclosed educational communities, and a certain sort of equality follows for every group of students face to face with a teacher. Add to this that every child goes to school, that there is a common curriculum, and that the enclosure is strong, and then the sphere of education is likely to be a highly egalitarian place.

But only for the students: students and teachers are not equals; indeed, the authority of teachers is necessary to the equality of students. The teachers are the guardians of the enclosure. In the Japanese case, Cummings argues, the crucial condition of educational equality has been the relative strength of the teachers' union.[14] It is, to be sure, a special feature of the case that this is a socialist union. But then, socialists, or people calling themselves socialists, have produced very different kinds of school. What has made for equality in Japan is that the union has been led by its ideology to resist the (inegalitarian) pressures of government officials, pressed themselves by the élite of corporate managers. The schools have been shaped less by socialist theory than by the natural results of that resistance—that is, the day-to-day practice of autonomy. Here are independent teachers, a body of knowledge, and students who need to know. What follows? I will quote and comment upon some of Cummings's conclusions.

1. "The schools are organically organized with a minimum of internal differentiation. . . . At the primary level there are no specialty teachers, and ability tracking is not practiced."[15] This simply enacts Aristotle's maxim for democratic schools: "Training for an end which is common should also itself be common."[16] Internal differentiation in the early grades is a sign of a weak school (or of teachers uncertain of their vocation), surrendering to the tyranny of race or class.

2. Teachers "try to bring all the students up [to a common standard] by creating a positive situation in which all [of them] receive rewards . . . by adjusting the classroom pace to the learning rates of students, and by relying on students to tutor each other."[17] It can't be said that the brighter children are held back by such procedures. Student-teaching is a form of recognition; and it is also a learning experience for the "teacher" as well as the student, an experience of real value for democratic politics. *Learn, then teach* is the practice of a strong school, capable of enlisting students in its central enterprise. The effect is to "minimize the incidence of exceptionally low achievers."

3. "The . . . curriculum is demanding, geared to the learning rate of the better-than-average student."[18] Another sign of strong schools and ambitious teachers. It is often said that the decision to educate everyone necessarily leads to a lowering of standards. But this is true only if the schools are weak, incapable of resisting the pressures of a hierarchical society. I include among these pressures not only the demands of business leaders for minimally educated and contented workers but also the apathy and indifference of many parents trapped at the lower levels of the hierarchy—and the arrogance of many other parents established at the upper levels. These groups, too, are socially reproductive, and democratic education is likely to succeed only insofar as it draws their children into its own enclosure. It may be an important feature of the Japanese case, then, that "students spend far more hours at school than do their counterparts in most other advanced societies."

4. "The relative equality of cognitive performance moderates the propensity of children to rank each other. . . . Instead, the children are disposed to see themselves as working together to master the curriculum."[19] This disposition may be further enhanced by the fact that all students—and teachers, too—share in the cleaning and repair of the school. There are virtually no maintenance personnel in Japanese schools: the educational community is self-contained, consisting only of teachers and students. "The maintenance of the school is everyone's

responsibility."[20] The shared learning and the shared working point alike to a world of citizens rather than to a division of labor. And so they discourage the comparisons that the division of labor, at least in its conventional forms, endlessly provokes.

I have omitted various complicating features of Cummings's analysis that are not immediately relevant here. My purpose has been to suggest the effects of normative schooling under democratic conditions. These effects can be summed up very simply. Everyone is taught the basic knowledge necessary for an active citizenship, and the great majority of students learn it. The experience of learning is itself democratic, bringing its own rewards of mutuality and camaraderie as well as of individual achievement. It is possible, of course, to gather children into schools for the sole purpose of not educating them there or of teaching them nothing more than a bare literacy. Then education, by the default of the schools, is in effect unmediated and is carried on in the family or on the streets; or it is mediated by television, the movies, and the music industry, and the schools are nothing but a (literal) holding operation until children are old enough to work. Schools of this sort may well have walls to keep the children in, but they have no walls to keep society and economy out. They are hollow buildings, not centers of autonomous learning; and then some alternative is necessary to train, not the citizens, but the managers and professionals of the next generation—thus reproducing in a new form the old distinction between direct and mediated education and maintaining the basic structure of a class society. But the distribution of educational goods within autonomous schools will make for equality.

Specialized Schools

Democratic education begins with simple equality: common work for a common end. Education is distributed equally to every child—or, more accurately, every child is helped to master the same body of knowledge. That doesn't mean that every child is treated in exactly the same way as every other child. Praise is plentifully distributed in Japanese schools, for example, but it is not equally distributed to all the children. Some of the children regularly play the part of student-teachers; some of them are always students. Backward and apathetic children probably receive a disproportionate share of the teachers' attention. What holds them all together is the strong school and the core curriculum.

But simple equality is entirely inappropriate as soon as the core has been grasped and the common end achieved. After that, education must be shaped to the interests and capacities of individual students. And the schools themselves must be more receptive to the particular requirements of the workaday world. Bernard Shaw has suggested that at this point schools should simply be dispensed with—precisely because they can no longer fix common goals for all their students. He identifies schooling with simple equality:

> When a child has learnt its social creed and catechism and can read, write, reckon, and use its hands: in short, when it is qualified to make its way about in modern cities and do ordinary useful work, it had better be left to find out for itself what is good for it in the direction of higher cultivation. If it is a Newton or a Shakespeare, it will learn the calculus or the art of the theater without having them shoved down its throat: all that is necessary is that it should have access to books, teachers, and theaters. If its mind does not want to be highly cultivated, its mind should be left alone on the grounds that its mind knows what is good for it.[21]

This is Shaw's version of "deschooling." Unlike the version advocated by Ivan Illich in the 1970s, it builds upon years of prior schoolwork, and so is not foolish.[22] Shaw is probably right to argue that young men and women should be allowed to sort themselves out and make their way in the world without official certification. We have come to overemphasize the importance, not of schooling itself, but of schooling indefinitely extended. The effect is to rob the economy of its only legitimate proletariat, the proletariat of the young, and to make promotion up the ranks more difficult than it need be for real proletarians.

But it is not at all clear just how long it takes to learn one's "social catechism" or what knowledge is included in knowing one's way around a modern city. Something more than street knowledge, certainly, else schooling would be unnecessary from the beginning. Nor would it be satisfactory from a democratic standpoint if some children moved quickly onto the streets while the parents of the others purchased a further education that gave them access to privileged places in the city. For this reason, every advance in the school-leaving age has been a victory for equality. At some point, however, that must cease to be true, for it can't be the case that a single life course is equally appropriate for all children. With regard to the course represented by the schools, the opposite claim is more plausible: there will never be a political community of equal citizens if schoolwork is the only path to adult responsibility. For some children, beyond a certain age, school is a kind of prison (but they have done nothing to deserve imprisonment!), endured because of legal requirements or for the sake of a diploma. Surely these children should be set free and then helped to learn the work they want to do on the job. Equal citizenship requires a common schooling—its precise length a matter for political debate; but it does not require a uniform educational career.

What about young men and women who want to continue in school for the sake, say, of a general and liberal education? We might most simply provide for them by maintaining open enrollments beyond the school-leaving age: do away with grading, permit no failures, and sort people out, if that is necessary, only at the end of the process. Students would study whatever they were interested in learning, and would continue to study until their interest in this or that subject (or in studying) was exhausted. Then they would do something else. But interests are at least potentially infinite; and on a certain view of human life, one should study as long as one has breath. There is little likelihood that the political community could raise the necessary money for an education of this sort, and no reason to suppose that the people who give up studying are morally required to support those who continue. Medieval monks and Talmudic sages were indeed supported by the work of ordinary men and women, and that may well have been a good thing. Such support is not morally required, however, not in a society like ours, not even if the chance to become a monk or a sage or the contemporary equivalent were equally available to everyone.

But if the community underwrites the general education of some of its citizens, as we do today for college students, then it has to do so for any of them who are interested—not only in colleges but also, as Tawney has argued, "in the midst of the routine of their working lives." Tawney, who devoted many years to the Workers' Educational Association, is entirely right to insist that a higher education of this sort should not be available solely on the basis of "a career of continuous school attendance from five to eighteen."[23] One can imagine a great variety of schools and courses, catering to students of different ages and educational histories, run at national and local levels, attached to unions, professional associations, factories, museums, old-age homes, and so on. In these settings, to be sure, schooling shades off into other, less formal sorts of teaching and learning. The "enclosed community" loses its physical reality, becomes a metaphor for critical distance. But insofar as we are distributing school places (the "college of hard knocks" has always had open enrollment), I don't think we should give up the idea of the enclosure or yield any more distance than we have to. The only extension of basic education appropriate to a democracy is one that provides real opportunities, real intellectual freedom, not just for some students conventionally gathered together, but for all the others, too.

I cannot specify any particular level of support for this provision. Here again, there is room for democratic debate. Nor is it the case, as some educational radicals have argued, that democracy itself is impossible without a public program of continuing education.[24] Democracy is in danger only if such a program is organized undemocratically, not if it isn't organized at all. As with monks and sages, so with ordinary citizens: it is a good thing if they are able to study indefinitely, without a professional purpose, for the sake of what Tawney calls "a reasonable and humane conduct of life"; but the only point critical for the theory of justice is that this sort of study not be the exclusive privilege of a few people, picked out by state officials through a system of examinations. To study the "humane conduct of life," no one needs to qualify.

The case is different, however, with regard to specialized or professional training. Here interest alone cannot serve as a distributive criterion; nor can interest and capacity serve: there are too many interested and capable people. Perhaps, in the best of all possible worlds, we would educate all such people for as long as they were educable. This, it might be said, is the only standard intrinsic to the idea of education—as if capable men and women were empty vessels that ought to be filled to the brim. But this is to conceive of an education abstracted from every particular body of knowledge and from every system of professional practice. Specialized schooling doesn't just go on and on until the student has learned everything he can possibly learn; it stops when he has learned something, when he is acquainted with the state of knowledge in a field. We will plausibly look in advance for some assurance that he can learn that much and learn it well. And if we have only a limited amount of money to spend, or if there are only a limited number of places requiring that particular training, we will plausibly look for some assurance that he can learn it especially well.

Educating citizens is a matter of communal provision, a kind of welfare. I would suggest that we commonly conceive of a more specialized education as a kind of office. Students must qualify for it. They qualify, presumably, by some display of interest and capacity; but these two yield nothing like a right to a specialized education, for the necessary specializations are a matter for communal decision, and so is the number of places available in the specialized schools. Students have the same right that citizens generally have with regard to office holding: that they be given equal consideration in the awarding of the available places. And students have this additional right: that insofar as they are prepared for office holding in the public schools, they should, so far as possible, be equally prepared.

The education of a gentleman, wrote John Milton, should fit the children who receive it "to perform justly, skillfully, magnanimously, all the offices both private and public of peace and war."[25] In a modern democratic state, citizens take on the prerogatives and obligations of gentility, but their education prepares them only to be voters and soldiers or (perhaps) presidents and generals, but not to advise presidents about the dangers of nuclear technology, not to advise generals about the risks of this or that strategic plan, not to prescribe medicines, design buildings, teach the next generation, and so on. These specialized offices require a further education. The political community will want to make sure that its leaders—and its ordinary members, too—get the best possible advice and service. And the corps of teachers has a parallel interest in the most apt students. Hence the need for a selection process aimed at locating within the set of future citizens a subset of future "experts." The standard form of this process is not difficult to discover: the universal civil service examination, which I have already described in chapter 5, is simply introduced into the schools. But this makes for deep strains in the fabric of a democratic education.

The more successful basic schooling is, the more apt the body of future citizens is, the more intense is the competition for advanced places in the educational system, and the deeper is the frustration of those children who fail to qualify.[26] Established élites are then likely to demand earlier and earlier selection, so that the schoolwork of the unselected is turned into a training in passivity and resignation. Teachers in strong schools will resist this demand, and so will the children—or, better, the parents of the children will resist, insofar as they are politically alert and capable. Indeed, equality of consideration would seem to require such resistance, for children learn at different rates and awaken intellectually at different ages. Any once-and-for-all selection process is certain to be unfair to some students; it will also be unfair to young people who have stopped studying and gone to work. And so there must be procedures for reconsideration and, more important, for lateral as well as upward movement into the specialized schools.

Assuming a limited number of places, however, these procedures will only multiply the number of ultimately frustrated candidates. There is no avoiding that, but it is morally disastrous only if the competition is not for school places and educational chances so much as it is for the status, power, and wealth conventionally joined to professional standing. The schools, however, need have nothing to do with this trinity of advantage. No feature of the educational process requires the link between higher education and hierarchical rank. Nor is there any reason to think that the most apt students would give up their educations were that link broken and future office holders paid, say, "workmen's wages." Some students, certainly, will make better engineers, surgeons, nuclear physicists, and so on, than their fellows will. It remains the task of the specialized schools to find these students, give them some sense of what they can do, and set them on their way. Specialized education is necessarily a monopoly of the talented or, at least, of those students most capable at any given moment of deploying their talents. But this is a legitimate monopoly. Schools cannot avoid differentiating among their students, advancing some and turning others away; but the differences they discover and enforce should be intrinsic to the work, not to the status of the work. They should have to do with achievement, not with the economic and political rewards of achievement; they should be inwardly focused, matters of praise and pride within the schools and then within the profession, but of uncertain standing in the larger world. Of uncertain standing: for achievement may still carry with it, given a little luck, not wealth and power but authority and prestige. I am describing not schools for saints but only centers of learning rather more insulated than at present from the business of "making it."

George Orwell's Schooldays

It might help at this point to consider a negative example; and in the vast literature on schools and schooling, there is no more perfectly negative example than Orwell's account of the English prep school that he attended in the 1910s. Some questions have been raised about the accuracy of the account, but on the points most relevant here we can, I think, assume its truth.[27] Orwell's "Crossgates" was designed to prepare students for admission to schools like Harrow and Eton, where England's upper civil servants and leading professional men were trained. A prep school is by definition not an autonomous center of learning, but Crossgates's dependency was doubled by the fact that it was not only an educational but also a commercial enterprise—and a rather precarious one at that. So the owners and the teachers shaped their work to the requirements of Harrow and Eton, on the one hand, and to the prejudices and ambitions of the parents of their pupils, on the other. The first of these external forces gave form to the curriculum. "Your job," wrote Orwell, "was to learn exactly those things that would give an examiner the impression that you knew more than you did know, and as far as possible to avoid burdening your brain with anything else. Subjects which lacked examination-value . . . were almost completely neglected." The second determined the government of the school and the character of social relations within it. "All the very rich boys were more or less undisguisedly favored. . . . I doubt that Sims [the Master] ever caned any boy whose father's income was much above 2000 pounds a year."[28] So the class system was reproduced —naïvely by the boys, with calculation by the masters.

These external forces—the élite public schools and the paying parents—did not always work to the same end. Crossgates had to provide some serious academic training, and its success in doing so had to be displayed, if it was to attract students. Hence it needed not only rich boys but bright ones, too. And since the parents most able to pay did not necessarily produce the children most likely to do well on the exams, the owners of Crossgates invested money in a small number of non-paying or reduced tuition students, looking for a return in the form of academic prestige. Orwell was one of these students. "If I had 'gone off,' as promising boys sometimes do, I imagine [Sims] would have got rid of me swiftly. As it was, I won him two scholarships when the time came, and no doubt he made full use of them in his prospectuses."[29] So, in the profoundly anti-intellectual setting of the prep school, there existed a few potential intellectuals, uneasy, intermittently grateful and sullen, occasionally rebellious. Tolerated for their brains, they were subjected to a hundred petty humiliations designed to teach them what the other boys took for granted: that no one really counted unless he was rich, and that the greatest virtue was not to earn money but simply to have it. Orwell was invited to qualify for educational advancement and then for bureaucratic or professional office—but only within a system where the highest qualifications were hereditary. Though wealthy parents were, in effect, buying advantages for their children, the children were taught to claim those advantages as a matter of right. They were not taught much else. Crossgates, as Orwell described it, is a perfect illustration of the tyranny of wealth and class over learning.

I suspect that any prep school, conceived as a commercial venture, will be the instrument of tyranny—indeed, of these particular tyrannies. For the market can never be a closed environment; it is (and should be) a place where money counts. Hence, again, the importance of a common "prep" for all children in strong and independent schools. But how can one prevent parents from spending their money on a little extra preparation? Even if all parents had the same income, some of them would be more ready than others to use what they had for their children's education. And even if schools like Crossgates were abolished, legally banned, parents could still hire tutors for their children. Or, if parents were knowledgeable enough, they could tutor their children themselves: professionals and office holders passing on their instincts for survival and advance, the folkways of their class.

Short of separating children from their parents, there is no way of preventing this sort of thing. It can, however, play a greater or a lesser role in social life generally. Parental support for schools like Crossgates, for example, will vary with the steepness of the social hierarchy and with the number of access points to specialized training and official positions. Orwell was told that he would either do well on the exams or end up as a "little office-boy at forty pounds a year."[30] His fate was to be decided, with no chance of reprieve, at the age of twelve. If that is an accurate picture, then Crossgates looks almost like a sensible institution—oppressive perhaps, but not irrational. But suppose the picture were different. Suppose that the sneer with which one said, and the shiver with which one heard, that awful phrase "office-boy at forty pounds a year" were both of them inappropriate. Suppose that offices were differently organized from the way they were in 1910, so that "boys" could move up (or around) within them. Suppose that the public schools were one—but not the only—way of finding interesting and prestigious work to do. Then Crossgates might begin to appear as unattractive to parents as it was to many of the children. The "prep" would be less critical, the exam less frightening, and the space and time available for learning would be greatly enhanced. Even specialized schools require some freedom from social pressure if they are to do their work—hence a society organized to yield that freedom. Schools can never be entirely free; but if they are to be free at all, there must be constraints in other distributive spheres, constraints roughtly of the sort I have already described, on what money can buy, for example, and on the extent and importance of office.

Association and Segregation

Basic education is a coercive business. At the lower levels, at least, schools are institutions that children must be required to attend:

> The whining school-boy, with his satchel,
> And shining morning face, creeping like snail
> Unwillingly to school

is a stock figure in many different cultures.[31] In Shakespeare's time, the will that drove the unwilling boy to school was a parental will; the state did not compel attendance. The education of children depended upon the wealth, ambition, and cultivation of their parents. That seems to us a wrongful dependency: first, because the community as a whole has an interest in education; and, second, because the children themselves are assumed to have an interest, though they may not understand it yet. Both these interests look to the future, to what children will be and to the work they will do, and not, or not simply, to what their parents are, or to how they stand in society, or to the wealth they hold. Communal provision best meets these interests; for it, too, is forward-looking, designed to enhance the competence of individuals and the integration of (future) citizens. But this is necessarily provision of a special sort, whose recipients are not enrolled but conscripted. Abolish the conscription, and children are thrown back, not—as advocates of "deschooling" like to suggest—upon their own resources but upon the resources of their parents.

Because they are conscripted, schoolchildren are like soldiers and prisoners, and they are unlike ordinary citizens who decide for themselves what they will do and with whom they will associate. But one should not make too much of either the resemblance or the difference.[32] Prisoners are sometimes "reformed," and the training that soldiers receive is sometimes useful in civilian life; but we would be lying to ourselves if we pretended that education was the chief purpose of prisons or armies. These institutions are shaped to the purposes of the community, not to those of the individuals who are dragged into them. Soldiers serve their country; prisoners "serve time." But schoolchildren in an important sense serve themselves. The distribution of prison places and, sometimes, of army places is a distribution of social bads, of pains and risks. But it isn't merely a pretence of adults that school places are social goods. Adults speak from their own experience when they say that, and they anticipate the views that children will one day hold. And, of course, the adults also remember that children in their after-school hours are free in ways that the adults themselves can only envy and never recapture.

Still, school attendance is compulsory; and because of that compulsion, it isn't only places that are distributed to children; children themselves are distributed among the available places. The public schools have no *a priori* existence; they must be constituted and their students assigned by a political decision. We require, then, a principle of association. Who goes to school with whom? This is a distributive question in two senses. It is distributive, first, because the content of the curriculum varies with the character of its recipients. If children are associated as future citizens, they will be taught the history and laws of their country. If they are associated as fellow believers in this or that religion, they will study ritual and theology. If they are associated as future workers, they will receive a "vocational" education; if as future professionals, an "academic" education. If bright students are brought together, they will be taught at one level; dull students, at another. The examples could be extended indefinitely to match the prevailing set of human differences and social distinctions. Even if we assume, as I have been doing, that children are associated as citizens and given a common education, it is still true that they can't all study together; they must be segregated into schools and classes. And how this is done remains a distributive question because, second, children are each others' resources: comrades and rivals, challenging one another, helping one another, forming what may well be the crucial friendships of their adult lives. The content of the curriculum is probably less important than the human environment within which it is taught. It is no surprise, then, that association and segregation are the most hotly contested issues in the sphere of education. Parents take a much livelier interest in the schoolmates than in the schoolbooks of their children. They are right to do so—and not only in the cynical sense that "whom you know matters more than what you know." Since so much of what we know we learn from our peers, whom and what always go together.

Randomness is the most obvious associative principle. If we were to bring children together without regard to the occupations and wealth of their parents, without regard to the political or religious commitments of their parents, and if, moreover, we were to bring them together in boarding schools, cut off from day-to-day contact with their parents, we might produce perfectly autonomous educational communities. The teacher would confront his students as if they were nothing but students, without a past and with an open future—whatever future their learning would make possible. This kind of association has occasionally been advocated by leftist groups in the name of (simple) equality, and it might well achieve that goal. Certainly, the opportunity to qualify for specialized training would be more equally distributed than under any alternative arrangement. But random association would represent a triumph not only for the school but also for the state. The child who is nothing but a student does not exist; he would have to be created; and this could only be achieved, I suspect, in a tyrannical society. Education, in any case, is more properly described as the training of particular persons, with identities, aspirations, lives of their own. This particularity is represented by the family, defended by parents. Autonomous schools are mediating institutions; they stand in a tension with parents (but not only with them). Abolish compulsory education, and one loses the tension; children become the mere subjects of their families and of the social hierarchy in which their families are implanted. Abolish the family, and the tension is lost again; children become the mere subjects of the state.

The crucial distributive problem in the sphere of education is to make children commoners of learning without destroying what is uncommon about them, their social as well as their genetic particularity. I shall argue that there is, given certain social conditions, a preferred solution to this problem, a form of complex equality that best fits the normative model of the school, on the one hand, and the requirements of democratic politics, on the other. But there is no unique solution. The character of a mediating institution can be determined only by reference to the social forces between which it mediates. A balance must always be struck, different in different times and places.

In discussing some of the possibilities, I shall draw my examples from the contemporary United States, a society considerably more heterogeneous than either Orwell's England or post-Second World War Japan. Here, more clearly than anywhere else, the requirements of basic education and equality of consideration come up against the facts of ethnic, religious, and racial pluralism, and the problems of association and segregation take an especially acute form. I want to stress in advance, however, that these problems also have a general form. Marxist writers have sometimes suggested that the advent of communism would bring an end to all differences rooted in race and religion. Maybe so. But even communist parents will not share a single philosophy of education (whatever else they share). They will disagree over what sorts of school are best for the community at large or for their own children, and so it will remain a question whether children whose parents have different educational philosophies should attend the same schools. In fact, that is a question today, though it is overshadowed by less intellectual differences.

If we stand inside the school, what associative principles seem most appropriate? What reasons do we have for bringing this particular group of children together? Except for a literal incapacity to learn, there are no reasons for exclusion that have to do with the school as a school. Reasons for inclusion are correlative with academic subjects. Specialized schools bring together qualified students, with special interests and capacities. In the case of basic education, the reason for bringing students together is need (we assume interest and capacity). What is crucial here is the need of every child to grow up within this democratic community and take his place as a competent citizen. Hence the schools should aim at a pattern of association anticipating that of adult men and women in a democracy. This is the principle that best fits the schools' central purpose, but it is a very general principle. It excludes randomness, for we can be sure that adults will not (by definition and in any community) associate randomly, without regard to their interests, occupations, blood relationships, and so on. But beyond that, there are a number of associative patterns and institutional forms that at least seem compatible with the education of democratic citizens.

Private Schools and Educational Vouchers

Neither compulsory education nor a common curriculum requires that all children go to the same sorts of school or that all schools stand in the same relation to the political community. It is a feature of American liberalism that educational entrepreneurs, like-minded parents, and religious organizations are all allowed to sponsor private schools. Here the associative principle is probably best described as parental interest and ideology—though these must be taken to include an interest in social standing and an ideology of social class. The claim is that parents should be able to get what they want, exactly what they want, for their children. This doesn't necessarily eliminate the mediating role of the school, for the state can still license private schools and set common curricular requirements. Nor do parents always want for their children exactly what they themselves can provide. Perhaps they are socially or intellectually or even religiously ambitious: eager that the children become more prominent, more sophisticated, or more devout than their parents are. And the teachers in many private schools have (what Orwell's teachers clearly lacked) a strong sense of corporate identity and intellectual mission. In any case, don't adults associate in exactly this way, on the basis of their social class or class aspiration or religious commitment (or their ideas about how to educate their children)?

But private schools are expensive, and so parents are not equally capable of associating their children as they please. This inequality seems wrong, especially if the associations are thought to be beneficial: why should children be denied such benefits simply because of the accident of their birth? With public support, the supposed benefits could be much more widely distributed. This is the thrust of the "voucher plan," a proposal that tax money available for educational purposes be turned over to parents in the form of vouchers that could be spent on the open market.[33] To absorb these vouchers, all sorts of new schools would be founded, catering to the full range of parental interests and ideologies. Some schools would still cater to class interests, requiring tuition payments over and above the voucher and so assuring wealthy parents that their children need associate only or chiefly with their social kind. But I will leave this point aside (there is an easy legislative remedy). What is more important is that the voucher plan would guarantee that children go to school with other children whose parents, at least, were very much like their own.

The voucher plan is a pluralist proposal, but it suggests a pluralism of a peculiar sort. For while the plan may well strengthen traditional organizations like the Catholic Church, the unit for which it is specifically designed is the organization of like-minded parents. It points toward, and would help to create, a society in which there was no strong geographic base or customary loyalty but, rather, a large and changing variety of ideological groups—or better, of groups of consumers brought together by the market. Citizens would be highly mobile, rootless, moving easily from one association to another. Their moves would be their choices, and so they would avoid the endless arguments and compromises of democratic politics whose participants are more or less permanently bound together. Citizens with vouchers in their hands could, in Albert Hirschman's terms, always choose "exit" over "voice."[34]

I doubt that there could possibly exist among such citizens a sufficient community of ideas and feelings to sustain the voucher plan—which is, after all, still a form of communal provision. Even a minimal welfare state requires deeper and stronger relationships. In any case, the actual experience that children would have in schools freely chosen by their parents hardly anticipates rootlessness and easy mobility. For most children, parental choice almost certainly means less diversity, less tension, less opportunity for personal change than they would find in schools to which they were politically assigned. Their schools would be more like their homes. Perhaps such an arrangement predicts their own future choices, but it hardly predicts the full range of their contacts, working relationships, and political alliances in a democratic society. Parental choice might cut across ethnic and racial lines in a way that political assignments sometimes don't. But even that is uncertain since ethnicity and race would surely be, as they are today, two of the principles around which private schools were organized. And even if these were acceptable principles, so long as they weren't the only ones, in a pluralist society, it has to be stressed that for particular children they would be the only ones.

The voucher plan assumes the activism of parents, not in the community at large but narrowly, on behalf of their own children. But its greatest danger, I think, is that it would expose many children to a combination of entrepreneurial ruthlessness and parental indifference. Even concerned parents are, after all, often busy elsewhere. And then children can be defended only by agents of the state, governmental inspectors enforcing a general code. Indeed, state agents may still have work to do even if parents are active and involved. For the community has an interest in the education of children, and so do the children, which neither parents nor entrepreneurs adequately represent. But that interest must be publicly debated and given specific form. That is the work of democratic assemblies, parties, movements, clubs, and so on. And it is the pattern of association necessary for this work that basic education must anticipate. Private schools don't do that. The communal provision of educational goods, then, has to take a more public form—else it won't contribute to the training of citizens. I don't think that there is any need for a frontal assault on parental choice, so long as its chief effect is to provide ideological diversity on the margins of a predominently public system. In principle, educational goods should not be up for purchase, but the purchase is tolerable if it doesn't carry with it (as it still does, for example, in Britain today) enormous social advantages. Here, as in other areas of communal provision, the stronger the public system, the easier one can be about the uses of money alongside it. Nor is there much reason to worry about those private schools that provide specialized education, so long as scholarships are widely available, and so long as there are alternative routes to public and private office. A voucher plan for specialized schooling and on-the-job training would make a lot of sense. But this would not serve to associate children in accordance with parental preference; it would allow them to follow their own preferences.

Talent Tracks

The career open to talents is a principle dear to American liberalism, and it has often been argued that schools should be shaped to the requirements of that career. Children who can move along quickly should be allowed to do so, while the work of slower students should be adjusted to the pace of their learning. Both groups will be happier, so the argument goes; and within each the children will find their authentic and future friends—and, indeed, their likely spouses. In later life, they will continue to associate with people of roughly similar intelligence. Parents who think their children especially bright tend to favor this sort of segregation, partly so that the children make the "right" contacts, partly so that they are not bored in school, partly in the belief that intelligence reinforced is even more intelligent. Just for this reason, however, there is often a counterdemand—that bright children be distributed throughout the school so as to stimulate and reinforce the others. This looks like using the bright students as a resource for the less bright, treating the former as means rather than as ends, much as we treat able-bodied young men when we conscript them to defend ordinary citizens. But such treatment seems wrong in the case of students, whose education is supposed to serve their own interests as well as those of the community. Whether distributing the bright students constitutes using them, however, depends upon what one takes as the natural starting point of their conscription. If the starting point is everyday residence and play, for example, then it is the segregation of the bright students that can plausibly be criticized: it looks now like a willful impoverishment of the educational experience of the others.

At the height of the Cold War, immediately after the Soviet Union sent its first rocket into space, tracking was advocated as a kind of national defense: the early recruitment of scientists and technicians, trained men and women whom we needed, or thought we needed, in large numbers. If the community that one wants to defend is a democracy, however, no form of recruitment can precede the "recruitment" of citizens. Certainly, citizens today require an education in modern science; without that, they will hardly be prepared for "all the offices both private and public of peace and war." And presumably this education will inspire some of them to pursue one or another scientific specialization; if many such people are required, additional inducements can be offered. There is no need, however, to pick out the future specialists early on, give them their proper names, as it were, before the others have had their chance at inspiration. To do so is simply to acknowledge defeat before the "recruitment" of citizens has half begun —and it will be resisted, as the Japanese example suggests, in strong schools, especially at the primary level.

Nor is it true that the tracks anticipate, though they may help to form, the associative patterns of adult citizens. The adult world is not segregated by intelligence. All sorts of work relationships, up and down the status hierarchy, require mixing; and, more important, democratic politics requires it. One could not conceivably organize a democratic society without bringing together people of every degree and kind of talent and lack of talent—not only in cities and towns but also in parties and movements (not to speak of bureaucracies and armies). The fact that people tend to marry at their intellectual level is of marginal interest, for public education in a democratic society is only incidentally a training for marriage or for private life generally. If there were no public life, or if democratic politics were radically devalued, then tracking by talent would be easier to defend.

More limited uses of segregation are permissible, however, even among future citizens. There are educational reasons for separating out children who are having special difficulties with mathematics, for example, or with a second language. But there are neither educational nor social reasons for making such distinctions across the board, creating a two-class system within the schools or creating radically different sorts of schools for different sorts of students. When this is done, and especially when it is done early in the educational process, it is not the associations of citizens that are being anticipated, but the class system in roughly its present form. Children are brought together chiefly on the basis of their pre-school socialization and home environments. It is a denial of the school's enclosure. In the United States today, this denial is likely to produce a hierarchy not only of social classes but also of racial groups. Inequality is doubled; and the doubling, as we have reason to know, is especially dangerous for democratic politics.

Integration and School Busing

We will not avoid racial segregation, however, by associating children on the basis of residence and play; for in the United States today, children of different races rarely live and play together. Nor do they receive a common education. These facts don't arise most importantly from differences in the amount of money spent on their schooling or in the quality of the teaching or the content of the curriculum; they have their origins in the social character and the expectations of the children themselves. In ghetto and slum schools, children are prepared, and prepare one another, for ghetto and slum life. The enclosure is never strong enough to protect them from themselves and from their immediate environment. They are labeled, and taught to label one another, by their social location. The only way to change all this, it is often said, is to shift the location, to separate schools from neighborhoods. This can be done by moving ghetto and slum children out of their local schools or by moving other children in. Either way, it is the associational pattern that is being changed.

The goal is the integration of future citizens, but it's not easy to say exactly what new patterns that goal requires. Logic presses us toward a public system where the social composition of every school would be exactly the same—not random but proportional association. Different sorts of children would be mixed in the same ratio in every school within a given area, the ratio varying from area to area with the overall character of the population. But how are we to identify the appropriate areas? And how are we to sort out the children: by race alone, or by religion, or ethnic group, or social class? A perfect proportionality would seem to require areas incorporating the largest possible range of groups and then the most detailed sorting out of members. But the federal judges who decided such questions in the 1970s focused their attention on established political units (cities and towns) and on racial integration alone. "In Boston," Judge William Garrity declared in a decision requiring extensive intracity busing, "the public school population is approximately two-thirds white and one-third black; ideally, every school would have the same proportions."[35] No doubt, there are good reasons for stopping at that point, but it is worth emphasizing that the principle of proportional association would require much more elaborate arrangements.

On the other hand, no form of proportional association anticipates the choices of democratic citizens. Consider, for example, the argument of many black activists in and around the civil rights movement. Even in a political community free of every taint of racism, they insisted, most black Americans would choose to live together, shaping their own neighborhoods and controlling local institutions. The only way to anticipate that pattern is to establish local control now. If the schools were run by black professionals and supported by black parents, the ghetto would cease to be a place of discouragement and defeat.[36] What equality requires, on this view, is that the association of black children with other black children carry with it the same mutual reinforcement as the association of white children with other white children. To opt for proportionality is to admit that such reinforcement is impossible—and to do so (again) before there has been any serious effort to make it work.

This is a powerful argument, but it faces in America today a major difficulty. The residential segregation of black Americans is very different from that of other groups: a great deal more thoroughgoing and a great deal less voluntary. It doesn't anticipate pluralism so much as it anticipates separatism. It isn't the pattern that we would expect to find among democratic citizens. Under such conditions, local control is likely to defeat the purposes of educational mediation. Given a political victory for the local activists, schooling will become a means of enforcing some very strong version of group identity, much as it is in the public schools of a new nation-state.[37] Children will be educated for an ideological rather than an actual citizenship. There is no reason for the larger community to pay for an education of that sort. But how far can we deviate from it while still respecting the associations that blacks would form even in a fully democratic community? Equally important, how far can we deviate from it while still respecting the associations that other people have already formed? I don't know exactly how to draw the line, but I am inclined to think that strict proportionality draws it badly.

I assume a pluralist society: so long as adults associate freely, they will shape diverse communities and cultures within the larger political community. They will certainly do this in a country of immigrants, but they will do it elsewhere, too. And then the education of children has to be group-dependent—at least in the sense that the particularity of the group, represented concretely by the family, is one of the poles between which the schools mediate. But the other pole is the larger community, represented concretely by the state, which rests upon the cooperation and mutual involvement of all the groups. So the schools, while they respect pluralism, must also work to bring children together in ways that hold open possibilities for cooperation. This is all the more important when the pluralist pattern is involuntary and distorted. It is not necessary that all schools be identical in social composition; it is necessary that different sorts of children encounter one another within them.

This necessity sometimes requires what is called (by those who oppose it) "forced busing"—as if public education must for some reason dispense with public transportation. The phrase is in any case unfair, since all school assignments are compulsory in character. So, for that matter, is schooling itself: forced reading and forced arithmetic. It may still be true that busing programs designed to meet the requirements of strict proportionality represent a more overt kind of coercion, a more direct disruption of everyday living patterns, than is desirable. The American experience suggests, moreover, that schools integrated by bringing together children who live entirely apart are unlikely to become integrated schools. Even strong schools may fail when they are forced to cope with social conflicts generated on the outside (and continually reinforced from the outside). On the other hand, it is clear that state officials have imposed racial separatism even when actual living arrangements called for, or at least allowed for, different associational patterns. This kind of imposition requires repair, and repair may now require busing. It would be foolish to rule it out. One would also hope for a more direct assault upon tyrannical distributions in the spheres of housing and employment—which no educational arrangement can possibly repair.

Neighborhood Schools

In principle, as I have already argued, neighborhoods have no admissions policies. Whether they are shaped originally by individuals and families who cluster together or by administrative decisions, highway placement, land speculation, industrial development, subway and bus routes, and so on, they will come in time, barring the use of force, to include a heterogeneous population—"not a selection, but rather a specimen of life as a whole," or at least of national life as a whole. A neighborhood school, then, does not—or not for long—serve a group of people who have chosen one another as neighbors. But insofar as different groups come to regard a school as their own, its existence may serve to heighten feelings of community. This was one of the purposes of the public school from its inception: each school was to be a little melting pot, and neighborliness was the first of its products, on the way, as it were, to citizenship. It was assumed that school districts geographically drawn would be socially mixed, and that the children who came together in the classroom would come from very different class and ethnic backgrounds. Because of protective covenants, zoning laws, and gerrymandered school districts, this was never consistently true across any particular city or town; I'm not sure whether it is more or less true now than it used to be. With regard to racial mixing, however, the evidence is clear: neighborhood schools keep black and white children apart. For this reason, the associative principle of neighborhood has come under harsh criticism.

It is, nevertheless, the preferred principle. For politics is always territorially based; and the neighborhood (or the borough, town, township, "end" of town: the contiguous set of neighborhoods) is historically the first, and still the most immediate and obvious, base for democratic politics. People are most likely to be knowledgeable and concerned, active and effective, when they are close to home, among friends and familiar enemies. The democratic school, then, should be an enclosure within a neighborhood: a special environment within a known world, where children are brought together as students exactly as they will one day come together as citizens. In this setting, the school most easily realizes its mediating role. On the one hand, children go to schools that their parents are likely to understand and support. On the other hand, political decisions about the schools are made by a diverse group of parents and non-parents, within limits set by the state. And these decisions are carried out by teachers educated (mostly) outside the neighborhood and professionally as well as politically responsible. It is an arrangement made for conflict—and, in fact, school politics in the United States has probably been the most lively and engaging kind of politics. Few parents are ever entirely satisfied by its outcomes, and children are almost certain to find a world at school different from the one they know at home. The school is simultaneously a "house of the young men and women" and a place with its own characteristic intellectual discipline.

Parents often try to defeat this discipline, and the corps of teachers is not always strong enough to maintain it. The actual distribution of schooling is shaped in significant ways by local political struggles over the size and the everyday government of the school district, the allocation of funds, the search for new teachers, the precise content of the curriculum, and so on. Neighborhood schools will never be the same across different neighborhoods. Hence the simple equality of one child/one place in the educational system makes for only a part of the story of justice in education. But I think it is fair to say that when neighborhoods are open (when racial or ethnic identity is not dominant over membership and place), and when every neighborhood has its own strong school, then justice has been done. The children are equals within a complex set of distributive arrangements. They receive a common education, even if there is some variation in the curriculum (and in the ways teachers stress or elide this or that area within the curriculum) from place to place. The cohesiveness of the faculty and the cooperative or critical zeal of the parents will vary, too; but these are variations intrinsic to the character of a democratic school, inevitable features of complex equality.

The same thing can be said of the patterns of student association. Some school districts will be more heterogeneous than others; some contacts across groups, more tense than others. The boundary conflicts endemic to a pluralist society will be faced in every school, but sometimes in a milder, sometimes in a more acute, form. It requires extraordinary ideological zeal or great priggishness to insist that they be faced in their most acute form everywhere and all the time. One could, indeed, arrange for that, but only by a radical use of state power. Now, the state has much to do with regard to education. It requires school attendance, establishes the general character of the curriculum, polices the certification process. But if the schools are to have any inward strength at all, there must be limits on the state's activity—limits fixed by the integrity of academic subjects, by the professionalism of teachers, by the principle of equal consideration—and by an associative pattern that anticipates democratic politics but is not dominated by the powers-that-be or the reigning ideologies. Just as success in the Cold War was never a reason for doing anything more than improving the quality and attractiveness of the specialized schools, so the goal of an integrated society was never a reason for going beyond the remedies required to end willful segregation. Any more radical subordination of schooling to political purpose undermines the strength of the school, the success of its mediation, and then the value of schooling as a social good. Ultimately, it makes for less, not greater, equality when students and teachers are subject to the tyranny of politics.

9

Kinship and Love

The Distributions of Affect

Kinship ties and sexual relations are commonly thought to constitute a domain beyond the reach of distributive justice. They are judged in other terms, or we are taught not to be judgmental. People love as best they can, and their feelings can't be redistributed. It might be true, as Samuel Johnson once said, that "Marriages would in general be as happy, and often more so, if they were all made by the Lord Chancellor."[1] But no one has seriously proposed extending the Lord Chancellor's power in this way, not even for the sake of greater happiness (and, if that, why not equal happiness?). It would, nevertheless, be a mistake to think of kinship and love as a sphere different from all the others, as a sacred precinct, like the Vatican in republican Italy, safe from philosophical criticism. In fact, it is closely connected to other distributive spheres, highly vulnerable to their interventions and itself pervasively influential. Its boundaries often have to be defended, if not against the Lord Chancellor, then against other sorts of tyrannical intrusion—the quartering of troops in private homes, for example, or the demand for child labor in factories and mines, or the "visits" of social workers, truant officers, policemen, and other agents of the modern state. And other spheres have to be defended against its intrusions, against nepotism and favoritism—which in our society, though not by any means in all societies, are blocked acts of love.

Important distributions are carried out within the family and through the alliance of families. Dowries, gifts, inheritances, alimony, mutual aid of many different kinds: all these are subject to customs and rules that are conventional in character and reflect deep, but never permanent, understandings. More important, love itself, and marriage too, and parental concern, and filial respect are similarly subject and similarly reflective. "Honor thy father and thy mother" is a distributive rule. So is the Confucian maxim about elder brothers.[2] So are the multitude of prescriptions that anthropologists have turned up, that attach children to their maternal uncles, for example, or wives to their mothers-in-law. These distributions, too, depend upon cultural understandings that change over time. If people love and marry freely, as we supposedly do, that is because of what love and marriage mean in our society. Nor are we entirely free, despite a succession of liberation struggles. Incest is still ruled out: "The sexual permissiveness of the contemporary western world has not done away with this restriction."[3] Polygamy is ruled out, too. Homosexual marriage remains legally unrecognized and politically controversial. Miscegenation carries with it social, if no longer legal, penalties. In each of these (very different) cases, "liberation" would be a redistributive act, a new arrangement of commitments, obligations, responsibilities, and alliances.

Throughout most of human history, love and marriage have been far more closely regulated than they are in the United States today. The rules of kinship are an anthropological feast, wonderfully various and highly seasoned. There are a hundred ways in which the basic distributive question—Who . . . whom?—is asked and answered. Who can sleep with whom? Who can marry whom? Who lives with whom? Who eats with whom? Who celebrates with whom? Who must show respect to whom? Who is responsible for whom? The answers to these questions constitute an elaborate system of rules, and it is a feature of the earliest understanding of political power that chiefs or princes who violate these rules are tyrants.[4] The deepest understanding of tyranny probably lies here: it is the dominance of power over kinship. Marriage is rarely what John Selden called it: "nothing but a civil contract."[5] It is part of a larger system, which legislators ordinarily deal with only at the margins or after the fact, for the moral and also the spatial arrangement of "private" life: homes, meals, visits, duties, expressions of feeling, and transfers of goods.

In many times and places, the determinations of kinship range even farther, shaping politics, too, and fixing the legal status and the life chances of individuals. Indeed, one view of human history has it that all the spheres of relationship and distribution, all the "companies" of men and women, spin off the family, much as the full set of state offices

Kinship and Love

and institutions spin off the king's house. But the opposition of kinship and politics is very old, perhaps primordial. "Every society," the contemporary anthropologist Meyer Fortes has written, ". . . comprises two basic orders of social relations . . . familial domain and politico-jural domain, kinship and polity."[6] It makes sense to say, then, that kinship rules don't encompass the social world but mark off the first set of boundaries within it.

The family is a sphere of special relationships. This child is the apple of its father's eye; that child is its mother's joy. This brother and sister love one another better than they should. That uncle dotes on a favorite niece. Here is a world of passion and jealousy, whose members frequently seek to monopolize each other's affections, while all of them have at the same time some minimal claim—at least as against outsiders who may well have no claim at all. The line between insiders and outsiders is often sharply drawn: inside, "the rule of prescriptive altruism" applies; outside, not.[7] Hence the family is a perennial source of inequality. This is so not only for the reason usually given, because the family functions (differently in different societies) as an economic unit within which wealth is hoarded and passed on, but also because it functions as an emotional unit within which love is hoarded and passed on. We might better say, passed around and then passed on, and initially at least for internal reasons. Favoritism begins in the family—as when Joseph is singled out from his brothers—and is only then extended into politics and religion, into schools, markets, and workplaces.

Plato's Guardians

The most radical egalitarian proposal, then, the simplest way to simple equality, is the abolition of the family. I have already considered this proposal in the sphere of education, where the school offers an immediate alternative. But the school, even the all-encompassing school, abolishes only the special relation of parents with children above a certain age; and it is worth considering a more radical abolitionism.* Imagine a society like that of Plato's Guardians where, within each generation, all the members are siblings, brothers and sisters who know nothing of their own blood ties and who produce through a kind of civic

---

*A certain straining toward abolitionism is common in egalitarian thought, even among writers who are visibly uneasy with the idea. For example, John Rawls says that "the principle of fair opportunity can be only imperfectly carried out, at least as long as the institution of the family exists."[8] The argument is repeated,[9] but not pursued. Presumably, Rawls does not want the distribution of parental love and concern to be governed by the second principle of justice. By what principle, then, ought it to be governed?

229

incest a new generation of children to whom they are only generalized, never particular, parents. Kinship is universal, hence effectively non-existent, assimilated to political friendship. We may expect that passion and jealousy will find their way even into the hearts of universal siblings. But without a clear sense of "mine" and "thine," without exclusive ties to persons or things, Plato argues, "a fit of passion is less likely to grow into a serious quarrel." The individual as we know him (and as Plato knew him), who "[drags] off whatever he can get for himself into a private home, where he [has] his separate family, forming a center of exclusive joys and sorrows," will no longer exist. Instead, men and women will experience pleasure and pain as common passions; the jealousies of family life will be replaced by an emotional, as well as a material, egalitarianism: the regime of "fellow feeling."[10] It is the triumph of equanimity over passionate intensity.

The triumph, too, of political community over kin; for, as Lawrence Stone has written in his study of the development of the contemporary family, "the distribution of affective ties . . . is something of a zero-sum game. . . . The highly personalized, inward-looking family was achieved in part at the cost of . . . a withdrawal from the rich and integrated community life of the past."[11] The same withdrawal seems to have occurred in earlier times, too. Perhaps the community life of the past is a golden age, and abolitionism a perennial utopia. In any case, the purpose of abolition is not to achieve some balance between kinship and community, but radically to reverse the outcome of the "game." To be sure, Plato imposes his egalitarian regime only on the Guardians. His own purpose is not to produce a truly universal *amour social* or to equalize the experience of love (though he attaches real value to equanimity); he wants to eliminate the effects of love in the politics of the city—"to free the Guardians from the temptation to prefer family interests to those of the whole community."[12] Orwell describes a similar purpose in his novel *Nineteen Eighty-Four:* the Anti-Sex League seeks to bar all kinship ties among party members, so as to bind them unequivocally to the party (and to Big Brother). But the proles are free to marry as they please and to love their own children. A democratic regime, I assume, could not tolerate such a division; kinship would have to be abolished entirely. It isn't accidental, however, that philosophers and novelists who have imagined the abolition have so often thought in terms of an élite, whose members could be compensated by special prerogatives for the loss of special affections.

For it is a loss, and one that is likely to be resisted by most men and women. What we might think of as the highest form of communal life—universal brotherhood and sisterhood—is probably incompatible with any process of popular decision making. The case is the same in moral philosophy. A number of writers have argued that the highest form of ethical life is one where the "rule of prescriptive altruism" applies universally, and there are no special obligations to kinfolk (or friends).[13] Faced with a choice between saving my own child or someone else's from an imminent and terrible danger, I would adopt a random decision procedure. It would be much easier, obviously, if I were not able to recognize my own children or if I had no children of my own. But this highest form of ethical life is available only to a few strong-minded philosophers or to monks, hermits, and platonic guardians. The rest of us must settle for something less, which we are likely to think of as something better: we draw the best line that we can between the family and the community and live with the unequal intensities of love. That means that some families will be warmer and more intimate than others. Some children will be better loved than others. Some men and women will move into the spheres of education, money, and politics with all the self-confidence that parental affection and respect can produce; while others will step forward hesitantly, full of self-doubt. (But we can still try to rule out favoritism in the schools and "family alliances" in the civil service.)

If we give up universal kinship, no arrangement of family ties seems to be theoretically required or even generally preferable. There is no single set of passional connections that is more just than all of the alternative sets. This point, I think, is commonly conceded by writers who nevertheless seek a highly specific and unitary justice in other spheres. But the argument is the same here as elsewhere. We don't know, for example, whether the political community should make the drama equally accessible to all its members, until we know what the drama means in this or that culture. We don't know whether the sale of guns should be a blocked exchange, until we know how guns are used on particular streets. And we don't know how much affection or respect is due to husbands, until we know the answer to the question with which Lucy Mair opens her anthropological study of marriage: "What are husbands for?"[14]

In each local setting, of course, there are objective principles, sometimes disputed, often violated, but commonly understood. Joseph's brothers resented their father's favoritism because it went beyond the bounds, so they thought, of patriarchal willfulness. In such cases, though often with unhappy consequences, we leave the enforcement of the relevant principles to the members of the family. We don't want government officials stepping in to make sure that everyone (or no one) gets a coat of many colors. Only when familial distributions undercut the promises of communal membership and welfare are interventions required, as in the case of neglected children, say, or of battered wives. The distribution of family wealth is also legally regulated; but these regulations are likely to represent, as I have already suggested in my discussion of gifts and inheritance, the external enforcement of principles originally internal to a particular understanding of family ties.

Family and Economy

In early modern political thought, the family is often described as a "little state" within which children are taught the virtues of obedience and prepared for citizenship (or, more often, subjection) in the larger state, the political community as a whole.[15] This looks like a formula for integration, but it also had another purpose. If the family was a little state, then the father was a little king, and the realm over which he ruled was a realm the king himself could not invade. The little states bounded and contained the larger one of which they were also the parts. Similarly, we can think of the family as an economic unit, partially integrated into, but also fixing the boundaries of, the sphere of money and commodities. Once, of course, the integration was perfect. The Greek word from which our *economy* derives means simply "household management"; it describes a single sphere distinct from that of politics. But whenever the economy takes on an independent character and makes for the company not of relatives but of strangers, whenever the market replaces the self-subsistent household, our understanding of kinship sets limits on the reach of exchange, establishing a space within which market norms don't apply. We can see this most clearly if we consider a period of rapid economic change, as in the early Industrial Revolution.

Manchester, 1844

Engels had a great deal to say about working-class families in his account of factory life in Manchester in 1844. He told a story not only of misery but also of moral catastrophe: men, women, and children working from dawn to dusk; infants left behind, locked up in tiny un-

Kinship and Love

heated rooms; a radical failure of socialization; a breakdown of the structures of love and mutuality; a loss of kinship feeling under conditions that allowed those feelings no room and no realization.[16] Historians today suggest that Engels underestimated the strength and resiliency of the family and the help it was able to provide, under all but the worst of conditions, to its members.[17] But I am less interested in the accuracy of Engels's account—it is accurate enough—than in what it reveals about the intentions of the early socialist writers and organizers. They saw capitalism as an assault on the family, a tyrannical disruption of domestic bonds: "all family ties among the proletarians are torn asunder, and their children transformed into simple articles of commerce and instruments of labor."[18] And to this tyranny they set themselves in opposition.

Manchester, as Engels described it, is another example of the unzoned city, money triumphant everywhere. So children are sold into the factories, women into prostitution; the family is "dissolved." There is no sense of hearth and home, no time for domestic arrangements and family celebrations, no rest, no intimacy. The family relation, Marx and Engels wrote in the *Manifesto,* is "reduced . . . to a mere money relation." Communism, they went on, will bring with it the abolition of the bourgeois family; but since the bourgeois family already represented, to their minds, the abolition of kinship and love—the enslavement of children and "the community of women"—what they really intended is something closer in its likely effects to a restoration. Or better, they argued that when production is finally and fully socialized, the family will emerge for the first time as an independent sphere, a sphere of personal relations, based on sexual love and free entirely from the tyranny of money—and also, they thought, from the closely related tyranny of fathers and husbands.[19]*

The response of trade unionists and reformers to the conditions that Engels described was more simply defensive. They wanted to "save" the existing family, and that is the purpose of a great deal of nineteenth-century factory legislation. Child-labor laws, the shorter working day, restrictions on the work that women might do: all these were designed to protect family ties against the market, to mark out a certain

*Although Engels plays heavily on the suffering of children in his dramatic account of working-class life in Manchester, his reconstituted family—and Marx's, too—seems to be limited to adults. Children will be cared for communally, so that both parents can share in social production. The proposal makes sense when the community is small and relationships are close, as in an Israeli kibbutz. But given the conditions of mass society, it is likely to result in a great loss of love—a loss, moreover, borne in the first instance by the weakest members. The family, under a great variety of arrangements, which include but extend far beyond the conventional bourgeois arrangements (why can't the parents share in social *re*production?), works to prevent that loss.[20]

space, to free some minimal time, for domestic life. A very old conception of domesticity underlay this effort. The space and time were meant primarily for mothers and children; the home was conceived to center on these two, while fathers were more distant protectors, who protected themselves only in order to protect their dependents. Hence "women were commonly excluded from trade unions, and male trade unionists demanded a wage that could support the entire family."[21] The domestic sphere was woman's place, children gathered around her, safe in her nurturing care. Victorian sentimentality is as much a proletarian as a bourgeois creation. The sentimental family is the first form that the distribution of kinship and love takes, in the West at least, once household and economy are pulled apart.

Marriage

But the establishment of the domestic sphere begins long before the Industrial Revolution and has long-term consequences very different from those suggested by the word *domesticity*. These are most clearly visible in the upper classes; they grow out of a twofold process of boundary drawing, not only between kinship and economic life but also between kinship and politics. The aristocratic and *haut bourgeois* families of the early modern period were little dynasties. Their marriages were complex matters of exchange and alliance, carefully planned and elaborately negotiated. This sort of thing persists in our own time, though the negotiations nowadays are rarely explicit. I suppose that marriage will always have this aspect, so long as families are differently placed in the social and the political worlds, so long as there are family businesses and well-established networks of relatives. Simple equality would eliminate exchange and alliance by eliminating familial difference. "If every family were brought up at the same cost," wrote Shaw, "we should all have the same habits, manners, culture, and refinement; and the dustman's daughter could marry the duke's son as easily as a stockbroker's son now marries a bank manager's daughter."[22] All marriages would be love matches—and this is indeed the tendency, the intention, as it were, of the kinship system as we currently understand it.

But Shaw overestimated the power of money. He would have to require not only that no child be brought up in a family with more money than other families, but also that no child be brought up in a family with more political influence or social status than other families. None of this is possible, I think, short of the abolition of the family itself. Something of the same effects can be had, however, through the separation of distributive spheres. If family membership and political influence are entirely distinct, if nepotism is ruled out, inheritance curtailed, aristocratic titles abolished, and so on, then there is much less reason to think of marriage as either an exchange or an alliance. And then sons and daughters can (and will) search for mates whom they find physically or spiritually attractive. So long as the family was integrated into political and economic life, romantic love had its place outside. What the troubadors celebrated was, so to speak, a marginal distribution. The independence of the family made for a relocation of love.

Or at least of romance: for love certainly existed in the older family, too, though it was often talked about in a rhetorically deflationary way. Now romantic love, more or less inflated, is conceived to be the sole satisfactory basis for marriage and married life. But that means that marriages are taken out of the hands of parents and their agents (matchmakers, for example) and delivered into the hands of children. The distributive principle of romantic love is free choice. I don't mean that free choice is the sole distributive principle in the sphere of kinship. That can never be the case; for though I choose my spouse, I don't choose my spouse's relatives, and the further obligations of marriage are always culturally and not individually determined. Nevertheless, romantic love focuses our attention on the couple who choose one another. And it has this crucial implication: the man and the woman are not only free but equally free. The feeling must be mutual, it takes two to tango, and so on.

Henceforth we call parents tyrants if they try to use their economic or political power to thwart the desires of their children. Once the children are of age, parents have indeed no legal right to punish or restrain them; and though sons and daughters who marry "badly" can still, as the saying goes, be cut off without a cent, this threat is no longer part of the family's moral arsenal (in some countries, it's not part of its legal arsenal either): in these matters, parents have little legitimate authority. They must play, if they can, on the feelings of their children. This is sometimes called, when it works, "emotional tyranny." But I think that phrase is wrong—or, it is used metaphorically, like Somerset Maugham's "human bondage." For the play of feeling, the experience of emotional intensity, is intrinsic to the sphere of kinship and not intrusive upon it. Freedom in love describes a choice made independently of the constraints of exchange and alliance, not of the constraints of love itself.

The Civic Ball

If children are free to love and marry as they please, there must be a social space, a set of arrangements and practices, within which they can make their choices. Among political and social theorists, Rousseau recognized this most clearly and, with that extraordinary foresight that so often marks his work, described what was to become one of the most common arrangements, a particular sort of public festival: "the ball for young marriageable persons." In his *Letter to D'Alembert on the Theater,* Rousseau wished that there were not so many "scrupulous doubts" about dancing among the Genevans. For what better way is there than this "agreeable exercise" in which young men and women can "show themselves off with the charms and the faults which they might possess, to the people whose interest it is to know them well before being obliged to love them?"[23] Rousseau to be sure, thought that mothers and fathers (and grandmothers and grandfathers!) should attend these balls, as spectators not participants; and this would, to say the least, impose a certain "gravity" upon the occasion. Still, the event that he describes has played a large part in the romantic life of the young over the past several centuries. It is often organized on a class basis—country club cotillions and "coming out" parties—but it also has more democratic forms, as in the high school prom, which carry forward into our own time Rousseau's cautiously expressed intentions: that "the inclinations of children would be somewhat freer; [their] first choice would depend somewhat more on their hearts; the agreements of age, temperament, taste, and character would be consulted somewhat more; and less attention would be paid to those of station and fortune." Social relations would become easier, and "marriages, less circumscribed by rank, would . . . temper excessive inequality."[24]

The implicit comparisons in the passage I have just quoted are with the system of arranged marriages, the exchange of children (and material goods, too), and the alliance of families. Rousseau's civic ball is designed to facilitate as well as express the new system of free choice. The parents are there, above all, to signal their acquiescence, though also no doubt to qualify the freedom in subtle and not so subtle ways. The city's endorsement has another purpose; it confirms the family's (partial) separation from political and economic life and guarantees, or at least protects, free choice in love. In exactly the same way, city magistrates might sponsor a fair or a market and guarantee free exchange. But the city doesn't in any sense fill in for the lost power of parents. Rousseau actually proposed that a "Queen of the Ball" be elected by a set of judges; but the magistrates don't vote, nor do the citizens, on who shall marry whom.

The Idea of the "Date"

I mean to dwell for a bit on these mechanisms for the distribution of love and marriage because they play such a crucial part in everyday life and so rarely figure in discussions of distributive justice. We think of them now almost entirely in terms of freedom, the right of individuals to do as they please within some moral and legal framework (which essentially establishes the rights of other individuals). Thus the old laws against copulation, extramarital sex, are understood simply as infringements of individual freedom. So they are, I suppose, at least to us; and we are inclined to believe that they are enacted solely for that purpose by small-minded legislators offended by other people's pleasures. But these laws—or, rather, the system of moral and legal restraint of which they constitute the tattered remains—are designed with larger goals in mind. They are so many efforts to defend social goods: the "honor" of a woman and her family, for example, or the value of marriage or of the exchange or the alliance that marriage embodies. And they become tyrannical only when physical love is publicly conceived (I have no doubt that it has always been privately conceived) as a good-in-itself. Or, when it is conceived as a good instrumental to free choice in marriage: "an agreeable exercise" by which young men and women "show themselves off . . . to the people whose interest it is to know them well before being obliged to love them." Were it not instrumental to married love (at least sometimes), I suspect that we would worry more than we do about the private assignation, where children are entirely free and the parental presence disappears.

The domesticated version of the assignation is the "date," probably the most common form of courtship in the West today. The early history of the date is staid enough. We can get some sense of it, for example, in the following brief account of courtship in rural Spain: "There young men choose their girls at the Sunday evening promenade where all the unmarried people of the village circulate together. The suitor first walks with his girl in the promenade, then goes with her to the corner of her street, and finally commits himself by asking to enter her house."[25] Here the promenade is a kind of market; the young people, but especially the girls, are the goods; and walking together is a tentative exchange. These general procedures have been extraordinarily stable over time, though they have also been marked in recent years by greater equality and greater intimacy in the exchange: both equality and intimacy are the consequences of freedom in love. The process still culminates, very often, in the family visit, introduction to parents, and so on. But it can obviously culminate differently, not in a marriage but in an affair, and then the family visit is likely to be avoided—then, indeed, the connection between love and kinship is likely to be broken off entirely.

Perhaps we should say that there is a sphere of private affairs, within which individual men and women are radically free, and where every kinship obligation is experienced as a kind of tyranny. In effect, there are no obligations—not, at least, until judges step in to enforce a kind of ersatz kinship, requiring alimony payments, for example, to former lovers. The sphere of private affairs is exactly like the market in commodities, except that these commodities own themselves: the gift of self and the voluntary exchange of selves are the model transactions. Love, affection, friendship, generosity, solicitude, and respect are not only initially but also continuously, at every point in time, matters of individual choice. The distributive mechanism through which these choices are made will be not the civic ball or the public promenade but something more like the singles' bar and the classified advertisement. The resulting distributions are obviously going to be very unequal, even if opportunities are more or less the same for everyone; more important, they are also going to be very precarious. Against this background, we can see that the family is a kind of welfare state, which guarantees to all its members some modicum of love, friendship, generosity, and so on, and which taxes its members for the sake of the guarantee. Familial love is radically unconditioned, whereas a private affair is a (good or bad) bargain.

Children are obviously a threat to the absclute freedom of the affair—which is, indeed, more perfectly represented by friendship than by heterosexual love. Anyone committed to the affair must find some way to liberate parents from children or men and women generally from parenting. Hence a variety of proposals have been brought forward, aiming, mostly, at one or another form of institutionalization. It is a hard argument, but a true one, that the integrity of private affairs requires a license for abandonment. And then if some children are abandoned to bureaucratic rearing, why not, in the name of equality, all of them? One might go farther still and liberate women from childbirth as well as parents from child care, by cloning the next generation, for example, or by purchasing babies from underdeveloped countries.[26] This is not the redistribution but the abolition of parental love, and I suspect that it would quickly produce a race of men and women incapable even of the commitment required for an affair. The strength of the family lies, again, in the guarantee of love. The guarantee isn't always effective; but for children, at least, no one has yet produced a substitute.

The sphere of private affairs can never be a stable place. The market in commodities works because the men and women who trade in commodities are connected elsewhere (most often to their families). But here men and women trade themselves, and they are radically disconnected, free-floating subjects. It is a way of life that most people will choose, if they have a choice, only for a time. From the point of view of society as a whole, private affairs are marginal to and parasitic upon marriages and families. Except at the margins, personal life is not usefully conceived as a private affair. It is focused on the family, even when the focus is tense and oppositional. To say this is not by any means to defend political interventions in private affairs. "Because we freely love, as in our will to love or not," all such interventions are barred: they represent the exercise of power outside its sphere.[27] I want only to reiterate that the constraints of kinship, though they are often burdensome and close, are not for that reason unjust. Because of what families are, freedom in love can rarely be anything more than a free acceptance of (a particular set of) domestic constraints.

The Woman Question

Freedom in love radically alters the standing of women, but it doesn't, certainly not in any automatic way, end their oppression. For that oppression is only partly situated within the family. As a little economy and a little state, ruled by a father-king, the family has long been a setting for the domination of wives and daughters (sons, too). It isn't difficult to collect stories of physical brutality or to describe customary practices and religious rites that seem designed, above all, to break the spirits of young women. At the same time, the family has long been woman's place; she was absolutely necessary to its existence and then to its well-being; and at some level, in most cultures, she had to be regarded as a valued member. Within the household, if only there, she often possessed considerable power. The real domination of women has less to do with their familial place than with their exclusion from all other places. They have been denied the freedom of the city, cut off from distributive processes and social goods outside the sphere of kinship and love.

Nepotism is the most readily understood of the forms of familial dominance, but it is by no means the most important. The family not only favors some of its members; it also disfavors others. It reproduces the structures of kinship in the larger world; it imposes what we currently call "sex roles" upon a range of activities to which sex is entirely irrelevant. Alongside nepotism—an expression of kinship preferences where preference has no proper place—there has long existed something like its opposite: a kind of political and economic misogyny—an expression of kinship constraints where constraint has no proper place. Thus the denial to women of the right to vote, or to hold office, or to own property, or to sue in court, and so on. In each case, the reasons given, when anyone bothers to give reasons, have to do with woman's place within the family.[28] So kinship patterns are dominant outside their sphere. And liberation begins outside, with a succession of claims that this or that social good should be distributed for its own, not for familial, reasons.

Consider just a few examples. In nineteenth-century China, one of the key demands of the Taiping rebels was that men and women alike should be eligible to take the civil service examinations.[29] How could women justly be excluded from a system aimed solely to discover meritorious or qualified individuals? I don't doubt that deep cultural transformations must have taken place before it became possible even to ask that question. After all, the exams had been around for a long time. But if they do not by themselves prompt the question, they do provide its moral basis—and the moral basis, too, for the extended answer that it receives. If women are to take the exams, then they must be allowed to prepare for them; they must be admitted to the schools, freed from concubinage, arranged marriages, foot binding, and so on. The family itself must be reformed so that its power no longer reaches into the sphere of office.

The women's suffrage movement in the West can be similarly described. Its leaders played on the meaning of citizenship in a democratic society. They had, to be sure, a great deal to say about the special values that women would bring to the performance of their political role, and these were essentially the values of the family: motherhood, nurturance, sympathy.[30] But it wasn't this sort of argument that made their claims ultimately unanswerable. Indeed, the counterarguments of the anti-suffragists may yet prove nearer to the truth: that the large-scale participation of women in politics will introduce new forms of conflict, new calculations of interest, into the kinship system. I suspect that when in 1927, out of a concern for peasant (male and female) sensibilities, Mao Tse-tung tried to slow down the communist attack on the traditional family, he was restraining some of his female comrades, who longed to introduce the class war into the domestic sphere. "The abolition of the clan system, of superstitions [that is, ancestor worship], and of inequality between men and women," he wrote, "will follow as a natural consequence of victory in political and economic struggles." And he warned against "crude and arbitrary" interventions in the daily conduct of family life.[31] Presumably, women will act like men in politics: that is, use what power they can muster for purposes of their own—not only as members of their sex (or of their families), but as members of other groups, too, and as individuals. It is just for this reason that democracy provides no basis for their exclusion.

The case is the same, finally, with contemporary demands for "affirmative action" in the economic sphere. Though these sometimes look like demands for preferential treatment, their deepest purpose is simply to establish woman's place in the free market. Just as market forces should not be allowed to disrupt family ties, so a particular set of family ties should not be allowed to constrain the play of market forces. Here, too, there has been some notion among feminists that women would (or that they should) change the terms of play: reduce the strains of competition, for example, or transform the discipline of a full-time job or the commitment hitherto entailed by a career. But what is most important right now is that the market, as it actually functions and as we understand its functioning, sets no internal bar to the participation of women. It is focused on the quality of goods and on the skill and energy of persons, not on kinship standing or sex—unless it is sex itself that is being sold: whether the merchandising of sex and sexuality will be undercut by the enhanced presence of women in the marketplace, or merely made more various, remains an open question. In any case, the company of the market, as of the forum, is a mixed company.

The family will certainly be a different place when it is no longer woman's exclusive place and when the structures of kinship are no longer reiterated in other distributive spheres. Thrown back upon its own resources, it may well prove a more fragile association than the kinship groups of other and older societies. Still, the sphere of personal relations, domestic life, reproduction, and childrearing remains, even among ourselves, the focus of enormously important distributions. The "rule of prescriptive altruism" is not a rule most people will willingly give up; the sharing of familial wealth (with women now assured of their rightful share) is a crucial safeguard, even in the welfare state. Rising divorce rates suggest, perhaps, that the bond of love, without the ancient reinforcements of power and interest, will not make for social stability. But we are at such an early point in the history of the independent family, man's as well as woman's place, that it would be foolish simply to project current trends. Nor, as I have already argued, is freely chosen love the sole basis even of the contemporary family. The love of siblings is important, too, for example; and though all the forces of modern life act to undermine it, so that "sibling solidarity would seem . . . to have little chance of outlasting early childhood . . . the evidence shows that it remains a dominant affective and moral force for most people throughout life."[32] And the nurturance and education of children centers the family in a new way: parents today are more likely to take pride in their children's achievements than are children in the status of their parents (or in the ancestors of their parents). This, too, is a product of the separation of the family from politics and economy, the decline of national and local dynasties, the triumph of complex equality. Today we protect our children as best we can, preparing them for school, examinations, marriage, and work. But we can't determine or guarantee their careers, assigning daughters to domesticity and motherhood, for example, and sons to the church or the law or the land. They make their own way, bearing the unequal burdens of parental expectations and the unequal grace of parental love. These last inequalities cannot be eliminated; indeed, the family exists, and will continue to exist, precisely in order to make a place for them.

10

Divine Grace

Grace is the gift presumably of a gracious God. He gives it to whomever He pleases, to those who deserve it (as if recognized by a jury of angels) or to those whom He makes deserving, for reasons known only to Himself. But we know nothing about these gifts. Insofar as men and women come to believe themselves saved, or are believed by others to be saved, they are the recipients of a social good, its distribution mediated by an ecclesiastical organization or a religious doctrine. This isn't a good available in all, perhaps not in most, cultures and societies. But it has been so important in the history of the West that I must take it up here. Grace has often been a disputed good, not because it is necessarily scarce and my having it diminishes your chances of getting it, but for two different reasons: first, its availability is sometimes thought to depend upon specific public arrangements; second, its possession by some people (and not others) is sometimes thought to carry with it certain political prerogatives. Both these beliefs are commonly denied today; but at various times in the past, it has taken some courage to deny them and then to resist their coercive implementation.

What makes the two denials so easy today is the generally held view that the pursuit of grace (and certainly its distribution by an omnipotent God) is necessarily free. The extreme version of this is the Protestant account of the relation between the individual and his God—the possessive pronoun is important—as an entirely private affair. "Each one stands for himself where the divine promise is concerned," Luther wrote. "His own faith is required. Each must respond for himself."[1] But even if we imagine grace to depend upon the social practice of communion, it is still thought that communion must be free, a matter of individual choice. Here is perhaps the clearest example in our own culture of an autonomous sphere. Grace cannot be purchased or inherited; nor can it be coerced. It cannot be had by passing an exam or by holding an office. It is not, though it once was, a matter of communal provision.

This autonomy didn't come easily. Of course, there were always political rulers in the West who argued that religion was a sphere apart—and then that priests should not interfere in politics. But even such rulers often found it useful to control, if they could, the machinery through which communion and the assurance of salvation were distributed. And other rulers, more pious perhaps (themselves the recipients of grace), or pliable in the hands of interfering priests, insisted that it was their duty to organize the political realm so as to make God's gift available, perhaps even equally available, to all their subjects, His children. Since these rulers were mortal men and women, they could do no more; since they bore the secular sword, they could do whatever they did with considerable effect, regulating the teaching of religious doctrine and the administration of the sacraments, requiring church attendance, and so on. I don't want to deny that it was their duty to do these things (though I would hope to draw the line well this side of burning heretics). Whether it was their duty depends upon the understandings of grace and political power that they shared with their subjects—not, it should be stressed, upon their private understandings.

From the beginning, however, political coercion and Christian doctrine sat uneasily together. Grace might be attained through good works freely chosen, or it might come only with faith, but it never seemed something with which princes had much to do. Hence princes who interfered in the worship of their subjects were often called tyrants—at least by those who suffered the interference. Protestants of various sorts, defending religious toleration in the sixteenth and seventeenth centuries, were able to draw upon latent but deep conceptions of what worship, good works, faith, and salvation really meant. When Locke, in his *Letter Concerning Toleration,* insisted that "no man can, if he would, conform his faith to the dictates of another," he was merely echoing Augustine's statement, quoted in turn by Luther, that "No one can or ought to be constrained to believe."[2]

Christian doctrine was shaped by that original distributive rule, "Render unto Caesar the things which are Caesar's; and unto God the things that are God's" (Matthew 22:21). Often overridden by imperial or crusading enthusiasms, the rule was regularly reasserted whenever God's servants or Caesar's found it useful. And, in one form or another,

Divine Grace

it survived to serve the purposes of the early modern opponents of religious persecution. Two "renderings," two jurisdictions, two distributive spheres: in the one, the magistrate presides, "procuring, preserving, and advancing," as Locke argued, the civil interests of his subjects;[3] in the other, God Himself presides, His power invisible, leaving His seekers and worshipers to advance their spiritual interests as best they can, and assure themselves or one another of divine favor. They can organize for that purpose in any way they please and submit themselves if they please to bishops, priests, presbyters, ministers, and so on. But the authority of all such officials is confined to the church, as the authority of magistrates is confined to the commonwealth, "because the church . . . is a thing absolutely separate and distinct from the commonwealth. The boundaries on both sides are fixed and immoveable. He jumbles heaven and earth together . . . who mixes these two societies."[4]

The Wall between Church and State

Within a century after it was written, Locke's *Letter* found legal expression in the first amendment to the United States Constitution: "Congress shall make no law respecting an establishment of religion, or prohibiting the free exercise thereof." This simple sentence bars any attempt at communal provision in the sphere of grace. The state is excluded from any concern with curing souls. The citizens cannot be taxed or coerced—not for the cure of their own souls and not for the cure of anyone else's either. State officials cannot even regulate entrepreneurial activity in the sphere of grace; they must watch without comment the steady proliferation of sects offering salvation on the cheap or, perhaps more excitingly, at an enormous expense of money and spirit. Consumers cannot be protected from fraud, for the First Amendment bars the state from recognizing fraud (nor is fraud easy to recognize in the sphere of grace where, as it is said, the most unlikely people may well be doing God's work).

All this is called religious liberty, but it is also religious egalitarianism. The First Amendment is a rule of complex equality. It does not distribute grace equally; indeed, it does not distribute it at all. Nevertheless, the wall that it raises has profound distributive effects. It makes, on the religious side, for the priesthood of all believers; that is, it leaves all believers in charge of their own salvation. They can acknowledge whatever ecclesiastical hierarchies they like, but the acknowledgment is theirs to give or refuse; it is not legally imposed or legally binding. And the wall makes, on the political side, for the equality of believers and non-believers, saints and worldlings, the saved and the damned: all are equally citizens; they possess the same set of constitutional rights. Politics is not dominant over grace nor grace over politics.

I want to stress the second of these negative propositions. Americans are very sensitive to the first. The willingness to tolerate (religious) conscientious objection has its origin in that sensitivity, and it certainly suggests a significant forbearance by the political authorities. People who believe that the safety of their immortal souls depends upon avoiding any sort of participation in warfare are exempt from the draft. Though the state cannot guarantee immortality, it at least refrains from taking it away. The state does not nourish souls; nor does it kill them. But the second negation rules out a kind of dominance that no one talks about today, in the West at least; and so we may well have forgotten its historical significance. For Locke, in the seventeenth century, it was still critically important to deny the claim that "dominion is founded in grace."[5] The claim had only recently been put forward, and with considerable vehemence, in the course of the Puritan Revolution. Indeed, Cromwell's first parliament, "the parliament of saints," was an attempt to give it political effect; and Cromwell opened the first session by asserting precisely what Locke wanted to deny: "God manifests this to be the day of the power of Christ; having, through so much blood and so much trial as hath been put upon these nations, made this to be one of the great issues thereof: to have His people called to the supreme authority."[6]

The Puritan Commonwealth

Cromwell acknowledged the inequality of this "call." Only the saints were invited to share in the exercise of power. And it would make no sense to submit the saints to a democratic election or even—what would have been more likely in seventeenth-century England—to an election by male property owners. In neither case would "His people" have won a majority of the votes. Cromwell hoped for a day when elections would be possible, that is, for a day when the people themselves, all of them, would be God's elect. "I would that all were fit to be called." But "who knows how soon God may fit the people for such a thing?"[7] Meanwhile, it was necessary to look for the outward signs of inner light. Hence members of Parliament were chosen by a search committee, not an electorate, and England was ruled by the monopolists of grace.

Locke's argument, and the argument embedded in the United States

Constitution, is that the saints are free to maintain their monopoly and to rule any society (church or sect) that they themselves establish. Grace is no doubt a great privilege, but there is no way to give it out to those who disbelieve in its existence, or who adopt a view of it radically different from that of the saints, or who hold the same view but with less fervor; nor is there any way to force upon the saints a more egalitarian understanding of their special gift. In any case, the monopoly of the saints is harmless enough so long as it doesn't reach to political power. They have no claim to rule the state, which they did not establish, and for whose necessary work divine assurance is no qualification. The purpose of the constitutional wall is the containment, not the redistribution, of grace.

Yet the state might be differently conceived, not as a secular but as a religious realm; civil interests might be understood as God's interests, too. The wall between church and state is, after all, a human construction; it might be torn down or, as in Islam, never raised in the first place. Then the rule of the saints would look rather different: who else—if not His people—should rule in a realm for which God Himself has legislated? It may be the case, moreover, that only the saints can establish the everyday social arrangements that make the good life, and then the eternal life, available to the rest of the population. For these arrangements, perhaps, have to be read out of Scripture, and it is the inner light that illuminates the Word. The argument has real force, given a sufficiently widespread commitment to the underlying religious doctrine. But if enough people are committed to the rule of the saints, then the saints should have no difficulty winning elections.

In any case, the force of the argument declines as soon as the commitment falters. The New England Puritans offer a nice example of this. Their whole educational system was bent to the task of religious conversion. Its chief end was to reproduce in the second generation the "experience of grace" that the founders had known. At first, there was no doubt at all that this was possible. "God has so cast the line of election," Increase Mather wrote, "that for the most part it runs through the loins of godly parents."[8] Teachers had little to do but enliven the latent spirit. But the gift of spiritual liveliness is not so easily passed on, not through the loins and not through the schools: neither nature nor nurture, apparently, can guarantee the inheritance. In the eyes of its elders—in its own eyes, too—the second generation of American Puritans, like many other second generations, turned out to be deficient in grace. Hence the compromise of the Half-Way Covenant of 1662, which permitted the children of the saints, even if they had no experience of grace, to maintain some loose connection with the church for the sake of the grandchildren. But this was only to postpone the obvious difficulty. Consider, writes a modern scholar, "the irony of a situation in which a chosen people cannot find enough chosen people to prolong its existence."[9] Secularism sneaks into the Puritan commonwealth in the form of religious discouragement. For membership in the commonwealth is indeed transmitted through the loins of godly *and ungodly* parents. And so the commonwealth soon included not only saints and worldlings—the first group ruling the second—but also worldlings who were the sons and daughters of the saints and saints who were the sons and daughters of the worldlings. The dominion of grace could not survive this entirely predictable and entirely unexpected outcome.

Alternatively, secularism sneaks into the Puritan commonwealth in the form of religious dissent: when the saints disagree about the everyday arrangements necessary for eternal life, or when they deny one another's saintliness. It is always possible, of course, to repress the dissent, to exile the dissenters, or even, as in the Europe of the Inquisition, to torture and kill them for the sake of their own (and everyone else's) salvation. But there are difficulties here, too, common, I think, to all the religions that preach salvation, and which I have already identified with regard to Christianity. The idea of grace seems deeply resistant to coercive distributions. Locke's assertion that "men cannot be forced to be saved,"[10] may represent the claim of a dissenter or even a skeptic, but it builds on an understanding of salvation shared by many believers. If that is so, then religious disagreement and dissent set limits on the use of force—limits that eventually take the form of a radical separation: the wall between church and state. And then efforts to breach the wall, to impose the arrangements or coerce the behavior that supposedly makes for salvation, are properly called tyrannical.

11

Recognition

The Struggle for Recognition

A Sociology of Titles

In a hierarchical society like that of feudal Europe, a title is the name of a rank attached to the name of a person. To call a person by his title is to place him in the social order and, depending on the place, to honor or dishonor him. Titles commonly proliferate in the upper ranks where they mark off fine distinctions and suggest the intensity and importance of the struggle for recognition. The lower ranks are more grossly titled, and the lowest men and women have no titles at all but are called by their first names or by some disparaging general name ("slave," "boy," "girl," and so on). There is a proper form of address for each and every person, one that simultaneously establishes the degree of recognition to which he is entitled and accords him just that degree.[1] Often the use of the title must be accompanied by such conventional gestures as kneeling, bowing one's head, doffing one's cap: these represent an extension of the title, the title mimed, as it were, and they serve the same double purpose. Similarly, people may wear their titles—velvet or corduroy, kneebreeches or sans-culottes—so that getting dressed is a kind of reflexive recognition, and walking in the street is a demand for respect or an acknowledgment of inferiority. If we know everyone's title, then we know the social order; we know to whom we must defer and who must defer to us; we are prepared for all encounters. It is the great convenience of a hierarchical society that this sort of knowledge is easy to come by and widely diffused.

Titles are instant recognitions. Insofar as there is a title for everyone, everyone is recognized; there are no invisible men. This is what Tocqueville means when he says that in aristocratic societies, "no one can either hope or fear that he will not be seen. No man's social standing is so low but that he has a stage of his own, and no man can, by his obscurity, avoid praise or blame."[2] But Tocqueville certainly misdescribes the position of slaves in all slave-holding aristocracies;* he is probably wrong about serfs and servants, who have in any case no very ample stage of their own; and he may well be wrong about the aristocrats themselves. He suggests that there are standards for each rank, even for the lowest, all the more so, then, for the highest, and that men and women who fail to live up to those standards may lose the honor of their titles. But that is just what the men and women of the aristocracy cannot do. One can say of the top of the hierarchy what Lord Melbourne said, admiringly, of the Most Noble Order of the Garter: "There is no damned merit about it." Praise and blame are irrelevant; there is nothing to test and nothing to prove.

Of course, aristocrats and gentlemen can behave badly, and often do, and their social inferiors are likely to notice this and comment on it among themselves. But they cannot comment more widely; they cannot mime their comments on public occasions. Short of rebellion or revolution, they have no choice but to yield the honor, respect, deference that is conventionally due to bad as to good aristocrats. The sentence, "You're no gentleman," is not likely to be spoken by a serf to his lord or by a servant to his master. In a hierarchical society, one can praise or blame equals and inferiors, but recognitions of superiority must be unqualified.

Rank, then, is dominant over recognition. If titles are hereditary, blood is dominant over rank; if they can be purchased, money is dominant; if they lie in the hands of the rulers of the state, political power is dominant. In none of these cases are praise and blame freely given. (In none of them, indeed, are love and hate freely given or likes and dislikes freely expressed, and this may well be more important; but I

*The whole point of enslavement, as Orlando Patterson has argued, is radically to degrade and dishonor the slave, to deny him a social place, a "stage of his own." Slaves, in the eyes of their masters, are base, irresponsible, shameless, infantile. They can be whipped or petted, but they cannot, in the proper sense of the words, be praised or blamed. Their value is the price they command at auction, and they are denied any other value or any recognition of value. But they do not themselves participate in this denial. "There is absolutely no evidence from the long and dismal annals of slavery," writes Patterson, "to suggest that any group of slaves ever internalized the conception of degradation held by their masters." Slaves and masters do not inhabit a world of shared meanings. The two groups are simply at war, as Hegel claimed, and the morality of their encounter is best approached through the theory of just and unjust wars, not through the theory of distributive justice.[3]

am concerned here with something else: with respect rather than love, with contempt rather than hate, with the way we value people and with the way they are valued in society as a whole.) Conceivably, the dominance of rank and blood, though not of wealth and power, can be so strong that it is impossible even to think about free recognition. In the Judeo-Christian world, however, the thought has always been possible because God provides a model, judging men and women without regard to their worldly standing and inspiring a certain social skepticism:

> When Adam delved and Eve span
> Who was then the gentleman?

But this was a subversive question. Religious doctrine more often ratified, and religious institutions quickly duplicated, the existing hierarchy; and both confirmed the fundamental truths of a hierarchical order. Recognitions depend not upon independent judgments but upon social prejudgments, embodied in names like "goodman," "esquire," "sir," "lord" (and "lord bishop"). And what reality lies behind these names we are not to talk about.

But though the struggle for recognition is always constrained by social prejudgments, it isn't wholly determined by them. People at the margins of a rank, nervous about snubs, are doubly insistent on their title; for them the title has an independent value, which they defend as if they had earned it. And within each rank, specific conceptions of honor are worked out. These will often look arbitrary and even fantastic to outsiders, but they fix the standards by which men and women who bear the same title distinguish themselves from one another. The distinctions are all the more bitterly disputed the less substance they seem to have. Hobbes took the disputes of contemporary aristocrats, and more particularly the duel, as one of the archetypal forms of the war of all against all. Men staked their lives for their honor, though the issues over which they fought were objectively of little importance—"trifles, as a word, a smile, a different opinion, and any other sign of undervalue."[4]

Such battles are fought only among equals, within ranks, not between them. When the lower ranks challenge the higher, we don't call it a duel; it's a revolution. It is possible to imagine many different sorts of revolution, but I shall consider here only the democratic revolutions of the modern period, which represent an attack on the whole system of social prejudgments and culminate in the substitution of a single title for the hierarchy of titles. The title that eventually wins out, though not the first that is chosen, derives from the lowest rank of aristocracy or gentility. In the English language, the common title is "master," elided to "Mr.," which became in the seventeenth century "the customary ceremonious prefix to the name of any man below the level of knight and above some humble but undefined level of social status. . . . As with other titles of courtesy, the inferior limit for its application has been continually lowered."[5] In the United States, though not yet in Britain, there is no upper limit for its application. Even in Britain, the universal title has been adopted by powerful men: "Mr. Pitt, like Mr. Pym," wrote Emerson, "thought the title of *Mister* good against any king in Europe."[6] During the first Congress, proposals were made to give the American President some higher title derived from the aristocratic past, but it was decided that the name of his office was sufficient; in direct address, he is "Mr. President."[7] Across Europe the outcome was the same: *monsieur, Herr, signor, señor,* all correspond to the English "master/Mr." In every case, a title of honor, though not of the highest honor, was made the general title. The revolutionary alternatives—"brother," "citizen," "comrade"—represent the refusal of this generalization; I shall come back to them later.

It is a matter of real importance that there is no title for women comparable to "Mr." for men. Even after the democratic revolution, women continued to be called by names (like "Miss" and "Mrs.") that described their place in the family, not in society at large. Women were "placed" by the place of their kin and were not expected to make their own way. The invention of "Ms." is a desperate remedy: an abbreviation for which there is no corresponding word. In part, the argument I am about to make applies to women as much as to men, but only in part. The absence of a universal title suggests the continued exclusion of women, or of many women, from the social universe, the sphere of recognition as it is currently constituted.

In a society of misters, careers are open to talents, recognitions to whoever can win them. To paraphrase Hobbes, the equality of titles breeds an equality of hope and then a general competition. The struggle for honor that raged among aristocrats, and that played such a large part in early modern literature, is now entered by everyman. It is not, however, aristocratic honor that everyman is after. As the struggle is broadened, so the social good at issue is infinitely diversified, and its names are multiplied. *Honor, respect, esteem, praise, prestige, status, reputation, dignity, rank, regard, admiration, worth, distinction, deference, homage, appreciation, glory, fame, celebrity:* the words represent an accumulation over time and were originally used in different social settings and for different purposes. But we can readily grasp their common element. They are the names of favorable recognitions, largely devoid now of any class specificity. Their opposites are either unfavorable recognitions *(dishonor)* or non-recognitions *(disregard)*. Tocqueville thought non-recognitions impossible under the old regime—and also unnecessary: one snubbed a man by letting him know (that you knew) his place. Under the new regime, no one has a fixed place; one snubs a man by denying that he is *there,* that he has any place at all. One refuses to recognize his personality or his moral or political existence. It is not difficult to see that this might well be worse than to be "placed" in the lowest possible rank. To be untouchable is (perhaps) not so awful as to be invisible. In some parts of India, not many years ago, "an untouchable had to shout a warning when entering a street so that all the holier folk could get out of the way of his contaminating shadow."[8] I can barely imagine what it would be like to shout that warning, but at least the person who shouts is a formidable presence, and he may get some satisfaction out of the fearful fleeing of the others. The invisible man doesn't get this sort of satisfaction. On the other hand, as soon as he sheds his alien or pariah status, he enters society not at this or that low rank but as an equal competitor for honor and reputation. And he announces his entrance by saying: "Call me mister."

He claims the general title and enters the general struggle. Since he has no fixed rank, since no one knows where he belongs, he must establish his own worth, and he can do that only by winning the recognition of his fellows. Each of his fellows is trying to do the same thing. Hence the competition has no social boundaries short of the national frontier; nor does it have any temporal limit. It just goes on and on, and the participants quickly learn that yesterday's honor is of little use on today's market. They can't relax or rest on their laurels; they must be alert to every slight. "Every man looketh that his companion should value him at the same rate he sets upon himself," wrote Hobbes, "and upon all signs of contempt, or undervaluing, naturally endeavors, as far as he dares . . . to extort a greater value from his contemners."[9] To speak only of extortion, however, is too stark. As the forms of recognition are various, so are the methods by which it can be won. The competitors speculate on the market, intrigue against near rivals, and bargain for small gains: I'll admire you if you'll admire me. They exercise power, spend money, display goods, give gifts, spread gossip, stage performances—all for the sake of recognition. And having done all this, they do it all again, reading their daily gains and losses in the eyes of their fellows, like a stockbroker with his morning paper.

But however complex the struggle, Hobbes's "extortion" does capture one of its central features. Recognitions must be won from people who, thinking of their own claims, are reluctant givers. I suspect, indeed, that most of us want, and even need, to give as well as to receive recognition; we need heroes, men and women whom we can admire without negotiation and without constraint.[10] But we are wary about finding such people among our friends and neighbors. Such discoveries are difficult because they challenge our own value and force unwelcome comparisons upon us. In a democratic society, recognitions are easiest at a distance. Sudden and temporary recognitions are easy, too: thus the celebrities-for-a-day created by the mass media. Our excitement at the rise of such figures is enhanced by the anticipation of their fall. Who are they, after all, but men and women like you and me, a little luckier perhaps? They have no permanent place, and it is an open question whether we will remember who they are tomorrow. The media make it look as if recognition is a good in plentiful supply; allocations are unstable but in principle unlimited. In practice, however, the good is scarce. Our everyday comparisons have the effect of transforming one person's gain into another's loss, even when nothing has been lost but relative standing. In the sphere of recognition, relative standing is very important.

There must be times when one longs for the comfort of a fixed place. A society of misters is a world of hope, effort, and endless anxiety. The image of a race, first worked out by Hobbes in the seventeenth century, has been a central feature of our social consciousness ever since. This is a democratic race, a participatory race; there are no spectators; everybody has to run. And all our feelings, about ourselves, about others, are a function of how well we are running:

> To consider them behind, is glory
> To consider them before, is humility
> To be in breath, hope
> To be weary, despair
> To endeavor to overtake the next, emulation
> To lose ground by little hinderances,
>   pusillanimity
> To fall on the sudden, is disposition to weep
> To see another fall, is disposition to laugh
> Continually to be outgone, is misery
> Continually to outgo the next before,
>   is felicity
> And to forsake the course, is to die.[11]

Why do we run? "There is no other goal, nor other garland," wrote

Recognition

Hobbes, "but being foremost."[12] But this claim draws too heavily upon the experience of the old aristocracy. Pascal was more prescient in one of his *Pensées:* "Such is our presumption that we should like to be known by the whole world, and even by people who will be born when we are no more: and we are so vain that the good opinion of five or six persons around us delights and contents us."[13] We run to be seen, recognized, admired by some subset of the others. If local victories were not possible, we would all be in despair long before we were done. On the other hand, the contentment that Pascal describes doesn't last long. Our presumption is soothed, repressed, reborn. There are very few people who hope in any serious way for eternal glory, but virtually everyone wants a little more recognition than he gets. Discontent is not permanent, but it is recurrent. And our anxieties are fed as much by our achievements as by our failures.

Though we are all called by the same title, we are not given the same degree of recognition. The Hobbesian race is more fluid and uncertain than the hierarchy; but at any given moment, the runners find themselves in an order, from first to last, winning or losing within the larger society and their own subset. Nor is there any easy appeal against losses, even if they seem unjust or undeserved. Wealth and commodities can always be redistributed, collected by the state and given out again in accordance with some abstract principle. But recognition is an infinitely more complex good. In some deep sense, it depends entirely upon individual acts of honoring and dishonoring, regarding and disregarding. There is, of course, such a thing as public recognition and public disgrace: I shall have something to say about both of these later. "The king," according to an old legal maxim, "is the fountain of honor." We might think of the good name of the king, or the legitimacy of the state, as a pool of recognition from which portions are distributed to individuals. But this sort of thing makes a small mark unless it is ratified and reiterated by ordinary men and women. Whereas money need only be accepted, recognition must be repeated if it is to have any value. Hence, the king does well if he honors only those people who are widely thought to be honorable.

No simple equality of recognition is possible; the idea is a bad joke. In the society of the future, Andy Warhol once said, "everyone will be world-famous for fifteen minutes." In fact, of course, in the future as in the past, some people will be more famous than others, and some people won't be famous at all. We can guarantee everyone's visibility (to government officials, say), but we can't guarantee his equal visibility (to his fellow citizens). We can insist as a matter of principle that everyone, from Adam and Eve on, is a gentleman; but we can't provide everyone with the same reputation for gentle—that is, "unrestrained yet delicate"—manners. Relative standing will still depend upon the resources that individuals can marshal in the ongoing struggle for recognition. As we can't redistribute fame itself, so we can't redistribute those resources; for they are nothing but the personal qualities, skills, and talents valued in a given time and place, with which particular men and women are able to command the admiration of their fellows. But there is no way to determine in advance what qualities, skills, and talents will be valued or who will possess them. And even if we could somehow identify and collect such things and then give them out in equal parts, they would instantly cease (because of the equality) to command admiration.

But if in the struggle for recognition there cannot be equality of outcomes, there can be—I have been writing as if there is—equality of opportunity. This is the promise of the society of misters. Has it, however, been achieved in any actual society? A contemporary sociologist warns us against confusing the status of individuals with their "reputational qualities." Status, Frank Parkin argues, is a function of place, profession, and office, not of particular recognitions of particular achievements.[14] The abolition of titles is not the abolition of classes. Conceptions of honor are more controversial than they were under the old regime, but distributions are still patterned, dominated now by occupation rather than by blood or rank. Hence, on the one hand, the insolence of office and, on the other, the degradation of the men and women who do society's hard and dirty work. In the Hobbesian race, many of the runners are running in place, unable to break through the constraints of the larger pattern. Nor can that pattern usefully be described as the product of their own valuations, a kind of social shorthand for the recognition of individuals. There is indeed such a shorthand, but it derives from the dominant ideology, itself a function of office and power—so that office holders command respect in the same way that they command high salaries, without having to prove their worth to their fellow workers or their clients.

But this dominant ideology is nothing other than the Hobbesian race, conceived now as a struggle for jobs and income rather than as a struggle for prestige and honor. Or, rather, the claim is that the two struggles are really one: a general competition for social goods in which merit, ambition, luck, whatever, win out in the end. We honor people in accordance with their victories because the qualities needed to win the general competition are roughly the same as the qualities we are likely to admire in any case. And if there are admirable qualities that don't come into play in the general competition, then we are free to admire them on the side, as it were, incidentally, locally, within this or that subset. So we can respect the kindness of a neighbor without letting that respect interfere with our more precise calculations of social status.

Status (standing in the race) dominates recognition. That is very different from the dominance of hierarchical rank, but it is not yet the free appraisal of each person by each other person. Free appraisal would require the disaggregation of social goods, the relative autonomy of honor. Exactly what autonomy might mean in this case is not easy to say, for honor is so closely tied to other sorts of goods. It comes along with the winning of an office, for example, or the achievement of a high score on the medical boards, or the successful establishment of a new business. These sorts of achievement will probably always command respect. But they will not always command the precise degree of respect that they do today, when each of them is seen as a crucial step on the road to wealth and power. What respect would they independently command? We don't know, in fact, what the social world would look like if each person's honor depended entirely on the freely given or freely withheld recognitions of each other person.* No doubt, there would be wide cultural variations. But even in our own society, it isn't difficult to imagine valuations very different from those that currently prevail—a new respect for socially useful work, say, or for physical effort, or for helpfulness in office rather than mere office holding.[16] Free appraisal would also generate, I think, a much more decentralized system of recognitions, so that the general ordering that Hobbes assumed would fade in importance or even cease to be discernible. Recall John Stuart Mill's complaint, "They like in crowds" (see page 7). So they do, but one can still make out the shapes of different crowds, with different or at least incipiently different standards for liking and disliking. These differences are suppressed for the sake of the general compe-

---

*For the moment (and for the foreseeable future), writes Thomas Nagel, "we have no way of divorcing professional status from social esteem and economic reward, at least not without a gigantic increase in social control."[15] But it isn't a question here of a divorce—or rather, divorce and increased control are required by simple but not by complex equality. The achievement of professional status surely entitles a man or a woman to *some* degree of social esteem and even to economic reward. The rest of us are prepared to acknowledge skill and talent and (individually or collectively) to pay for services rendered. But we want to be able to acknowledge a wide range of skills and talents and to pay no more than a market price or, in the case of conscripted services, a fair wage. It is only the illegitimate conversion of professional status into esteem and wealth that we ought to rule out—and then the techniques of conversion: restricted access, intellectual mystification, and so on; and that will require something considerably less than a "gigantic increase in social control."

tition. But if the general competition were broken up, if wealth did not entail office—or office, power—then recognitions, too, would be free.

This would be complex equality in the sphere of recognition, and it would certainly result in a distribution of honor and dishonor very different from the prevailing one. But individual men and women would still be differentially honored, and I am not sure that the competition would be less keen than in the world Hobbes described. If there were more winners (and a greater variety of possible victories), there would still, inevitably, be some losers. Nor does complex equality guarantee that recognitions would be distributed to individuals who were in some objective sense worthy of receiving them. Of course, there are objective standards, at least for some of the forms of recognition. There are novelists, say, who deserve critical attention and novelists who don't. And critics freed from the constraints of the social hierarchy and the market would be more likely to attend to the right novelists. More generally, however, recognitions would go to individuals thought to be worthy by some number of their fellows, and thoughts would be free. We would honor, respect, esteem, value freely those men and women who seemed to us deserving—and sometimes we would value men and women exactly as we love them, without regard to objective desert at all. So the deserving poor would still be with us. To paraphrase Marx: if a person is not able, by the manifestation of himself as a worthy person, to make himself a valued person, then his worth is impotent and a misfortune. Such misfortunes would no longer be the monopoly of a particular class or caste or occupational group. But against their general incidence, I can imagine no plausible form of social insurance.

But perhaps some minimal respect is in fact a common property in the society of misters. We might usefully distinguish what I will call *simple recognition* from the more complex forms of *recognition as this or that*. Simple recognition is today a moral requirement: we have to acknowledge that every person we meet is at least a potential recipient of honor and admiration, a competitor, even a threat. The phrase, "Call me mister," stakes a claim, not to any particular degree of honor, but to the possibility of honor. Here is someone we don't know and who appears before us without the markers of birth and rank. Still, we can't rule him out of the game. He is worthy at least of our appraisal, and we are vulnerable to his. These facts of our social life add to contemporary forms of politeness a certain wariness, which is not without its excitement. The eagerness of Americans to drop the "mister" and use first names derives from a desire to reduce the level of excitement, to find some way to relax a bit. We think the eagerness dishonest when-ever we know that neither party really intends to relax. This negative intention represents a minimal and basic respect. "They recognize themselves," Hegel wrote, "as mutually recognizing each other."[17] But this can be a very tense business.

Public Honor and Individual Desert

I have been writing about the sphere of recognition as if it were a free enterprise system. Honors are like commodities; they circulate among individuals through exchange, extortion, and gift; supply is only clum-sily and inadequately responsive to demand. There is no welfare state, no redistribution of wealth, no guaranteed minimum (beyond the bare acknowledgment that every individual is a competitor). And this ap-pears to be the best possible arrangement. Most often, the flow of rec-ognition is distorted by the dominance of other goods and the monop-oly power of old families, castes, and classes. If we break free of these distortions, we find ourselves in a loosened version of the Hobbesian race. At best, we will be entrepreneurs in the sphere of recogni-tion—some of us flush, others destitute.

All this is true, but it is only a part of the truth. For alongside the individual distributions, there are a variety of collective distributions: rewards, prizes, medals, citations, wreaths of laurel. Public honors, as I have said, are likely to be ineffective unless they conform to the stan-dards of private individuals. But it is important to note now that indi-viduals set rather more exacting standards for recognitions granted on their behalf than for those they grant themselves. The crucial standard for public honor is desert. Not desert casually or parochially conceived, not the desert of personal friends and enemies: public honor is endorsed and reiterated by private individuals only if it is thought to conform to an objective measure. Hence it is distributed by juries, whose mem-bers deliver not an opinion but a verdict—a "true speech" about the qualities of the recipients. And on juries thought is not free; it is bound by evidence and rules. What is called for is an absolute judgment. When the church designates its saints or the state its heroes, questions are asked that have to be answered with a Yes or a No. The miracle did or did not occur; the courageous action was or was not performed.

The purpose of public honor is to search out not the deserving poor but simply the deserving, whether they are poor or not. But the search will certainly turn up men and women whose heroic action, singular achievement, or public service has, for whatever reason, been neglected by their fellows. Hence it is in some sense a remedial distribution—not because it evens up the balance of honor but because it gets the unevenness right. Its agents (ideally) are more tightly tied to the standards they espouse than private persons are. Public honor is indeed distributed for public reasons; but the public reasons, unlike the private ones, come into play only when we choose the qualities that are worthy of honor, not when we choose the people. If state officials systematically selected men and women whom it was politically expedient to honor, they would devalue the honors they distributed. Hence the phenomenon of the mixed distribution, where a few deserving individuals are added to the honors list in order to cover those who are honored for political reasons; mostly, the cover doesn't work.

It is not only state officials who distribute public honor, but also privately organized societies, foundations, and committees. All sorts of achievements are or can be honored; those that are useful to the state, those that are socially useful, and those that are simply memorable, superior, distinguished, or exciting. So long as the choice conforms to some objective measure, so long as it isn't a matter of individual will or whim, we can properly think of it as a form of public honoring. The standard is desert, and what is being rewarded is merit: this or that performance, accomplishment, good deed, job well done, fine piece of work attributed to an individual or a group of individuals.*

In the distribution of most social goods, desert plays little part. Even in the cases of office and education, it figures only minimally and indirectly. With membership, welfare, wealth, hard work, leisure, familial love, and political power, it doesn't figure at all (and with divine grace we don't know how it figures). Desert isn't disqualified, however, because the adjective *deserving* cannot or does not accurately characterize individual men and women; it can and does. Advocates of equality have often felt compelled to deny the reality of desert.[18] The people we call deserving, they argue, are simply lucky. Born with certain capacities,

---

*But do people deserve the rewards that come not because of some achievement but because of some state of being? Is the winner of a beauty contest *honored?* The organizers of contemporary beauty contests seem to have a dim and embarrassed sense that the winner would not be honored were she chosen merely for her natural endowments, for they have introduced a variety of "talent" criteria. Honor is (for us) the recognition of an action; and displaying one's physical beauty or, for that matter, announcing one's noble birth and blood does not qualify as an action in the proper sense. It is necessary to use one's endowments in some socially valued way. But it's obviously not difficult to imagine societies founded on different conceptions of honor.

raised by loving or exacting or stimulating parents, they then find themselves living, quite by chance, in a time and place where their particular capacities, so carefully fostered, are also valued. For none of this can they claim any credit; in the deepest sense, they are not responsible for their own achievements. Even the effort they expend, the painful training they undergo, is no evidence of personal merit; for the capacity to make an effort or to endure pain is, like all their other capacities, only the arbitrary gift of nature or nurture. But this is an odd argument, for while its purpose is to leave us with persons of equal entitlement, it is hard to see that it leaves us with *persons* at all. How are we to conceive of these men and women once we have come to view their capacities and achievements as accidental accessories, like hats and coats they just happen to be wearing? How, indeed, are they to conceive of themselves? The reflexive forms of recognition, self-esteem and self-respect, our most important possessions, which I shall come to only at the end of this chapter, must seem meaningless to individuals all of whose qualities are nothing but the luck of the draw.

The impulse at work here is closely related to the impulse that leads contemporary philosophers to ignore the concrete meaning of social goods. Persons abstracted from their qualities and goods abstracted from their meanings lend themselves, of course, to distributions that accord with abstract principles. But it seems doubtful that such distributions can possibly do justice to persons as they are, in search of goods as they conceive them. We don't encounter other people as moral and psychological blanks, neutral bearers of accidental qualities. It isn't as if there is X and then there are X's qualities, so that I can react separately to the one and the other. The problem that justice poses is precisely to distribute goods to a host of Xs in ways that are responsive to their concrete, integrated selves. Justice, that is, begins with persons. More than this, it begins with persons-in-the-social-world, with goods in their minds as well as in their hands. Public honor is one such good, and we don't have to think about it long or deeply to realize that it literally cannot exist as a good unless there are deserving men and women. This is the unique place where desert has to count if there is to be any distribution at all or any value in what gets distributed.

We could, of course, give out public honors for utilitarian reasons, so as to encourage politically or socially useful performances. Such reasons will always play a part in the practice of honoring, but I don't see how they can stand alone. How will we know whom to honor unless we are committed to attend to personal desert? Anyone will do, so long as the encouragement turns out to be effective. Indeed, the authorities might well think it best to invent a performance and to "frame" an appropriate performer so as to make sure that they are encouraging exactly what they want to encourage. This possibility (which mirrors an old argument against the utilitarian account of punishment) suggests that there are good reasons for sticking to the common understanding of individual desert. Otherwise, honor is simply available for tyrannical use. Because I have power, I shall honor so and so. It doesn't matter whom I choose, because no one really deserves to be honored. And it doesn't matter what the occasion is, for I don't recognize any intrinsic (social) connection between honor and some particular set of performances. This sort of thing won't work unless the tyrant stays in power long enough to transform the common understanding of an honorable performance. But that is precisely his purpose.

Stalin's Stakhanovites

Stakhanov was not an invention, though he might well have been. He was a coal miner of unusual strength and energy who produced more coal than the official quota required. Surely, in a socialist society, a proletarian state, this was an honorable performance. Just as surely, Stakhanov's strength and energy were, in the contemporary phrase, "arbitrary from a moral point of view"—no reason to single him out from other workers, less well endowed, who also worked hard. (Nor would there be any reason, given this view of arbitrariness, to single out those who worked hard from those who merely worked.) But in choosing Stakhanov, not just to be honored, but to serve as the living symbol of socialist honor, Stalin was presumably endorsing the idea of desert. Stakhanov deserved to be honored because he had done what he did, and what he did was honorable. In fact, Stalin himself almost certainly did not believe the first of these propositions, and Stakhanov's fellow workers did not believe the second.

The idea of desert implies some conception of human autonomy. Before an individual can perform honorably, he must be responsible for his performances; he must be a moral agent; the performances must be his own. There were Soviet philosophers and psychologists in the 1930s who held such a view of human agency; but when Stalin finally announced his own position on these matters, in the period immediately after the Second World War, he took a very different stand. He adopted then a radical Pavlovianism, according to which "man is a reactive mechanism whose behavior, including all the higher mental processes, can be exhaustively understood through a knowledge of the laws

of conditioning and . . . controlled through application of this knowledge."[19] This is only one of the psychological theories that plausibly
underpins the denial of individual desert, but it has to be said that it
underpins it very well. Stalin probably held some such view in the 1930s
when the Stakhanovite experiment was launched. But if Stakhanov's
energetic activity (I'll leave aside now his physical strength) is the product of his conditioning, then in what sense does he deserve to be honored for it? Stalin singled him out only for utilitarian reasons: the purpose of Stakhanovism was to condition other workers to perform in
a similar fashion—so that quotas could be raised, assembly lines
speeded up, and so on. The Stakhanovite award was not a recognition
but an incentive, a goad, one of those offers that turns very easily into
a threat. That's all an award can be, I think, in the absence of a theory
of desert.

Naturally, the other workers objected. The utilities that Stalin had
in mind were not their own utilities. But their objection went deeper
than that. For whatever they thought of Stakhanov himself, they
clearly did not think that his successors, the Stakhanovites of the middle 1930s, deserved to be honored. The award winners had (let's assume) worked hard, but they had also violated the norms of their class,
broken its solidarity. By all accounts, they were taken to be opportunists
and renegades, the proletarian equivalents of Uncle Toms; they were
snubbed, ostracized, harassed on the job.[20] Stalin's honoring was the
occasion for individual and communal dishonoring. No doubt, the dishonoring was intended in part as a disincentive, but I suspect that the
workers would also have said that they were responding to the dishonorable character of the Stakhanovite performances and of the performers.
They would have said, that is, that they believed in giving people what
they (really) deserved.

But it is a hard question whether that is possible. Even if we refuse
Hamlet's "Who would 'scape whipping?" and assume that there are
some people who deserve public honor, it remains to be seen whether
there is any way of finding the right people. Can juries really deliver
verdicts that are not merely opinions? Won't awards still be arbitrary
even when we agree that achievements are not? It is important here
not to set our standards too high. We are not gods, and we never know
enough to speak with perfect truth about the qualities and performances of other human beings. What counts, however, is the aspiration. We aim at verdicts, not opinions, and we design certain arrangements for the sake of that aim. Thus (again) the jury, a company of
men and women sworn to seek the truth. Sometimes the truth lies be-

yond their reach, and they find themselves choosing among competing approximations. Sometimes they make mistakes; sometimes individual members are corrupt or partisan. Sometimes disagreements are too deep and no verdict is possible; sometimes the members merely strike a bargain. But the criticisms that we commonly make of juries serve in effect to ratify their purpose. For what we say is that they should have done better, or that we could have done better, not that there is nothing to be done. In principle, at least, true speech is possible.

The Nobel Prize in Literature

Consider now one of the most respected and controversial of public honors. Alfred Nobel's will established in 1896 a prize for literary achievement, but its stipulations were brief and by no means entirely clear. The prize was to go "to the person who shall have produced in the field of literature the most outstanding work of an idealist tendency."[21] The successive juries have had to decide how to constitute "the field of literature" for the purpose of the prize and how to understand "idealism" with reference to that field. And then they have had to choose among the extraordinary variety of candidates, writing in different genres, in different languages, within different literary traditions. How could the juries even come close to a verdict? "It is absolutely impossible," wrote Carl David af Wirsén, the leading member of the first jury, "to decide whether a dramatist, an epic or a lyric poet . . . a ballad writer or man of ideas, ranks the highest. It is like deciding on the relative merits of the elm, the linden, the oak, the rose, the lily, or the violet."[22] And yet the records of the jury meetings indicate that Wirsén had very strong views about who should get the prize. Nor have critics of the successive juries—and there have been many critics—pressed the idea of impossibility. If, on the one hand, it seems foolish even to attempt a rank ordering of all the world's writers, it seems, on the other hand, almost natural to recognize a very small number of pre-eminent writers. And then critics and readers seem to fall readily into arguments about who is the very best.

I suppose there never is a single answer to that question. Over a span of time, however, there might well be a series of answers that more or less exhausts the field. And it was the purpose of the successive juries to provide such a series. The fact that Tolstoy, Ibsen, Strindberg, Hardy, Valéry, Rilke, and Joyce never received the prize suggests that they were not entirely successful. But critics don't have a great deal of difficulty naming the omissions that constitute the juries' failure. We have, of course, the advantage of hindsight; and it is important to remember that the prize is, and should be, an immediate recognition of a writer thought by his contemporaries to be pre-eminent, not an effort to record the judgments of history. Still, Tolstoy, Ibsen, Strindberg, Hardy, Valéry, Rilke, and Joyce were thought by many of their contemporaries to be pre-eminent. . . . Perhaps the members of the jury sometimes feel constrained by political factors; perhaps they think that the prizes have to reflect a certain geographical distribution. So they slide into the role of a search committee, looking for candidates to fill slots. And then the standard criticism is that they should behave more like a jury. In any case, it is possible to behave like a jury; and the history of the Nobel Prize, and of the controversies that have attended particular awards, suggests powerfully that we all believe there are writers who deserve to be honored.

It is not necessary, however (except for Alfred Nobel's will), that we aim only at the "most outstanding" achievements; we can aim simply at all achievements that stand out. This is the most common form of public honor in modern societies, where the honors list is always published, the honor roll always called, with implicit apologies to anyone inadvertently left off, who deserves to be on. There is perhaps a certain tension between the extended list and the grand prize. In his *Government of Poland*, Rousseau exploited this tension to make a democratic point. He described a Board of Censors that "would draw up accurate and complete lists of persons of all ranks who had so conducted themselves as to merit some distinction or reward"—and went on to say that the Board

> should look much more to the agents than to the isolated deeds. The truly good deed is that done with little display. Sustained day-to-day behavior, the virtues a man practices in his private and domestic life, the faithful discharge of the duties that attach to [his] station . . . these are the things for which a man deserves to be honored, rather than the spectacular feats he performs only on occasion—which for the rest, will already have their rewards in public admiration. Sensation-mongering philosophers have a great fondness for deeds that make noise.[23]

That last point is probably true, though I can see no reason to go out of one's way to avoid endorsing the general public's admiration for this or that "spectacular feat." But Rousseau is right to have insisted on the importance of recognizing the virtues of ordinary people, especially in a democratic regime. Stalin's Stakhanovite awards are a vicious parody of what needs to be done, but a parody in which the need remains visible. It is most commonly filled in contemporary armies, where the award of the highest honor for some heroic performance doesn't preclude lesser honors for lesser performances. On the other hand, the need isn't filled at all in occupations whose social prestige is low: "the sometimes incredible heroism displayed by miners and fishermen," as Simone Weil wrote, "barely awakens an echo among miners and fishermen themselves."[24] Here public honor is obviously remedial—and educational, too: it invites ordinary citizens to look beyond their prejudgments and to recognize desert wherever it is found, even among themselves.

Roman and Other Triumphs

This sort of distribution is not politically neutral. If democracy seems to require it, other regimes endure it only at some risk. In monarchies and oligarchies, desert is a subversive principle, and this is true even when it is only "spectacular feats" that are at issue. This is an old argument in political theory, but it is worth rehearsing because it helps us understand why the autonomy of distributive spheres is always relative. The standard reference is to the Roman triumph, "the highest point of honor," Jean Bodin has written, "that a Roman citizen could aspire unto. . . . He that triumphed made his entry more honorable than a king could do in his realm." Clothed in purple and gold, crowned with bay leaves, riding in a chariot at the head of his army, his captives in chains before him, the victorious commander paraded to the Capitol, "ravishing the hearts of all men, partly with incredible joy, and partly with amazement and admiration." The triumph is suitable only in a popular state (with a strong sense of citizenly virtue). A king, by contrast, has to be jealous of honor; he is a miserly fountain, a monopolist of glory. He can permit no one but himself to ravish the hearts of his people. "And therefore," Bodin went on, "we never see monarchs, and much less tyrants, to grant triumphs and honorable entries unto his subjects, what victory soever they have gotten of the enemy . . . the honor of the victory is always due unto the prince, although he be absent the day of the battle."[25] Francis Bacon made the same point in his *Essays*: "But that honor [of the triumph] perhaps were not fit for monarchies, except it be in the person of the monarch himself or his sons."[26]

As Bodin suggested, the argument holds even more strongly for tyrants. That's why rulers like Stalin and Mao always claimed for themselves the honor of great achievements, not only in war but also in science, linguistics, medicine, poetry, agriculture, and so on. And that's why poor Stakhanov couldn't be honored for anything that his fellow workers thought honorable, lest "the sweet enticing bait of honor" should draw him to seek a representative or a leadership role. Tyrants dispense honors for manipulative or whimsical reasons, so as to undercut the value of the gift. But they themselves demand to be honored for their putative deserts. In an earlier time, of course, kings were honored for their birth and blood or for their kingship: things honorable in themselves. Neither Bodin nor Bacon made the claim in those terms; their arguments are appeals to political prudence. For them as for us, honor belongs to deserving people. The king's honor is therefore a politic lie. Though Bodin and Bacon would never have said so, every king is a usurper and a tyrant. "For . . . honor which is the only reward of virtue is taken away, or at least much restrained, from them that deserve it."[27] The recognition of deserving men and women, and of all deserving men and women, is possible only in a democracy.

And recognition, so we are told, works wonders. Democracies have more heroes, more enterprising citizens, more citizens willing to sacrifice themselves for the common good, than any other regime—all of them enticed, as Bodin said, by the sweet bait of honor. At the same time, however, honor must never be distributed so widely that it is devalued. Egalitarian philosophers commonly hold that in a democratic community the citizens are entitled to equal respect.[28] I shall try later to find some sense in which that claim is justified; but in terms of my argument thus far, it would make more sense to deny it. The law is no respecter of persons. When citizens petition their government, they are entitled to equal attention; when offices are available, to equal consideration; when welfare is distributed, to equal concern. But when respect is at issue, "deferential esteem," special regard, ritual eminence, they are entitled to none at all until they have been found to deserve it.

That finding is, to be sure, different from the "findings" of the market and the Hobbesian race, since it is in principle free from every sort of bargaining and extortion. Public honor is not a gift or a bribe but a true speech about distinction and value. But the values asserted in the speech must be comprehensible to the ordinary participants in the market and the race, and the distinctions it upholds must be ones that they are prone to make. Public honor cannot be egalitarian, then, any more than private honor can be—not, at least, in any simple sense of that term. Even when men and women ordinarily ignored are recognized and honored—by a Rousseauian board of censors, say—it is for some achievement or record of achievement that, if widely known, would in any case have brought them the admiration of their fellow citizens. The acknowledgement that honor can be deserved by those who are not conventionally honorable is a crucial feature of complex equality, but it doesn't reduce or annul the singularity of honor.

Punishment

The case is the same with punishment, the most important example of public dishonor. All citizens are innocent until proven guilty, but this maxim does not call for universal respect but the universal absence of disrespect. The law is no disrespecter of persons. It does not (or it should not) prejudge individuals because they are wellborn and bear a noble title or have a lot of money or hold this or that set of political opinions. Punishment requires a specific judgment, a jury's verdict; and that suggests that we punish people only when they deserve to be punished. Punishment, like honor, is a singling out. Indeed, punishment is more like a grand prize than an honors list, in that we punish individuals for single acts (and especially severely for "spectacular feats"), not for a bad life. It might be possible to work out an analogue to Rousseauian honor, some sort of public recognition for non-criminal viciousness, but nothing like this plays a part—or, so far as I know, has ever played a part—in the institution of punishment.

Punishment is a powerful stigma; it dishonors its victim. According to the Biblical account, God put a mark on Cain in order to protect him; but the mark branded him a murderer, and so it was a punishment; and though all of us would be grateful for divine protection, no one wants to bear the mark of Cain. There is no way of punishing that doesn't mark and stigmatize those who are punished. This is as true for utilitarian punishments as it is for retribution. Whatever the aim of the punishment, however it is justified, the distributive effect is the same. If our aim in punishing is to deter other people from crime, we cannot do that without singling out a particular criminal; deterrence requires an example, and examples must be specific. If our aim is to condemn certain sorts of action, we cannot do that without condemning an actor; the expression must be concrete if it is to be understood. If our aim is to reform the man or the woman who has broken the law, we cannot do that without naming this particular man or woman as someone in need of reformation. In the first two of these cases (though not in the third), we could pick someone at random, forge the evidence, and "frame" him of whatever crime we wished to deter or condemn. If individuals are not responsible for their character and their conduct, it wouldn't matter whom we chose. There would be no question of a just distribution, however, for persons without responsibilities are not the appropriate subjects of justice. Nor would punishment of this sort, if we all understood it for what it was, be in any sense dishonorable. But if punishment is dishonorable, as it is, then it must be the case that individual men and women deserve or do not deserve to be dishonored. And then it is critically important that we find the right people, that we put the mark of Cain *on Cain*. Once again, we are not gods and can never really be sure, but we must design distributive institutions so as to bring us as close to surety as possible.

There is a kind of moral anxiety that attends the practice of punishment and probably has as much to do with the dishonor as with the coercion and pain that punishment involves. Coercion and pain are also a feature of military service, where they don't generate the same anxiety or set us looking for deserving men and women. But military service is not dishonorable, and it is not or should not be a punishment. We try to distribute it fairly; but we do that, and we can do it, without worrying about desert at all. Conscription does not rest upon a series of verdicts. Similarly, punishment does not rest upon the general designation of an age cohort; we do not choose prisoners by lottery or exempt individuals with asthma or varicose veins. We conscript the able-bodied, men and women deemed capable of bearing the rigors of war. But we punish only the deserving: not those people most able to bear the stigma of punishment or some random selection of them, but those who ought to bear it. We aim at an extraordinary and difficult precision.

And we decide who the right people are through the mechanism of the trial, a public inquiry into the truth of a particular action. Differently organized in different cultures, the trial is a very old institution; one finds it almost everywhere, always marked off as a special procedure whose aim is not a common opinion or a political decision but a judgment, a proof, a verdict. Except in Alice's Wonderland, the punishment follows the verdict and is impossible without it. We might even say that the verdict is the punishment, for it attaches the stigma, which the subsequent coercion and pain symbolize and enforce. Without the verdict, the coercion and pain are nothing but malevolence and, assuming the malevolence is known, carry no stigma at all. Similarly, if the trial is a fraud, its victims are more likely to be honored than dishonored by their "punishment."

If we distributed punishment differently, it would not be punishment at all. We can see this best if we consider two different distributive mechanisms, which I will call the "election" and the "search." We might vote for the people we punish, as the ancient Athenians did when they chose citizens for ostracism; or we might look for the most qualified candidates, as contemporary advocates of preventive detention would have us do. Both of these are eminently practical arrangements; but insofar as they distribute dishonor, they do so, I think, tyrannically.

Ostracism in Athens

Exile was a form of punishment in the ancient world, and it was often used for the most serious crimes. It carried with it the loss of political membership and civil rights, and there was no Greek or Roman writer who took Hobbes's view that "a mere change of air is no punishment."[29] That sentiment belongs to another age, when the sense of place and community had lost its keenness. But exile, in Athens at least, was a punishment only when it followed upon a trial and a verdict. Ostracism was something very different, and it was different precisely because the exiled citizen was not judged but elected by his peers. The procedure was designed in the very early days of the democratic regime to permit the citizens to get rid of powerful or ambitious individuals, who might aim at tyranny or whose rivalries threatened the peace of the city. Hence ostracism was a kind of political defeat, one of the risks of democratic politics. There was no implication that the individuals chosen deserved their exile; only, it was best for the city, in the opinion of the citizens, that they should be exiled. There was no accusation and no defense. The law went so far as to rule out nominations and debate—perhaps with the conscious intent of avoiding anything that looked like a trial. The citizens simply wrote the name of anyone they wanted to ostracize on a potsherd or tile (thousands of these have been found by contemporary archaeologists), and the person receiving a plurality of their votes was banished, without appeal, for ten years. It followed from this procedure, as Finley says, that ostracism was an "honorary exile . . . without loss of property and without social disgrace."[30]

But when the practice of ostracism was dropped in the very late fifth century, Finley goes on, "ordinary exile on 'criminal charges' remained a possibility."[31] It was possible, that is, to use the jury system to inflict the same sort of political defeat upon an opponent or a rival. For the Athenian jury was a little assembly, with the jurors numbering in the thousands; and the criminal process was readily politicized. But when opponents and rivals rather than criminals were convicted and sent into what could no longer be called an "honorary exile," the conviction was plainly an act of tyranny. Because I have political power and can command enough votes, I will punish you. The distinction between ostracism and punishment drew a nice line between popular opinion and a jury's verdict, between political defeat and criminal desert; and it teaches a nice lesson. Social disgrace, if it is to be justly distributed, must follow upon a verdict, must be a function of desert.

Preventive Detention

As the Athenians ostracized dangerous citizens, so we are sometimes invited to imprison them. If there were a form of "honorary imprisonment," this might be an attractive arrangement. But no such form currently exists, and the advocates of preventive detention have not managed to describe anything that is as different from ordinary imprisonment as ostracism was from ordinary exile. Nor are the prospects promising, for what they have in mind is a criminal, not a political, danger; and it isn't easy to see how we might honorably detain men and women whom we have designated as potential criminals.[32]

The idea behind preventive detention is that we should fill our prisons through a search for qualified candidates—men and women likely to act badly—just as we fill our offices through a search for men and women likely to act well. What is called for is not a judgment but a prediction: hence not a jury but a search committee. Perhaps the committee must make some claim to expert knowledge (a jury makes no such claim); at least, it must consult with experts. If its predictions are accurate, then it should be possible to detain people before it becomes necessary to arrest them, and so the security of everyday life would be greatly enhanced. Of course, a prediction is not the same thing as a verdict; though one might argue, given the vagaries of juries and the putative competence of search committees, that the one is as likely to be a "true speech" as the other. But this misses the crucial difference between the two. Once one acts on a prediction, it is impossible ever to know whether it was a true speech. The incidence of crime may well drop sharply once a program of preventive detention has been instituted; indeed, it is certain to drop if enough people are detained.

But we will never know whether this particular person, now locked up, would or would not have committed a crime.

We tolerate this sort of uncertainty in the case of offices because we have no choice. There is no way of knowing whether that failed candidate would have performed better than this successful one. The performances that offices require, unlike those that punishment presupposes, only come after the distribution has been made. Some degree of honor no doubt comes with the office, in advance of any performance, but I have tried to suggest that under conditions of complex equality, the highest honors will go only to office holders who perform well. Now, punishment is a negative honor, not a negative office. It follows upon actions, not qualifications; we punish individuals who have already performed badly. One might defend this view of punishment by reference to the value of freedom: even men and women of whom it can be said that they probably will commit crimes have a right to choose for themselves whether they will actually do so.[33] But I think it makes more sense to put the argument somewhat differently. If we valued freedom less, we would have devised a form of honorary detention, like the quarantine of people with contagious diseases, for which individuals might qualify (though we assume that they would prefer not to qualify). It is because we haven't done that—haven't chosen to, haven't been able to—that preventive detention is unjust. Detained men and women are punished for reasons that don't connect with our ordinary understanding of what punishment is and how it ought to be distributed. The detention, then, is an act of tyranny.

Self-Esteem and Self-Respect

Honor and dishonor are especially important because they so readily take the reflexive form. Indeed, it is an old argument that conceptions of the self are nothing but internalized social judgments. There is no self-knowledge without the help of the others. We see ourselves in a mirror formed by their eyes. We admire ourselves when we are admired by the people around us. Yes, but it has to be added: not only then, and not always even then. The circle of recognition is problematic. Consider someone who is conceited or puffed up: he admires himself more than the rest of us do. Consider someone with a deep inferiority complex: he thinks himself inferior, and the rest of us don't. Perhaps someone else once idolized the first person or humiliated the second. Still, these are breaks in the circle, and they should alert us to the difficulties of the reflexive form. What we distribute to one another is esteem, not self-esteem; respect, not self-respect; defeat, not the sense of defeat; and the relation of the first to the second term in each of these pairs is indirect and uncertain.

Self-esteem may well be greatest in hierarchical societies—except in the lowest rank of the hierarchy. The members of all the other ranks, looking, as Rousseau says, "rather below than above," relish the deference they receive more than they dislike the deference they yield. In this sense, hierarchical societies reiterate again and again, for each successive rank except the last, the joy that Tertullian claimed the saints would feel when they watched the sufferings of the damned. And this is not merely a sensual but also a mental joy, a heightened self-esteem that has to do with the social (or spiritual) heights the saints think they have attained. They would cease to be happy, as Rousseau says of the rich and the powerful, the moment the people below them "ceased to be wretched."[34] But the wretchedness of those below is not always or necessarily reflected in a diminished sense of self-esteem. The lower ranks imitate the higher and search for some comparative advantage. Thus Indian sweepers, according to a contemporary anthropologist, acknowledge their place in the hierarchical system, but also "associate their work . . . with a toughness that they admire in both men and women, with drinking and eating 'hot' substances, meat and strong liquor. Linked with this is their belief that they are hot-blooded and highly-sexed."[35] We can call this compensation, if we like, as if to say that it has only subjective value: but that is value nonetheless. From their own heights, the sweepers look down upon the pallid abstemiousness of the "higher" castes.

I don't want to pretend that the sweepers wouldn't have greater self-esteem if the hierarchy were abolished. I assume that they would. It might be true, however, that the overall quantity of self-esteem, could it be measured, would be less (this is not an argument in favor of hierarchy). In the society of misters, we should expect to find a more uniform kind of self-esteem, more widely but also more nervously held, so that men and women would grasp at every opportunity to distinguish themselves from the others. "It is impossible in our condition of society," Thackeray wrote in the 1840s, "not to be sometimes a snob."[36] Snobbery is the pride of those who are no longer sure just where they stand, and so it is a peculiarly democratic vice. We say of a snob that he "rides a high horse" and "gives himself airs." He acts as if he were an aristocrat; he claims a title he doesn't have. It is hard to see how this sort of thing can be avoided, even if, as the memory of aristocracy fades, it begins to take forms rather different (though surprisingly, not yet very different) from those that Thackeray described. If we eliminate rank as the basis of snobbery, then people will be snobs on the basis of wealth, or office, or schooling and cultivation. If it's not one thing, it will be something else, for men and women value themselves—just as they are valued—in comparison with others. "The sight of contrast," writes Norbert Elias, "heightens joy in living."[37] Self-esteem is a relational concept. Under conditions of complex equality, the pattern of relationships will be loosened and freed from the dominance of rank and wealth; the special joys of aristocracy will be abolished; snobbery on one basis or another will be universally available. But self-esteem will still be a relational concept.

The case is different, however, with regard to self-respect. This is a difference clearly marked in our language but not often attended to in the work of contemporary philosophers. According to the dictionary, self-esteem is "a favorable appreciation or opinion of oneself," while self-respect is "a proper regard for the dignity of one's person or one's position."[38] The second of these is, and the first is not, a normative concept, dependent upon our moral understanding of persons and positions. The same difference does not show up in the nonreflexive forms, esteem and respect simply. Those latter terms both belong to the world of interpersonal comparisons, but self-respect belongs to a world apart. The concept of honor, like that of a "good name," seems to belong to both worlds. I respect myself not with reference to other people but with reference to a standard; at the same time, other people can judge, by the same standard, whether I have a right to respect myself.

Consider an example from my discussion of schooling. "To serve educational needs," wrote R. H. Tawney, "without regard to the vulgar irrelevancies of class and income, is a part of the teacher's honor" (see page 202). The appeal here is to some shared understanding of what a teacher is, to an (implicit) professional code. The individual teacher is supposed to think of his honor in terms of that code; he ought not to respect himself unless his conduct conforms to its terms. And if it does, he should. The meaning is the same in sentences like these:

No self-respecting doctor would treat a patient like that.
No self-respecting trade unionist would agree to such a contract.

What is at stake is the dignity of the position and the integrity of the person who holds it. He ought not to lower himself for some personal advantage; he ought not to sell himself short; he ought not to endure such-and-such an affront. And what counts as lowering, selling, and enduring depends upon the social meaning of the role and of the work. No substantive account of self-respect will also be a universal account.

But it is entirely possible that every teacher, doctor, and trade unionist will refuse to lower himself, sell himself short, and so on, expressing in his every act a proper regard for his person and position. The norm of proper regard may come into dispute, of course, and the dispute may generate competitive behavior. But the practice of respecting oneself isn't a competitive practice. Once we know what the norm is, we measure ourselves against that; and my sense (or other people's sense) that I have measured up, while it may prick someone else's conscience and make him uncomfortable, is no bar to his success, and his success is no diminution of my own. One can, I suppose, be too scrupulous in these measurements. Self-respect makes for prigs as self-esteem makes for snobs. But the values the prig exaggerates, unlike those the snob exaggerates, can be shared. Self-respect is a good we can all have—and it is still very much worth having.

In a hierarchical society, there are different norms and different measurements for each rank. A gentleman may value himself because of his vast lands or his near relation to a great lord: this is self-esteem, and it is instantly diminished if someone who owns still more land, or is related to a greater lord, moves into the neighborhood. Or he may value himself because he lives up to some standard of gentility: this is self-respect; and though it can be lost, I don't think it can be diminished. Both these reflexive forms are tricky, but self-esteem sticks more closely to hierarchical rank (even when the lower ranks cultivate in secret a counterhierarchy). Aristocrats and gentlemen enjoy greater self-esteem than do artisans, serfs, or servants. So we commonly assume, at any rate. But the case is different again with self-respect, which can be grasped as firmly by the lower as by the higher ranks, though the standards by which they measure themselves are different. Nor are the standards necessarily different. The philosopher slave Epictetus measured himself by his conception of humanity and sustained his self-respect. Religious universalism provides for similar measurements, which have greater appeal, no doubt, to slaves than to masters but apply equally to both. I am more interested here, however, in the way hierarchies generate distinct models of self-respect appropriate to each rank: the proud aristocrat, the honest artisan, the loyal servant, and so on. These are conventional types, and they serve to uphold the hierarchy. Still, we shouldn't be too quick to denigrate such self-conceptions, even if we hope to replace them. For they have played a large part in the moral life of mankind—a larger part, through much of human history, than their philosophical or religious alternatives.

So self-respect is available to anyone possessed of some understanding of his "proper" dignity and some capacity to act it out. The standards are different for different social positions, varying among ranks in a hierarchy just as they vary among occupations in the society of misters. But in the latter society, there is also a common social position, named (for men) by the title "mister." What standard is appropriate there? Tocqueville suggested that this question is equivalent to the question, What does it mean to be a self-respecting (or an honorable) person?

> The prescriptions of honor will . . . always be less numerous among a people not divided into castes than among any other. If ever there come to be nations in which it is hard to discover a trace of class distinctions, honor will then be limited to a few precepts, and these precepts will draw continually closer to the moral laws accepted by humanity in general.[39]

But this suggestion moves too quickly, I think, from class and nation to "humanity in general." We have indeed some idea of what it might mean to be a self-respecting person—a "man," a *Mensch*, a human being. But the notion lacks concreteness and specificity. By itself, it is too vague, like morality in general when it is abstracted from roles and relationships and social practices. It is for this reason that the title "mister" is available for competitive definition and has come to represent little more than a minimal standing in the general competition. The revolutionaries who challenged the old order did not call themselves "mister." Nor was equal humanity their most immediate demand, but rather equal membership was. They would have understood Simone Weil's claim that "honor has to do with a human being considered not simply as such, but from the point of view of his social surroundings."[40] Their preferred titles were "brother," "citizen," "comrade." These words were used, of course, to describe self-respecting persons, but they gave at the same time a more specific meaning to the description.

Now imagine—to take the easiest of these—a society of citizens, a political community. The self-respect of citizens is incompatible, I think, with the kinds of self-respect available in a hierarchy of ranks. The self-respecting servant, who knows his place and measures up to its norms (and stands on his dignity when his master behaves badly), may well be an attractive figure, but he is not likely to make a good citizen. The two belong to different social worlds. In the world of masters and servants, citizenship is unimaginable; in the world of citizens, personal service is demeaning. The democratic revolution doesn't so much redistribute as reconceptualize self-respect, tying it, as Tocqueville suggests, to a single set of norms. It remains possible, of course, to be a self-respecting teacher, doctor, trade unionist—and also a self-respecting scavenger, dishwasher, hospital orderly; and these occupational roles provide, probably, the most immediate experience of self-respect. But the experience is connected now to a sense of one's ability to shape and control the work (and the life) one shares with others. Hence:

> No self-respecting citizen would endure such treatment at the hands of state officials (or corporate officials, or bosses, supervisors, and foremen).

Democratic citizenship is a status radically disconnected from every kind of hierarchy. There is one norm of proper regard for the entire population of citizens. Men and women who aim at a more strenuous version of citizenship—telling us that we should abandon every private pleasure and, in Rousseau's words, "fly to the public assemblies"[41]—are more like prigs than snobs. They are trying to tighten the standards by which citizens measure themselves and one another. But it is the minimal standards intrinsic to the practice of democracy that set the norms of self-respect. And as these standards spread throughout civil society, they make possible a kind of self-respect that isn't dependent on any particular social position, that has to do with one's general standing in the community and with one's sense of oneself, not as a person simply but as a person effective in such and such a setting, a full and equal member, an active participant.[42]

The experience of citizenship requires the prior acknowledgment that everyone is a citizen—a public form of simple recognition. This is probably what is meant by the phrase "equal respect." One can give this phrase some positive content: every citizen has the same legal and political rights, everyone's vote is counted in the same way, my word in a court of law has the same weight as yours. None of this constitutes a necessary condition of self-respect, however, for substantive inequalities in the courts and in the political arena persist in most democracies, whose citizens are nonetheless capable of respecting themselves. What is necessary is that the idea of citizenship be shared among some group of people who recognize one another's title and provide some social space within which the title can be acted out. Similarly, the idea of doctoring as a profession and of trade unionism as a commitment must be shared by a group of people before there can be self-respecting doctors or trade unionists. Or, more forcefully, "for the need of honor to be satisfied in professional life, every profession [must] have some association really capable of keeping alive the memory of all the . . . nobility, heroism, probity, generosity, and genius spent in the exercise of that profession."[43] Self-respect can not be an idiosyncrasy; it is not a matter of will. In any substantive sense, it is a function of membership, though always a complex function, and depends upon equal respect among the members. Once again, though now with intimations of cooperative rather than competitive activity: "they recognize themselves as mutually recognizing each other."

Self-respect requires, then, some substantial connection to the group of members, to the movement that champions the idea of professional honor, class solidarity, or citizen rights, or to the larger community within which these ideas are more or less well established. That's why expulsion from the movement or exile from the community can be so serious a punishment. It attacks both the external and the reflexive forms of honor. Prolonged unemployment and poverty are similarly threatening: they represent a kind of economic exile, a punishment that we are loathe to say that anyone deserves. The welfare state is an effort to avoid this punishment, to gather in the economic exiles, to guarantee effective membership.[44] But even when it does this in the best possible way, meeting needs without degrading persons, it doesn't guarantee self-respect; it only helps to make it possible. This is, perhaps, the deepest purpose of distributive justice. When all social goods, from membership to political power, are distributed for the right reasons, then the conditions of self-respect will have been established as best they can be. But there will still be men and women who suffer from a lack of self-respect.

In order to enjoy self-esteem, we probably have to convince ourselves (even if this means deceiving ourselves) that we deserve it, and we can't do that without a little help from our friends. But we are judges in our own case; we pack the jury as best we can, and we fake the verdict whenever we can. About this sort of thing, no one feels guilty; such trials are all-too-human. But self-respect brings us closer to the real thing; it more nearly resembles the system of public honor and dishonor than the Hobbesian race. Now conscience is the court, and conscience is a shared knowledge, an internalized acceptance of communal standards. The standards are not all that high; we are required to be brethren and citizens, not saints and heroes. But we can't ignore the standards, and we can't juggle the verdict. We do measure up, or we don't. Measuring up is not a matter of success in this or that enterprise, certainly not of relative success or the reputation of success. It is rather a way of being in the community, holding one's head high (which is very different from riding a high horse).

In order to enjoy self-respect, we must believe ourselves capable of measuring up, and we must accept responsibility for the acts that constitute measuring up or not measuring up. Hence, self-respect depends upon a deeper value that I will call "self-possession," the ownership not of one's body but of one's character, qualities, and actions. Citizenship is one mode of self-possession. We hold ourselves responsible, and we are held responsible by our fellow citizens. From this mutual holding, the possibility of self-respect and also of public honor follows. These two do not, however, always go together. If I believe myself wrongly dishonored, I can retain my self-respect. And I can also retain my self-respect by accepting dishonor honorably, by "owning up" to my own actions. What is dishonorable, above all, is the claim of irresponsibility, the denial of self-possession. It's not that the self-respecting citizen never fails to fulfill the obligations of citizenship, but rather that he acknowledges his failures, knows himself capable of fulfilling his obligations, and remains committed to do so. Self-esteem is a matter of what Pascal called "borrowed" qualities; we live in the opinion of others.[45] Self-respect is a matter of our own qualities: hence of knowledge, not opinion, and of identity, not relative standing. This is the most profound meaning of Mark Antony's line

> . . . If I lose mine honor
> I lose myself.[46]

The self-respecting citizen is an autonomous person. I don't mean autonomous in the world; I don't know what that would involve. He is autonomous in his community, a free and responsible agent, a participating member. I think of him as the ideal subject of the theory of justice. He is at home *here,* and he knows his place; he "reigns in his own [company], not elsewhere" and he doesn't "desire power over the whole world." He is the very opposite of the tyrant, who uses his noble birth, or his wealth or office, or even his celebrity, to claim other goods that he has not earned, to which he has no right. Plato characterized the tyrant, in psychological terms, as a person ruled by a master passion.[47] In terms of the moral economy that I have been describing, the tyrant is a person who exploits a master good to master the men and women around him. He is not content with self-possession; but rather, through the mediation of money or power, he possesses himself of other selves. "I am ugly, but I can buy the most beautiful women for myself. Consequently, I am not ugly, for the effect of ugliness . . . is annulled by money. . . . I am a detestable, dishonorable, unscrupulous, and stupid man, but money is honored and so also is its possessor."[48] I don't want to suggest that a self-respecting detestable man would never seek such honor—though a similar idea may lie behind a certain sort of proud misanthropy. More generally, the self-respecting citizen will not seek what he cannot honorably have.

But he will certainly seek recognition from the other runners of the Hobbesian race (he isn't a dropout) and public honor from his fellow citizens. These are good things to have, social goods, and self-respect is not a replacement for them. One can no more abolish the relativity of value than the relativity of motion. I should think, however, that self-respect would lead one to want only the freely given recognitions and the honest verdicts of one's peers. In this sense, it is a way of acknowledging the moral meaning of complex equality. And we might assume in turn that the experience of complex equality will breed, though it can never guarantee, self-respect.

12

Political Power

Sovereignty and Limited Government

I shall begin with sovereignty, political command, authoritative decision making—the conceptual foundation of the modern state. Sovereignty by no means exhausts the field of power, but it does focus our attention on the most significant and dangerous form that power can take. For this is not simply one among the goods that men and women pursue; as *state power*, it is also the means by which all the different pursuits, including that of power itself, are regulated. It is the crucial agency of distributive justice; it guards the boundaries within which every social good is distributed and deployed. Hence the simultaneous requirements that power be sustained and that it be inhibited: mobilized, divided, checked and balanced. Political power protects us from tyranny . . . and itself becomes tyrannical. And it is for both these reasons that power is so much desired and so endlessly fought over.

Much of the fighting is unofficial, the guerrilla skirmishes of everyday life through which we (ordinary citizens) defend or struggle to revise the boundaries of the various distributive spheres. We try to prevent illegitimate crossings; we make accusations, organize protests, sometimes even attempt what can be called, in settled democratic regimes, a "citizen's arrest." But our ultimate appeal on all these occasions, short of revolution, is to the power of the state. Our political rulers, the agents of sovereignty, have a great deal of work to do (and undo). In their official capacity, they are, and they have to be, active everywhere. They abolish hereditary titles, recognize heroes, pay for the prosecution—but also for the defense—of criminals. They guard the wall between church and state. They regulate the authority of parents, provide civil marriages, fix alimony payments. They define the jurisdiction of the school and require the attendance of children. They declare and cancel public holidays. They decide how the army is to be recruited. They guarantee the fairness of civil service and professional examinations. They block illegitimate exchanges, redistribute wealth, facilitate union organization. They fix the scope and character of communal provision. They accept and reject applicants for membership. And finally, in all their activities, they restrain their own power; they subject themselves to constitutional limits.

Or so they should. Ostensibly, they act on our behalf and even in our names (with our consent). But in most countries most of the time, political rulers function, in fact, as agents of husbands and fathers, aristocratic families, degree holders, or capitalists. State power is colonized by wealth or talent or blood or gender; and once it is colonized, it is rarely limited. Alternatively, state power is itself imperialist; its agents are tyrants in their own right. They don't police the spheres of distribution but break into them; they don't defend social meanings but override them. This is the most visible form of tyranny, and the first with which I shall deal. The immediate connotations of the word *tyrant* are political; its pejorative sense derives from centuries of oppression by chiefs and kings—and, more recently, by generals and dictators. Throughout most of human history, the sphere of politics has been constructed on the absolutist model, where power is monopolized by a single person, all of whose energies are devoted to making it dominant not merely at the boundaries but across them, within every distributive sphere.

Blocked Uses of Power

Precisely for this reason, a great deal of political and intellectual energy has gone into the effort to limit the convertibility of power and restrain its uses, to define the blocked exchanges of the political sphere. As there are, in principle at least, things that money can't buy, so there are things that the representatives of sovereignty, the officials of the state, can't do. Or better, in doing them, they exercise not political power properly speaking but mere force; they act nakedly, without authority. Force is power used in violation of its social meaning. That it is commonly so used should never blind us to its tyrannical character. Thomas Hobbes, the great philosophical defender of sovereign power, argued that tyranny is nothing but sovereignty misliked.[1] That's not inaccurate so long as we recognize that the "misliking" is not idiosyncratic but is common to the men and women who create and inhabit a particular political culture; it derives from a shared understanding of what sovereignty is and what it is for. This understanding is always complex, nuanced, at many points controversial. But it can be presented in the form of a list, like the list of blocked exchanges. In the United States today, that list has something like this form:

1. Sovereignty does not extend to enslavement; state officials cannot seize the persons of their subjects (who are also their fellow citizens), compel their services, imprison or kill them—except in accordance with procedures agreed to by the subjects themselves or by their representatives and for reasons derived from the shared understandings of criminal justice, military service, and so on.

2. The feudal rights of wardship and marriage, briefly taken over by absolutist kings, lie outside the legal and moral competence of the state. Its officials cannot control the marriages of their subjects or interfere in their personal or familial relations or regulate the domestic upbringing of their children;[2] nor can these officials search and seize their subjects' personal effects or quarter troops in their homes—except in accordance with procedures, and so on.

3. State officials cannot violate the shared understandings of guilt and innocence, corrupt the system of criminal justice, turn punishment into a means of political repression, or employ cruel and unusual punishments. (Similarly, they are bound by the shared understandings of sanity and insanity and required to respect the meaning and purpose of psychiatric therapy.)

4. State officials cannot sell political power or auction off particular decisions; nor can they use their power to advance the interests of their families or distribute government offices to relatives or "cronies."

5. All subjects/citizens are equal before the law, and so state officials cannot act in ways that discriminate against racial, ethnic, or religious groups, nor even in ways that degrade or humiliate individuals (except as a result of a criminal trial); nor can they cut anyone off from whatever goods are communally provided.

6. Private property is safe against arbitrary taxation and confiscation, and state officials cannot interfere with free exchange and gift giving within the sphere of money and commodities, once that sphere has been properly marked off.

7. State officials cannot control the religious life of their subjects or attempt in any way to regulate the distributions of divine grace—or,

for that matter, of ecclesiastical or congregational favor and encouragement.

8. Though they can legislate a curriculum, state officials cannot interfere in the actual teaching of that curriculum or constrain the academic freedom of the teachers.

9. State officials cannot regulate or censor the arguments that go on, not only in the political sphere but in all the spheres, about the meaning of social goods and the appropriate distributive boundaries. Hence they must guarantee free speech, free press, free assembly—the usual civil liberties.

These limits fix the boundaries of the state and of all the other spheres vis-à-vis sovereign power. We commonly think of the limits in terms of freedom, and not wrongly, but they also have powerful egalitarian effects. For the overbearingness of officials is not only a threat to liberty, it is also an affront to equality: it challenges the standing and overrides the decisions of parents; church members; teachers and students; workers, professionals, and office holders; buyers and sellers; citizens generally. It makes for the subordination of all the companies of men and women to the one company that possesses or exercises state power. Limited government, then, like blocked exchange, is one of the crucial means to complex equality.

Knowledge/Power

But limited government tells us nothing about who governs. It does not settle the distribution of power within the sphere of politics. In principle, at least, the limits might be respected by a hereditary king, a benevolent despot, a landed aristocracy, a capitalist executive committee, a regime of bureaucrats, or a revolutionary vanguard. There is, indeed, a prudential argument for democracy: that the different companies of men and women will most likely be respected if all the members of all the companies share political power. This is a strong argument; at its substantive base it connects closely with our shared understanding of what power is and what it is for. But it isn't the only argument that makes or pretends to make that connection. In the long history of political thought, the most common claims about the meaning of power have been anti-democratic in character. I want to examine those claims carefully. For there is no other social good whose possession and use is more important than this one. Power is not the sort of thing that one can hug to oneself or admire in private, like a miser with his money or ordinary men and women with their favorite possessions. Power has to be exercised to be enjoyed; and when it is exercised, the rest of us are directed, policed, manipulated, helped, and hurt. Now, who should possess and exercise state power?

There are only two answers to this question that are intrinsic to the political sphere: first, that power should be possessed by those who best know how to use it; and second, that it should be possessed, or at least controlled, by those who most immediately experience its effects. The wellborn and the wealthy make what are properly called extrinsic claims, which don't link up with the social meaning of power. That's why both these groups are likely to reach, if they can, for one or another form of the argument from knowledge—pretending to possess, for example, a special understanding of the fixed and long-term interests of the political community, an understanding unavailable to upstart families or to men and women without a "stake" in the country. The claim of divine installation is also an extrinsic argument, except, perhaps, in those communities of believers where all authority is conceived to be a gift from God. Even in such places, it is commonly said that when God chooses His earthly deputies, He also inspires them with the knowledge necessary to govern their fellows: so divine-right kings pretended to a unique insight into the "mysteries of state," and Puritan saints systematically confused inner light with political understanding. All arguments for exclusive rule, all anti-democratic arguments, if they are serious, are arguments from special knowledge.

The Ship of State

Power is assimilated, then, to office; and we are invited to look for qualified people, to choose political rulers through co-option rather than election, relying on search committees and not on parties, campaigns, and public debates. But there is an earlier assimilation that more perfectly captures the essence of the argument from special knowledge: Plato's account of politics as a *techné,* an art or a craft similar to, though infinitely more difficult than, the ordinary specializations of social life.[3] Just as we buy our shoes from a craftsman skilled in shoemaking, so we should receive our laws from a craftsman skilled in ruling. Here, too, there are "mysteries of state"—where *mystery* refers to the secret (or at least not readily available) knowledge that underlies a profession or trade, as in the phrase "art and mystery," a common formula in indentures of apprenticeship. But these are mysteries known by training or education rather than by inspiration. In politics, as in shoemaking, medicine, navigation, and so on, we are urged to look to the few who know the mysteries and not to the ignorant many.

Consider the case of the pilot or navigator who stands at the helm of a ship and guides its course (our word *governor* derives from a Latin translation of the Greek for "helmsman"). Whom should we choose to play that part? Plato imagines a democratic ship:

> The sailors are quarreling over the control of the helm; each thinks he ought to be steering the vessel, though he has never learned navigation and cannot point to any teacher under whom he has served his apprenticeship; what is more, they assert that navigation is a thing that cannot be taught at all, and are ready to tear in pieces anyone who says it can.

A dangerous ship to be on, and for two reasons: because of the physical struggle for control, which has no obvious or certain end; and because of the likely incompetence of each (temporary) victor. What the sailors don't understand is "that the genuine navigator can only make himself fit to command a ship by studying the seasons of the year, sky, stars, and winds, and all that belongs to his craft."[4] The case is the same with the ship of state. Democratic citizens quarrel over control of the government, and so put themselves in danger, whereas they ought to yield the government to that person who possesses the special knowledge that "belongs to" the exercise of power. Once we understand what the helm is, and what it is for, we can move easily to a description of the ideal pilot; and once we understand what political power is, and what it is for, we can move easily (as in the *Republic*) to a description of the ideal ruler.

In fact, however, the more deeply we consider the meaning of power, the more likely we are to reject Plato's analogy. For we entrust ourselves to the navigator only after we have decided where we want to go; and that, rather than the setting of a particular course, is the decision that best illuminates the exercise of power. "The true analogy," as Renford Bambrough has written in a well-known analysis of Plato's argument, "is between the choice of a policy by a politician and the choice of a destination by the owner or passengers of a ship."[5] The pilot doesn't choose the port; his *techné* is simply irrelevant to the decision that the passengers have to make, which has to do with their individual or collective purposes and not with "the seasons of the year, sky, stars, and winds." In an emergency, of course, they will be guided by the maxim, "any port in a storm," and then by the judgment of the pilot about the most accessible place. But even in such a case, if the choice is hard and the risks difficult to measure, the decision might well be left to the passengers. And once the storm has subsided, they will surely want to be delivered from their necessary refuge to their chosen destination.

Destinations and risks are what politics is about, and power is simply the ability to settle these matters, not only for oneself but for others. Knowledge is obviously crucial to the settlement, but it is not and cannot be determining. The history of philosophy, the Platonic *techné*, is a history of arguments about desirable destinations and morally and materially acceptable risks. These are arguments carried on, as it were, in front of the citizens; and only the citizens can settle them with any authority. So far as policy is concerned, what politicians and pilots need to know is what the people or the passengers want. And what empowers them to act on that knowledge is the authorization of the people or the passengers themselves. (The case is the same with shoemakers: they can't repair my shoes merely because they know how to do so, without my agreement.) The crucial qualification for exercising political power is not some special insight into human ends but some special relation to a particular set of human beings.

When Plato defended the distribution of power to philosophers, he claimed that he was expounding the meaning of power—or, better, of the exercise of power, ruling, on analogy with shoemaking, doctoring, navigating, and so on. But he clearly wasn't expounding the common meaning, the political understanding of his fellow Athenians. For they, or the great bulk of them, practicing members of a democracy, must have believed what Pericles asserted in his funeral oration and what Protagoras argued in the Socratic dialogue that bears his name: that ruling involved the choice of ends, "joint decision in the field of civic excellence"; and that the knowledge necessary for this was widely shared.[6] "Our ordinary citizens, though occupied with the pursuits of industry, are still fair judges of public matters."[7] More strongly, there are and can be no better judges, because the proper exercise of power is nothing more than the direction of the city in accordance with the civic consciousness or public spirit of the citizens. For special tasks, of course, specially knowledgeable people must be found. Thus, the Athenians elected generals and public physicians—rather than choosing them by lot—much as they might "shop around" before settling on a shoemaker or hiring a navigator. But all such people are the agents of the citizens, not their rulers.

Disciplinary Institutions

Pericles and Protagoras articulate the democratic understanding of power, which is commonly focused on what I have called—anachronistically now when talking of the Athenians—"sovereignty": state power, civic power, collective command. Power in this sense is constituted by the decision-making capacities of the citizens, by their conjoined wills. It issues in laws and policies, which are simply the articulations of power. But the effectiveness of these articulations remains an open question, and it is increasingly argued in these latter days that knowledge makes for a kind of power that sovereignty cannot control. This is to revive Plato's argument in a new form (and most often with a different animus). Plato claimed that persons conversant in the arts and mysteries were entitled to power; rational men and women would bow to their authority. Today it is said that technical knowledge itself constitutes a power over and against sovereignty, to which we all in fact bow, even though we are democratic citizens and supposedly share in the "constituted authority" of the state. On what Michel Foucault calls "the underside of the law," philosophy has at last won out—or science and social science have won out; and we are ruled by experts in military strategy, medicine, psychiatry, pedagogy, criminology, and so on.[8]

When they justify themselves, the experts use Platonic arguments, but they don't claim to rule the state (they are not in fact Platonic philosophers); they are content to rule the army, the hospital, the asylum, the school, and the prison. With regard to these institutions, ends—or at least some minimal set of ends—seem to be given. So contemporary experts are like pilots of ships whose destination has already been determined; pending emergencies that might require some change of course, they are in command. But armies, hospitals, prisons, and so on have this special feature: that their members or inmates are, though for different reasons, barred from full participation in decision making, even (or particularly) in emergencies. Decisions have to be made on their behalf by the citizens generally, who do not resemble passengers so much as possible passengers, and who are unlikely to devote much time to the enterprise. Hence the power of the experts is especially great, very much like that of Plato's philosopher-kings, who stand to their subjects like teachers to children or, in another of Plato's analogies, like shepherds to sheep.

The distribution of power in armies, hospitals, prisons, and schools

Political Power

(Foucault includes factories, but power claims in factories are ultimately based not on knowledge but on ownership, and I will take them up separately) is indeed different from that required in a democratic state. Knowledge has a distinctive role to play; we require qualified people and find them through a search rather than an election. In the course of the search, we attend to education and experience, the institutional equivalents of the helmsman's grasp of seasons, sky, stars, and winds. And it is undoubtedly true that educated and experienced men and women are partially shielded from lay criticism. The more recondite and mysterious their knowledge, as I argued in chapter 5, the more effective the shield—a powerful argument for democratic education, whose purpose is not, however, to make all citizens experts but to mark off the boundaries of expertise. If special knowledge makes for power, it does not make for unlimited power. Here, too, there are blocked uses of power, which derive from the reasons we have for establishing armies, hospitals, prisons, and schools, and from our common sense of the activities appropriate to their officials.

The agreement on destination which leaves the helmsman in command of his ship also sets limits to what he can do: he must finally bring the ship to such-and-such a place. Similarly, our understanding of the purpose of a prison (and the meaning of punishment and the social roles of judges, wardens, and prison guards) sets limits to the exercise of power within its walls. I am sure that those limits are often violated. In the best of circumstances, a prison is a brutal place; the daily routine is cruel, and the warden and the guards are often tempted to intensify the cruelty. Sometimes when they do so, they express their own fear; sometimes—for the same walls that imprison the convicts set warden and guards free—they express a particularly virulent form of the insolence of office. The rest of us can, nevertheless, recognize the violations. Given a factual account of prison conditions, we can say whether the warden has acted beyond his powers. And when the prisoners claim that he has done so, they appeal to the sovereign and the law and, ultimately, to the civic consciousness of the citizens. The warden's special knowledge of criminology is no argument against that appeal.

The case is the same with hospitals and schools. Patients and children are especially vulnerable to the exercise of power by a competent professional who claims, not wrongly, to be acting on their behalf, in their interests, for their own (future) good, and so on. And this or that medical doctrine or pedagogic technique may well require a harsh and uncomfortable discipline, a seemingly bizarre regimen, strict control of the subject. Here, too, however, limits are set by our firm conviction that therapy is the cure of a *person* (it's not, for example, like fixing a machine), and that education is the training of a *citizen*. Laws that require the consent of patients, or that make school records available to students, are so many efforts to enforce these convictions. They bind professional men and women to a close understanding of their callings. So science and social science generate a kind of power, useful and even necessary in particular institutional settings; but this power is always limited by sovereignty, itself generated and informed by the larger knowledge of social meanings. Doctors and teachers (and wardens and even generals) are submitted to the "discipline" of citizens.

Or so (again) they ought to be. A decent state, whose citizens and officials are committed to complex equality, will act to maintain the integrity of its various institutional settings: to make sure that its prisons are places for criminal internment and not for preventive detention or scientific experiment; that its schools are not like prisons; that its asylums house (and care for) the mentally ill and not the politically deviant. A tyrannical state, by contrast, will reproduce tyranny in all its institutions. Perhaps it distributes power to the wrong people; more likely, it permits or actually fosters the use of power outside its limits. At one time or another in our lives, we all experience subjection to knowledgeable professionals; we are all laymen to someone else's expertise. This is not only or primarily because of political weakness—even wealthy citizens in a capitalist society are students, patients, soldiers, madmen, and (though less often than other people) prisoners; nor does it necessarily issue in a permanent loss of power. Mostly, the experience has a fixed duration and a known endpoint: graduation, recovery, and so on. And we are protected by the autonomy of the various institutional settings in which it occurs. Imitation across settings, as in Foucault's "carceral continuum" where all disciplinary institutions look like prisons, blurs the lines that make for freedom and equality. So does top-down coordination by state officials. Both imitation and coordination bring tyrannical rule to bear on everyday life in a peculiarly intense way.[9] But special knowledge is not itself tyrannical.

Property/Power

Ownership is properly understood as a certain sort of power over things. Like political power, it consists in the capacity to determine destinations and risks—that is, to give things away or to exchange them (within limits) and also to keep them and use or abuse them, freely deciding on the costs in wear and tear. But ownership can also bring with it various sorts and degrees of power over people. The extreme case is slavery, which far exceeds the usual forms of political rule. I am concerned here, however, not with the actual possession, but only with the control, of people—mediated by the possession of things; this is a kind of power closely analogous to that which the state exercises over its subjects and disciplinary institutions over their inmates. Ownership also has effects well short of subjection. People engage with one another, and with institutions too, in all sorts of ways that reflect the momentary inequality of their economic positions. I own such-and-such book, for example, and you would like to have it; I am free to decide whether to sell or lend or give it to you or keep it for myself. We organize a factory commune and conclude that so-and-so's skills do not suit him for membership. You gather your supporters and defeat me in the competition for a hospital directorship. Their company squeezes out ours in intense bidding for a city contract. These are examples of brief encounters. I see no way to avoid them except through a political arrangement that systematically replaces the encounters of men and women with what Engels once called "the administration of things"—a harsh response to what are, after all, normal events in the spheres of money and office. But what sovereignty entails, and what ownership sometimes achieves (outside its sphere), is sustained control over the destinations and risks of other people; and that is a more serious matter.

It's not easy to make out just when the free use of property converts into the exercise of power. There are difficult issues here, and much political and academic controversy.[10] Two further examples, very much of the kind that figure in the literature, will illuminate some of the problems.

1. Beset by market failures, we decide to close down or relocate our cooperatively owned factory, thereby causing considerable harm to local merchants. Are we exercising power over the merchants? Not in any sustained way, I think, though our decision may well have serious effects on their lives. We certainly don't control their response to the

new conditions we have created (nor are the new conditions entirely our creation: we didn't decide to fail on the market). Still, given our commitment to democratic politics, it might be argued that we should have included the merchants in our decision making. Inclusion is suggested by the medieval maxim, much favored by modern democrats, *What touches all should be decided by all.* But once one begins including all the people who are touched or affected by a given decision, and not just those whose daily activities are directed by it, it is hard to know where to stop. Surely the merchants in the various towns where the factory might relocate must be included as well. And all the people affected by the well-being of all the merchants, and so on. So power is drained away from local associations and communities and comes more and more to reside in the one association that includes all the affected people—namely, the state (and ultimately, if we pursue the logic of "touching," the global state). But this argument only suggests that affecting others cannot be a sufficient basis for distributing inclusion rights. It doesn't amount to exercising power in the relevant political sense.

By contrast, the state's decision to relocate the district offices of one of its bureaucracies must, if challenged, be fought through the political process. These are public offices, paid for out of public funds, providing public services. Hence the decision is clearly an exercise of power over the men and women who are taxed to make up the funds and who depend upon the services. A private firm, whether individually or collectively owned, is different. Its relations with its customers are more like brief encounters. If we tried to control these relations, insisting, for example, that every decision to locate or relocate had to be fought out politically, the sphere of money and commodities would effectively be eliminated, together with its attendant freedoms. All such attempts lie beyond the rightful range of (limited) government. But what if our factory is the only one, or by far the largest one, in town? Then our decision to close down or relocate might well have devastating effects; and in any genuine democracy, the political authorities would be pressed to step in. They might seek to alter market conditions (by subsidizing the factory, for example), or they might buy us out, or they might look for some way to attract new industry to the town.[11] These choices, however, are a matter more of political prudence than of distributive justice.

2. We run our factory in such a way as to pollute the air over much of the town in which we are located and so to endanger the health of its inhabitants. Day after day, we impose risks on our fellow citizens,

and we decide, for technical and commercial reasons, what degree of risk to impose. But to impose risks, or at least risks of this sort, is precisely to exercise power in the political sense of the phrase. Now the authorities will have to step in, defending the health of their constituents or insisting on the right to determine, on behalf of those constituents, the degree of risk they will accept.[12] Even here, however, the authorities won't involve themselves in any sustained way in factory decision making. They will simply set or reset the limits within which decisions are made. If we (the members of the factory commune) were able to stop them from doing that—by threatening to relocate, for example—and so maintain an unlimited ability to pollute, then it would make sense to call us tyrants. We would be exercising power in violation of the common (democratic) understanding of what power is and how it is to be distributed. Would it make a difference if we weren't aiming to maintain our profit margins but just struggling to keep the factory afloat? I am not sure; probably we would be bound, either way, to inform the local authorities of our financial condition and to accept their view of acceptable risks.[13]

These are hard cases, the second more so than the first; and I shall not attempt any detailed resolution of them here. In a democratic society, the boundary of the sphere of money and commodities is likely to be drawn, roughly, between the two, so as to include the first but not the second. I have, however, radically simplified my accounts of the cases by assuming a cooperatively owned factory; and I need now to consider, at rather greater length, the more common example of private ownership. Now the workers in the factory are no longer economic agents, licensed to make a set of decisions; only the owners are agents of that sort; and the workers, like the townspeople, are threatened by the factory's failures and by its pollution. But they aren't merely "touched," more or less seriously. Unlike the townspeople, they are participants in the enterprise that causes the effects; they are bound by its rules. Ownership constitutes a "private government," and the workers are its subjects.* So I must take up again, as in my earlier discussion of wage determination, the character of economic agency.

The classic setting for private government was the feudal system,

*There is an extensive literature on private governments, much of it the work of contemporary political scientists, reaching (rightly) for new fields.[14] But I think the decisive words were written by R. H. Tawney in 1912: "What I want to drive home is this, that the man who employs, governs, to the extent of the number of men employed. He has jurisdiction over them. He occupies what is really a public office. He has power, not of pit and gallows . . . but of overtime and short time, full bellies and empty bellies, health and sickness. The question *who* has this power, how is he qualified to use it, how does the state control his liberties . . . this is the question which really matters to the plain man today."[15]

where property in land was conceived to entitle the owner to exercise direct disciplinary (judicial and police) powers over the men and women who lived on the land—and who were, moreover, barred from leaving. These people were not slaves, but neither were they tenants. They are best called "subjects"; their landlord was also their lord, who taxed them and even conscripted them for his private army. It took many years of local resistance, royal aggrandizement, and revolutionary activity before a clear boundary was drawn between the estate and the realm, between property and polity. Not until 1789 was the formal structure of feudal rights abolished and the disciplinary power of the lords effectively socialized. Taxation, adjudication, and conscription: all these dropped out of our conception of what property means. The state was emancipated, as Marx wrote, from the economy.[16] The entailments of ownership were redefined so as to exclude certain sorts of decision making that, it was thought, could only be authorized by the political community as a whole. This redefinition established one of the crucial divisions along which social life is organized today. On one side are activities called "political," involving the control of destinations and risks; on the other side are activities called "economic," involving the exchange of money and commodities. But though this division shapes our understanding of the two spheres, it does not itself determine what goes on within them. Indeed, private government survives in the post-feudal economy. Capitalist ownership still generates political power, if not in the market, where blocked exchanges set limits at least on the legitimate uses of property, then in the factory itself, where work seems to require a certain discipline. Who disciplines whom? It is a central feature of a capitalist economy that owners discipline non-owners.

What justifies this arrangement, we are commonly told, is the risk taking that ownership requires, and the entrepreneurial zeal, the inventiveness, and the capital investment through which economic firms are founded, sustained, and expanded. Whereas feudal property was founded on armed force and sustained and expanded through the power of the sword (though it was also traded and inherited), capitalist property rests upon forms of activity that are intrinsically non-coercive and non-political. The modern factory is distinguished from the feudal manor because men and women come willingly to work in the factory, drawn by the wages, working conditions, prospects for the future, and so on that the owner offers, while the workers on the manor are serfs, prisoners of their noble lords. All this is true enough, at least sometimes, but it doesn't satisfactorily mark off property rights from political power. For everything that I have just said of firms and factories might also be said of cities and towns, if not always of states. They, too, are created by entrepreneurial energy, enterprise, and risk taking; and they, too, recruit and hold their citizens, who are free to come and go, by offering them an attractive place to live. Yet we should be uneasy about any claim to own a city or a town; nor is ownership an acceptable basis for political power within cities and towns. If we consider deeply why this is so, we shall have to conclude, I think, that it shouldn't be acceptable in firms or factories either. What we need is a story about a capitalist entrepreneur who is also a political founder and who tries to build his power on his property.

The Case of Pullman, Illinois

George Pullman was one of the most successful entrepreneurs of late nineteenth century America. His sleeping, dining, and parlor cars made train travel a great deal more comfortable than it had been, and only somewhat more expensive; and on this difference of degree, Pullman established a company and a fortune. When he decided to build a new set of factories and a town around them, he insisted that this was only another business venture. But he clearly had larger hopes: he dreamed of a community without political or economic unrest—happy workers and a strike-free plant.[17] He clearly belongs, then, to the great tradition of the political founder, even though, unlike Solon of Athens, he didn't enact his plans and then go off to Egypt, but stayed on to run the town he had designed. What else could he do, given that he owned the town?

Pullman, Illinois, was built on a little over four thousand acres of land along Lake Calumet just south of Chicago, purchased (in seventy-five individual transactions) at a cost of eight hundred thousand dollars. The town was founded in 1880 and substantially completed, according to a single unified design, within two years. Pullman (the owner) didn't just put up factories and dormitories, as had been done in Lowell, Massachusetts, some fifty years earlier. He built private homes, row houses, and tenements for some seven to eight thousand people, shops and offices (in an elaborate arcade), schools, stables, playgrounds, a market, a hotel, a library, a theater, even a church: in short, a model town, a planned community. And every bit of it belonged to him.

A stranger arriving at Pullman puts up at a hotel managed by one of Mr. Pullman's employees, visits a theater where all the attendants are in Mr. Pullman's service, drinks water and burns gas which Mr. Pullman's water

and gas works supply, hires one of his outfits from the manager of Mr. Pullman's livery stable, visits a school in which the children of Mr. Pullman's
employees are taught by other employees, gets a bill charged at Mr. Pullman's bank, is unable to make a purchase of any kind save from some tenant
of Mr. Pullman's, and at night he is guarded by a fire department every
member of which from the chief down is in Mr. Pullman's service.[18]

This account is from an article in the *New York Sun* (the model
town attracted a lot of attention), and it is entirely accurate except for
the line about the school. In fact, the schools of Pullman were at least
nominally run by the elected school board of Hyde Park Township.
The town was also subject to the political jurisdiction of Cook County
and the State of Illinois. But there was no municipal government.
Asked by a visiting journalist how he "governed" the people of Pullman, Pullman replied, "We govern them in the same way a man governs his house, his store, or his workshop. It is all simple enough."[19]
Government was, in his conception, a property right; and despite the
editorial "we," this was a right singly held and singly exercised. In his
town, Pullman was an autocrat. He had a firm sense of how its inhabitants should live, and he never doubted his right to give that sense practical force. His concern, I should stress, was with the appearance and
the behavior of the people, not with their beliefs. "No one was required
to subscribe to any set of ideals before moving to [Pullman]." Once
there, however, they were required to live in a certain way. Newcomers
might be seen "lounging on their doorsteps, the husband in his shirt-
sleeves, smoking a pipe, his untidy wife darning, and half-dressed children playing about them." They were soon made aware that this sort
of thing was unacceptable. And if they did not mend their ways, "company inspectors visited to threaten fines."[20]

Pullman refused to sell either land or houses—so as to maintain "the
harmony of the town's design" and also, presumably, his control over
the inhabitants. Everyone who lived in Pullman (Illinois) was a tenant
of Pullman (George). Home renovation was strictly controlled; leases
were terminable on ten days' notice. Pullman even refused to allow
Catholics and Swedish Lutherans to build churches of their own, not
because he opposed their worship (they were permitted to rent rooms),
but because his conception of the town called for one rather splendid
church, whose rent only the Presbyterians could afford. For somewhat
different reasons, though with a similar zeal for order, liquor was available only in the town's one hotel, at a rather splendid bar, where ordinary workers were unlikely to feel comfortable.

I have stressed Pullman's autocracy; I could also stress his benevolence. The housing he provided was considerably better than that generally available to American workers in the 1880s; rents were not unreasonable (his profit margins were in fact quite low); the buildings were kept in repair; and so on. But the crucial point is that all decisions, benevolent or not, rested with a man, governor as well as owner, who had not been chosen by the people he governed. Richard Ely, who visited the town in 1885 and wrote an article about it for *Harper's Monthly*, called it "unAmerican . . . benevolent, well-wishing feudalism."[21] But that description wasn't quite accurate, for the men and women of Pullman were entirely free to come and go. They were also free to live outside the town and commute to work in its factories, though in hard times Pullman's tenants were apparently the last to be laid off. These tenants are best regarded as the subjects of a capitalist enterprise that has simply extended itself from manufacturing to real estate and duplicated in the town the discipline of the shop. What's wrong with that?

I mean the question to be rhetorical, but it is perhaps worthwhile spelling out the answer. The inhabitants of Pullman were guest workers, and that is not a status compatible with democratic politics. George Pullman hired himself a metic population in a political community where self-respect was closely tied to citizenship and where decisions about destinations and risks, even (or especially) local destinations and risks, were supposed to be shared. He was, then, more like a dictator than a feudal lord; he ruled by force. The badgering of the townspeople by his inspectors was intrusive and tyrannical and can hardly have been experienced in any other way.

Ely argued that Pullman's ownership of the town made its inhabitants into something less than American citizens: "One feels that one is mingling with a dependent, servile people." Apparently, Ely caught no intimations of the great strike of 1894 or of the courage and discipline of the strikers.[22] He wrote his article early on in the history of the town; perhaps the people needed time to settle in and learn to trust one another before they dared oppose themselves to Pullman's power. But when they did strike, it was as much against his factory power as against his town power. Indeed, Pullman's foremen were even more tyrannical than his agents and inspectors. It seems odd to study the duplicated discipline of the model town and condemn only one half of it. Yet this was the conventional understanding of the time. When the Illinois Supreme Court in 1898 ordered the Pullman Company (George Pullman had died a year earlier) to divest itself of all property not used for manufacturing purposes, it argued that the ownership of a town, but not of a company, "was incompatible with the theory and spirit of our institutions."[23] The town had to be governed democratically—not so much because ownership made the inhabitants servile, but because it forced them to fight for rights they already possessed as American citizens.

It is true that the struggle for rights in the factory was a newer struggle, if only because factories were newer institutions than cities and towns. I want to argue, however, that with regard to political power democratic distributions can't stop at the factory gates. The deep principles are the same for both sorts of institution. This identity is the moral basis of the labor movement—not of "business unionism," which has another basis, but of every demand for progress toward industrial democracy. It doesn't follow from these demands that factories can't be owned; nor did opponents of feudalism say that land couldn't be owned. It's even conceivable that all the inhabitants of a (small) town might pay rent, but not homage, to the same landlord. The issue in all these cases is not the existence but the entailments of property. What democracy requires is that property should have no political currency, that it shouldn't convert into anything like sovereignty, authoritative command, sustained control over men and women. After 1894, at least, most observers seem to have agreed that Pullman's ownership of the town was undemocratic. But was his ownership of the company any different? The unusual juxtaposition of the two makes for a nice comparison.

They are not different because of the entrepreneurial vision, energy, inventiveness, and so on that went into the making of Pullman sleepers, diners, and parlor cars. For these same qualities went into the making of the town. This, indeed, was Pullman's boast: that his " 'system' which had succeeded in railroad travel, was now being applied to the problems of labor and housing."[24] And if the application does not give rise to political power in the one case, why should it do so in the other?*

Nor are the two different because of the investment of private capital in the company. Pullman invested in the town, too, without thereby acquiring the right to govern its inhabitants. The case is the same with men and women who buy municipal bonds: they don't come to own

---

*But perhaps it was Pullman's expertise, not his vision, energy, and so on, that justified his autocratic rule. Perhaps factories should be assimilated to the category of disciplinary institutions and run by scientific managers. But the same argument might be made for towns. Indeed, professional managers are often hired by town councils; they are subject, however, to the authority of the elected councilors. Factory managers are subject, though often ineffectively, to the authority of owners. And so the question remains: Why owners rather than workers (or their elected representatives)?

Political Power

the municipality. Unless they live and vote in the town, they cannot even share in decisions about how their money is to be spent. They have no political rights; whereas residents do have rights, whether they are investors or not. There seems no reason not to make the same distinction in economic associations, marking off investors from participants, a just return from political power.

Finally, the factory and the town are not different because men and women come willingly to work in the factory with full knowledge of its rules and regulations. They also come willingly to live in the town, and in neither case do they have full knowledge of the rules until they have some experience of them. Anyway, residence does not constitute an agreement to despotic rules even if the rules are known in advance; nor is prompt departure the only way of expressing opposition. There are, in fact, some associations for which these last propositions might plausibly be reversed. A man who joins a monastic order requiring strict and unquestioning obedience, for example, seems to be choosing a way of life rather than a place to live (or a place to work). We would not pay him proper respect if we refused to recognize the efficacy of his choice. Its purpose and its moral effect are precisely to authorize his superior's decisions, and he can't withdraw that authority without himself withdrawing from the common life it makes possible. But the same thing can't be said of a man or a woman who joins a company or comes to work in a factory. Here the common life is not so all-encompassing and it does not require the unquestioning acceptance of authority. We respect the new worker only if we assume that he has not sought out political subjection. Of course, he encounters foremen and company police, as he knew he would; and it may be that the success of the enterprise requires his obedience, just as the success of a city or a town requires that citizens obey public officials. But in neither case would we want to say (what we might say to the novice monk): if you don't like these officials and the orders they give, you can always leave. It's important that there be options short of leaving, connected with the appointment of the officials and the making of the rules they enforce.

Other sorts of organizations raise more difficult questions. Consider an example that Marx used in the third volume of *Capital* to illustrate the nature of authority in a communist factory. Cooperative labor requires, he wrote, "one commanding will," and he compared this will to that of an orchestra conductor.[25] The conductor presides over a harmony of sounds and also, Marx seems to have thought, over a harmony of musicians. It is a disturbing comparison, for conductors have often been despots. Should their will be commanding? Perhaps it should, since an orchestra must express a single interpretation of the music it plays. But patterns of work in a factory are more readily negotiated. Nor is it the case that the members of an orchestra must yield to the conductor with regard to every aspect of the life they share. They might claim a considerable voice in the orchestra's affairs, even if they accept when they play the conductor's commanding will.

But the members of an orchestra, like the workers in a factory, while they spend a great deal of time with one another, don't live with one another. Perhaps the line between politics and economics has to do with the difference between residence and work. Pullman brought the two together, submitted residents and workers to the same rule. Is it enough if residents rule themselves while only workers are submitted to the power of property, if the residents are citizens and the workers metics? Certainly the self-rule of residents is commonly thought to be a matter of the first importance. That's why a landlord has so much less power over his tenants than a factory owner over his workers. Men and women must collectively control the place where they live in order to be safe in their own homes. *A man's home is his castle.* I will assume that this ancient maxim expresses a genuine moral imperative. But what the maxim requires is not political self-rule so much as the legal protection of the domestic sphere—and not only from economic but also from political interventions. We need a space for withdrawal, rest, intimacy, and (sometimes) solitude. As a feudal baron retired to his castle to brood over public slights, so I retire to my home. But the political community is not a collection of brooding places, or not only that. It is also a common enterprise, a public place where we argue together over the public interest, where we decide on goals and debate acceptable risks. All this was missing in Pullman's model town, until the American Railway Union provided a forum for workers and residents alike.

From this perspective, an economic enterprise seems very much like a town, even though—or, in part, because—it is so unlike a home. It is a place not of rest and intimacy but of cooperative action. It is a place not of withdrawal but of decision. If landlords possessing political power are likely to be intrusive on families, so owners possessing political power are likely to be coercive of individuals. Conceivably the first of these is worse than the second, but this comparison doesn't distinguish the two in any fundamental way; it merely grades them. Intrusiveness and coercion are alike made possible by a deeper reality—the usurpation of a common enterprise, the displacement of collective decision making, by the power of property. And for this, none of the standard justifications seems adequate. Pullman exposed their weaknesses by claiming to rule the town he owned exactly as he ruled the factories he owned. Indeed, the two sorts of rule are similar to one another, and both of them resemble what we commonly understand as authoritarian politics. The right to impose fines does the work of taxation; the right to evict tenants or discharge workers does (some of) the work of punishment. Rules are issued and enforced without public debate by appointed rather than by elected officials. There are no established judicial procedures, no legitimate forms of opposition, no channels for participation or even for protest. If this sort of thing is wrong for towns, then it is wrong for companies and factories, too.

Imagine now a decision by Pullman or his heirs to relocate their factory/town. Having paid off the initial investment, they see richer ground elsewhere; or, they are taken with a new design, a better model for a model town, and want to try it out. The decision, they claim, is theirs alone since the factory/town is theirs alone; neither the inhabitants nor the workers have anything to say. But how can this be right? Surely to uproot a community, to require large-scale migration, to deprive people of homes they have lived in for many years; these are political acts, and acts of a rather extreme sort. The decision is an exercise of power; and were the townspeople simply to submit, we would think they were not self-respecting citizens. What about the workers?

What political arrangements should the workers seek? Political rule implies a certain degree of autonomy, but it's not clear that autonomy is possible in a single factory or even in a group of factories. The citizens of a town are also the consumers of the goods and services the town provides; and except for occasional visitors, they are the only consumers. But workers in a factory are producers of goods and services; they are only sometimes consumers, and they are never the only consumers. Moreover, they are locked into close economic relationships with other factories that they supply or on whose products they depend. Private owners relate to one another through the market. In theory, economic decisions are non-political, and they are coordinated without the interventions of authority. Insofar as this theory is true, worker cooperatives would simply locate themselves within the network of market relations. In fact, however, the theory misses both the collusions of owners among themselves and their collective ability to call upon the support of state officials. Now the appropriate replacement is an industrial democracy organized at national as well as local levels. But how, precisely, can power be distributed so as to take into account both the necessary autonomy and the practical linkage of companies and factories? The question is often raised and variously answered in the literature on workers' control. I shall not attempt to answer it again, nor do I mean to deny its difficulties; I only want to insist that the sorts of arrangements required in an industrial democracy are not all that different from those requred in a political democracy. Unless they are independent states, cities and towns are never fully autonomous; they have no absolute authority even over the goods and services they produce for internal consumption. In the United States today, we enmesh them in a federal structure and regulate what they can do in the areas of education, criminal justice, environmental use, and so on. Factories and companies would have to be similarly enmeshed and similarly regulated (and they would also be taxed). In a developed economy, as in a developed polity, different decisions would be made by different groups of people at different levels of organization. The division of power in both these cases is only partly a matter of principle; it is also a matter of circumstance and expediency.

The argument is similar with regard to the constitutional arrangements within factories and companies. There will be many difficulties working these out; there will be false starts and failed experiments exactly as there have been in the history of cities and towns. Nor should we expect to find a single appropriate arrangement. Direct democracy, proportional representation, single-member constituencies, mandated and independent representatives, bicameral and unicameral legislatures, city managers, regulatory commissions, public corporations—political decision making is organized and will continue to be organized in many different ways. What is important is that we know it to be political, the exercise of power, not the free use of property.

Today, there are many men and women who preside over enterprises in which hundreds and thousands of their fellow citizens are involved, who direct and control the working lives of their fellows, and who explain themselves exactly as George Pullman did. I govern these people, they say, in the same way a man governs the things he owns. People who talk this way are wrong. They misunderstand the prerogatives of ownership (and of foundation, investment, and risk taking). They claim a kind of power to which they have no right.

To say this is not to deny the importance of entrepreneurial activity. In both companies and towns, one looks for people like Pullman, full of energy and ideas, willing to innovate and take risks, capable of organizing large projects. It would be foolish to create a system that did not bring them forward. They are of no use to us if they just brood in their castles. But there is nothing they do that gives them a right to rule over the rest of us, unless they can win our agreement. At a certain point in the development of an enterprise, then, it must pass out of entrepreneurial control; it must be organized or reorganized in some political way, according to the prevailing (democratic) conception of how power ought to be distributed. It is often said that economic entrepreneurs won't come forward if they cannot hope to own the companies they found. But this is like saying that no one would seek divine grace or knowledge who did not hope to come into hereditary possession of a church or "holy commonwealth," or that no one would found new hospitals or experimental schools who did not intend to pass them on to his children, or that no one would sponsor political innovation and reform unless it were possible to own the state. But ownership is not the goal of political or religious life, and there are still attractive and even compelling goals. Indeed, had Pullman founded a better town, he might have earned for himself the sort of public honor that men and women have sometimes taken as the highest end of human action. If he wanted power as well, he should have run for mayor.

Democratic Citizenship

Once we have located ownership, expertise, religious knowledge, and so on in their proper places and established their autonomy, there is no alternative to democracy in the political sphere. The only thing that can justify undemocratic forms of government is an undifferentiated conception of social goods—of the sort, roughly, that theocrats and plutocrats might hold. Even a military regime, which seems to rest on nothing more than an assertion of force, must make a deeper claim: that military force and political power are really the same thing, that men and women can only be ruled by threats and physical coercion, and hence that power should be given to (even if it hasn't yet been seized by) the most efficient soldiers. This, too, is an argument from special knowledge; for it's not just any soldier who should rule, but rather the one soldier who best knows how to organize his troops and use his weapons. But if we conceive of military force more narrowly, as Plato did when he submitted guardians to philosophers, then we can also set limits on military rule. The best soldier rules the army, not the state. And similarly, if we conceive of philosophy more narrowly than

Plato did, we will conclude that the best philosophers, while they may rule our speculations, cannot govern our persons.

The citizens must govern themselves. "Democracy" is the name of this government, but the word doesn't describe anything like a simple system; nor is democracy the same thing as simple equality. Indeed, government can never be simply egalitarian; for at any given moment, someone or some group must decide this or that issue and then enforce the decision, and someone else or some other group must accept the decision and endure the enforcement. Democracy is a way of allocating power and legitimating its use—or better, it is *the political way* of allocating power. Every extrinsic reason is ruled out. What counts is argument among the citizens. Democracy puts a premium on speech, persuasion, rhetorical skill. Ideally, the citizen who makes the most persuasive argument—that is, the argument that actually persuades the largest number of citizens—gets his way. But he can't use force, or pull rank, or distribute money; he must talk about the issues at hand. And all the other citizens must talk, too, or at least have a chance to talk. It is not only the inclusiveness, however, that makes for democratic government. Equally important is what we might call the rule of reasons. Citizens come into the forum with nothing but their arguments. All non-political goods have to be deposited outside: weapons and wallets, titles and degrees.

Democracy, according to Thomas Hobbes, "is no more than an aristocracy of orators, interrupted sometimes with the temporary monarchy of one orator."[26] Hobbes was thinking of the Athenian assembly and of Pericles. Under modern conditions, one would have to attend to a much greater variety of settings—committees, caucuses, parties, interest groups, and so on—and then to a greater variety of rhetorical styles. The great orator has long since lost his dominance. But Hobbes was certainly right to insist that individual citizens always share in decision making to a greater or a lesser degree. Some of them are more effective, have more influence, than others. Indeed, if this were not true, if all citizens had literally the same amount of influence, it is hard to see how any clear-cut decisions could ever be reached. If the citizens are to give the law to themselves, then their arguments must somehow issue in a *law*. And though this law may well reflect a multitude of compromises, it will also in its final form be closer to the wishes of some citizens than to those of others. A perfectly democratic decision is likely to come closest to the wishes of those citizens who are politically most skillful. Democratic politics is a monopoly of politicians.

The Athenian Lottery

One way to avoid this monopoly is to choose office holders by lot. This is simple equality in the sphere of office, and I have already discussed some of its modern versions. But it is worth focusing for a moment on the Athenian example, because it suggests very clearly how political power escapes this sort of equality. This is not to deny the impressive egalitarianism of Athenian democracy. A wide range of officials were chosen by lot and entrusted with important civic responsibilities. They were, indeed, submitted to a kind of examination before being allowed to take up those responsibilities. But the questions posed were the same for all citizens and for all offices, intended only to establish that potential office holders were citizens in good standing and that they had performed their political and familial duties. The examination "did not in any sense test [the individual's] capacity to perform the office for which he had been selected by lot."[27] This capacity, it was assumed, all citizens possessed. And that assumption seems to have been justified; at any rate, the work was done, and effectively done, by one randomly selected citizen after another.

The most important offices, however—those that required the widest discretion—were not distributed in this way. What was more important, laws and policies were not chosen in this way. No one ever suggested that every citizen should be allowed to "nominate" a policy or draft a law for a general lottery. That would have seemed an irresponsible and arbitrary procedure for determining the goals and risks of the community. Instead, the assembly debated the various proposals; or, rather, the aristocracy of orators debated them, and the bulk of the citizens listened and voted. The lot distributed administrative but not, properly speaking, political power.

Political power in a democracy is distributed by arguing and voting. But isn't the vote itself a kind of power, distributed by the rule of simple equality? A kind of power, perhaps, but something well short of the capacity to determine destinations and risks. Here is another example of how the rule of simple equality devalues the goods it governs. A single vote, as Rousseau argued, represents a $1/n$ share of sovereignty.[28] In an oligarchy, that is a considerable share; in a democracy, and especially in a modern mass democracy, it is a very small share indeed. The vote is important nonetheless because it serves both to symbolize membership and to give it concrete meaning. "One citizen/one vote" is the functional equivalent, in the sphere of politics, of the rule against exclusion and degradation in the sphere of welfare, of the principle of equal consideration in the sphere of office, and of the guarantee of a school place for every child in the sphere of education. It is the foundation of all distributive activity and the inescapable framework within which choices have to be made. But choices still have to made; and these depend not on single votes but on the accumulation of votes—hence on influence, persuasion, pressure, bargaining, organization, and so on. It is through their involvement in activities like these that politicians, whether they appear as leaders or as middlemen, exercise political power.

Parties and Primaries

Power "belongs to" persuasiveness, and therefore politicians are not tyrants—so long as their reach is suitably limited and their persuasiveness is not constituted by "money talking" or by deference to birth and blood. Nevertheless, democrats have always been suspicious of politicians and have long searched for some way to make simple equality more effective in the sphere of politics. We might, for example, handicap the most persuasive of our fellow citizens, limiting the number of times they can intervene in a discussion or requiring that they speak at meetings, like Demosthenes practicing on the beach, with pebbles in their mouths.[29] Or, more plausibly, we might eliminate meetings altogether and ban the clubs and parties that politicians organize to make their persuasiveness effective. This is the intent of Rousseau's argument that the citizens would always reach a good decision if, "being furnished with adequate information . . . [they] had no communication with one another." Then each individual would think "only his own thoughts." There would be no room for persuasion or organization, no premium on speechmaking and committee skills; instead of an aristocracy of orators, a genuine democracy of citizens would take shape.[30] But who would furnish the necessary information? And what if disagreements arose over what information was "adequate"?

In fact, politics is unavoidable; and politicians are unavoidable, too. Even if we don't talk with one another, someone must talk to all of us, not only supplying facts and figures but also defending positions. Modern technology makes possible something like this, bringing individual citizens into direct contact, or what seems as good as direct contact, with policy decisions and candidates for office. Thus, we might organize push-button referenda on crucial issues, the citizens alone in their living rooms, watching television, arguing only with their spouses, hands hovering over their private voting machines. And we could organize national nominations and elections in exactly the same way: a television debate and an instant ballot. This is something like simple equality in the sphere of politics (there are, of course, those other people arguing on television). But is it the exercise of power? I am inclined to say, instead, that it is only another example of the erosion of value— a false and ultimately degrading way of sharing in the making of decisions.

Compare for a moment the primary and the party convention, two very different methods of choosing presidential candidates. Democrats and egalitarians have pressed for more primaries, more open primaries (in which voters are free to select the party contest in which they will participate), and then for regional or national rather than state primaries. Here again, the intent is to minimize the influence of party organizations, machines, entrenched politicians, and so on, and to maximize the influence of individual citizens. The first effect is certainly achieved. Once primaries are established, and especially once open primaries are established, state and local organizations lose their hold. The candidate makes his appeal not through an articulated structure but through the mass media. He does not negotiate with local leaders, speak to caucuses, form alliances with established interest groups. Instead, he solicits votes, as it were, one by one, among all the registered voters without regard to their attachment to the party, loyalty to its programs, or willingness to work for its success. In turn, the voters encounter the candidate only on the television screen, without political mediation. Voting is lifted out of the context of parties and platforms; it is more like impulse buying than political decision making.

A primary campaign in the United States today is like a commando raid. The candidate and his personal entourage, together with a few attached professionals, advertising men, make-up artists for the face and mind, descend upon a state, fight a brief battle, and are quickly off again. No local ties are necessary; grass-roots organization and the endorsement of local notables are alike superfluous. The whole business is enormously strenuous for a few people, who are here and gone; while the residents of the state are mere spectators and then, miraculously, citizen-sovereigns, choosing their favorites. Party politics, by contrast, is not a raid but a long-term struggle. Though punctuated by elections, it has a more steady pace than a primary campaign has; it requires commitment and endurance. It involves more people for more time; but it is only the people who get involved who make the key decisions, choosing the party's candidates and designing its platform through caucuses and conventions. People who sit at home are excluded. Party politics is a matter of meetings and arguments, and going to the meetings and listening to the arguments are crucial; passive citizens enter the process only later, not to nominate but to choose among the nominees.

Caucuses and conventions are commonly taken to be less egalitarian than primaries, but that view falls short of the whole truth. The more intense forms of participation actually reduce the distance between leaders and followers, and they serve to maintain the centrality of argument—without which political equality quickly becomes a meaningless distribution. Candidates chosen in caucuses and conventions will almost certainly be better known to more people than will candidates chosen in primaries. For the former, unlike the latter, will have been seen at close quarters without their make-up; they will have worked the wards and precincts, taken stands, committed themselves in particular ways to particular men and women. Their victory will be the party's victory, and they will exercise power in something more like a collective fashion, not so much over their supporters as together with them. Caucuses and conventions are the crucial setting for the negotiations that shape this common effort, bringing together the divided forces of the party—notables, machines, sects, ginger groups—into a larger union. At worst, this is a politics of local bosses (rather than the national celebrities required and produced by the primary system); at best, it is a politics of party organizers, activists, and militants, going to meetings, debating issues, making deals. Primaries are like elections: every citizen is a voter, and every voter is equal to every other. But all the voters do is . . . vote. Caucuses and conventions are like parties generally: citizens come with the power they can muster, and the mustering of power involves them more deeply in the political process than voting alone can ever do. The citizen/voter is crucial to the survival of democratic politics; but the citizen/politician is crucial to its liveliness and integrity.

The argument for the stronger forms of participation is an argument for complex equality. No doubt, participation can be widely dispersed, as it is, for example, in the jury system. But even though juries are selected by lot, and even though each member has one—and only one—vote, the system works more like a caucus or convention than like a primary. The jury room is one more setting for the unequal exercise of power. Some of the members have more rhetorical skill, or personal charm, or moral force, or simple stubbornness than others, and they are more likely to determine the verdict. We might think of such people as "natural leaders" in the sense that their leadership doesn't hang on their wealth or birth or even their education; it is intrinsic to the political process. If the jurors never met or talked with one another but simply listened to the arguments of the lawyers, thought their own thoughts, and then voted, natural leaders would never appear. The power of the more passive jurors would certainly be enhanced by such a procedure; whether verdicts would be better or worse, I don't know. But I suspect that the jury system as a whole would be devalued, and that individual jurors would value their own roles less. For we commonly think of truth emerging from discussion—much as we think of policy emerging from the give-and-take of political debate. And it is better, more satisfying, to share in the discussions and debates, even if unequally, than to abolish them for the sake of simple equality.

Democracy requires equal rights, not equal power. Rights here are guaranteed opportunities to exercise minimal power (voting rights) or to try to exercise greater power (speech, assembly, and petition rights). Democratic theorists commonly conceive the good citizen as someone who is constantly trying to exercise greater power, though not necessarily on his own behalf. He has principles, ideas, and programs, and he cooperates with like-minded men and women. At the same time, he finds himself in intense, sometimes bitter, conflict with other groups of men and women who have their own principles, ideas, and programs. He probably relishes the conflict, the "fiercely agonistic" character of political life, the opportunity for public action.[31] His aim is to win—that is, to exercise *unequaled* power. In pursuit of this aim, he and his friends exploit whatever advantages they have. They make good account of their rhetorical skill and organizational competence; they play on party loyalties and memories of old struggles; they seek the endorsement of readily recognized or publicly honored individuals. All this is entirely legitimate (so long as recognition doesn't translate directly into political power: we don't give the people we honor a double vote or a public office). It would not be legitimate, however, for reasons I have already worked through, if some citizens were able to win their political struggles because they were personally wealthy or had wealthy backers or powerful friends and relatives in the existing government. There are some inequalities that can, and others that cannot, be exploited in the course of political activity.

Even more important, it would not be legitimate if, having won, the winners used their unequal power to cut off the voting and participation rights of the losing side. They can rightly say: because we argued and organized, persuaded the assembly or carried the election, we shall rule over you. But it would be tyrannical to say: we shall rule over you forever. Political rights are permanent guarantees; they underpin a process that has no endpoint, an argument that has no definitive conclusion. In democratic politics, all destinations are temporary. No citizen can ever claim to have persuaded his fellows once and for all. There are always new citizens, for one thing; and old citizens are always entitled to reopen the argument—or join an argument from which they have previously abstained (or to kibitz endlessly from the sidelines). This is what complex equality means in the sphere of politics: it is not power that is shared, but the opportunities and occasions of power. Every citizen is a potential participant, a potential politician.

That potentiality is the necessary condition of the citizen's self-respect. I have already had something to say about the connection between citizenship and self-respect, and I want now briefly to conclude the argument. The citizen respects himself as someone who is able, when his principles demand it, to join in the political struggle, to cooperate and compete in the exercise and pursuit of power. And he also respects himself as someone who is able to resist the violation of his rights, not only in the political sphere but in the other spheres of distribution, too: for resistance is itself an exercise of power, and politics is the sphere through which all the others are regulated. The casual or arbitrary exercise of power won't generate self-respect; that's why push-button participation would make for a morally unsatisfying politics. The citizen must be ready and able, when his time comes, to deliberate with his fellows, listen and be listened to, take responsibility for what he says and does. Ready and able: not only in states, cities, and towns but wherever power is exercised, in companies and factories, too, and in unions, faculties, and professions. Deprived permanently of power, whether at national or local levels, he is deprived also of this sense of himself. Hence the reversal of Lord Acton's maxim, attributed to a variety of twentieth-century politicians and writers: "Power corrupts, but the lack of power corrupts absolutely."[32] This is an insight available, I think, only in a democratic setting, where the sense of potential power can be recognized as a form of moral health (rather than as a threat of political subversion). Citizens without self-respect dream of a tyrannical revenge.

The most common form of powerlessness in the United States today derives from the dominance of money in the sphere of politics. The endless spectacle of property/power, the political success story of the rich, enacted and re-enacted on every social stage, has over time a deep and pervasive effect. Citizens without money come to share a profound conviction that politics offers them no hope at all. This is a kind of practical knowledge that they learn from experience and pass on to their children. With it comes passivity, deference, and resentment.[33] But we must guard, again, against drawing the circle too tight—from powerlessness to a loss of self-respect to a deeper and deeper loss of power, and so on. For the struggle against the dominance of money, against corporate wealth and power, is perhaps the finest contemporary expression of self-respect. And the parties and the movements that organize the struggle and carry it forward are breeding grounds of self-respecting citizens. The struggle is itself a denial of powerlessness, an acting out of citizenly virtue. What makes it possible? A surge of hope, generated perhaps by a social or an economic crisis, a shared understanding of political rights, an impulse toward democracy latent in the culture (not in every culture).

But I can't say that victory is any guarantee of self-respect. We can recognize rights, we can distribute power or at least the occasions of power, but we cannot guarantee the prideful activity that rights and occasions make possible. Democratic politics, once we have overthrown every wrongful dominance, is a standing invitation to act in public and know oneself a citizen, capable of choosing destinations and accepting risks for oneself and others, and capable, too, of patrolling the distributive boundaries and sustaining a just society. But there is no way to make sure that you or I, or anyone, will seize the opportunity. This, I suppose, is the secular version of Locke's proposition that no one can be forced to be saved. But citizenship, as distinct from salvation, does depend upon certain public arrangements, which I have tried to describe. And the dominion of citizenship, unlike the dominion of grace (or money, or office, or education, or birth and blood), is not tyrannical; it is the end of tyranny.

13

Tyrannies
and Just Societies

The Relativity and the Non-Relativity of Justice

The best account of distributive justice is an account of its parts: social
goods and spheres of distribution. But I want now to say something
about the whole: first, with regard to its relative character; second, with
regard to the form it takes in our own society; and third, with regard
to the stability of that form. These three points will conclude my argument. I shall not attempt here to consider the question whether societies where goods are justly distributed are also good societies. Certainly,
justice is better than tyranny; but whether one just society is better
than another, I have no way of saying. Is there a particular understanding (and then a particular distribution) of social goods that is *good* simply? That is not a question that I have addressed in this book. As a
singular conception, the idea of the good does not control our arguments about justice.

Justice is relative to social meanings. Indeed, the relativity of justice
follows from the classic non-relative definition, giving each person his
due, as much as it does from my own proposal, distributing goods for
"internal" reasons. These are formal definitions that require, as I have
tried to show, historical completion. We cannot say what is due to this

person or that one until we know how these people relate to one another through the things they make and distribute. There cannot be a just society until there is a society; and the adjective *just* doesn't determine, it only modifies, the substantive life of the societies it describes. There are an infinite number of possible lives, shaped by an infinite number of possible cultures, religions, political arrangements, geographical conditions, and so on. A given society is just if its substantive life is lived in a certain way—that is, in a way faithful to the shared understandings of the members. (When people disagree about the meaning of social goods, when understandings are controversial, then justice requires that the society be faithful to the disagreements, providing institutional channels for their expression, adjudicative mechanisms, and alternative distributions.)

In a society where social meanings are integrated and hierarchical, justice will come to the aid of inequality. Consider again the caste system, which has served me before as a test of theoretical coherence. Here is the summary of a detailed account of the distribution of grain in an Indian village:

> Each villager participated in the division of the grain heap. There was no bargaining, and no payment for specific services rendered. There was no accounting, yet each contributor to the life of the village had a claim on its produce, and the whole produce was easily and successfully divided among the villagers.[1]

This is the village as commune, an idealized though not an absurd picture. But if everyone had a claim on the communal grain heap, some people had greater claims than others. The villagers' portions were unequal, significantly so; and the inequalities were tied to a long series of other inequalities, all of them justified by customary rules and an overarching religious doctrine. Distributions were public and "easily" made, so it can't have been difficult to recognize unjust seizures and acquisitions, not only of grain. A landowner, for example, who brought in hired labor to replace the lower caste members of the village community would violate their rights. The adjective *just*, applied to this community, rules out all such violations. But it does not rule out the inequality of the portions; it cannot require a radical redesign of the village against the shared understandings of the members. If it did, justice itself would be tyrannical.

But perhaps we should doubt that the understandings governing village life were really shared. Perhaps the lower caste members were angry and indignant (though they repressed these feelings) even with landowners who took only their "rightful" portions. If that were so, then it would be important to seek out the principles that shaped their anger and indignation. These principles, too, must have their part in village justice; and if they were known among the lower castes, they were not unknown (though perhaps repressed) among the higher. Social meanings need not be harmonious; sometimes they provide only the intellectual structure within which distributions are debated. But that is a necessary structure. There are no external or universal principles that can replace it. Every substantive account of distributive justice is a local account.*

It will be useful at this point to return to one of the questions that I set aside in my preface: By virtue of what characteristics are we one another's equals? One characteristic above all is central to my argument. We are (all of us) culture-producing creatures; we make and inhabit meaningful worlds. Since there is no way to rank and order these worlds with regard to their understanding of social goods, we do justice to actual men and women by respecting their particular creations. And they claim justice, and resist tyranny, by insisting on the meaning of social goods among themselves. Justice is rooted in the distinct understandings of places, honors, jobs, things of all sorts, that constitute a shared way of life. To override those understandings is (always) to act unjustly.

Assume now that the Indian villagers really do accept the doctrines that support the caste system. A visitor to the village might still try to convince them—it is an entirely respectable activity—that those doctrines are false. He might argue, for example, that men and women are created equal not across many incarnations but within the compass of this one. If he succeeded, a variety of new distributive principles would come into view (depending on how occupations were reconceptualized to match the new understanding of persons). More simply, the imposition of a modern state bureaucracy over the system of castes immediately introduces new principles and lines of differentiation. Ritual purity is no longer integrated with office holding. The distribution of state jobs involves different criteria; and if outcastes, say, are excluded, we can begin, because they will begin, to talk about injustice. Indeed, the talk has a familiar form, for it includes (in India today) argu-

*At the same time, it may be the case, as I suggested in chapter 1, that certain internal principles, certain conceptions of social goods, are reiterated in many, perhaps in all, human societies. That is an empirical matter. It cannot be determined by philosophical argument among ourselves—nor even by philosophical argument among some ideal version of ourselves.

ments about the reservation of particular offices, which some people see as a mutation of the caste system, others as a necessary remedy for it.[2] Exactly how to draw the line between old castes and new bureaucracy is bound to be a contentious matter, but some line will have to be drawn once the bureaucracy is in place.

Just as one can describe a caste system that meets (internal) standards of justice, so one can describe a capitalist system that does the same thing. But now the description will have to be a great deal more complex, for social meanings are no longer integrated in the same way. It may be the case, as Marx says in the first volume of *Capital,* that the creation and appropriation of surplus value "is peculiar good fortune for the buyer [of labor power], but no injustice at all to the seller."[3] But this is by no means the whole story of justice and injustice in capitalist society. It will also be crucially important whether this surplus value is convertible, whether it purchases special privileges, in the law courts, or in the educational system, or in the spheres of office and politics. Since capitalism develops along with and actually sponsors a considerable differentiation of social goods, no account of buying and selling, no description of free exchange, can possibly settle the question of justice. We will need to learn a great deal about other distributive processes and about their relative autonomy from or integration into the market. The dominance of capital outside the market makes capitalism unjust.

The theory of justice is alert to differences, sensitive to boundaries. It doesn't follow from the theory, however, that societies are more just if they are more differentiated. Justice simply has more scope in such societies, because there are more distinct goods, more distributive principles, more agents, more procedures. And the more scope justice has, the more certain it is that complex equality will be the form that justice takes. Tyranny also has more scope. Viewed from the outside, from our own perspective, the Indian Brahmins look very much like tyrants—and so they will come to be if the understandings on which their high position is based cease to be shared. From the inside, however, things come to them naturally, as it were, by virtue of their ritual purity. They don't need to turn themselves into tyrants in order to enjoy the full range of social goods. Or, when they do turn themselves into tyrants, they merely exploit the advantages they already possess. But when goods are distinct and distributive spheres autonomous, that same enjoyment requires exertion, intrigue, and violence. This is the crucial sign of tyranny: a continual grabbing of things that don't come naturally, an unrelenting struggle to rule outside one's own company.

The highest form of tyranny, modern totalitarianism, is only possible in highly differentiated societies. For totalitarianism is the *Gleichschaltung*, the systematic coordination, of social goods and spheres of life that ought to be separate, and its peculiar terrors derive from the force of that "ought" in our lives. Contemporary tyrants are endlessly busy. There is so much to do if they are to make their power dominant everywhere, in the bureaucracy and the courts, in markets and factories, in parties and unions, in schools and churches, among friends and lovers, kinfolk and fellow citizens. Totalitarianism gives rise to new and radical inequalities, but it is perhaps the one redeeming feature of these inequalities that the theory of justice can never come to their aid. Here injustice takes on a kind of perfection, as if we have conceived and created a multitude of social goods and drawn the boundaries of their proper spheres only so as to provoke and enlarge the ambitions of tyrants. But at least we can recognize the tyranny.

Justice in the Twentieth Century

Justice as the opposite of tyranny speaks, then, to the most terrifying experiences of the twentieth century. Complex equality is the opposite of totalitarianism: maximum differentiation as against maximum coordination. It is the special value of complex equality for us, here and now, that it makes this opposition clear. For equality cannot be the goal of our politics unless we can describe it in a way that protects us against the modern tyranny of politics, against the domination of the party/state. I need to focus, then, on how that protection works.

Contemporary forms of egalitarian politics have their origin in the struggle against capitalism and the particular tyranny of money. And surely in the United States today it is the tyranny of money that most clearly invites resistance: property/power rather than power itself. But it is a common argument that without property/power, power itself is too dangerous. State officials will be tyrants, we are told, whenever their power is not balanced by the power of money. It follows, then, that capitalists will be tyrants whenever wealth is not balanced by a strong government. Or, in the alternative metaphor of American political science, political power and wealth must check one another: since armies of ambitious men and women push forward from one side of the boundary, what we require are similar armies pushing forward from the other side. John Kenneth Galbraith developed this metaphor into a theory of "countervailing powers."[4] There is also a competing argument according to which freedom is served only if the armies of capitalism are always and everywhere unopposed. But that argument can't be right, for it isn't only equality but freedom, too, that we defend when we block a large number of (the larger number of) possible exchanges. Nor is the theory of countervalence right without qualification. Boundaries must, of course, be defended from both sides. The problem with property/power, however, is that it already represents a violation of boundaries, a seizure of ground in the sphere of politics. Plutocracy is an established fact not only when rich men and women rule the state but also when they rule the company and the factory. When these two sorts of rule go together, it is commonly the first that serves the purposes of the second: the second is paramount. So the National Guard is called in to save the local power and the real political base of owners and managers.

Still, the tyranny of money is less frightening than the kinds of tyranny that have their origins on the other side of the money/politics divide. Certainly, plutocracy is less frightening than totalitarianism; resistance is less dangerous. The chief reason for the difference is that money can buy power and influence, as it can buy office, education, honor, and so on, without radically coordinating the various distributive spheres and without eliminating alternative processes and agents. It corrupts distributions without transforming them; and then corrupt distributions coexist with legitimate ones, like prostitution alongside married love. But this is tyranny still, and it can make for harsh forms of domination. And if resistance is less heroic than in totalitarian states, it is hardly less important.

Resistance will require at some point a concentration of political power that matches the concentration of plutocratic power—hence a movement or a party that seizes or, at least, uses the state. But once plutocracy is defeated, will the state wither away? It won't do that, not for all the promises of revolutionary leaders; nor should it. Sovereignty is a permanent feature of political life. The crucial question, as always, concerns the boundaries within which sovereignty operates, and these will depend upon the doctrinal commitments, the political organization, and the practical activity of the successful movement or party. That means, the movement must recognize in its everyday politics the real autonomy of distributive spheres. A campaign against plutocracy that doesn't respect the full range of social goods and social meanings is likely enough to end in tyranny. But other sorts of campaign are possible. Faced with the dominance of money, what one wants, after all, is a declaration of distributive independence. In principle, the movement and the state are agents of independence; and so they will be in practice if they are firmly in the hands of self-respecting citizens.

A great deal depends upon the citizens, upon their ability to assert themselves across the range of goods and to defend their own sense of meaning. I don't want to suggest that there are no institutional arrangements that might make complex equality easier (though it can never be as "easy" as the caste system). The appropriate arrangements in our own society are those, I think, of a decentralized democratic socialism; a strong welfare state run, in part at least, by local and amateur officials; a constrained market; an open and demystified civil service; independent public schools; the sharing of hard work and free time; the protection of religious and familial life; a system of public honoring and dishonoring free from all considerations of rank or class; workers' control of companies and factories; a politics of parties, movements, meetings, and public debate. But institutions of this sort are of little use unless they are inhabited by men and women who feel at home within them and are prepared to defend them. It may be an argument against complex equality that it requires a strenuous defense—and a defense that begins while equality is still in the making. But this is also an argument against liberty. Eternal vigilance is the price of both.

Equality and Social Change

Complex equality might look more secure if we could describe it in terms of the harmony, rather than the autonomy, of spheres. But social meanings and distributions are harmonious only in this respect: that when we see why one good has a certain form and is distributed in a certain way, we also see why another must be different. Precisely because of these differences, however, boundary conflict is endemic. The principles appropriate to the different spheres are not harmonious with one another; nor are the patterns of conduct and feeling they generate. Welfare systems and markets, offices and families, schools and states are run on different principles: so they should be. The principles must somehow fit together within a single culture; they must be comprehensible across the different companies of men and women. But this doesn't rule out deep strains and odd juxtapositions. Ancient China was ruled by a hereditary divine-right emperor and a meritocratic bureaucracy. One has to tell a complex story to explain that sort of coexistence. A community's culture is the story its members tell so as to make sense of all the different pieces of their social life—and justice is the doctrine that distinguishes the pieces. In any differentiated society, justice will make for harmony only if it first makes for separation. Good fences make just societies.

We never know exactly where to put the fences; they have no natural location. The goods they distinguish are artifacts; as they were made, so they can be remade. Boundaries, then, are vulnerable to shifts in social meaning, and we have no choice but to live with the continual probes and incursions through which these shifts are worked out. Commonly, the shifts are like sea changes, very slow, as in the story that I told in chapter 3 about the cure of souls and the cure of bodies in the medieval and modern West. But the actual boundary revision, when it comes, is likely to come suddenly, as in the creation of a national health service in Britain after the Second World War: one year, doctors were professionals and entrepreneurs; and the next year, they were professionals and public servants. We can map a program of such revisions, based on our current understanding of social goods. We can set ourselves in opposition, as I have done, to the prevailing forms of dominance. But we can't anticipate the deeper changes in consciousness, not in our own community and certainly not in any other. The social world will one day look different from the way it does today, and distributive justice will take on a different character than it has for us. Eternal vigilance is no guarantee of eternity.

It isn't likely, however, that we (or our children or grandchildren) will live through changes on such a scale as to call into doubt the fact of differentiation and the argument for complex equality. The forms of dominance and domination, the precise ways in which equality is denied, may well change. Indeed, it is a common argument among social theorists today that education and technical knowledge are increasingly the dominant goods in modern societies, replacing capital and providing the practical base for a new ruling class of intellectuals.[5] That argument is probably wrong, but it nicely suggests the possibility of large-scale transformations that still leave intact the range of goods and social meanings. For even if technical knowledge takes on a new importance, we have no reason to think that it will be so important as to require us to dispense with all the other distributive processes in which it currently plays no part at all—and then to give people exams, for example, before allowing them to serve on juries, or raise children, or take vacations, or participate in political life. Nor will the importance of knowledge be such as to guarantee that only intellectuals can make money or receive divine grace or win the respect of their fellow citizens. We can assume, I think, that social change will leave more or less intact the different companies of men and women.

And that means that complex equality will remain a lively possibility even if new opponents of equality take the place of old ones. The possibility is, for all practical purposes, permanent . . . and so is the opposition. The establishment of an egalitarian society will not be the end of the struggle for equality. All that one can hope for is that the struggle might get a little easier as men and women learn to live with the autonomy of distributions and to recognize that different outcomes for different people in different spheres make a just society. There is a certain attitude of mind that underlies the theory of justice and that ought to be strengthened by the experience of complex equality: we can think of it as a decent respect for the opinions of mankind. Not the opinions of this or that individual, which may well deserve a brusque response: I mean those deeper opinions that are the reflections in individual minds, shaped also by individual thought, of the social meanings that constitute our common life. For us, and for the foreseeable future, these opinions make for autonomous distributions; and every form of dominance is therefore an act of disrespect. To argue against dominance and its accompanying inequalities, it is only necessary to attend to the goods at stake and to the shared understandings of these goods. When philosophers do this, when they write out of a respect for the understandings they share with their fellow citizens, they pursue justice justly, and they reinforce the common pursuit.

In his *Politics*, Aristotle argued that justice in a democracy requires the citizens to rule and be ruled in turn. They take turns governing one another.[6] That is not a likely picture of a political community that includes tens of millions of citizens. Something like it might be possible for many of them, ruling not only in the state but also in cities and towns, companies and factories. Given the number of citizens, however, and the shortness of life, there simply is not time enough, even if there is will and capacity enough, for everyone to have his turn. If we consider the sphere of politics by itself, inequalities are bound to appear. Politicians, orators, activists, and militants—subject, we can hope, to constitutional limits—will exercise more power than the rest of us do. But politics is only one (though it is probably the most important) among many spheres of social activity. What a larger conception of justice requires is not that citizens rule and are ruled in turn, but that they rule in one sphere and are ruled in another—where "rule" means not that they exercise power but that they enjoy a greater share than other people of whatever good is being distributed. The citizens cannot be guaranteed a "turn" everywhere. I suppose, in fact, that they cannot be guaranteed a "turn" anywhere. But the autonomy of spheres will make for a greater sharing of social goods than will any other conceivable arrangement. It will spread the satisfaction of ruling more widely; and it will establish what is always in question today—the compatibility of being ruled and of respecting oneself. For rule without domination is no affront to our dignity, no denial of our moral or political capacity. Mutual respect and a shared self-respect are the deep strengths of complex equality, and together they are the source of its possible endurance.

NOTES

Preface

1. Frank Parkin, *Class, Inequality, and Political Order* (London, 1972), p. 183.
2. Karl Marx, *Economic and Philosophical Manuscripts*, in *Early Writings*, trans. T. B. Bottomore (London, 1963), p. 153.
3. Cf. John Stuart Mill, *On Liberty*, in *The Philosophy of John Stuart Mill*, ed. Marshall Cohen (New York, 1961), p. 198.
4. Michael Walzer, *Just and Unjust Wars: A Moral Argument with Historical Illustrations* (New York, 1977), especially chaps. 4 and 8.

Chapter 1

1. See John Rawls, *A Theory of Justice* (Cambridge, Mass., 1971); Jürgen Habermas, *Legitimation Crisis*, trans. Thomas McCarthy (Boston, 1975), esp. p. 113; Bruce Ackerman, *Social Justice in the Liberal State* (New Haven, 1980).
2. Robert Nozick makes a similar argument in *Anarchy, State, and Utopia* (New York, 1974), pp. 149–50, but with radically individualistic conclusions that seem to me to miss the social character of production.
3. Ralph Waldo Emerson, "Ode," in *The Complete Essays and Other Writings*, ed. Brooks Atkinson (New York, 1940), p. 770.
4. John Stuart Mill, *On Liberty*, in *The Philosophy of John Stuart Mill*, ed. Marshall Cohen (New York, 1961), p. 255. For an anthropological account of liking and not liking social goods, see Mary Douglas and Baron Isherwood, *The World of Goods* (New York, 1979).
5. William James, quoted in C. R. Snyder and Howard Fromkin, *Uniqueness: The Human Pursuit of Difference* (New York, 1980), p. 108.
6. Karl Marx, *The German Ideology*, ed. R. Pascal (New York, 1947), p. 89.
7. Bernard Williams, *Problems of the Self: Philosophical Papers, 1956–1972* (Cambridge, England, 1973), pp. 230–49 ("The Idea of Equality"). This essay is one of the starting points of my own thinking about distributive justice. See also the critique of Williams's argument (and of an earlier essay of my own) in Amy Gutmann, *Liberal Equality* (Cambridge, England, 1980), chap. 4.
8. See Alan W. Wood, "The Marxian Critique of Justice," *Philosophy and Public Affairs* 1 (1972): 244–82.
9. Michael Young, *The Rise of the Meritocracy, 1870–2033* (Hammondsworth, England, 1961)—a brilliant piece of social science fiction.
10. Rawls, *Theory of Justice* [1], pp. 75ff.
11. See Marx's comment, in his "Critique of the Gotha Program," that the democratic republic is the "form of state" within which the class struggle will be fought to a conclusion: the struggle is immediately and without distortion reflected in political life (Marx and Engels, *Selected Works* [Moscow, 1951], vol. II, p. 31).
12. Blaise Pascal, *The Pensées*, trans. J. M. Cohen (Hammondsworth, England, 1961), p. 96 (no. 244).
13. Karl Marx, *Economic and Philosophical Manuscripts*, in *Early Writings*, ed. T. B. Bottomore (London, 1963), pp. 193–94. It is interesting to note an earlier echo of Pascal's argument in Adam Smith's *Theory of Moral Sentiments* (Edinburgh, 1813), vol. I, pp. 378–79; but Smith

The numbers in brackets refer to the original complete citation of a particular reference in each chapter.

seems to have believed that distributions in his own society actually conformed to this view of appropriateness—a mistake neither Pascal nor Marx ever made.

14. See the summary account in Jean Bodin, *Six Books of a Commonweale*, ed. Kenneth Douglas McRae (Cambridge, Mass., 1962), pp. 210–18.

15. Cf. Nozick on "patterning," *Anarchy, State, and Utopia* [2], pp. 155 ff.

16. Marx, "Gotha Program" [11], p. 23.

17. J. H. Hutton, *Caste in India: Its Nature, Function, and Origins* (4th ed., Bombay, 1963), pp. 127–28. I have also drawn on Célestin Bouglé, *Essays on the Caste System*, trans. D. F. Pocock (Cambridge, England, 1971), esp. Part III, chaps. 3 and 4; and Louis Dumont, *Homo Hierarchus: The Caste System and Its Implications* (revised English ed., Chicago, 1980).

18. Hutton, *Caste in India* [17], p. 125.

19. See Charles Beitz, *Political Theory and International Relations* (Princeton, 1979), part III, for an effort to apply Rawlsian ideal contractualism to international society.

Chapter 2

1. John Rawls, *A Theory of Justice* (Cambridge, Mass., 1971), p. 115. For a useful discussion of mutual aid as a possible right, see Theodore M. Benditt, *Rights* (Totowa, N. J., 1982), chap. 5.

2. Rawls, *Theory of Justice* [1], p. 339.

3. John Winthrop, in *Puritan Political Ideas: 1558–1794*, ed. Edmund S. Morgan (Indianapolis, 1965), p. 146.

4. On zoning, see Robert H. Nelson, *Zoning and Property Rights: An Analysis of the American System of Land Use Regulation* (Cambridge, Mass., 1977), pp. 120–21.

5. See the U.S. Supreme Court's decision in *Village of Belle Terre* v. *Boraas* (October term, 1973).

6. Bernard Bosanquet, *The Philosophical Theory of the State* (London, 1958), p. 286.

7. Henry Sidgwick, *Elements of Politics* (London, 1881), pp. 295–96.

8. Ibid., p. 296.

9. Cf. Maurice Cranston, on the common understanding of the right to move, in *What Are Human Rights?* (New York, 1973), p. 32.

10. See John Higham's account of these debates, *Strangers in the Land* (New York, 1968).

11. Winthrop, *Puritan Political Ideas* [3], p. 145.

12. Thomas Hobbes, *The Elements of Law*, ed. Ferdinand Tönnies (2nd ed., New York, 1969), p. 88, (part I, chap. 17, para. 2).

13. Bauer made his argument in *Die Nationalitätenfrage und die Sozialdemokratie* (1907); parts of it are excerpted in *Austro-Marxism*, ed. Tom Bottomore and Patrick Goode (Oxford, England, 1978), pp. 102–25.

14. Sidgwick, *Elements of Politics* [7], p. 295. Cf. John Stuart Mill's letter to Henry George on Chinese immigration to America, quoted in Alexander Saxton, *The Indispensable Enemy: Labor and the Anti-Chinese Movement in California* (Berkeley, 1971), p. 103.

15. Thomas Hobbes, *Leviathan*, part II, chap. 30.

16. Quoted in H. I. London, *Non-White Immigration and the "White Australia" Policy* (New York, 1970), p. 98.

17. Hobbes, *Leviathan*, part I, chap. 15.

18. Sidgwick, *Elements of Politics* [7], pp. 296–97.

19. Bruce Ackerman, *Social Justice in the Liberal State* (New Haven, 1980), p. 95.

20. E. C. S. Wade, and G. Godfrey Phillips, *Constitutional and Administrative Law*, 9th ed. revised by A. W. Bradley (London, 1977), p. 424.

21. For the whole ugly story, see Nikolai Tolstoy, *The Secret Betrayal: 1944–1947* (New York, 1977).

22. Victor Ehrenberg, *The People of Aristophanes* (New York 1962), p. 153; I have drawn on the entire discussion of foreigners in fifth-century Athens, pp. 147–64.

23. David Whitehead, *The Ideology of the Athenian Metic*, Cambridge Philological Society supplementary volume no. 4 (1977), p. 41.

24. Aristotle, *The Politics* 1275a and 1278a; I have used the translation of Eric Havelock in

Notes

The Liberal Temper in Greek Politics (New Haven, 1957), pp. 367–69.

25. Isocrates, quoted in Whitehead, *Athenian Metic* [23], pp. 51–52.
26. Whitehead *Athenian Metic* [23], p. 174.
27. Ibid., pp. 57–58.
28. Ibid., pp. 154ff.
29. Aristotle, *The Politics* 1326b, trans. Ernest Barker (Oxford, 1948), p. 343.
30. In my account of guest workers, I rely chiefly on Stephen Castles and Godula Kosack, *Migrant Workers and Class Structure in Western Europe* (Oxford, England, 1973); and also on Cheryl Bernard, "Migrant Workers and European Democracy," *Political Science Quarterly* 92 (Summer 1979): 277–99, and John Berger, *A Seventh Man* (New York, 1975).
31. I have taken the term "communities of character" from Otto Bauer (see *Austro-Marxism* [13], p. 107).

Chapter 3

1. Jean-Jacques Rousseau, "A Discourse on Political Economy," in *The Social Contract and Discourses*, trans. G. D. H. Cole (New York, 1950), pp. 302–3.
2. Edmund Burke, *Reflections on the French Revolution* (London, 1910), p. 75.
3. Cf. David Hume, *A Treatise of Human Nature*, bk. III, part II, chap. 8.
4. The quotation is from the Greek geographer Pausanias, in George Rosen, *A History of Public Health* (New York, 1958), p. 41.
5. Simone Weil, *The Need for Roots*, trans. Arthur Wills (Boston, 1955), p. 21.
6. Charles Fried, *Right and Wrong* (Cambridge, Mass., 1978), p. 122.
7. Michael Walzer, "Philosophy and Democracy," *Political Theory* 9 (1981): 379–99. See also the thoughtful discussion in Amy Gutmann, *Liberal Equality*, (Cambridge, England, 1980) especially pages 197–202.
8. Louis Cohn-Haft, *The Public Physicians of Ancient Greece* (Smith College Studies in History, vol. 42, Northampton, Mass., 1956), p. 40.
9. Ibid., p. 49.
10. Aristotle, *The Constitution of Athens*, in *Aristotle and Xenophon on Democracy and Oligarchy*, trans. J. M. Moore (Berkeley, 1975), pp. 190–92 (secs. 49–52); M. I. Finley, *The Ancient Economy* (Berkeley, 1973), p. 170.
11. Aristotle, *Constitution* [10], p. 191 (50.2).
12. Ibid., p. 190 (49.4).
13. Kathleen Freeman, *The Murder of Herodes, and Other Trials from the Athenian Law Courts* (New York, 1963), p. 167.
14. A. H. M. Jones, *Athenian Democracy* (Oxford, England, 1957), p. 6.
15. Finley, *Ancient Economy* [10], p. 173.
16. S. D. Goitein, *A Mediterranean Society*, vol. II: *The Community* (Berkeley, 1971).
17. Salo Wittmayer Baron, *The Jewish Community* (Philadelphia, 1942), pp. 248–56; H. H. Ben-Sasson, "The Middle Ages," in Ben-Sasson, ed., *A History of the Jewish People* (Cambridge, Mass., 1976), p. 551.
18. Baron, *Jewish Community* [17], p. 333.
19. Goitein, *Mediterranean Society* [16], p. 142.
20. Ibid.
21. Baron, *Jewish Community* [17], p. 172; see also Ben-Sasson, "Middle Ages" [17], pp. 608–11.
22. The strongest philosophical defense of this position is Robert Nozick, *Anarchy, State, and Utopia* (New York, 1974).
23. Morris Janowitz, *Social Control of the Welfare State* (Chicago, 1977), p. 10.
24. See Baron, *Jewish Community* [17], pp. 177–79.
25. Goitein, *Community* [16], p. 186.
26. Freeman, *Murder of Herodes* [13], p. 169.
27. For an account of the famine and the British response, see C. B. Woodham-Smith, *The Great Hunger: Ireland 1845–1849* (London, 1962).
28. Burke, *French Revolution* [2], p. 57.

Notes

29. John Rawls, *A Theory of Justice* (Cambridge, Mass., 1971), part I, chaps. 2 and 3.

30. T. H. Marshall, *Class, Citizenship, and Social Development* (Garden City, New York, 1965), p. 298.

31. See Judith Walzer Leavitt, *The Healthiest City: Milwaukee and the Politics of Health Reform* (Princeton, 1982), chap. 5.

32. See the careful discussion in Harold L. Wilensky, *The Welfare State and Equality* (Berkeley, 1975), pp. 87–96.

33. P. H. J. H. Gosden, *Self-Help: Voluntary Associations in the Nineteenth Century* (London, 1973), chap. 9.

34. See, for example, Harry Eckstein's discussion of conceptions of community and welfare policies in Norway: *Division and Cohesion in Democracy: A Study of Norway* (Princeton, 1966), pp. 85–87.

35. Rousseau, *Social Contract* [1], pp. 250–52.

36. Louis Dumont, *Homo Hierarchus: The Caste System and Its Implications* (revised English ed., Chicago, 1980), p. 105.

37. Wilensky, *Welfare State* [32], chaps. 2 and 3.

38. See Whitney North Seymour, *Why Justice Fails* (New York, 1973), especially chap. 4.

39. René Descartes, *Discourse on Method*, trans. Arthur Wollaston (Hammondsworth, England, 1960), p. 85.

40. For a brief account of these developments, see Odin W. Anderson, *The Uneasy Equilibrium: Private and Public Financing of Health Services in the United States, 1875–1965* (New Haven, 1968).

41. Bernard Williams, "The Idea of Equality," in *Problems of the Self* (Cambridge, England, 1973), p. 240.

42. See Robert Nozick, *Anarchy, State, and Utopia* (New York, 1974), pp. 233–35.

43. Thomas Scanlon, "Preference and Urgency," *Journal of Philosophy* 57 (1975): 655–70.

44. Monroe Lerner, "Social Differences in Physical Health," John B. McKinley, "The Help-Seeking Behavior of the Poor," and Julius Roth, "The Treatment of the Sick," in *Poverty and Health: A Sociological Analysis*, ed. John Kosa and Irving Kenneth Zola (Cambridge, Mass., 1969), summary statements at pp. 103, 265, and 280–81.

45. Also, supposedly, a cheaper form of welfare: see Colin Clark, *Poverty before Politics: A Proposal for a Reverse Income Tax* (Hobart Paper 73, London, 1977).

46. See *The New York Times*, 2 July 1978, p. 1, col. 5.

47. Marcel Mauss, *The Gift*, trans. Ian Cunnison (New York, 1967), p. 63.

48. Richard Titmuss, *The Gift Relationship: From Human Blood to Social Policy* (New York, 1971).

49. The quoted phrase is from *Social Work, Welfare, and The State*, ed. Noel Parry, Michael Rustin, and Carole Satyamurti (London, 1979), p. 168; for a similar argument, see Janowitz, *Social Control* [23], pp. 132–33.

Chapter 4

1. William Shakespeare, *Timon of Athens*, IV:3, as quoted in Karl Marx's *Economic and Philosophical Manuscripts*, in *Early Writings*, trans. and ed., T. B. Bottomore (London, 1963), p. 190.

2. Marx, *Early Writings* [1], p. 191.

3. William Shakespeare, *Henry VI, Part II*, IV:2.

4. On the scale of the war and the manpower required, see Walter Mills, *Arms and Men: A Study of American Military History* (New York, 1958), pp. 102–4.

5. Marcus Cunliffe, *Soldiers and Civilians: The Martial Spirit in America, 1775–1865* (New York, 1973), pp. 205–6.

6. James McCague, *The Second Rebellion: The Story of the New York City Draft Riots of 1863* (New York, 1968), p. 54.

7. Ibid., p. 18.

8. Arthur Okun, *Equality and Efficiency: The Big Tradeoff* (Washington, D.C., 1975), pp. 6ff.

9. Ibid., p. 20.

Notes

10. Douglas M. MacDowell, *The Law in Classical Athens* (Ithaca, N.Y., 1978), pp. 171–73.

11. Samuel Butler, *Hudibras*, part III, chap. 3, l. 1279

12. On the importance of "things," see Mary Douglas and Baron Isherwood, *The World of Goods* (New York, 1979), esp. chap. 3: and Mikaly Csikszentmikalyi and Eugene Rochberg-Halton, *The Meaning of Things: Domestic Symbols and the Self* (Cambridge, England, 1981).

13. John Locke, *Second Treatise of Government*, chap. 5, paras. 25–31.

14. Lee Rainwater, *What Money Buys: Inequality and the Social Meaning of Income* (New York, 1974), p. *xi*.

15. An entirely individualized valuation, a private language of goods, is, of course, impossible: see, again, Douglas and Isherwood, *World of Goods* [12], chaps. 3 and 4.

16. See Louis O. Kelso and Mortimer J. Adler, *The Capitalist Manifesto* (New York, 1958), pp. 67–77, for an argument that makes the distribution of wealth on the basis of contribution analogous to the distribution of office on the basis of merit. Economists like Milton Friedman are more cautious, but this is surely the popular ideology of capitalism: success is a deserved reward for "intelligence, resolution, hard work, and a willingness to take risks" (George Gilder, *Wealth and Poverty* [New York, 1981], p. 101).

17. See Robert Nozick's distinction between entitlement and desert, *Anarchy, State, and Utopia* (New York, 1974), pp. 155–60.

18. Walt Whitman, *Complete Poetry and Selected Prose*, ed. James E. Miller, Jr. (Boston, 1959), p. 471 n.

19. On the bazaar economy, see Clifford Geertz, *Peddlers and Princes: Social Development and Economic Change in Two Indonesian Towns* (Chicago, 1963), pp. 35–36.

20. Ralph M. Hower, *History of Macy's of New York, 1858–1919: Chapters in the Evolution of the Department Store* (Cambridge, Mass., 1943), chaps. 2–5 tell the story of Macy's failures and his eventual success.

21. Ibid., pp. 141–57; see also Michael B. Miller, *The Bon Marché: Bourgeois Culture and the Department Store* (Princeton, 1981).

22. Ezra Vogel, *Japan as Number One: Lessons for America* (New York, 1980), p. 123; a number of European countries have similar laws.

23. Hower, *History of Macy's* [20], pp. 298, 306.

24. André Gorz, *Socialism and Revolution*, trans. Norman Denny (Garden City, N.Y., 1973), p. 196.

25. Ibid., pp. 195–97.

26. Ibid., p. 196.

27. For a critique of "the consumer society" in these terms, see Charles Taylor, "Growth, Legitimacy, and the Modern Identity," in *Praxis International* 1 (July 1981): 120

28. See Alfred E. Kahn, "The Tyranny of Small Decisions: Market Failures, Imperfections, and the Limits of Economics," in *KYKLOS: International Review of Social Sciences* 19 (1966).

29. Gorz, *Socialism and Revolution* [24], p. 195.

30. Henry Phelps Brown has a useful discussion of these different factors in *The Inequality of Pay* (Berkeley, 1977), pp. 322ff; see also p. 13.

31. For a review of current arguments, see Mark Granovetter, "Toward a Sociological Theory of Income Differences," in *Sociological Perspectives on Labor Markets*, ed. Ivar Berg (New York, 1981), pp. 11–47.

32. Adolph Sturmthal, *Workers Councils: A Study of Workplace Organization on Both Sides of the Iron Curtain* (Cambridge, Mass., 1964), p. 106.

33. Martin Carnoy and Derek Shearer, *Economic Democracy: The Challenge of the 1980s* (White Plains, N.Y., 1980), p. 175.

34. *R. H. Tawney's Commonplace Book*, ed. J. M. Winter and D. M. Joslin (Cambridge, England, 1972), pp. 33–34.

35. See the discussion of "pooling" in Marshall Sahlins, *Stone Age Economics* (Chicago, 1972), chap. 5. I should stress that pooling does not necessarily make for equal shares; see Walter C. Neale, "Reciprocity and Redistribution in an Indian Village: Sequel to Some Notable Discussions," in *Trade and Market in the Early Empires*, ed. Karl Polanyi, Conrad M. Arensberg, and Harry W. Pearson (Chicago, 1971), pp. 223–28.

36. Robert Kuttner, *Revolt of the Haves: Tax Rebellions and Hard Times* (New York, 1980).

37. See, for example, Henri Pirenne, *Economic and Social History of Medieval Europe* (New York, 1958), pp. 172–74.

Notes

38. Benjamin Franklin, *Poor Richard's Almanac,* April 1735.
39. Jack Barbash, *The Practice of Unionism* (New York, 1956), p. 195.
40. Bronislaw Malinowski, *Argonauts of the Western Pacific* (New York, 1961).
41. Ibid., p. 95.
42. Ibid., p. 81.
43. Ibid., pp. 96, 81.
44. Sahlins, *Stone Age Economics* [35], p. 169.
45. Malinowski, *Argonauts* [40], pp. 189–90.
46. John P. Dawson, *Gifts and Promises: Continental and American Law Compared* (New Haven, 1980), pp. 48–50.
47. John Stuart Mill, *Principles of Political Economy,* book II, chap. 2, sec. 5, in *Collected Works of John Stuart Mill,* vol. II, ed. J. M. Robson (Toronto, 1965), p. 226n.
48. Ibid., p. 225.
49. Ibid., p. 226.
50. Ibid., p. 223.

Chapter 5

1. For an account of this process through one of its critical moments, see G. Tellenbach, *Church, State, and Society at the Time of the Investiture Contest* (Oxford, England, 1940).
2. State of Massachusetts, "Civil Service Announcements" (1979), mimeo. Frederick C. Mosher, *Democracy and the Public Service* (New York, 1968) chap. 3, provides a useful history of American conceptions of office holding.
3. John Rawls, *A Theory of Justice* (Cambridge, Mass., 1971), p. 83.
4. Emile Durkheim, *The Division of Labor in Society,* trans. George Simpson (New York, 1964), p. 377.
5. Ibid.
6. William Shakespeare, *Henry VI, Part II,* IV:7.
7. For Rousseau, see *The Government of Poland,* trans. Willmoore Kendall (Indianapolis, 1972), p. 20. For Andrew Jackson, see Mosher, *Democracy and Public Service* [2], p. 62. For Lenin, *State and Revolution* (New York, 1932), p. 38; see also pp. 83–84.
8. See Ying-Mao Kau "The Urban Bureaucratic Elite in Communist China: A Case Study of Wuhan, 1949–1965," in *Chinese Communist Politics in Action,* ed. A. Doak Barnett (Seattle, 1969), pp. 221–60.
9. See Michael Young, *The Rise of the Meritocracy, 1870–2033* (Baltimore, 1961), for a fictionalized account of the working out of this purpose; and Barry R. Gross, *Discrimination in Reverse: Is Turnabout Fair Play?* (New York, 1978), for a philosophical defense.
10. John Dryden, trans. of Virgil's *Georgics* IV. 136, in *The Poetical Works of Dryden,* ed. George Noyes (Cambridge, Mass., 1950), p. 478.
11. Chung-Li Chang, *The Chinese Gentry: Studies on Their Role in Nineteenth-Century Chinese Society* (Seattle, 1955), pp. 165ff. I have also relied on Ping-Ti Ho, *The Ladder of Success in Imperial China: Aspects of Social Mobility, 1368–1911* (New York, 1962); and Ichisada Miyazaki, *China's Examination Hell: The Civil Service Examinations of Imperial China,* trans. Conrad Schirokauer (New Haven, 1981).
12. Ho, *Ladder of Success* [11], p. 258.
13. Ibid., chap. 4.
14. Ibid., p. 11.
15. Miyazaki, *Examination Hell* [11], pp. 43–49.
16. Quoted in Chang, *Gentry* [11], p. 172.
17. Ibid., p. 182.
18. William Cowper, *The Task,* book IV, l.788.
19. But it was officially condemned only in 1567 in the papal bill *Admonet nos;* see *The New Catholic Encyclopedia* (1967), s.v. "nepotism."
20. For helpful discussions of this issue, see Alan H. Goldman, *Justice and Reverse Discrimination* (Princeton, 1979); Robert K. Fullinwider, *The Reverse Discrimination Controversy: A Moral and Legal Analysis* (Totowa, N. J. 1980); and Gross, *Discrimination in Reverse* [9].

Notes

21. See the account of this argument in Goldman, *Reverse Discrimination* [20], pp. 188–94. Any argument about the rights of groups—like that, for example, of Owen Fiss, "Groups and the Equal Protection Clause," in *Philosophy and Public Affairs* 5 (1976): 107–77—would seem to invite the use of proportionality as a standard for measuring the violation of rights or the failure of equal protection.

22. Arend Lijphart, *Democracy in Plural Societies: A Comparative Exploration* (New Haven, 1977), pp. 38–41 and passim.

23. See Harold Isaacs, *India's Ex-Untouchables* (New York, 1974), pp. 114ff.

24. See the discussion in Fullinwinder, *Controversy* [20], pp. 45ff.; also Judith Jarvis Thomson, "Preferential Hiring," in *Philosophy and Public Affairs* 2 (1973): 364–84.

25. Ronald Dworkin, *Taking Rights Seriously* (Cambridge, Mass., 1977), p. 227; see also Dworkin, "Why Bakke Has No Case," in *The New York Review of Books*, 10 November 1977, pp. 11–15.

26. See Boris J. Bittker, *The Case for Black Reparations* (New York, 1973); and Robert Amdur, "Compensatory Justice: The Question of Costs," in *Political Theory* 7 (1979): 229–44.

27. Magali Sarfatti Larson, *The Rise of Professionalism: A Sociological Analysis* (Berkeley, 1977), especially introduction and chap. 6.

28. T. H. Marshall, *Class, Citizenship, and Social Development* (Garden City, N. Y., 1965), p. 177.

29. Tom Levin, *American Health: Professional Privilege vs. Public Need* (New York, 1974), p. 41.

30. See Henry Phelps Brown, *The Inequality of Pay* (Berkeley, 1977), pp. 322–28.

31. R. H. Tawney, *The Acquisitive Society* (New York, n.d.), p. 178.

32. Larson, *Professionalism* [27], p. 9 (quoting Everett Hughes). Cf. the somewhat different argument of Adam Smith, *An Inquiry into the Nature and Causes of the Wealth of Nations*, ed. Edwin Cannan (New York, 1937), p. 105.

33. Karl Marx, *The Civil War in France*, in Marx and Engels, *Selected Works* (Moscow, 1951), vol. 1, p. 471.

34. Brown, *Inequality of Pay* [30], p. 84 (table 3.4). For an argument in favor of this sort of equalization, see Norman Daniels, "Merit and Meritocracy," in *Philosophy and Public Affairs* 7 (1978): 206–23.

35. George Bernard Shaw, "The Socialist Criticism of the Medical Profession," in *Transactions of the Medico-Legal Society* 6 (London, 1908–1909): 210.

36. Smith, *Wealth of Nations* [32], p. 100.

37. Blaise Pascal, *The Pensées*, trans. J. M. Cohen (Hammondsworth, England, 1961), p. 62 (no. 104).

Chapter 6

1. Oscar Wilde, "The Soul of Man under Socialism," reprinted in *The Artist as Critic: Critical Writings of Oscar Wilde*, ed. Richard Ellmann (New York, 1969), p. 269.

2. John Ruskin, *The Crown of Wild Olive: Four Lectures on Industry and War* (New York, 1874), pp. 90–91.

3. See the discussion of Fourier's system in Frank E. Manuel, *The Prophets of Paris* (Cambridge, Mass., 1962), p. 229.

4. George Orwell, *The Road to Wigan Pier* (New York, 1958), p. 44.

5. Ibid., pp. 32–33.

6. Jean-Jacques Rousseau, *The Social Contract*, book III, chap. 15, in *Social Contract and Discourses*, trans. G. D. H. Cole (New York, 1950), p. 93.

7. Melford E. Spiro, *Kibbutz: Venture in Utopia* (New York, 1970), pp. 16–17.

8. Ibid., p. 77.

9. Ibid. For an analysis of the sexual division of labor on the kibbutz, see Joseph Raphael Blasi, *The Communal Future: The Kibbutz and the Utopian Dilemma* (Norwood, Pa., 1980), pp. 102–3.

10. Spiro, *Kibbutz* [7], p. 69.

11. Bernard Shaw, *The Intelligent Woman's Guide to Socialism, Capitalism, Sovietism, and Fascism* (Hammondsworth, England, 1937), p. 106.

12. Harold R. Isaacs, *India's Ex-Untouchables* (New York, 1974), pp. 36–37.

13. Walt Whitman, "Song of the Exposition," in *Complete Poetry and Selected Prose*, ed. James E. Miller, Jr. (Boston, 1959), p. 147.

14. See Michael Walzer, *The Revolution of the Saints: A Study in the Origin of Radical Politics* (Cambridge, Mass., 1965), p. 214.

15. Stewart E. Perry, *San Francisco Scavengers: Dirty Work and the Pride of Ownership* (Berkeley, 1978), p. 7.

16. Shaw, *Woman's Guide* [11], p. 105.

17. Ibid., p. 109.

18. Perry, *Scavengers* [15], p. 197.

19. Wilde, "Soul of Man" [1], p. 268.

20. Perry, *Scavengers* [15], p. 8.

21. Ibid., pp. 188–91.

22. Studs Terkel, *Working* (New York, 1975), p. 168.

23. Bernard Shaw, "Maxims for Revolutionists," *Man and Superman*, in *Seven Plays* (New York, 1951), p. 736.

24. W. H. Auden, "In Time of War" (XXV), in *The English Auden: Poems, Essays, and Dramatic Writings 1927–1939*, ed. Edward Mendelson (New York, 1978), p. 261.

25. Everett Hughes, *The Sociological Eye* (Chicago, 1971), p. 345.

26. Ibid., p. 314.

27. Ibid.

28. Shaw, *Woman's Guide* [11], p. 107.

29. Terkel, *Working* [22], p. 153.

Chapter 7

1. Thorstein Veblen, *The Theory of the Leisure Class* (New York, 1953), p. 47.

2. James Boswell, *The Life of Samuel Johnson*, ed. Bergen Evans (New York, 1952), p. 206.

3. See the discussions of these words in Sebastian de Grazia, *Of Time, Work, and Leisure* (New York 1962), p. 12; and Martin Buber, *Moses: The Revelation and the Covenant* (New York, 1958), p. 82.

4. T. H. Marshall, *Class, Citizenship, and Social Development* (Garden City, N. Y., 1965), p. 159.

5. Alfred Zimmern, *The Greek Commonwealth* (Oxford, 1961) p. 271, paraphrasing a passage from G. Salvioli, *Le Capitalisme dans le monde antique* (Paris, 1906), p. 148.

6. Aristotle, *Nicomachean Ethics* X. 7.

7. Karl Marx, quoted in Stanley Moore, *Marx on the Choice between Socialism and Communism* (Cambridge, Mass., 1980), p. 42. See *The Grundrisse*, ed. and trans. by David McLellan (New York, 1971), p. 124.

8. Karl Marx, *Capital* (New York, 1967), vol. III, p. 820; cf. Moore, *Choice* [7], p. 44.

9. Marx, *Capital* [8], vol. I, pp. 234–35.

10. Ibid., vol. I, pp. 264–65.

11. Ibid., I, 264.

12. De Grazia, *Time* [3], pp. 89–90; Neil H. Cheek and William R. Burch, *The Social Organization of Leisure in Human Society* (New York, 1976), pp. 80–84; William L. Parish and Martin King Whyte, *Village and Family in Contemporary China* (Chicago, 1980), p. 274. The calculations in the case of China are those of a communist opponent of traditional forms of leisure (see later in this book, page 195).

13. Marx, *Capital* [8], I, 264.

14. William Shakespeare, *Henry V*, IV:1.

15. Bernard Shaw, *The Intelligent Woman's Guide to Socialism, Capitalism, Sovietism, and Fascism* (Hammondsworth, England, 1965), p. 340.

16. Ibid., p. 342.

17. De Grazia, *Time* [3], p. 467 (table 12).

18. *Ibid.*, p. 66. I am indebted to de Grazia's discussion here and also on pp. 116ff.

19. Cheek and Burch, *Social Organization* [12], chap. 3.

Notes

20. Buber, *Moses* [3], p. 84.
21. Max Weber, *Ancient Judaism*, trans. H. H. Gerth and Don Martindale (New York, 1967), p. 33.
22. See Louis Ginzberg, *The Legends of the Jews* (Philadelphia, 1954), vol. IV, p. 201.
23. Quoted in Isadore Twersky, *Introduction to the Code of Maimonides* (New Haven, 1980), pp. 113–14.
24. Leo Baeck, *This People Israel: The Meaning of Jewish Existence*, trans. Albert H. Friedlander (New York, 1964), p. 138.
25. See E. Wright Bakke, *Citizens Without Work* (New Haven, 1940), pp. 13–18.
26. William Shakespeare, *Henry IV, Part I*, I:2.
27. Ginzberg, *Legends* [22] vol. III, p. 99.
28. Parish and Whyte, *Village and Family* [12], p. 274.
29. Ibid., p. 287.
30. United Nations' International Covenant on Economic, Social, and Cultural Rights, part I, art. 8; see discussion in Maurice Cranston, *What Are Human Rights?* (New York, 1973), chap. 8.

Chapter 8

1. Aristotle *The Politics*, 1337a. trans. Ernest Barker (Oxford, 1948), p. 390.
2. See Samuel Bowles and Herbert Gintis, *Schooling in Capitalist America* (New York, 1976), p. 12.
3. John Dewey, *Democracy and Education* (New York, 1961), pp. 18–22.
4. Cf. Rousseau's proposals in *The Government of Poland*, trans. Willmoore Kendall (Indianapolis, 1972), p. 20: "Above all, do not make the mistake of turning teaching into a career." That seems to me exactly wrong.
5. G. C. Vaillant, *The Aztecs of Mexico* (Hammondsworth, England, 1950), p. 117.
6. Jacques Soustelle, *The Daily Life of the Aztecs*, trans. Patrick O'Brian (Hammondsworth, England, 1964), pp. 178, 175, respectively.
7. Aristotle, *The Politics* 1332b [1], p. 370
8. The story is retold in Aaron H. Blumenthal, *If I Am Only for Myself: The Story of Hillel* (n. pl., 1974), pp. 2–3.
9. See the appendix ("Selected Cases . . .") to Ping-Ti Ho, *The Ladder of Success in Imperial China: Aspects of Social Mobility, 1368–1911* (New York, 1962), pp. 267–318.
10. R. H. Tawney, *The Radical Tradition* (New York, 1964), p. 69.
11. Aristotle, *The Politics* 1332b [1], p. 370
12. Hence it is commonly argued that the value of, say, a high school education is "debased" as it is more widely distributed; see the useful discussion by David K. Cohen and Barbara Neufeld, "The Failure of High Schools and the Progress of Education," in *Daedalus*, Summer 1981, p. 79 and generally.
13. William Cummings, *Education and Equality in Japan* (Princeton, 1980), pp. 4–5.
14. Ibid., p. 273.
15. Ibid., p. 274; see also p. 154.
16. Aristotle, *The Politics* 1337a [1], p. 391
17. Cummings, *Japan* [13], p. 274; see also p. 127.
18. Ibid., p. 275.
19. Ibid.
20. Ibid., p. 117.
21. Bernard Shaw, *The Intelligent Woman's Guide to Socialism, Capitalism, Sovietism, and Fascism* (Hammondsworth, England, 1937), pp. 436–37.
22. See Ivan Illich, *Deschooling Society* (New York, 1972), who has nothing to say about how elementary education would be carried out in a "deschooled" society.
23. Tawney, *Radical Tradition* [10], pp. 79–80, 73.
24. See David Page, "Against Higher Education for Some," in *Education for Democracy*, ed. David Rubinstein and Colin Stoneman (2nd ed., Hammondsworth, England, 1972), pp. 227–28.

25. John Milton, "Of Education," in *Complete Prose Works of John Milton,* vol. II, ed. Ernest Sirluck (New Haven, 1959), p. 379.

26. See the discussion in Cummings, *Japan* [13], chap. 8, of the growing numbers of Japanese children competing for university positions.

27. Bernard Crick, *George Orwell: A Life* (Boston, 1980), chap. 2, reviews the evidence.

28. George Orwell, "Such, Such Were the Joys," in *The Collected Essays, Journalism, and Letters of George Orwell,* ed. Sonia Orwell and Ian Angus (New York, 1968), vol. III, p. 336.

29. Ibid., p. 343.

30. Ibid., p. 340.

31. William Shakespeare, *As You Like It,* II:5.

32. See Michel Foucault's account of the "carceral continuum," which includes prisons, asylums, armies, factories, and schools, in *Discipline and Punish: The Birth of the Prison,* trans. Alan Sheridan (New York, 1979), pp. 293–308. Foucault makes too much of the resemblance.

33. John E. Coons and Stephen D. Sugarman, *Education by Choice: The Case for Family Control* (Berkeley, 1978).

34. Albert O. Hirschman, *Exit, Voice, and Loyalty: Responses to Decline in Firms, Organizations, and States* (Cambridge, Mass., 1970).

35. See the critical discussion of the Garrity decision and of "statistical parity" in general, in Nathan Glazer, *Affirmative Discrimination: Ethnic Inequality and Public Policy* (New York, 1975), pp. 65–66.

36. Congress of Racial Equality (CORE), "A Proposal for Community School Districts" (1970), in *The Great School Bus Controversy,* ed. Nicolaus Mills (New York, 1973), pp. 311–21.

37. This is especially clear when the local activists speak a "foreign" language; see Noel Epstein *Language, Ethnicity, and the Schools* (Institute for Educational Leadership, Washington, D.C., 1977).

Chapter 9

1. James Boswell, *The Life of Samuel Johnson,* ed. Bergen Evans (New York, 1952), p. 285.

2. *The Analects of Confucius,* trans. Arthur Waley (New York, n.d.), p. 83 (I:2).

3. Lucy Mair, *Marriage* (New York, 1972), p. 20.

4. See Eugene Victor Walter's discussion of kinship constraints on political power in *Terror and Resistance: A Study of Political Violence, with Case Studies of Some Primitive African Communities* (New York, 1969), chap. 4; and then his description of the attack on kinship by Shaka, the "terrorist despot" of the Zulus, especially pp. 152–54.

5. John Selden, *Table Talk,* ed. Frederick Pollack (London, 1927), p. 75.

6. Meyer Fortes, *Kinship and the Social Order: The Legacy of Lewis Henry Morgan* (Chicago, 1969), p. 309.

7. The quoted phrase is from Fortes, *Kinship and Social Order* [6], p. 232.

8. John Rawls, *A Theory of Justice* (Cambridge, England, 1971), p. 74.

9. Ibid., p. 511.

10. Plato, *The Republic,* trans. F. M. Cornford (New York, 1945), pp. 165–66 (V. 463–64).

11. Lawrence Stone, *The Family, Sex, and Marriage in England: 1500–1800* (New York, 1979), p. 426.

12. Plato, *The Republic* [10], p. 155 (Cornford's commentary).

13. See Lawrence Kohlberg, "The Claim to Moral Adequacy of a Highest Stage of Moral Development," *Journal of Philosophy* 70 (1975), pp. 631–47.

14. Mair, *Marriage* [3], p. 7.

15. See Gordon J. Schochet, *Patriarchalism in Political Thought* (New York, 1975), chaps. 1–3.

16. Frederick Engels, *The Condition of the Working Class in England* (1844), in Karl Marx and Frederick Engels, *Collected Works* (New York, 1975), vol. 4, especially pp. 424–25 on the "neglect of all domestic duties." See also Steven Marcus, *Engels, Manchester, and The Working Class* (New York, 1974), pp. 238ff.

17. Jane Humphries, "The Working Class Family: A Marxist Perspective," in Jean Bethke Elshtain, ed., *The Family in Political Thought* (Amherst, Mass., 1982), p. 207.

Notes

18. *Manifesto of the Communist Party,* in Karl Marx and Frederick Engels, *Selected Works* (Moscow, 1951), vol. I, p. 48.
19. See also Frederick Engels, *The Origin of the Family, Private Property, and the State,* in *Selected Works,* vol. II; and the discussion in Eli Zaretsky, *Capitalism, the Family, and Personal Life* (New York, 1976), pp. 90–97.
20. See the discussion of Marx's views in Phillip Abbott, *The Family on Trial: Special Relationships in Modern Political Thought* (University Park, Pa., 1981), pp. 72–85.
21. Zaretsky, *Capitalism* [19], pp. 62–63.
22. Bernard Shaw, *The Intelligent Woman's Guide to Socialism, Capitalism, Sovietism, and Fascism* (Hammondsworth, England, 1937), p. 87.
23. Jean-Jacques Rousseau, *Politics and the Arts: Letter to M. D'Alembert on the Theater,* trans. Allan Bloom (Glencoe, Ill., 1960), p. 128.
24. Ibid., p. 131.
25. Mair, *Marriage* [3], p. 92.
26. These and other examples of "liberation" are nicely characterized by Abbott, *Family on Trial* [20], esp. pp. 153–54.
27. The quotation is from John Milton, *Paradise Lost,* book V, l.538.
28. This is one of the main points of Susan Moller Okin, *Women in Western Political Thought* (Princeton, 1979); see pp. 274–75 for a summary statement.
29. Hugh D. R. Baker, *Chinese Family and Kinship* (New York, 1979), p. 176.
30. Jean Bethke Elshtain, *Public Man, Private Woman: Women in Social and Political Thought* (Princeton, 1981), pp. 229–35.
31. Quoted in Baker, *Chinese Family* [29], p. 182.
32. Quoted in Fortes, *Kinship and Social Order* [6], p. 79, from Elaine Cumming and David Schneider, "Sibling Solidarity: A Property of American Kinship," *American Anthropologist* 63 (1961): 498–507.

Chapter 10

1. Martin Luther, *The Pagan Servitude of the Church,* in *Martin Luther: Selections from His Writings,* ed. John Dillenberger (Garden City, N. Y., 1961), p. 283.
2. John Locke, *A Letter Concerning Toleration,* intro. Patrick Romanell (Indianapolis, 1950), p. 18; Luther, *Secular Authority,* in *Selections* [1], p. 385.
3. Locke, *Letter* [2], p. 17.
4. Ibid., p. 27.
5. Ibid.
6. Oliver Cromwell, *Oliver Cromwell's Letters and Speeches,* ed. Thomas Carlyle (London, 1893), p. 354 (speech to the parliament of saints, 4 July 1653).
7. Ibid., p. 355.
8. Increase Mather, *Pray for the Rising Generation* (1618), quoted by Edmund S. Morgan, *The Puritan Family* (New York, 1966), p. 183; see the discussion in J. R. Pole, *The Pursuit of Equality in American History* (Berkeley, 1978), chap. 3.
9. Alan Simpson, *Puritanism in Old and New England* (Chicago, 1961), p. 35.
10. Locke, *Letter* [2], p. 35.

Chapter 11

1. For a nice review of the remains of this system, see "Armiger," *Titles and Forms of Address: A Guide to Their Correct Use* (7th ed., London, 1949).
2. Alexis de Tocqueville, *Democracy in America,* trans. George Lawrence (New York, 1966), p. 601.
3. Orlando Patterson, *Slavery and Social Death: A Comparative Study* (Cambridge, Mass., 1982), p. 97 and chap. 3 generally.
4. Thomas Hobbes, *Leviathan,* part I, chap. 13.

5. *Oxford English Dictionary*, s.v. "Mr." See also the entry "Titles of Honour" in the *Encyclopedia Britannica* (11th ed., 1911).

6. Ralph Waldo Emerson, *Conduct of Life*, in *The Complete Essays and Other Writings of Ralph Waldo Emerson*, ed. Brooks Atkinson (New York, 1940), p. 729.

7. H. L. Mencken, *The American Language* (4th ed., New York, 1938), p. 275.

8. Harold R. Isaacs, *India's Ex-Untouchables* (New York, 1974), pp. 27–28.

9. Hobbes, *Leviathan* part I, chap. 13.

10. This is one of the main points of William J. Goode's *The Celebration of Heroes: Prestige as a Social Control System* (Berkeley, 1978).

11. Thomas Hobbes, *The Elements of Law* (ed. Ferdinand Tönnies [2nd ed., New York, 1969], pp. 47–48), part I, chap. 9, para. 21 (I have omitted some of the definitions).

12. Ibid.

13. Blaise Pascal, *Pensées*, no. 151, trans. J. M. Cohen (Hammondsworth, England, 1961).

14. Frank Parkin, *Class, Inequality, and Political Order* (London, 1972), pp. 34–44.

15. Thomas Nagel, *Mortal Questions* (Cambridge, 1979), p. 104.

16. Parkin argues that such valuations already exist, though they are subordinate to other "meaning-systems" (*Class* [14], p. 97).

17. George Friedrich Hegel, *The Phenomenology of Mind*, trans. J. B. Baillie (London, 1949), p. 231.

18. See John Rawls, *A Theory of Justice* (Cambridge, Mass., 1971), pp. 103–4, also 72–74. Rawls's arguments are my chief concern here. I partly follow the criticisms of Robert Nozick, *Anarchy, State, and Utopia* (New York, 1974), pp. 213–16 and 228.

19. Robert C. Tucker, "Stalin and Psychology," in *The Soviet Political Mind* (New York, 1963), p. 101.

20. Isaac Deutscher, *Stalin: A Political Biography* (New York, 1960), pp. 270–71.

21. Anders Österling, "The Literary Prize," in H. Schück, et al., *Nobel: The Man and His Prizes* (Amsterdam, 1962), p. 75.

22. Ibid., p. 87.

23. Jean-Jacques Rousseau, *Government of Poland*, trans. Wilmoore Kendall (Indianapolis, 1972), pp. 95–96.

24. Simone Weil, *The Need for Roots*, trans. Arthur Wills (Boston, 1955), p. 20.

25. Jean Bodin, *The Six Books of a Commonweale*, ed. Kenneth Douglas McRae (Cambridge, Mass., 1962), p. 586.

26. Francis Bacon, *Essays*, no. 29, "Of the True Greatness of Kingdoms and Estates."

27. Bodin, *Six Books* [25], p. 586.

28. See Ronald Dworkin's argument that Rawlsian justice rests ultimately on the claim that "all men and women" have a right to equal respect (*Taking Rights Seriously* [Cambridge, Mass., 1977], chap. 6).

29. Thomas Hobbes, *Leviathan*, part II, chap. 28.

30. M. I. Finley, *The Ancient Greeks* (Hammondsworth, England, 1977), p. 80. For an account of the history and procedures of ostracism, see *Aristotle and Xenophon on Democracy and Oligarchy*, trans. with commentary by J. M. Moore (Berkeley, 1975), pp. 241–44.

31. Finley, *Greeks* [30], p. 80.

32. See the useful discussion of "dangerousness" as a reason for imprisonment, in Norval Morris, *The Future of Imprisonment* (Chicago, 1974), pp. 63–73.

33. H. L. A. Hart, *Punishment and Responsibility* (Oxford, England, 1968), pp. 21–24.

34. Jean-Jacques Rousseau, *A Discourse on the Origins of Inequality*, in *The Social Contract and Discourses*, trans. G. D. H. Cole (New York, 1950), p. 266. For a nice discussion of Tertullian's attitude, see Max Scheler, *Ressentiment*, ed. Lewis A. Coser (New York, 1961), p. 67.

35. Mary Searle-Chatterjee, "The Polluted Identity of Work: A Study of Benares Sweepers," in Sandra Wallman, ed. *The Social Anthropology of Work* (London, 1979), pp. 284–85.

36. William Makepeace Thackeray, *The Book of Snobs* (Garden City, N. Y., 1961), p. 29.

37. Norbert Elias, *The Civilizing Process: The History of Manners* (New York, 1978), p. 210; see also Nozick, *Anarchy* [18], pp. 243–44.

38. *Oxford English Dictionary*, s.v. "self-esteem," "self-respect." David Sachs is one of the few contemporary philosophers who has written about this distinction; see "How to Distinguish Self-Respect from Self-Esteem," *Philosophy and Public Affairs* 10 (Fall 1981): 346–60.

39. Tocqueville, *Democracy in America* [2], p. 599.

40. Weil, *Need for Roots* [24], p. 19.

Notes

41. Jean-Jacques Rousseau, *The Social Contract*, book III, chap. 15, in *Social Contract and Discourses* [34], p. 93.

42. See Rawls's discussion of these issues—though under the head of "self-esteem" (*Theory of Justice* [18], p. 234).

43. Weil, *Need for Roots* [24], p. 20.

44. See Robert Lane's argument that work is more important than politics in sustaining "self-esteem" ("Government and Self-Esteem," *Political Theory* 10 [February 1982]: 13).

45. Pascal, *Pensées* [13], nos. 145, 306.

46. William Shakespeare, *Anthony and Cleopatra*, III:4.

47. Plato, *The Republic* IX. 571–76.

48. Karl Marx, *Economic and Philosophical Manuscripts*, in *Early Writings*, trans. T. B. Bottomore (London, 1963), p. 191.

Chapter 12

1. Thomas Hobbes, *Leviathan*, part II, chap. 19.

2. See Lucy Mair's discussion of chiefly and monarchic wardships in *Marriage* (New York, 1972), pp. 76–77.

3. The key texts of Plato's are *The Republic* I. 341–47, IV. 488–89; *Gorgias*, 503–8; *Protagoras*, 320–28.

4. Plato, *The Republic* VI. 488–89; trans. F. M. Cornford (New York, 1945), pp. 195–96.

5. Renford Bambrough, "Plato's Political Analogies," in *Philosophy, Politics, and Society*, ed. Peter Laslett (Oxford, 1967), p. 105.

6. Plato, *Protagoras* 322; see the translation and discussion of this passage in Eric A. Havelock, *The Liberal Temper in Greek Politics* (New Haven, 1957), p. 169.

7. Thucydides, *History of the Peloponnesian War*, trans. Richard Crawley (London, 1910), p. 123 (II. 40).

8. Michel Foucault, *Discipline and Punish: The Birth of the Prison*, trans. Alan Sheridan (New York, 1979), p. 223; see also Foucault, *Power/Knowledge: Selected Interviews and Other Writings, 1972–1977*, ed. Colin Gordon (New York, 1980), especially, nos. 5 and 6.

9. Foucault, *Discipline and Punish* [8], pp. 293–308.

10. See the useful discussions of Steven Lukes, *Power: A Radical View* (London, 1974); and William E. Connolly, *The Terms of Political Discourse* (Lexington, Mass., 1974), chap. 3.

11. For an example, see Martin Carnoy and Derek Shearer, *Economic Democracy: The Challenge of the 1980s* (White Plains, N.Y., 1980), pp. 360–61.

12. For an argument that we should rely on the market and the courts rather than on executive or legislative action, see Robert Nozick, *Anarchy, State, and Utopia* (New York 1974), pp. 79–81; cf. the case study by Matthew Crenson, *The Unpolitics of Air Pollution: A Study of Non-Decisionmaking in Cities* (Baltimore, 1971).

13. For a possible further complication, see Connolly on threats and predictions, *Political Discourse* [10], pp. 95–96.

14. For an excellent beginning, see Grant McConnell, *Private Power and American Democracy* (New York, 1966).

15. *R. H. Tawney's Commonplace Book*, ed. J. M. Winter and D. M. Joslin (Cambridge, England, 1972), pp. 34–35.

16. Karl Marx, "On the Jewish Question," in *Early Writings*, trans. T. B. Bottomore (London, 1963), pp. 12–13.

17. Stanley Buder, *Pullman: An Experiment in Industrial Order and Community Planning, 1880–1930* (New York, 1967).

18. Ibid., pp. 98–99.

19. Ibid., p. 107.

20. Ibid., p. 95; see also William M. Carwardine, *The Pullman Strike*, intro. Virgil J. Vogel, (Chicago, 1973), chaps. 8, 9, 10.

21. Richard Ely, quoted in Buder, *Pullman* [17], p. 103.

22. Ibid.; see also Carwardine, *Pullman Strike* [20], chap. 4.

23. Carwardine, *Pullman Strike* [20], p. XXXIII.

24. Buder, *Pullman* [17], p. 44.

25. Karl Marx, *Capital* (New York, 1967), vol. III, pp. 383, 386. Lenin repeats the argument, suggesting "the mild leadership of a conductor of an orchestra" as an example of communist authority; see "The Immediate Tasks of the Soviet Government," in *Selected Works* (New York, n.d.), vol. VII, p. 342.

26. Thomas Hobbes, *The Elements of Law*, ed. Ferdinand Tönnies (2nd ed., New York, 1969), pp. 120–21 (part 2, chap. 2, para. 5).

27. *Aristotle and Xenophon on Democracy and Oligarchy*, trans. with commentary J. M. Moore (Berkeley, 1975), p. 292 (the quote is from Moore's commentary).

28. Jean-Jacques Rousseau, *The Social Contract*, trans. G. D. H. Cole (New York, 1950), p. 56 (book III, chap. 1).

29. Jane J. Mansbridge, *Beyond Adversary Democracy* (New York, 1980), p. 247.

30. Rousseau, *Social Contract* [28], p. 27 (book II, chap. 3).

31. Hannah Arendt, *The Human Condition* (Chicago, 1958), p. 41.

32. The preferred attribution, according to the *Oxford Dictionary of Quotations*, 3rd ed. (1979), is to Adlai Stevenson.

33. See John Gaventa, *Power and Powerlessness: Quiesence and Rebellion in an Appalachian Valley* (Champaign, Ill., 1982).

Chapter 13

1. Walter C. Neale, "Reciprocity and Redistribution in the Indian Village: Sequel to Some Notable Discussions," in *Trade and Market in the Early Empires*, ed. Karl Polanyi, Conrad M. Arensberg, and Harry W. Pearson (Chicago, 1971), p. 226.

2. Harold R. Isaacs, *India's Ex-Untouchables* (New York, 1974), chaps. 7 and 8.

3. Karl Marx, *Capital*, ed. Frederick Engels (New York, 1967), p. 194; I have followed the translation and interpretation of Alan W. Wood, "The Marxian Critique of Justice," *Philosophy and Public Affairs* 1 (1972): 263ff.

4. John Kenneth Galbraith, *American Capitalism* (Boston, 1956), chap. 9.

5. See, for example, Alvin W. Gouldner, *The Future of Intellectuals and the Rise of the New Class* (New York, 1979).

6. Aristotle, *The Politics*, 1283, trans. Ernest Barker (Oxford, England, 1948), p. 157.

INDEX

Index

Index

Index

343

Index